International Counterterrorism and Organized Crime Conventions

International Counterterrorism and Organized Crime Conventions

By

Usman Hameed and Beata Polok

Cambridge Scholars Publishing

International Counterterrorism and Organized Crime Conventions

By Usman Hameed and Beata Polok

This book first published 2024

Cambridge Scholars Publishing

Lady Stephenson Library, Newcastle upon Tyne, NE6 2PA, UK

British Library Cataloguing in Publication Data
A catalogue record for this book is available from the British Library

ISBN (10): 1-5275-5650-6
ISBN (13): 978-1-5275-5650-8

TABLE OF CONTENTS

TABLE OF CASES

International and Regional Cases

- S.S. Lotus (Fr. v. Turk.), 1927 P.C.I.J. (ser. A) No. 10 (Sept.7)
- Questions of Interpretation and Application of the 1971 Montreal Convention Arising from the Aerial Incident at Lockerbie (Libyan Arab Jamahiriya v. United Kingdom), Provisional Measures, 1992 ICJ Reports 3 (Apr 14)
- Case Concerning Military and Paramilitary Activities in and Against Nicaragua (Nicaragua v. United States of America); Merits, International Court of Justice (ICJ), Judgement of 27 June1986 [1986] ICJ Rep 14
- Questions relating to the Obligation to Prosecute or Extradite (Belgium v. Senegal), ICJ Reports 2012, Judgement of July 20, 2012
- Othman (Abu Qatada) v. the United Kingdom – 8139/09 [2012] ECHR 56
- Soering v. The United Kingdom, 1/1989/161/217, Council of Europe: European Court of Human Rights, 7 July 1989
- Chitat Ng v. Canada, Communication No. 469/1991, U.N. Doc. CCPR/C/49/D/469/1991 (1994)
- Case of Babar Ahmad and Others v. the United Kingdom (Applications nos. 24027/07, 11949/08, 36742/08, 66911/09 and 67354/09) ECtHR (Fourth Section) Admissibility Decision of 6 July 2010
- Case of Babar Ahmad and Others v. the United Kingdom EctHR (Fourth Section) Strasbourg Judgment 10 April 2012
- Kafkaris v. Cyprus [GC], no. 21906/04 ECHR 2008
- Saadi v. Italy, No. 32201/06, 128 (Eur.Ct. H.R. Feb 2, 2008

Domestic Cases

- MacLeod v Attorney General for New South Wales [1891] AC 455, 458
- Somchai Liangsiriprasert v. United States Government [1990] 2 ALL ER 866
- US v. Alvarez Machain 504 US 655 (1992)

- US v. Yunis (1988) 681 F. Supp (D.D.C) 909
- A.-G. Israel v. Eichmann, (1968) 36 ILR 5 (District Court, Jerusalem)
- In re Stupp 23 F.Cas.281 (C.C.S.D.N.Y.1873) (No.13562)
- In re Lo Dolce 106 F. Supp. 455 (W.D.N.Y. 1952)
- In re ryat, Unreported, QDB,1989
- R. V. Bow Street Metropolitan Stipendiary Magistrate exparte Pinochet Urgate (Amnesty International and others intervening) (No.3), 2 ENG. Rep 97,170 (H.L 1999) [1999] 2 W.L.R 827
- R. (on the application of Bermingham) v Director of the Serious Fraud Office and Bermingham and others v the Government of the United States of America and the Secretary of State for the Home Department [2006] E.W.H.C. 200 (Admin); [2007] Q.B. 727; [2007] 2 W.L.R. 635
- Abu Daud case, Judgement of Jan.11, 1977, Chambre d' Accusation De La CourD' appel Paris
- McKinnon v United States (2007) EWHC 762 (Admin); (2007) 157 N.L.J. 554; McKinnon v Government of the USA, [2008] U.K.H.L. 59
- Strassheim v. Daily, 221 U.S. 280 (1911)
- Assarsson case, 635 F.2d 1237 (7th Cir 1979)
- Factor v. Laubenheimer 90 U.S. 276 (1933)
- US V. Khashoggi 717 F. Supp.1048 (1989)
- Steven Ivan Ross v. State of Israel (1973) (II) 27 P.D. 365
- Riley and Butler v. Commonwealth, 260 ALR 106 (Austrl. 1985)
- Canada v. Aronson [1989] 2 All E.R. 1025
- R. v. Parisien [1988] 1 S.C.R. 950
- Kim Dotcom, et al., v. United States of America Judgement of 29 May 2012 in the District Court at North Shore in the matter of a request by the Government of United States of America for the surrender of persons in New Zealand
- United States of America v. Kim Dotcom, et al., Criminal no. 1:12 CR 3 US District Court Alexandra Virginia, Indictment 5 January, 2012
- Regina v. Bartle and the Commissioner of Police for the Metropolis and Others Ex Parte Pinochet & Regina v. Evans and Another and the Commissioner of Police for the Metropolis and Others Ex Parte Pinochet (On Appeal from a Divisional Court of the Queen's Bench Division)
- In re John Anderson, 20 U.C.Q.B.R. 124 (1860)
- Canada v. Schmidt [1987] 1 S.C.R 500 AT 501-502(CAN)
- Jeffrey Phillip Kamrin v. United States of America, 725 F.2d 1225, Decided by United States Court of Appeals Ninth Circuit on Feb 14, 1984

- Judgment of Swiss Magistrate in SGS, Cotecna case <http://www.assetrecovery.org/kc/node/2fb39f42-5114-11de-bacd-a7d8a60b2a36.8>
- Pakistan v. Zardari et al, [2006] EWHC 2411 (Comm)
- Dr Mobashir Hassan etc v. Federation of Pakistan etc (PLD 2010 SC 265)
- Muhammad Azhar Siddique vs. Federation of Pakistan etc. Judgement of the Supreme Court of Pakistan dated 19th June, 2012 passed in Constitution Petition No. 40/2012
- In re Castioni [1891] 1 QB 149, UK Court of Appeal (England and Wales) 10 Nov, 1890
- US v. Usama Bin Laden S(2) 98 Cr.1023(LSB)(SDNY 4 Nov.1998)
- Swystun v. United States of America (1988) 40 C.C.C (3d) 222, 227-228 (Man. Q.B)
- U.S v. Noriega 746 F. Supp. 1541 (1990)
- R (Wellington) v. Secretary of State for the Home Department [2008] UKHL 72
- United States v. Burns, 2001 SCC 7, [2001] 1 SCR 283

Table of Treaties

International / Regional Conventions

- 1979 International Convention against the Taking of Hostages 1979; 1316 UNTS 205/ [1990] ATS 17/ 18 ILM 1456(1979)
- 1979 Vienna Convention on the Physical protection of Nuclear Materials; 1456 UNTS 246/ 18 ILM 1419(1980)/ [1987] ATS 16
- 1988 United Nations Convention against Illicit Traffic in Narcotic Drugs and Psychotropic Substances; UN Doc. E/CONF.82/15(1988)/28 ILM 493(1989)
- 1997 International Convention for the Suppression of Terrorist Bombings; 2149 UNTS 256/ [2002] ATS 17/UN Doc. A/Res/52/164
- 1999 International Convention for the Suppression of the Financing of Terrorism; 2178 UNTS 197/39 ILM 270(2000)/ [2002] ATS 23
- 2000 Protocol to Prevent, Suppress and Punish Trafficking in Persons, Especially Women and Children, supplementing the United Nations Convention against Transnational Organised Crime; 40 ILM 335(2001)/ UN Doc. A/55/383 (Annex II, p.53) / [2005] ATS 27
- 2000 United Nations Convention against Transnational Organised Crime (UNTOC) 40 ILM 335 (2001)/ UN Doc. A/55/383 at 25(2000)/ [2004] ATS 12
- 2001 Protocol against the Illicit Manufacturing of and Trafficking in Firearms, their Parts and Components and Ammunition, supplementing the United Nations Convention against Transnational Organised Crime; 40 ILM 335(2001)/ [2202] ATNIF 7
- 2003 United Nations Convention against Corruption (UNCAC); UN Doc. A/58/422(2003)/ (2004) 43 ILM 37
- 2005 International Convention for the Suppression of Acts of Nuclear Terrorism: UN Doc. A/Res/59/290(2005)/[2005]ATNIF 20
- 2006 Protocol against the Smuggling of Migrants by Land, Sea and Air, supplementing the United Nations Convention against Transnational Organised Crime; 40 ILM 384(2001) / UN Doc. A55/383(Annex III P.62) / [2004] ATS 11
- 2010 Convention on the Suppression of Unlawful Acts Relating to International Civil Aviation, (Not yet in force)

- Charter of the United Nations Signed on 26 June 1945 at San Francisco
- Convention Against Torture and Other Cruel, Inhuman or Degrading Treatment or Punishment 1984,1465 UNTS 85/ [1989] ATS 21
- Convention for the Suppression of Unlawful Acts against the Safety of Maritime Navigation 1988; 1618 UNTS 201/ [1993] ATS 16/ 10 ILM 672(1988)
- Convention for the Suppression of Unlawful Acts Against the Safety of Civil Aviation, ICAO Doc. 8966/974 UNTS 177 / [1973] ATS 24 / 10 ILM 1151 (1971)
- Convention on the prevention and punishment of crimes against Internationally Protected Persons 1973; UNTS vol.1035 p.167
- European Convention on Human Rights (ECHR), signed at Rome on 4 November 1950
- Hague Convention / Hijacking Convention / Unlawful Seizure Convention, ICAO Doc. 8920/ 860 UNTS 105 / [1972] ATS 16 / 10 ILM 133 (1971)
- International Convention for the Suppression of Counterfeiting Currency, adopted in Geneva on 20 April 1929
- International Covenant on Civil and Political Rights (ICCPR), Adopted by the General Assembly of the United Nations with resolution 2200A (XXI) of 16 December 1966
- Rome Statute of the ICC 1998, 2187 UNTS 90/37 ILM 1002 (1998)/[2002] ATS
- Second Optional Protocol to the ICCPR, adopted by the General Assembly with resolution 44/128 of 15 December 1989

Extradition and Mutual Legal Assistance Treaties and Conventions

- Spain and Canada Treaty of Extradition. Signed at Madrid on 31 May 1989
- Treaty of Extradition Between the Government of India and the Government of Nepal signed at Kathmandu on 2 October 1953
- Agreement Between the Government of the Hong Kong Special Administrative Region of the People's Republic of China and the Government of the Republic of Singapore for the Surrender of Fugitive offenders. Signed at Hong Kong 11 November 1997
- Extradition Treaty Between the Government of the United States and the Government of the Republic of South Africa, Signed at Washington on September 16,1999

- Extradition Treaty Between Australia and the Republic of India signed at Canberra on 23 June 2008
- France and Canada Extradition Treaty. Signed at Ottawa on 17 November 1988
- The European Convention on Extradition 1957. Signed at Paris on 13.XII.1957
- UN Model Treaty on Extradition 1990 G.A. Res 116, U.N. GAOR, 45th Sess., Annex, at 211-15, U.N. Doc. A/RES/45/116 (1990)
- Extradition Treaty Between Israel and France signed in 1958, ratified by France in 1971
- Extradition Treaty between the United States of America and France. Signed at Paris on April 23, 1996
- Treaty between Australia and Federal Republic of Germany Concerning Extradition. Signed on 1/04/1987
- Extradition Treaty between the Government of the United Kingdom of Great Britain and Northern Ireland and the Government of the United States of America. Signed at Washington 31 March 2003
- Extradition Treaty between United States of America and India. Signed at Washington on June 25,1997
- Treaty between Australia and the Republic of Indonesia on Mutual Assistance in Criminal Matters. Signed at Jakarta on 7 October 1995
- United States of America and Italy Extradition Treaty. Signed at Rome on 13 October 1983
- Convention on Extradition between the Government of United States and the Government of the State of Israel. Signed at Washington on December 10, 1962
- Treaty on Extradition between Australia and United States of America. Signed at Washington on 14 May1974, entered into force 1976
- Treaty on Mutual Legal Assistance in Criminal Matters. Signed on 29 November 2004 in Kuala Lampur, Malaysia
- Treaty on Extradition between the United States of America and New Zealand. Signed at Washington on January 12, 1970
- Treaty on Extradition between the Republic of Korea and the People's Republic of China. Signed at Seoul October 18, 2000
- A treaty to settle and define the boundaries of the US and the possessions of Her Britannic Majesty in North America for final suppression of African slave trade and for giving up criminals, fugitives from justice in certain cases, Aug 9, 1842, US-UK, article X, 8 Stat.572,12 Bevans 82 [Webster Ashburton Treaty 1842]

- Extradition Treaty between the Government of United States of America and the Government of Swiss Confederation. Signed at Washington on November 14, 1990
- Agreement for the Surrender of Fugitive Offenders between the Government of Hong Kong and the Government of the Republic of India. Signed at Hong Kong on June 28, 1997
- Extradition Treaty between the United Kingdom of Great Britain and Northern Ireland and United Arab Emirates. Signed at London on 6 December 2006. Instruments of Ratification were exchanged on 3rd March 2008 and the Treaty entered into force on 2nd April 2008.
- Agreement for the Surrender of Accused and the Convicted Persons between the Government of Australia and the Government of Hong-Kong. Signed at Hong Kong on 15 November 1993.
- Treaty between the Kingdom of Thailand and People's Republic of China on Extradition. Signed at Beijing on 26 August 1993.
- Convention on Laundering, Search, Seizure and Confiscation of the Proceeds of Crime. Strasbourg, 8.XI.1990
- Mutual Legal Assistance Treaty Between the United States of America and France, Signed at Paris December 10, 1998
- Treaty on Mutual Legal Assistance in Criminal Matters between the United Kingdom of Great Britain and Northern Ireland and the Republic of the Philippines. Signed at London 18 September 2009
- UN Model Treaty on Mutual Legal Assistance in Criminal Matters 1990 G.A. Res. 117, 45th Sess., Annex, at 215-19, U.N. Doc. A/RES/117 (1990)

TABLE OF NATIONAL LEGISLATIONS

National laws on Terrorism, Organised Crime and Criminal procedure

Laws of Pakistan

- Pakistan Penal Code (PPC) 1860, Act XLV of 1860
- Control of Narcotics Substances Act (CNSA) 1997, Act No.XXV of 1997
- Anti-Terrorism Act (ATA), Act No. XXVII of 1997
- Anti-Money Laundering Act 2010, Act No. VII of 2010
- National Accountability Bureau (NAB) Ordinance 1999, Act XVIII of 1999 as modified on 26-03-2010
- The Constitution of Islamic Republic of Pakistan, 12th April 1973
- The National Reconciliation Ordinance (NRO), October 5 2007
- Code of Criminal Procedure, Act V of 1898 as amended by Act II of 1997

Laws of India

- Indian Penal Code (IPC) 1860, Act No.45 of 1860
- The Narcotics Drugs and Psychotropic Substances Act 1985, Act No.61 of 1985
- The Unlawful Activities (Prevention) Act 1967, Act No. 37 of 1967 as amended in 2008
- The Anti- Hijacking Act 1982, Act 65 of 1982
- Prevention of Corruption Act 1988, Act No.49 of 1988
- the Prevention of Money Laundering Act 2002, Act 15 of 2003

Laws of the US

- United States Code, Title 18 - Crimes and Criminal Procedure Chapter 113B-Terrorism
- 18 USC Sc. 2332B, Acts of Terrorism Transcending National Borders
- 18 USC Sc. 2332-f (Bombing of places)
- 18 USC Sc. 2332-a use of radioactive dispersal devices
- 18 USC Sc. 2332-d financing of terrorism

- 18 U.S.C. Sc. 2339A, Providing Material Support to Terrorists
- 18 U.S.C. Sc. 2339B, Providing Material Support or Resources to Designated Foreign Terrorist Organizations
- 18 U.S.C. Sc. 1203, Hostage Taking
- 21 U.S.C. Ss.846 & 963, the Controlled Substances Act
- 18 USC S.1961-1968, RICO (Racketeer-Influenced and Corrupt Organizations) Act
- 18 U.S.C Chapter 46 Forfeiture Sc. 981(1991) Civil Forfeiture
- 31 U.S.C Ss.5316,5317 (1991) Search and Forfeiture of Monetary Instruments
- 21 USC S.881 (1991): Forfeitures
- 21 U.S.C Chapter 13 Sc.801 (The Controlled Substances Act)
- 18 U.S.C. 3286 (a) Extension of Statutes of Limitation for certain Terrorism Offences
- Restatement of the Law, Third, Foreign Relations Law of the United States 1987
- U.S.C 1782 Assistance to foreign and International Tribunals and to Litigants before such Tribunals
- U.S.C 1602 (1991) Seizure: Report to Customs officer

Laws of the UK

- Explosive Substances Act 1883; 46 Vict. Ch.13
- Terrorism Act 2000, 2000 Chapter 11
- Taking of Hostages Act 1982 s.1, 1982 Chapter 28
- Aviation Security Act 1982, 1982 Chapter 36
- Proceeds of Crime Act (POCA) 2002, 2002 Chapter 29
- The Bribery Act 2010, 2010 Chapter 23
- Criminal Justice Act of 1988, 1988 Chapter 33 Halsbury's Stat.1154, 1183 (1989 Reissue)
- Criminal Justice (International Cooperation Act) of 1990, 1990 Chapter 5
- Prevention of Terrorism (Temporary Provisions) Act of 1989 F1 (Repealed) 1989 Chapter 4
- The Drugs Act 2005, 2005 Chapter 17
- State Immunity Act 1978, 1978 Chapter 33
- Diplomatic Privileges Act 1964, 1964 Chapter 81
- Drug Trafficking Offences Act 1986, 1986 Chapter 32, 12 Halsbury's Stats 933 (1989 re-issue)

Laws of other states

- Strafgesetzbuch, StGB 1998 [German Criminal Code]
- Code Penal 1810 [French Penal Code]
- Terrorism Suppression Act 2002, Act No. 34 of 2002 [New Zealand's anti-terrorism law]
- Criminal Code of Canada, R.S.C 1985, cC-46
- Swiss Criminal Code of 21 December 1937, SR 311.0
- Criminal Code of the Azerbaijan Republic 2005
- Código Penal de Panamá, Ley No.14, of 18 May 2007

National laws on Extradition and Mutual Legal Assistance

- Singapore's Extradition Act, Chapter 103, Original Enactment: Act 14 of 1968, Revised Edition 2000
- Indian Extradition Act 1962, Act No.34 of 1962
- French Extradition Law of 10 March 1927
- 18 U.S.C. Chapter 209 – Extradition, Ss. 3181 to3184
- Federal Act on International Mutual Assistance in Criminal Matters, Mutual Assistance Act, IMAC of 20 March 1981 [Swiss Law on Mutual Legal Assistance]
- L.S.I 144 - Israel's Extradition Law of 1954
- Israel's Extradition Regulations 1970 (Law, Procedures and Rules of Evidence in Petitions) 5731
- Extradition Law of the People's Republic of China 2000 (Order of President No.42 of 2000)
- The Extradition Act, 1972 of Pakistan, Act No. XXI of 1972
- Extradition Act 2003 of UK, 2003 Chapter 41
- Bulgaria's Extradition and European Arrest Warrant Act 2005, in force since 01/07/2005
- Australian Extradition Act 1988, Act No.4 of 1988
- Extradition Law 5714-1954 and the Extradition Regulations of Israel (Law, Procedures and Rules of Evidence in Petitions) 5731-1970
- New Zealand's Extradition Act 1999 (1999 No. 55)
- Swedish Extradition For Criminal Offences Act (1957: 668)
- Australian Proceeds of Crimes Act 1987 (CWLTH), Act No.87 of 1978 as amended on 3 march 2005
- Australian Criminal Property Confiscation Act 2000, the Act as at 9 December 2005
- Canadian Mutual Assistance in Criminal Matters Act 1998, 36-37 Eliz II, Vol II

TABLE OF UNITED NATIONS RESOLUTIONS

- A/RES/60/288, resolution on Global Counterterrorism Strategy (2006), adopted by the General Assembly at its 60th session on 08 September 2006
- S/RES/1267 (1999), resolution on Al-Qaeda Sanctions Committee, adopted by the Security Council at its 4051st meeting on 15 October 1999
- S/RES/1373(2001), resolution on threats to international peace and security caused by terrorist acts, adopted by the Security Council at its 4385th meeting, on 28 September 2001
- S/RES/1456 (2003), resolution on combating terrorism adopted by the Security Council at its 4688th meeting, on 20 January 2003
- S/RES/1566 (2004), resolution concerning threats to international Peace and Security, adopted by the Security Council at its 5053 meeting, on 8 October 2004
- S/RES/1624 (2005), resolution on the incitement and glorification of terrorist acts, adopted by the Security Council at its 5261st meeting, on 14 September 2005
- S/RES/1817(2008), resolution on the Production and trafficking of drugs in Afghanistan, adopted by the Security Council at its 5907th meeting, on 11 June 2008
- U.N. GAOR, 51ST Sess., Supp. No.10 U.N. Doc. A/ 51/10(1996) Draft Code of Crimes against Peace and Security of Mankind 1996

ABBREVIATIONS

-/AC.../-	Adhoc Committee
-/Add.../-	Addendum
-/CN..../-	Commission
-/CONF.../-	Conference
-/CRP.../-	Conference Room Paper
-/RES.../-	Resolution
-/Rev.../-	Revision
-/SR.../-	Summary Record of meeting
-/WP.../-	Working Group
[GC]	Grand Chamber of the European Court of Human Rights
A.C.	Appeals Cases
A.L.R	American Law Reports
A/-	Document Symbol for the UN General Assembly
S/-	Document Symbol for the United Nations Security Council
AJIL	American Journal of International Law
ALL ER	All England Law Report
ALR	Australian Law Reports
ANI	Asia News International
Annex	Annexure
ASILS	Association of Student International Law Societies
ATA	Anti-Terrorism Act 1997
ATNIF	Australian Treaties not yet in force
ATS	Australian Treaty Series
BBC	British Broadcasting Corporation
Berkeley J. Int'l L	Berkley Journal of International Law
Brook J. Int'l L.	Brooklyn Journal of International Law
Brown J. World Aff.	Brown Journal of World Affairs
BYBIL	British Yearbook of International Law
C.C.C	Canadian Criminal Cases Canada
Cal W.Int'l.L.J	California Western International Law Journal
CAN	Canada

CAT	United Nations Convention against Torture 1984
CCE	Continuing Criminal Enterprise
CCPR/C/	Document Symbol for UN Human Rights Committee
CCSDNY	Circuit Court of the United States for the Southern District of New York
CIL	Centre for International Law
Cir.	Circuit Court
CNSA	Control of Narcotics Substance Act 1997 of Pakistan
COE	Council of Europe
Colum. J. Trannsnat'l L	Columbia Journal of Transnational Law
Cornell Int'l L.J	Cornell International Law Journal
Crim Law Forum	Criminal Law Forum
CRS	Congressional Research Service
CTC	UN Counterterrorism Committee
CWLTH	Commonwealth
Denv. J. Int'l L. & Poly	Denver Journal of International Law and Policy
DePaul L. Rev	Depaul Law Review
E/CN.4/	Document Symbol for UN Commission for Human Rights
E/CONF	Document symbol for the UN Economic and Social Council
ECHR	European Convention on Human Rights
ECR	European Court Reports
ECtHR	European Court of Human Rights
Edn	Edition
EJIL	European Journal of International Law
Eliz II	Queen Elizabeth II
Emory Intl L. Review	Emory International Law Review
Eng. Rep	The English Reports
EWHC (Admin)	High Court (Administrative Court)
EWHC (Comm)	High Court (Commercial Division)
F.2d	Federal Reporter, 2nd Series
F.Supp (DDC)	Federal Supplement District of Columbia Circuit
F.Supp., F.Supp.2d.	Federal Supplement
F.Supp.2d	Federal Supplement, 2nd Series
FATF	Financial Action Task Force
Fr. v. Turk.	France v. Turkey

FRY	Federal Republic of Yugoslavia
H.L	House of Lords
Halsbury's Stat.	Halsbury's Statutes of England and Wales
Harv.Int'l .LJ	Harvard International Law Journal
I.C.J	International Court of Justice
ICAO	International Civil Aviation Organization
ICC	International Criminal Court
ICCPR	International Covenant on Civil and Political Rights
ICJ Rep.	ICJ Reports
ICLQ	International and Comparative Law Quarterly
ICTY	International Criminal Tribunal for the former Yugoslavia
ILC	International Law Commission
ILM	International Legal Materials
ILR	International Legal Reports
IMAC	Federal Act on International Mutual Assistance in Criminal Matters 1981
Int'l. J. of Refugee law	International Journal of Refugee Law
Int'l Enforcement L. Rep.	International Enforcement Law Report
IPC	Indian Penal Code 1860
Isr. L. Rev	Israel Law Review
J. Crim. L. & Criminology	Journal of Criminal Law and Criminology
J. Int'l L & Econ	Journal of International Law and Economics
L.S.I	Laws of the state of Israel
Maastricht J. Eur. & Comp. L.	Maastricht Journal of European and Comparative Law
Man (QB)	Court of Queen's Bench of Manitoba
MLAT	Mutual Legal Assistance Treaty
mtg.	meeting
NAB Ordinance 1999	National Accountability Bureau Ordinance 1999
New Eng. L. Rev	New England Law Review
NLJ	New Law Journal
NRO	National Reconciliation Ordinance 2007
NY Times	New York Times
P.D.	Decisions of Israeli Supreme Court (Piskei Din shel Bet HaMishpat HaElyon LeYisrael)
Pace Y.B.Int'l L.	Pace Yearbook of International Law
Para	Paragraph

PCIJ	Permanent Court of International Justice
PLD	Pakistan Law Digest
POCA	Proceeds of Crimes Act
PPC	Pakistan Penal Code 1860
PTI	Press Trust of India
QDB	Queen's Bench Division
R.S.C	The Revised Statutes of Canada
RICO	Racketeer Influenced Corrupt Organisations Act
S.D.N.Y	US District Court for the Southern District of New York
Sc.	A section of a legal enactment
SC.	Supreme Court of Pakistan
SCR	Supreme Court of Canada Reports
Sess.	Session
Ss.	Sections of a legal enactment
StGB	Strafgesetzbuch- German Criminal Code
Supp.	Supplementary
Syracuse J.Int'l L. & Comm	Syracuse Journal of International Law and Commerce
Transp. L.J.	Transportation Law Journal
U.C.Q.B.R.	Upper Canada Queen's Bench Reports
U.S.	United States Reports
U.S.C	United States Code
UCQB	Upper Canada Queen's Bench Reports 1841-1882
UKHL	United Kingdom House of Lords
UNCAC	UN Convention against Corruption 2003
UNGAOR	United Nations General Assembly Official Records
UNODC	United Nations Office on Drugs and Crime
UNTOC	UN Convention on Transnational Organised Crime 2000
UNTS	United Nations Treaty Service
USCA	United States Code Annotated
USCS	United States Code Service
UST	United States Treaties and other international Agreements
W.D.N.Y	Western District of New York
WLR	Weekly Law Reports
Yale J. Int'l L.	Yale Journal of International Law
YBILC	Yearbook of International Law Commission

Glossary

Aut Dedere Aut Judicare Duty to Extradite or Prosecute.

Double criminality The act in respect of which state cooperation is sought must constitute a crime under the laws of both the requesting and requested states.

Double punishability The act in respect of which state cooperation is sought must fulfil the standards of criminal responsibility of each cooperating state.

forum conveniens Place most convenient to hold a trial.

Jus Cogens Peremptory norm of international law.

Legality No one shall be prosecuted or punished without there being a previous violation of law; it is used inter-changeably for *nullum cimen.*

nemo debet bis vexari No one to be tried or punished twice for the same act.

nullum crimen sine lege No crime without law.

Predicate Crime The act through which the proceeds of crime are generated.

Refouler A refugee shall not be returned to a state where his life is in danger.

Relator A person whose extradition or interrogation is sought by the requesting state.

Res Judicata A rule that a final judgement on the merits by a court having jurisdiction is conclusive between the parties to a suit as to all matters that were litigated or that could have been litigated in that suit.

Special use of double criminality When the extradition is sought in respect of a crime taking place outside state territory, the theory of jurisdiction applied by the requesting state must correspond to the rules of jurisdiction applied by the requested state.

Speciality An extraditee shall not be prosecuted for crimes committed before extradition, other than those for which his extradition is granted.

Transnational crimes Crimes spreading across national frontiers in terms of perpetration or nationality or location of the victim or offenders.

Transnational offenders The offenders involved in crimes spreading across national frontiers.

Value and Substitute Confiscation Modern theories of confiscation whereby the proceeds which have been lost or converted into new property can be confiscated.

INTRODUCTION

Transnational terrorism and organized crimes pose severe threats to international security and stability. Transnational crimes are characterized by criminal activities that transcend national borders and therefore make it difficult for individual states to address these crimes on their own.

Combating transnational crimes effectively requires international cooperation among states. Currently, there are over 200 international conventions dealing with the phenomenon of transnational crimes. The United Nations has also responded to this challenge by supporting the development of international conventions on terrorism and organized crime, which aim to facilitate law enforcement cooperation among States-Parties. These conventions have established certain mandatory obligations that are designed to ensure harmony among the legal systems of States-Parties with a view to making them conducive to law enforcement cooperation.

The objective of these international, multilateral conventions is to suppress transnational crimes through state cooperation in extradition and mutual legal assistance. To achieve this aim, the conventions have established certain mandatory obligations that ensure harmony among the legal systems of States-Parties. The obligations are designed to bring harmony in national justice systems to enable the parties to satisfy the requirements of law enforcement cooperation. This is necessary to further satisfy the requirements of extradition and mutual legal assistance proceedings, which necessitate similarity in the legal systems of the requesting and requested states. These requirements can be classified into distinct categories of conditions and procedures.

Conditions refer to conditions associated with the principle of reciprocity or exchange of comparable favours, upon which the laws and treaties on extradition and mutual legal assistance are based. It demands similar legal prescriptions or equivalent conceptions of justice under the laws of the requesting and requested state with respect to the act concerning which surrender or interrogation is sought. To enable the parties to satisfy conditions, the international conventions impose mandatory obligations to implement their rules concerning jurisdiction, criminalisation and fair treatment.

Procedure implies the procedure of applying or executing the enforcement devices of aut dedere aut judicare and confiscation of the proceeds of crime. The application of both these devices necessitates similarity in the laws of the requesting and requested states with respect to procedure of enforcement. Similarity is needed to ensure that a foreign request may not be refused due to the requested state lacking enabling procedural rules or the request not being consistent with its procedural law. To establish similarity, the conventions impose mandatory obligations to implement the mechanisms of aut dedere aut judicare and confiscation of the proceeds of crimes. This book critically examines the impact of these obligations on state cooperation in bringing to justice transnational offenders.

This book provides a comprehensive analysis of the mandatory obligations established under 12 major counterterrorism and organized crime conventions to facilitate inter-state cooperation in law enforcement. The book examines in depth the obligations to establish extraterritorial jurisdiction, criminalize offenses, provide fair treatment, and implement the aut dedere aut judicare and confiscation frameworks. The author rigorously explores how these mandatory obligations aim to overcome barriers to cooperation posed by conflicting domestic laws and procedures across states.

By assessing the implementation of these mandatory obligations in domestic laws and treaties worldwide, the book reveals both promising trends as well as ongoing challenges and limitations. The author pays attention to the fact that, despite decades of efforts by states to strengthen cooperation in combating these transnational crimes, critical gaps and inconsistencies remain in the implementation of international counterterrorism and organized crime conventions. This book critically examines the impact of mandatory obligations under the counterterrorism and organized crime conventions on state cooperation in bringing transnational offenders to justice. The central argument of this book is that the mandatory obligations under the counterterrorism and organized crime conventions are required to be implemented in accordance with, and to the extent permissible, under the national law of state parties. The book further proves that although the international counterterrorism and organized crime conventions establish mandatory obligations, they also include exceptions, qualifications, and allowances that provide parties with enough flexibility to alter their obligations according to their legal systems. These exceptions and qualifications often take the form of safeguard or savings clauses, which permit parties to deviate from their obligations in certain circumstances, and reservations, which allow parties to opt out of certain provisions altogether. As a result, the obligations may not be as strict as they appear on paper, leading to inconsistent implementation and enforcement across different states. Accordingly, when they are translated domestically, they do not achieve a level of harmony sufficient to facilitate the fulfillment of the requirements of extradition and mutual legal assistance, i.e., 'double conditions' and procedural similarity needed to enforce aut dedere aut judicare and confiscation. Resultantly, discretion rests with the requested state to grant or refuse cooperation depending upon its political and diplomatic relations with the requesting state. This contradicts the objective of facilitating law enforcement cooperation in the specific context of borderless or transnational crimes. Following this approach, state cooperation concerning transnational crimes remains as discretionary and as unregulated as cooperation in regard to ordinary crimes. This calls into question the utility of reliance on mandatory obligations as tools to facilitate law enforcement cooperation.

As an alternative, some bilateral and regional treaties and domestic laws adopt the strategy of relaxing 'double conditions' and simplifying the procedure of applying aut dedere aut judicare and confiscation. This strategy also aims at facilitating law enforcement cooperation; however, it takes the route of regulating the requirements of extradition and mutual legal assistance rather than harmonizing national justice systems to make them conducive to their demands. Given that this system carries greater potential for facilitating law enforcement cooperation, this book recommends that the makers of the international counterterrorism and organized crime conventions should substitute or complement the mandatory obligations with it. Significantly, states have, by agreeing not to apply political and fiscal offense exceptions to extradition and interrogation proceedings involving these crimes, shown their willingness to accept this approach of facilitating law enforcement cooperation in the specific context of transnational crimes.

The book comprises five chapters, each of which addresses a specific aspect of the impact of mandatory obligations on state cooperation in bringing transnational offenders to justice.

Part one of the thesis concerns the mandatory obligations to establish jurisdiction, criminalize offenses and provide fair treatment to the offenders. The obligations are designed to harmonize national legal systems with a view to facilitating the fulfilment of 'double conditions' applicable to extradition and mutual legal assistance proceedings. This part consists of chapters 2, 3, and 4.

Chapter 2 relates to the mandatory obligation to establish jurisdiction over the crimes established by the conventions. The obligation is directed at facilitating the fulfilment of certain conditions of extradition laws and treaties which stipulate that when surrender is requested in respect of a crime taking place outside state territory, the requesting state must not only have jurisdiction over crime but the theory of jurisdiction applied by it must also correspond to the theory applied by the requested state with respect to the act in question.

Chapter 3 relates to the obligation to legislate against universal definitions of crimes. The laws and treaties on extradition and mutual legal assistance require that the act in respect of which cooperation is sought must constitute a crime under the laws of both the requesting and requested state. The condition is known as double criminality. To enable the parties to meet this condition, international counterterrorism and organized crime conventions impose a duty on states to legislate against universal definitions of crimes.

Chapter 4 relates to the obligation to provide fair treatment to persons facing extradition and mutual assistance proceedings. The obligation responds to a condition under extradition and mutual assistance laws which stipulates that the act in respect of which surrender or interrogation is sought must not be considered nonpunishable under the laws of either the requesting or the requested state due to actual or possible violation of human rights of the offender.

Part two of the thesis concerns the obligations under the international counterterrorism and organized crime conventions to implement the enforcement mechanisms of aut dedere aut judicare and confiscation of the proceeds of crime. The application of both these measures demands similarity in the laws of the requesting and requested states with respect to the procedure of enforcement. To establish similarity, the international conventions impose mandatory obligations to implement these mechanisms. This part comprises chapters 5 and 6.

Chapter 5 of the thesis looks into the question of the extent to which the mandatory obligation to implement aut dedere aut judicare facilitates its application. The application of both alternative measures underlying the maxim, i.e. extradition and prosecution depends upon the requested state having enabling procedural rules or the request being consistent with its procedural law. To establish similarity in national laws, the international conventions oblige the parties to implement the mechanism.

Chapter 6 analyses the question of the extent to which the obligation to implement the mechanism of confiscation upon foreign request facilitates its application. The application of confiscation upon foreign request depends upon the requested state having enabling procedural rules or the request being consistent with its national laws. To establish similarity in national legal systems, the international conventions impose mandatory obligations to implement the mechanism.

Chapter 7 is the concluding chapter which evaluates the general conclusions made within the study at the end of each chapter. This includes suggestions for improving established provisions of the conventions with a view to make them more effective in facilitating state cooperation in law enforcement.

This fascinating book offers a fresh perspective on the challenges of bringing transnational criminals to justice. Unlike previous publications, which only looked at differences in national laws compared to international conventions, this book takes a more comprehensive approach. It examines three key areas: international conventions on transnational crimes, national laws, and treaties related to extradition and legal assistance.

The book not only highlights inconsistencies in how countries implement international obligations but also delves into the complex world of state cooperation in extradition and legal assistance. It explores the obstacles created by differing national laws when trying to apprehend or question suspects involved in transnational crimes.

To make the topic even more engaging, the book includes real-life court cases that demonstrate the potential problems that can arise during the extradition and questioning of transnational criminals due to inconsistent implementation of international obligations. This book is perfect for anyone interested in understanding the intricacies of international law and the challenges faced in bringing transnational offenders to justice.

This book definitely aims to contribute to the ongoing debate on the most effective approach to facilitating law enforcement cooperation in the specific context of transnational crimes.

It also proposes a range of prescriptive recommendations to strengthen the effectiveness of international conventions in enabling cooperative responses to transnational security threats. Governments and policymakers will find this an invaluable guide to modernizing their legal and operational frameworks for inter-state cooperation in law enforcement

By assessing the implementation of these mandatory obligations in domestic laws and treaties worldwide, the book reveals both promising trends as well as ongoing challenges and limitations. It proposes a range of prescriptive recommendations to strengthen the effectiveness of international conventions in enabling cooperative responses to transnational security threats. Governments and policymakers will find this an invaluable guide to modernizing their legal and operational frameworks for inter-state cooperation in law enforcement

CHAPTER 1

OVERVIEW OF INTERNATIONAL CONVENTIONS ON OBLIGATIONS, COUNTER-TERRORISM, AND ORGANISED CRIME

The UN-sponsored international conventions on terrorism and organised crime deal with a specific genre of crime which spreads across national frontiers.[1] Accordingly, the conventions have been collectively named by some scholars as 'transnational treaties' and the crimes established by them 'transnational crimes'.[2] Although the nature and motivation of these crimes differ, the means adopted by the offenders to carry them out are more or less the same.[3] For example, the offenders involved in these crimes purposely spread their operations in more than one state to defeat territorially restricted national laws. Furthermore, they paralyse administrative machinery of states through violence, corruption and obstruction of justice with a view to ensure non-enforcement of law.[4]

Reflecting the similarity of the means adopted by the offenders to commit the crimes,[5] the conventions establishing these crimes provide identical measures for their repression.[6] The primary method relied upon by the

---

[1] See Cherif Bassiouni, 'Effective National and International Action against Organised Crime and Terrorist Criminal Activities' 4 Emory International Law Review (1990) 9 at 36; For relevant treaty provisions see (n 22) Chapter 2 below

[2] Carrie Lyn Donigan Guymon, 'International Legal Mechanisms for Combating Transnational Organised Crime: The Need for a Multilateral Convention' 18 Berkeley J. Int'l L (2000) 53 at 86-87; See also Neil Boister, 'Transnational Criminal Law' 14 EJIL (2003) 953 at 953; Roger S. Clarke, 'The United Nations Convention against Transnational Organised Crime' 50 Wayne State Law Review (2004) 161 at 166

[3] Bassiouni (n 1) 10

[4] Guymon (n 2) 87 See also Cherif Bassiouni, 'Policy Considerations on Interstate Cooperation in Criminal Matters' 4 Pace Y.B. Int'l L. (1992) 123 at 127

[5] Bassiouni, 'Effective Action' (n 1) 13

[6] Boister (n 2); Guymon (n 2); D.W. Sproule and Paul St-Denis, 'The UN Drug Trafficking Convention: An Ambitious Step' 27 Canadian Yearbook of International

conventions is state cooperation in law enforcement, which is required to be carried out through the measures of extradition, mutual legal assistance, *aut dedere aut judicare* and confiscation of the proceeds of crime.[7]

The laws and treaties regulating these measures require harmony in the legal systems of the requesting and requested states.[8] The international counterterrorism and organised crime conventions do not supersede these laws and treaties. Instead, they aim to make national legal systems responsive to their demands through establishing harmony.[9] To bring about harmony, the conventions establish certain mandatory obligations.[10] The obligations represent a shift in the traditional role of international law which had previously been confined to establishing 'general obligations'. General obligations refer to provisions which do not require the parties to legislate; their purpose is to provide guidelines for the legislators.[11] Hence, they are akin to statements of policy.[12] As observed by Lambert, general obligations are based on the premise that 'international law imposes obligation not of way but of result.'[13] Mandatory obligations, on the other hand, imply binding duties whose non-compliance could entail state responsibility.[14]

Law (1989) 263 at 266; Kofi A Annan, Foreword to the Organized Crime Convention 2000 at iii; UNODC's Technical Assistance Guide 2009 for the implementation of the UN Convention against Corruption 2003 at 133

[7] The purpose of promoting state cooperation has been reiterated in a majority of international counter-terrorism and organised crime conventions under consideration. See (n 4) Chapter 3 below

[8] Lech Gardocki, 'Double Criminality in Extradition Law' 27 Isr. L. Rev. (1993) 288

[9] See UNODC's Legislative Guide 2004 for implementing the Organised Crime Convention 2000 at 130 <http://www.unodc.org/pdf/crime/legislative_guides/Legislative%20guides_Full%20version.pdf> [date accessed 21/03/23]

[10] ibid

[11] Olympia Beku, 'A Case for the Review of Article 88 of the ICC Statute: Strengthening a Forgotten Provision' 12 New Criminal Law Review (2009) 468 at 475

[12] Vaughan Lowe, *International Law* (New York: Oxford University Press 2007) 119

[13] Joseph J Lambert, *Terrorism and Hostages in International Law, A Commentary on Hostages Convention 1979* (Cambridge: Grotius Publications Limited 1990) 101

[14] Lowe (n 12)

The extraordinary nature of these obligations has led some scholars to claim that the international counterterrorism and organised crime conventions have established a new regime of state cooperation directed at subjecting sovereign discretion to collective law enforcement.[15] This book looks into the impact of these obligations on state cooperation in law enforcement.

The requirements of law enforcement cooperation which necessitate harmony in national legal systems can be classified into distinct categories of *conditions* and *procedure*. *Conditions* refer to 'double conditions' applicable to extradition and mutual legal assistance proceedings and *procedure* denotes the procedure of applying the enforcement devices of *aut dedere aut judicare* and confiscation. To establish harmony, the international conventions on terrorism and organised crime impose certain mandatory obligations. In keeping with the requirements of law enforcement cooperation necessitating harmony, the obligations established by the conventions can be classified into distinct categories of obligations responding to 'double conditions' and those concerning enforcement devices. In line with these, the book has been divided into two parts. I shall now provide an overview of each of the two parts and the issues disused thereunder.

1.1) Introduction to part one: mandatory obligations to establish jurisdiction, criminalise offences and provide fair treatment

Part one of the book concerns the mandatory obligations established by the international counterterrorism and organised crime conventions to establish jurisdiction, criminalise offences and provide fair treatment. The obligations respond to a series of 'double conditions' applicable to extradition and mutual legal assistance proceedings necessitating similarity in national justice systems concerning areas such as jurisdiction, criminalisation and fair treatment.

Extradition and mutual legal assistance proceedings are governed by the traditional principle of reciprocity.[16] According to this principle, states provide assistance to each other on reciprocal basis with a view to ensure that if circumstances are reversed in future and the requested state steps into the shoes of requesting state, it must be entitled to obtain similar assistance with respect to the act in question.[17] Since there is no rule of

[15] Sproule (n 6); Boister (n 2); Guymon (n 2)
[16] See Edward M Wise, 'Some Problems of Extradition' 15 Wayne State L. Rev. (1968-1969) 709 at 713
[17] ibid

general international law which compels a state to extradite or to provide mutual legal assistance in the absence of a treaty, these proceedings are carried out on the basis of bilateral treaties which are premised on reciprocity.[18] The principle necessitates similar legal prescriptions or equivalent concepts of justice in the requesting and requested states, with respect to the act concerning which surrender or interrogation is sought. It is generally expressed in the form of a series of 'double conditions' necessitating harmony in national legal systems with respect to areas such as jurisdiction, criminalisation and human rights.[19] The double conditions are commonly referred to using the generic title of 'double criminality' and are found amongst the grounds for refusal of assistance in the laws and treaties on extradition and mutual legal assistance.[20]

The international counterterrorism and organised crime conventions do not supersede these laws and treaties; instead they aim to make national legal systems responsive to their demands through establishing harmony. To facilitate the fulfilment of 'double conditions', the conventions establish mandatory obligations to implement their rules concerning jurisdiction, criminalisation and fair treatment.

This book criticises the approach of satisfying 'double conditions' of extradition and mutual assistance proceedings through establishing mandatory obligations under the international conventions. Since the obligations are required to be implemented to the extent permissible under national law, when they are translated domestically, they reflect the diversity of national legal systems. As a result, enough discrepancies arise in the laws of the requested and requesting states to allow refusal of surrender or interrogation based upon non-fulfilment of 'double conditions', which are applied in multiple ways as grounds for refusal of assistance under extradition and mutual assistance laws and treaties.

The satisfaction of various applications of 'double conditions' requires considerable harmony in the justice systems of cooperating states. This necessitates the establishment of mandatory obligations without any qualification or exception. However, states parties to the international

---

[18] ibid

[19] Gardocki (n 8)

[20] ibid; See also SZ Fellar, 'The Significance of the Requirement of Double Criminality in the Law of Extradition' 10 Isr. L. Rev. (1975) 51 at 71-75

conventions are unwilling to accept such absolute and overriding obligations.[21]

Some bilateral and regional treaties adopt the technique of requiring the parties to relax the application of 'double conditions' considering the specific nature of transnational or borderless crimes.[22] This strategy is also aimed at facilitating state cooperation in law enforcement; however, it takes the route of regulating the requirements of extradition and mutual legal assistance rather than harmonising national justice systems to make them conducive to their demands. This book recommends that the makers of the international counterterrorism and organised crime conventions adopt this technique as a substitute or complement to the strategy of establishing mandatory obligations.

1.2) Introduction to part two: mandatory obligations to implement enforcement devices of *aut dedere aut judicare* and confiscation of the proceeds of crime

Part two of the book relates to mandatory obligations established by the international counterterrorism and organised crime conventions to implement law enforcement devices of *aut judicare aut judicare* and confiscation of the proceeds of crime. The two devices are specifically designed to promote inter-state cooperation for bringing to justice transnational offenders. *Aut dedere aut judicare* refers to the obligation to extradite or prosecute, whereas, confiscation implies forfeiture of the proceeds of crime upon foreign request.

Since the two devices are regulated by same laws and treaties which govern extradition and mutual legal assistance, their application makes similar demands, i.e. harmony in the laws of requesting and requested states. Nonetheless, in addition to harmony necessitated by 'double conditions' applicable to extradition and mutual assistance proceedings underlying these devices, they also require harmony with respect to *procedure* of their enforcement. Procedural harmony is needed to ensure that a foreign request may not be refused due to the requested state lacking enabling procedural rules or the request not being consistent with its procedural law. To establish harmony, the counterterrorism and organised crime conventions impose mandatory obligations upon the parties to

---

[21] See for instance ICAO Doc 8979-LC/165-2 at 81, SA Doc. No.33, Rev.1 (1972)

[22] See also Guy Stessens, *Money Laundering: A New International Law Enforcement Model* (UK Cambridge University Press 2004) 291-292

implement the mechanisms of *aut dedere aut judicare* and confiscation of the proceeds of crimes upon foreign request.

The book will explain that as per the existing scheme of the conventions, the *procedure* of applying *aut dedere aut judicare* and confiscation of the proceeds of crime is to be determined in accordance with the national law of the requested state party. Consequently, the obligations to implement these mechanisms may only bring harmony to the extent of their inclusion in national laws, which is insufficient to facilitate their application. For such facilitation to occur, it is essential that an elaborate procedure be provided for applying or executing these devices.

In contrast to the counterterrorism and organised crime conventions, some bilateral/regional treaties and domestic laws provide extensive guidelines on the procedure of applying *aut dedere aut judicare* and confiscation of the proceeds of crime upon foreign request.[23] Guidelines on the pattern of these laws and treaties reduce dissimilarities in national laws and ensure that the requested state has enabling rules at its disposal to carry out the request. The book recommends that identical provisions should be imported into the international conventions in order to complement or replace their mandatory obligations.

1.3) Counterterrorism and organised crime conventions under consideration

According to Bassiouni, there are over 200 international conventions dealing with the phenomenon of transnational crimes, however, for the purposes of this book only those conventions have been chosen which proscribe the acts of transnational terrorism and organised crime.[24] The rationale of choosing these conventions is the similarity of the rules established by them. Their commonalities include:

1. Regulation of crimes committed by non-state actors and reliance on domestic legal processes for repression of the crimes. In other words, there is no international court or tribunal vested with the jurisdiction to try these crimes and the conventions rely on

---

[23] ibid

[24] Cherif Bassiouni, 'The Sources and Contents of International Criminal Law: A Theoretical Framework' in 1 International Criminal Law: Crimes (2nd Edn. 1999) at 32-33 & 62-69

domestic courts and legal processes for their prosecution and punishment.[25]

2. The crimes established by all these conventions spread across national frontiers in terms of their perpetration or nationality or location of the victims or offenders. Since it is not possible for any one state to prevent and punish these crimes single handedly, the objective of the conventions is to facilitate state cooperation in criminal law enforcement.[26]
3. Each of these conventions sets forth mandatory obligations for the parties to criminalise offences, establish jurisdiction, provide fair treatment and to implement law enforcement devices of *aut dedere aut judicare* and mutual legal assistance.[27]

Below is given a brief description of 13 Conventions chosen for the purposes of this book.

1.3.1) Convention for the Suppression of Unlawful Seizure of Aircraft Signed at The Hague, on 16 December 1970 [hereinafter the Hague Convention 1970][28]

The Convention is concerned with preventing and punishing the unlawful acts of hijacking, i.e. seizure and control, directed against an aircraft in flight.[29]

1.3.2) Convention for the Suppression of Unlawful Acts against the Safety of Civil Aviation, Signed at Montreal, on 23 September1971 [hereinafter the Montreal Convention 1971][30]

The Convention responds to the acts against the safety of civil aviation.

It establishes as criminal offences the acts of sabotage of aircraft committed in flight as well as directed from the ground through interference with air navigational facilities.[31]

---

[25] Bassiouni, 'Policy Considerations' (n 4)
[26] See (n 1); See also (n 21-30 & 37-39) Chapter 5 below
[27] Legislative Guide for implementing Organised Crime Convention 2000 (n 9)
[28] ICAO Doc. 8920 / 860 UNTS 105 / [1972] ATS 16 / 10 ILM 133 (1971)
[29] See preamble of the Hague Convention 1970
[30] ICAO Doc. 8966 / 974 UNTS 177 / [1973] ATS 24 / 10 ILM 1151 (1971)
[31] See article 1 (b) and (c) of the Montreal Convention 1971

1.3.3) Convention for the Prevention and Punishment of Crimes against Internationally Protected Persons, including Diplomatic Agents, Adopted by the General Assembly of United Nations on 14 December 1973 [hereinafter the Protection of Diplomats Convention 1973][32]

The need for the Protection of Diplomats Convention 1973 was felt when it was realised that attacks against diplomatic agents and other internationally protected persons create a serious threat to the maintenance of normal international relations which are necessary for cooperation among states. It establishes as crimes the acts of violence committed against heads of states, their families, government representatives and diplomatic agents.[33]

1.3.4) International Convention against the Taking of Hostages Adopted by the General Assembly of the United Nations on 17 December 1979 [hereinafter the Hostages Convention 1979][34]

The Convention is aimed at preventing and punishing the act of taking of hostages, the act being targeted at compelling a state or an international organisation to do or abstain from doing something as a condition for the release of hostages.[35]

1.3.5) Convention on Physical Protection of Nuclear Materials, Signed at Vienna on 3 March 1980 [hereinafter the Nuclear Materials Convention 1980][36]

The Convention was adopted to avert the potential dangers posed by the unlawful taking and the use of nuclear material including its theft, robbery, illegal import, and export and trafficking.[37]

---

[32] UNTS vol.1035 p.167

[33] See Preamble and article 2 of the Protection of Diplomats Convention 1973

[34] 1316 UNTS 205 / [1990] ATS 17/ 18 ILM 1456 (1979)

[35] See article 1(1) of the Hostages Convention 1979

[36] 1456 UNTS 246 / 18 ILM 1419(1980) / [1987] ATS 16

[37] See article 7 of the Nuclear Materials Convention 1980

1.3.6) Convention for the Suppression of Unlawful Acts against the Safety of Maritime Navigation, concluded at Rome on 10 March 1988 [hereinafter the Rome Convention 1988][38]

The Convention is designed to prevent and punish unlawful acts jeopardising the freedom of maritime navigation and the safety of the persons and property on board.[39]

1.3.7) International Convention for the Suppression of Terrorist Bombings, Signed at New York on 15 December 1997 [hereinafter the Terrorist Bombings Convention 1997][40]

The Convention aims at suppressing terrorist attacks involving the use of explosives or other lethal devices intended to provoke a state of terror in the general public for the achievement of political objectives.[41]

1.3.8) International Convention for the Suppression of the Financing of Terrorism, Adopted by the General Assembly of United Nations on 9 December 1999 [hereinafter the Terrorism Financing Convention 1999][42]

The Convention focuses on combating the financing of terrorists and terrorist organisations. It establishes as crimes the acts of collecting and providing funds with the intention and knowledge that they will be used to carry out terrorist attacks.[43]

1.3.9) International Convention for the Suppression of Acts of Nuclear Terrorism, Adopted at New York on 13 April 2005 [hereinafter Nuclear Terrorism Convention 2005][44]

The Convention aims at preventing and punishing the use and possession of radioactive material or devices intended to cause death, injury, damage to property or to a nuclear facility in order to compel a state or an organization to do or abstain from doing something.[45]

---

[38] 1618 UNTS 201 / [1993] ATS 16 / 10 ILM 672 (1988)
[39] See preamble of the Rome Convention 1988
[40] 2149 UNTS 256 / [2002] ATS 17 / UN Doc. A / RES / 52 /164
[41] See article 2 of the Terrorist Bombings Convention 1997
[42] 2178 UNTS 197/39 ILM 270 (2000) / [2002] ATS 23
[43] See preamble and article 2 of the Terrorism Financing Convention 1999
[44] UN Doc. A / RES / 59 / 290 (2005) / [2005] ATNIF 20
[45] See article 2 of the Nuclear Terrorism Convention 2005

1.3.10) Convention on the Suppression of Unlawful Acts Relating to International Civil Aviation, Adopted at Beijing on 10 September 2010 [hereinafter the Beijing Convention 2010][46]

The Convention deals with new kinds of threats to International Civil Aviation such as bio- terrorism and cyber terrorism that jeopardise the safety and security of the persons and property on board and affect the operation of air services.[47]

1.3.11) United Nations Convention against Illicit Traffic in Narcotic Drugs and Psychotropic Substances 1988, Adopted at Vienna on 20 December 1988 [hereinafter the Drugs Convention 1988][48]

The Convention is concerned with countering the illegal production of, demand for and traffic in narcotic drugs and psychotropic substances.[49]

1.3.12) United Nations Convention against Transnational Organized Crime, Adopted at New York on 15 November 2000 [hereinafter the Organized Crime Convention 2000][50]

The Convention aims at defeating the organised criminality of any type by making unlawful the acts of participation in the activities of an organised criminal group with common purpose.[51]

1.3.13) United Nations Convention against Corruption, Adopted at New York on 31 October 2003 [hereinafter the UN Convention against Corruption 2003][52]

The Convention responds to the phenomenon of transnational corruption which undermines democracies and creates political instability by depriving the affected nations of their resources and wealth.[53]

---

[46] Not yet in force

[47] See article 1 the Beijing Convention 2010; also see Ruwantissa Abeyratne, 'The Beijing Convention of 2010 on the Suppression of Unlawful Acts Relating to International Civil Aviation—an Interpretative Study' 4 Journal of Transport Security (2011) 131 at 135, 136

[48] UN Doc. E/CONF.82/15 (1988) / 28 ILM 493 (1989)

[49] See preamble of the Drugs Convention 1988

[50] 40 ILM 335 (2001) / UN Doc. A / 55 / 383 at 25 (2000) / [2004] ATS 12

[51] See article 5 the Organized Crime Convention 2000

[52] UN Doc. A/ 58 / 422 (2003) / (2004) 43 ILM 37

[53] See preamble of the UN Convention against Corruption 2003

In addition to similarities mentioned above, a majority of these conventions are widely ratified and hence are considered to have established obligations of universal scope.[54] For example, out of 193 UN member states, 185 are party to the Hague Convention 1970,[55] 188 have ratified the Montreal Convention 1971,[56] 168 are party to the Hostages Convention 1979,[57] 167 are party to the Protection of Diplomats Convention 1973,[58] 156 are party to the Rome Convention 1988,[59] 142 are party to the Nuclear Materials Convention 1980,[60] 165 are party to the Terrorist Bombings Convention 1997,[61] 173 are party to the Terrorism Financing Convention 1999,[62] 188 are party to the Drugs Convention 1988,[63] 174 are party to the Organised Crime Convention 2000 [64] and 165

---

[54] M. Cherif Bassiouni & Edward M Wise, *'Aut dedere Aut Judicare: The duty to extradite or prosecute in international law'* (Netherlands: Matinus Nijhoff Publishers 1995) 20, 21

[55] International Civil Aviation Organization (ICAO) Secretariat <http://www.icao.int/secretariat/legal/List%20of%20Parties/Hague_EN.pdf> [Date accessed 21/03/23]

[56] Centre for International Law (CIL) National University of Singapore <http://cil.nus.edu.sg/1971/1971-convention-for-the-suppression-of-unlawful-acts-against-the-safety-of-civil-aviation/> [Date accessed 21/03/23]

[57] United Nations Treaty Collection <http://treaties.un.org/Pages/ViewDetails.aspx?src=TREATY&mtdsg_no=XVIII-5&chapter=18&lang=en> [Date accessed 21/03/23]

[58] United Nations Treaty Collection <http://treaties.un.org/Pages/ViewDetails.aspx?src=IND&mtdsg_no=XVIII-7&chapter=18&lang=en> [Date accessed 21/03/23]

[59] Centre for International Law (CIL) National University of Singapore <http://cil.nus.edu.sg/1988/1988-convention-for-the-suppression-of-unlawful-acts-against-the-safety-of-maritime-navigation/> [Date accessed 21/03/23]

[60] Centre for International Law (CIL) National University of Singapore <http://cil.nus.edu.sg/1979/1979-vienna-convention-on-the-physical-protection-of-nuclear-materials/> [Date accessed 21/03/23]

[61] United Nations Treaty Collection <http://treaties.un.org/doc/publication/mtdsg/volume%20ii/chapter%20xviii/xviii-9.en.pdf> [Date accessed 21/03/23]

[62] Centre for International Law (CIL) National University of Singapore <http://cil.nus.edu.sg/1999/1999-international-convention-for-the-suppression-of-the-financing-of-terrorism/> [Date accessed 21/03/23]

[63] Ratification status of the UN Convention against Narcotics Drugs and Psychotropic substances 1988 <http://treaties.un.org/doc/publication/mtdsg/volume%20i/chapter%20vi/vi-19.en.pdf> [Date accessed 21/03/23]

[64] United Nations Treaty Collection

have ratified the UN Convention against Corruption 2003.[65] Only two of the selected conventions have lesser ratifications namely the Beijing Convention 2010 and Nuclear Terrorism Convention 2005. The former has three [66] parties and the latter 84 parties.[67]

1.4) Distinction between Security Council's counterterrorism regime and the regime set forth by the international counterterrorism and organised crime conventions

Any discussion of the international conventions regulating the acts of transnational terrorism and organised crime is incomplete without mentioning the Security Council's counterterrorism regime complementing the counterterrorism conventions. The Security Council as the organ charged with primary responsibility of maintaining international peace and security has been the architect of UN's response to terrorism.[68] Through a series of resolutions, the Security Council has established a comprehensive counterterrorism regime. Resolution 1373 (2001) is of particular significance in this respect. It calls upon states to become parties to international conventions relating to terrorism.[69] Moreover, it obliges states to criminalise financing of terrorism, freeze assets belonging to terrorists and prohibit their nationals or legal entities operating in their territories from making funds available to terrorists.[70] Additionally, it establishes a Committee to monitor the implementation of the resolution.[71]

<http://treaties.un.org/Pages/ViewDetails.aspx?src=TREATY&mtdsg_no=XVIII-12&chapter=18&lang=en> [Date accessed 21/03/23]

65 United Nations Treaty Collection <http://treaties.un.org/doc/publication/mtdsg/volume%20ii/chapter%20xviii/xviii-14.en.pdf> [Date accessed 21/03/23]

66 International Civil Aviation Organization (ICAO) Secretariat <http://www.icao.int/secretariat/legal/List%20of%20Parties/Beijing_Conv_EN.pdf> [Date accessed 21/09/23]

67 United Nations Treaty Collection <http://treaties.un.org/Pages/ViewDetailsIII.aspx?&src=TREATY&mtdsg_no=XVIII%7E15&chapter=18&Temp=mtdsg3&lang=en> [Date accessed 21/03/23]

68 See article 24, the Charter of the United Nations Signed on 26 June 1945 at San Francisco [hereinafter the UN Charter]

69 See Para 3(d) S / RES / 1373 (2001), adopted by the Security Council at its 4385th meeting, on 28 September 2001 [hereinafter S/RES/1373(2001)]

70 See Para 1 ibid

71 See Para 6 ibid

The book therefore makes explicit references to various resolutions of the Security Council including SCR 1373 (2001) supporting the obligations set forth by counterterrorism conventions. However, the Security Council's regime differs fundamentally from the so called regime set forth by the international counterterrorism and organised crime conventions. The former seeks direct enforcement of international law by virtue of specific powers granted to the Security Council under chapter vii of the UN Charter; the latter, on the other hand, seeks to enforce international law indirectly, through domestic justice systems and domestic procedures.

For example, in resolution 1267, the Security Council determined that the Taliban's actions in Afghanistan of providing sanctuary to Bin Laden constituted a threat to international peace and security.[72] Thus, acting under Chapter vii of the UN Charter, the Security Council established a sanctioning regime to freeze financial resources of Taliban and to enforce an air embargo against Afghanistan.[73]

On the other hand, the measures of law enforcement set forth by the counterterrorism and organised crime conventions, such as extradition and mutual legal assistance are inherently bilateral and consent based processes. The enforcement of these measures depends upon the requested state having voluntarily undertaken the obligation to apply them, through the medium of a bilateral/regional treaty or unilateral legislation. Since these laws and treaties are based on the principle of reciprocity or exchange of comparable favours, they are not subject to the control of Security Council's counterterrorism regime. The argument draws support from the wording of resolution 1373 which calls upon states to '[c]ooperate, particularly through *bilateral and multilateral arrangements* and agreements, to prevent and suppress terrorist attacks and take action against perpetrators of such acts.' [74]

The mandate of Counterterrorism Committee (CTC) established pursuant to SCR 1373 is to bolster the capacity of states to fight terrorism.[75] It includes monitoring of state compliance with the obligations to criminalise offences, establish jurisdiction, freeze assets and deny safe heavens; it does not however extend to supervising cooperative arrangements arrived

---

[72] S / RES / 1267 (1999), Adopted by the Security Council at its 4051st meeting on 15 October 1999 [hereinafter S / RES / 1267 (1999)]

[73] See Para 4 ibid

[74] See Para 3(c) S / RES / 1373 (2001)

[75] Security Council, Counter Terrorism Committee <http://www.un.org/en/sc/ctc/> [date accessed 21/03/23]

at by states concerning extradition and mutual legal assistance. These arrangements are entrenched in the rules of comity and reciprocity, the supervision of which is beyond the control of CTC. Thus, it was held in the joint declaration of four judges of the ICJ in *Lockerbie* case that, in general international law there is no duty to extradite or prosecute in the absence of a bilateral/regional treaty.[76] Other law enforcement measures outlined by the conventions such as confiscation are also governed by the same principle because they are recent in origin and borrow the rules applicable to extradition.[77]

Since this book views the mandatory obligations set forth by the counterterrorism and organised crime conventions as attempts at facilitating state cooperation in law enforcement i.e. extradition and mutual legal assistance, an in-depth study of the Security Council's counterterrorism regime is outside its purview.

1.5) Do international conventions on terrorism and organised crime establish a supra national regime?

Scholars commenting upon the obligations set forth by the international counterterrorism and organised crime conventions can broadly be classified into two distinct groups: supra-national regime advocates and proponents of complementary and subsidiary regime. According to the first group, the obligations set forth by the conventions are designed to override national laws because the objective of the conventions is to bring sovereign discretion subject to collective law enforcement. This group comprises scholars like Shehu, Gurule, Boister, Guymon, Sproule and Abramovsky.[78] The writings of these scholars suggest that they are

---

[76] See Joint Declaration of Judges Evensen, Tarassov, Guillaume and Aguilar Mawdsley in *Lockerbie* Case 1992 I.C.J 136 (Apr 14) Para 2

[77] M. Cherif Bassiouni, '*International Criminal Law, Volume II: Multilateral and Bilateral Enforcement Mechanisms*' (3[rd]edn, Martinus Nijhoff, Netherlands, 2008) 17

[78] See Guymon (n 2); Boister (n 2); Clarke (n 2); Sproule (n 6); Abraham Abramovsky, 'Multilateral Conventions for the Suppression of Unlawful Seizure and Interference with Aircraft part-II: The Montreal Convention' 14 Colum. J. Trannsnat'l L. (1975) 268 at 294; According to Shehu, the international regime focusing transnational criminality asserts universal application of specific rules aiming at replacing diversity with uniformity, particularism with universalism. See Abdullah Y. Shehu, 'International Initiatives against Corruption and Money Laundering: an Overview' 12 Journal of Financial Crime (2005) 221 at 231 and Jimmy Gurule, 'The 1988 UN Convention against Illicit Traffic in Narcotic Drugs

disappointed at exceptions and safeguards included in the convention obligations pertaining to jurisdiction, criminalisation, human rights, *aut dedere aut judicare* and confiscation. To them, these exceptions have turned the obligations into hortatory or persuasive rules unlikely to produce the level of harmony needed to facilitate state cooperation in law enforcement.[79] Obviously, these scholars were expecting a broader regime targeted at facilitating law enforcement cooperation through establishing unqualified obligations.

The second group consists of scholars such as Bassiouni, Blakesley, Galdocki, Wise, Fellar, Williams, Dugard and Abelson.[80] According to this group, law enforcement cooperation is an inherently consent-based process, embedded in the principles of comity and reciprocity. It is therefore unlikely that such uniformity could be brought in national legal systems by imposing international obligations as to limit the discretion available to states to refuse extradition or interrogation.

In the opinion of these scholars, viewing the counterterrorism and organised crime conventions as instruments directed at subordinating sovereign discretion amounts to suggesting that the conventions may transform the consent-based and reciprocal nature of law enforcement

---

and Psychotropic Substances-A Ten Years Perspective: Is International Cooperation Merely Illusory?' 22 Fordham International Law Journal (1998-1999) 74

[79] See (n 169) Chapter 3 below

[80] See Adam Abelson, 'The Prosecute / Extradite Dilemma: Concurrent Criminal Jurisdiction and Global Governance'16 University of California, Davis (2010) 102 at 124. See also Roger O'Keefe, 'Universal Jurisdiction - Clarifying the Basic Concept' 2 Journal of International Criminal Justice (2004) 735; J. Dugard and Christine Van den Wyngaert, 'Reconciling Extradition with Human Rights' 92 AJIL (1998) 187 at 187; Christopher L. Blakesley, 'The Autumn of the Patriarch: The Pinochet Extradition Debacle and Beyond- Human Rights Clauses Compared to Traditional Derivative Protections Such as Double Criminality' 91 Journal of Criminal Law and Criminology (200-2001) 1; Cherif Bassouni, 'Theories of Jurisdiction and their Application in Extradition Law and Practice' 5 Cal W. Int'l L.J 1 (1974-75) 1; Christopher L. Blakesley, 'Wings For Talon: The Case for Extraterritorial Jurisdiction Over Sexual Exploitation of Children Through Cyberspace' 50 Wayne State L. Rev (2004) 109 at 119; Bassiouni, 'Policy Considerations' (n 4) 127; [80] Cherif Bassiouni, 'The "Political Offence Exception" Revisited: Extradition between the US and the UK- A Choice between Friendly Cooperation among Allies and Sound Law and Policy' 15 Denv. J. Int'l L. Pol'y (1986-1987) 255 at 260; Gardocki (n 8) 288; Sharon A Williams, 'Human Rights Safeguards and International Cooperation in Extradition: Striking in Balance' 3 Criminal Law Forum (1992) 191 at 200 and Wise (n 16) 709 at 713

cooperation into an obligatory one, an argument refuted by the conventions themselves. Furthermore, when the conventions are viewed as instruments overriding national laws, the solutions which are presented to address various problems arising in the extradition and interrogation of offenders involved in crimes set forth by the conventions, do not consider the reciprocal and consent-based nature of these measures. As a result, more often than not, such solutions turn out to be impracticable. For example, to resolve the issue of competing jurisdictions in the application of *aut dedere aut judicare*, it had been proposed that a system of priority be established in the bases of jurisdiction. This suggestion was put to vote and rejected by states parties to some counterterrorism conventions.[81] Similarly, a proposal of forfeiting the option not to extradite was also rejected.[82] To paraphrase the words of Bassiouni and Wise, right of the states not to extradite is so deeply rooted in practice of states that there is something fundamentally wrong with the suggestion that it could be restricted by imposing international obligations.[83]

The book while agreeing with the latter group of scholars, suggests that establishment of mandatory obligations may not produce the level of harmony needed to satisfy the requirements of law enforcement cooperation, i.e. 'double conditions' and similarity in the procedures of enforcing *aut dedere aut judicare* and confiscation. Since these requirements are governed by domestic laws and bilateral treaties, their application differs from state to state and region to region, necessitating unqualified obligations at the international level for their fulfilment through harmony. However, states parties have repeatedly shown their reluctance to accept such absolute obligations. Given the nature of these requirements, the best course is to simplify and relax them by regulating their use.

Simplification does not mean that the requirements of law enforcement cooperation should be altogether abolished or replaced. This would be akin to suggesting that the international counterterrorism and organised crime conventions can override bilateral treaties and domestic laws on extradition and mutual legal assistance. Instead, simplification means that the international conventions should regulate and clarify these requirements on the pattern of some bilateral/regional treaties and domestic laws with a

---

[81] See (n 197-198) Chapter 5 below
[82] See (n 160) Chapter 5 below
[83] Bassiouni & Wise (n 54) 66

view to ensuring their consistent application and providing better models for domestic legislation.

1.5.1) Distinction between the existing and proposed techniques of facilitating law enforcement cooperation and willingness of states to accept proposed technique

It can be argued that the proposed technique of facilitating law enforcement cooperation suffers from same weaknesses which are found in the existing technique. If the obligations of the conventions are ineffective in regard to making national legal systems conducive to the demands of extradition, mutual legal assistance, *aut dedere aut judicare* and confiscation they are unlikely to be productive in making states agree to collectively lower the barriers to law enforcement cooperation.

The argument fails to take stock of the fact that the existing technique is directed at harmonising the 'entire justice systems' of states parties to make them conducive to extradition and mutual legal assistance. For example, it requires states to implement convention obligations with respect to areas such as jurisdiction, criminalisation and treatment of offenders. This amounts to circumscribing the discretion available to states to conduct criminal proceedings in accordance with their local norms. On the other hand, the proposed technique impacts only one aspect of national justice systems i.e. state cooperation in law enforcement. Hence, it is less likely to be resisted by states. Furthermore, states have time and again shown their willingness to collectively lower the barriers to law enforcement cooperation in the specific context of transnational crimes. For example, by agreeing not to apply political and fiscal offence exception to extradition and mutual assistance proceedings involving these crimes, states have indicated that they are willing to dispense with the traditional hurdles in the specific context of transnational crimes. The proposed technique represents a step in that direction.

Simplification of the traditional requirements of extradition and mutual legal assistance has also been advocated by some noted scholars. For example Dugard and Wyngaert maintain that international law is not well served by a system that allows a state to refuse surrender or interrogation for non-fulfilment of certain requirements but provides no common standards for application and interpretation of those requirements.[84] Similarly, Bassiouni suggests that facilitation of law enforcement

---

[84] See Dugard and Wyngaert (n 80) at 66

cooperation calls for international regulation of the ‘double conditions’ associated with the principle of reciprocity which tend to hinder extradition and mutual legal assistance on account of the disparity between national legal systems.[85]

[85] See Bassiouni 'Policy Considerations' (n 4) 128, 143, 144, Gardocki (n 8) 288, Bassiouni 'Political Offence Exception' (n 80) 260 and Bassiouni 'Theories of Jurisdiction' (n 80) 3

PART ONE

ESTABLISHMENT OF JURISDICTION, CRIMINALISING OFFENCES AND ENSURING FAIR TREATMENT

CHAPTER 2

MANDATORY OBLIGATIONS TO ESTABLISH JURISDICTION, CRIMINALISE OFFENSES AND PROVIDE FAIR TREATMENT

The international conventions on terrorism and organised crime oblige the parties involved to establish extraterritorial jurisdiction. The objective of the conventions is to facilitate state cooperation in law enforcement because the crimes set forth by them transcend national frontiers in terms of their perpetration, nationality or location of victims and offenders. The element of transnationality, makes it difficult for any one state to handle prevent and punish these crimes. Hence, the conventions encourage states parties to cooperate with each other in prevention, suppression and prosecution of these crimes.

To effectuate state cooperation, the conventions rely on law enforcement measures of extradition and mutual legal assistance. Both these measures require a state, seeking surrender or interrogation of a person with respect to a crime taking place outside its territory, to have laws with extraterritorial reach. Thus, the obligation to establish extraterritorial jurisdiction under the international conventions can be said to have been designed to enable states parties to meet jurisdictional requirements of extradition and mutual legal assistance laws concerning crimes spreading across national frontiers.

There are three basic requirements of extradition and mutual legal assistance laws in regard to jurisdiction: 1- principle of legality 2- crime having occurred on state territory and 3- special use of double criminality. This chapter looks into the usefulness of the obligation to establish extraterritorial jurisdiction in facilitating the fulfilment of these requirements.

It will be argued that the obligation does facilitate the fulfilment of the principle of legality and the condition of crime having occurred on state territory; however, it provides little support with respect to the fulfilment of special use of double criminality. The reason is that the former conditions only require extraterritorial reach of national laws while the latter also requires harmony in national theories of jurisdiction. However, the obligation to establish extraterritorial jurisdiction allows diversity in national theories of jurisdiction. Consequently, a requested state applying special use condition in its extradition or mutual assistance laws remains free to reject a request for surrender or interrogation despite the imposition of an international duty to establish extraterritorial jurisdiction.

Special use condition requires the requesting and requested states to have identical theories of jurisdiction when the assistance is sought in respect of a crime taking place outside the territory of the requesting state. A number of extradition requests have had to remain unsatisfied due to the non-fulfilment by the requesting state of special use of double criminality condition. For example, in *Abu Daoud* case, Israel requested extradition of an offender from France by asserting jurisdiction over his crime on passive personality basis. The crime in question was not punishable in France under the passive personality theory at the time of its commission. Consequently, Israel's request for extradition had to be refused for lack of correspondence in the jurisdictional theories of the requesting and requested states. Similarly, in *Pinochet* case, Spain requested extradition of General Pinochet from the UK under the universality theory in regard to the acts of torture committed since 1984. The UK criminalised torture under the universality theory in 1988. Accordingly, the House of Lords held that Pinochet could not be extradited for crimes committed prior to 1988 when torture was not punishable in the UK under the principle of universal jurisdiction.

It will be suggested that in order to facilitate the fulfilment of the special use condition, the international conventions on terrorism and organised crime can recommend that parties relax the application of the special use condition in their laws and treaties on extradition and mutual legal assistance to accommodate the inherently extraterritorial nature of the crimes established by them. This technique has been adopted in some bilateral and regional treaties and appears more effective in facilitating extradition and mutual legal assistance as compared to the obligation to establish extraterritorial jurisdiction.

The chapter has been divided into four sections. Section 1 will discuss the purpose of the obligation to establish extraterritorial jurisdiction under the international conventions on terrorism and organised crime. Section 2 will consider the bases provided by the conventions to give extraterritorial effect to national laws and the impact of the obligation to implement those bases. Section 3 will examine the effectiveness of the obligation to establish extraterritorial jurisdiction in facilitating the fulfilment of legality principle and the requirement of crime having occurred in state territory. Section 4 will analyse the usefulness of the obligation in facilitating the fulfilment of special use of double criminality condition.

Section 1: Purpose of the obligation to establish extraterritorial jurisdiction under the international conventions on terrorism and organised crime

1.1) Territoriality of crime no longer an option

According to Professor Mann, the term jurisdiction refers to the competence of a state to make persons, events and goods subject to its laws and legal processes.[1] With respect to criminal jurisdiction, historically, there has been a consensus among states that the ambit of criminal law is primarily territorial.[2] This implies that the legal authority to make a crime subject to national legal processes belongs to the state in the territory of which the crime has taken place.[3] In the words of Lords Halsbury: 'All crime is local. The jurisdiction over the crime belongs to the country where it is committed.' [4]

With the advent of globalisation and modern technology, crime has started reflecting an inter-jurisdictional flavour.[5] It became easier for the offenders to plan, organise or finance their crimes in one state and to carry them out in another.[6] Just as faster means of communication facilitated global commerce, they also enabled offenders to evade territorially restricted national laws.[7] According to Sornarajah, electronic and other means of banking and commerce have diminished the significance of territorial boundaries. The proceeds of crime can now be generated in one state and transferred instantly to offshore banks. Accelerated means of transportation can now be used to smuggle narcotics and other contraband

---

[1] F.A. Mann, 'The Doctrine of Jurisdiction In International Law' 111 Recuil Des Cours (1964) 1 at 9

[2] Geoff Gilbert, 'Crimes Sans Frontiers: Jurisdictional Problems in English Law' 63 BYBIL (1992) 415 at 416

[3] ibid

[4] *MacLeod v Attorney General for New South Wales* [1891] AC 455, 458

[5] M. Sornarajah, 'Extraterritorial Criminal Jurisdiction: British, American and Commonwealth Perspectives' 2 Singapore Journal of International and Comparative Law (1998) 1 at 1, 4

[6] ibid at 1

[7] ibid at 6

substances. Threats of terrorist activities have increased alarmingly as a result of the interlinking of the politics of separate regions. Criminal groups previously operating in one region have found it profitable to establish worldwide networks.[8]

Due to the rise of this new form of criminality, which spreads across national frontiers, a strictly territorial view of jurisdiction has become outdated.[9] The ensuing situation demanded the extraterritorial reach of criminal laws.[10] As observed by Lord Griffith, 'unfortunately, in this century, crime has ceased to be largely local in origin and effect. Crime is now established on an international scale and common law must face this new reality'.[11]

1.1.1) *Lotus* Case

The most famous international case concerning the legality of jurisdiction beyond state territory was the *Lotus* case of 1927.[12] According to the facts, the French steamer, Lotus collided in high seas with the Turkish vessel, Boz-Kurtz, killing eight persons on board the latter.[13] Thereafter, when Lotus entered Turkish territorial waters, Turkish authorities arrested its captain and charged him with the crime of manslaughter under its national law.[14] France took the matter to the Permanent Court of International Justice (PCIJ), where it challenged Turkish jurisdiction on the ground that the crime had occurred in a French vessel and the alleged offender held French nationality. Therefore, France argued it had exclusive jurisdiction to try the captain.[15] The PCIJ dismissed France's claim in view of its failure to show any prohibitory rule of international law which prevented

---

[8] ibid

[9] Neil Boister, 'Treaty Crimes, International Criminal Court?' 12 New Criminal Law Review (2009) 341 at 342

[10] Christopher L. Blakesley, 'Wings For Talon: The Case for Extraterritorial Jurisdiction Over Sexual Exploitation of Children Through Cyberspace' 50 Wayne State L. Rev (2004) 109 at 119; See also Anthony J. Colangelo, 'Constitutional Limits on Extraterritorial Jurisdiction' 48 HJIL (2007) 121 at 128

[11] *Somchai Liangsiriprasert v. United States Government* [1990] 2 ALL ER 866 at 878

[12]*S.S. Lotus (Fr. v. Turk)* 1927 P.C.I.J. (ser. A) No. 10 (Sept.7) <http://www.worldcourts.com/pcij/eng/decisions/1927.09.07_lotus.htm> [Date accessed 21/03/23]

[13] ibid at Para 14-23

[14] ibid

[15] ibid at Para [28] 3

Turkey from applying its own criminal law beyond Turkish territory.[16] Since the result of the crime had occurred on a Turkish vessel, Turkey was entitled to establish concurrent jurisdiction over the crime.[17] On the basis of this ruling, many consider international law to be permissive with respect to the extraterritorial application of criminal laws.[18]

1.2) Significance of extraterritorial jurisdiction for combating crimes established by the international conventions on terrorism and organised crime

The crimes established by the international conventions on terrorism and organised crime essentially include the element of extraterritoriality. A prime example of these crimes is international drug trafficking which may involve as many as three states, i.e. the producer state, the transit state and the consumer state.[19] Similarly, acts of international terrorism can be plotted, prepared and financed in one state and executed in another.[20] Therefore, majority of the conventions under consideration establish these crimes as a distinct genre of crimes by providing that the conventions will have no application when each element of the crime takes place in a single state. For instance, article 13 of the Hostages Convention 1979 provides:

> This Convention shall not apply where the offence is committed within a single State, the hostage and the alleged offenders are nationals of that State and the alleged offender is found in the territory of that State.[21]

---

[16] ibid at Para 73

[17] ibid at Para 86

[18] See Roger O'Keefe, 'Universal Jurisdiction - Clarifying the Basic Concept' 2 Journal of International Criminal Justice (2004) 735 at 740; See also Blakesley (n 11) 114, 141

[19] D.W. Sproule and Paul St-Denis, 'The UN Drug Trafficking Convention: An Ambitious Step' 27 Canadian Yearbook of International Law (1989) 263 at 266

[20] Nathan Rasiah, 'To Prosecute or to Extradite? A Duty to Consider the Appropriate Venue in Cases of Concurrent Criminal Jurisdiction' Law Reform Essay Competition 2008 1 at 2 <www.barcouncil.org.uk/media/61922/nathan_rasiah__32_.pdf> [Date accessed 21/03/23]

[21] See article 13 the Hostages Convention 1979. Also see, article 3 the Nuclear Terrorism Convention 2005, article 3 the Terrorist Bombing Convention 1997, article 3 the Terrorism Financing Convention 1999, article 5 Beijing Convention 2010 and article 3(2) the Organised Crime Convention 2000. In the conventions dealing with crimes committed in aircrafts and vessels, their applicability to transnational crimes is expressed differently. According to their wording, the Convention applies only if the crime takes place in the aircraft or vessel destined

Thus, for the application of these conventions, it is necessary that either the crime takes place in more than one state or the victim or offenders hold nationalities of states other than the one where the crime is committed or are found outside its territory. In view of this, a number of scholars have coined the term 'transnational crimes' to refer to the offences established by these conventions.[22]

Since it is not possible to bring these crimes under national legal processes by relying on a strictly territorial view of jurisdiction, the conventions regulating these crimes oblige the parties to establish extraterritorial jurisdiction.[23] That is to say, the reach of their laws must not be confined to national territories; it must rather extend to any area beyond their borders where a crime having an impact on their territory has taken place.[24]

The obligation is meant to ensure that the offenders may not escape punishment by benefiting from territorially restricted national laws.[25] Another objective could be to enable the parties to punish individual parts of crimes.[26]

As observed by the Privy Council in *Somchai Liangsiriprasert v. United States Government*:

---

for a country other than the one which represents the place of their departure or registration. See article 4(1) the Rome Convention 1988, article 4(2) the Montreal Convention 1971 and article 3(3) of the Hague Convention 1970. For definition of transnationality, see Chapter 3 (n 26) below.

22 See Neil Boister, 'Transnational Criminal Law' 14 EJIL (2003) 953 at 953; See also Philip C Jessup quoted in Roger S. Clarke, 'The United Nations Convention against Transnational Organised Crime' 50 Wayne State Law Review (2004) 161 at 166; Carrie Lyn Donigan Guymon, 'International Legal Mechanisms for Combating Transnational Organised Crime: The Need for a Multilateral Convention' 18 Berkeley J. Int'l L (2000) 53 at 86-89

23 See Boister 'Treaty Crimes' (n 10) 342

24 M. Cherif Bissouni, 'Theories of Jurisdiction and their Application in Extradition Law and Practice' 5 Cal W. Int'l L.J 1 (1974-75) 1 at 1; see also Sami Shubber, 'Aircraft Hijacking under the Hague Convention 1970 - A New Regime?' 22 ICLQ (1973) 687 at 706-707; O'Keefe (n 19) at 736

25 See UNODC's Legislative Guide 2004 for implementation of the Organized Crime Convention 2000 at 104 <http://www.unodc.org/pdf/crime/legislative_guides/Legislative%20guides_Full%20version.pdf> [Date accessed 21/03/23]

26 ibid

> Their Lordships can find nothing in precedent, comity or good sense that should inhibit the common law from regarding as justiciable in England inchoate crimes committed abroad which are intended to result in the commission of criminal offences in England.[27]

1.3) Meanings of extraterritorial jurisdiction

1.3.1) Argument that extraterritorial jurisdiction includes legislation, enforcement and adjudication

The academic debate concerning the various meanings of extraterritorial jurisdiction divides scholars into two rival camps. On one side are commentators such as Shubber and Sornarajah who maintain that extraterritorial jurisdiction embraces all three aspects of jurisdiction: legislative, adjudicatory and enforcement.[28] To support their view, they refer to various clauses of the international conventions on terrorism and organised crime. First of all, they argue that preambles of several conventions indicate that one of their objectives is to punish the offenders.[29] Since punishment is an attribute of law enforcement, the term jurisdiction, wherever used in the conventions, should be deemed to include the authority to enforce laws.[30] Secondly, they suggest that the bases of jurisdiction outlined by the conventions include the basis of the offender's presence in state territory. In other words, the conventions require states to establish jurisdiction when the offender arrives in their territory after committing his crimes abroad. This basis further obliges a state in the territory of which the offender is found to either prosecute him itself or extradite to a state having jurisdiction over crime and willing to prosecute. Since, these two actions pertain to adjudicatory and enforcement aspects of jurisdiction, the requirement to establish extraterritorial jurisdiction must be understood to encompass both.[31]

The claim of these scholars is not without support in state practice. For example, in the US, national courts are competent to determine the limits of the extraterritorial operation of its national laws.[32] On more than one occasion, they upheld the legality of the trial of an offender who had been

---

[27] *Somchai Liangsiriprasert* (n 12)

[28] According to Sornarajah, it is wrong to suggest that extraterritorial criminal law enforcement is unlawful in all offences. See Sornarajah (n 6) at 31; See also Shubber (n 25) at 707

[29] Shubber (n 25) 707

[30] ibid

[31] ibid

[32] See Colangelo (n 11) 159

abducted from abroad, through undertaking an extraterritorial enforcement operation.[33]

1.3.2) Argument that extraterritorial jurisdiction refers to the legislative jurisdiction alone

The second group includes scholars like O'Keefe and Bassiouni who maintain that the term jurisdiction, when used in extraterritorial sense, refers to legislative jurisdiction only, that is, the authority of states to enact laws having extraterritorial scope.[34] To substantiate their claim, they allude to the impermissibility of extraterritorial police powers.[35] The police of one state may not investigate crimes and arrest suspects in the territory of another state. Similarly, the courts of one state may not sit in another state to examine witnesses in the absence of an express agreement with the territorial sovereign.[36] The argument finds support from the facts of the *Lotus* case according to which Turkey did not take the offender into custody straightaway when the collision took place in the high seas. Rather, Turkey waited for the French steamer to enter Turkish territorial waters and whereupon it enforced its laws by charging the captain of the Lotus with the crime of manslaughter and took him into custody.[37] The ensuing judgement of the PCIJ confirmed the view that although states were competent to extend the application of their laws and jurisdiction of their courts to persons, property and acts outside their territory, they were not entitled to enforce their laws in a foreign territory. The relevant parts of the judgement are reproduced below:

> [45] Now the first and foremost restriction imposed by international law upon a State is that – failing the existence of a permissive rule to the contrary – it may not exercise its power in any form in the territory of another State. In this sense jurisdiction is certainly territorial; it cannot be exercised by a State outside its territory [p19] except by virtue of a permissive rule derived from international custom or from a convention.
>
> [46] It does not, however, follow that international law prohibits a State from exercising jurisdiction in its own territory, in respect of any case

---

33 See for instance *US v. Alvarez Machain* 504 US 655 (1992); See also *US v. Yunis* (1988) 681 F. Supp (D.D.C) 909

34 O'Keefe (n 19) 740; See also Bassiouni (n 25) 2

35 O'Keefe ibid at 741

36 ibid; See also Charles Doyle, 'Extraterritorial Application of American Criminal Law' CRS Report to Congress 2010 <http://www.fas.org/sgp/crs/misc/94-166.pdf> [Date accessed 21/03/23]

37 *S.S. Lotus* (n 13) at Para's 15-23

> which relates to acts which have taken place abroad, and in which it cannot rely on some permissive rule of international law. Such a view would only be tenable if international law contained a general prohibition to States to extend the application of their laws and the jurisdiction of their courts to persons, property and acts outside their territory, and if, as an exception to this general prohibition, it allowed States to do so in certain specific cases. But this is certainly not the case under international law as it stands at present. Far from laying down a general prohibition to the effect that States may not extend the application of their laws and the jurisdiction of their courts to persons, property and acts outside their territory, it leaves them in this respect a wide measure of discretion, which is only limited in certain cases by prohibitive rules; as regards other cases, every State remains free to adopt the principles which it regards as best and most suitable.[38]

The writings of publicists also endorse the argument that international law prohibits enforcement of laws in foreign territories. For example, when the US in *Alvarez*[39] and Israel in *Eichman*[40] enforced their laws in foreign territories by abducting offenders, their actions were condemned by the majority of scholars.[41] The criticism was mainly centred on article 2(4) of the UN Charter which prohibits the UN members from violating the political independence and territorial integrity of any state. It is often seen as classic example of *Jus Cogens* or peremptory norm of international law. The term *Jus Cogens* was used by the International Court of Justice (ICJ) with reference to article 2(4) of the UN Charter in *Nicaragua* case.[42]

---

[38] ibid at Para 45-46

[39] *US v. Alvarez Machain* (n 34)

[40] *A.-G. Israel* v. *Eichmann*, (1968) 36 ILR 5 (District Court, Jerusalem)

[41] See Blakesley (n 11) 140; See also Abraham Abramovsky, 'Extraterritorial Jurisdiction: The United States Unwarranted Attempt to Alter International Law' 15 Yale J. Int'l L. (1990) 121; M. Cherif Bassiouni, *International Criminal Law, Volume II: Multilateral and Bilateral Enforcement Mechanisms* (3rdedn, Martinus Nijhoff, Netherlands, 2008) 324; Abdul Ghaffar Hamid, 'Jurisdiction Over Person Abducted From a Foreign Country: Alvarez Machain Case Revisited' 31 Journal of Malaysian and Comparative Law (2004) 69. Ronald J. Rychlak, '*Humberto Alvarez-Machain v. United States*: The Ninth Circuit Panel Decision of September 11' <http://www.fed-soc.org/publications/detail/humberto-alvarez-machain-v-united-states-the-ninth-circuit-panel-decision-of-september-11> [Date accessed 21/03/23]

[42] See *Case Concerning Military and Paramilitary Activities in and Against Nicaragua (Nicaragua v. United States of America); Merits*, International Court of Justice (ICJ), Judgement of 27 June1986 [1986] ICJ Rep 14, para 188

Significantly, this peremptory norm also appears in a number of international conventions on terrorism and organised crime. For example, article 2(2) of the Drugs Convention 1988 provides:

> The parties shall carry out their obligations under this Convention in a manner consistent with the principles of sovereign equality and territorial integrity of states and that of non-intervention in the domestic affairs of other states.[43]

More specifically, article 2(3) provides:

> A Party shall not undertake in the territory of another Party the exercise of jurisdiction and performance of functions which are exclusively reserved for the authorities of that other Party by its domestic law.[44]

It is thus clear that the enforcement of laws in foreign territories without the consent of the territorial sovereign has been designated by the international conventions on terrorism and organised crime as in violation of territorial sovereignty. Hence, it is difficult to defend the argument that the conventions, when using the term jurisdiction, always refer to all three aspects of jurisdiction (legislative, adjudicative and enforcement). The inescapable conclusion is when the conventions require the parties to establish extraterritorial jurisdiction, they envisage prescriptive jurisdiction only, i.e. the authority to enact laws having extraterritorial scope.[45] It does, however, include the subject matter jurisdiction of national courts, which means the extraterritorial acts made punishable by a domestic law shall be triable by the national courts of the legislating state, once the offender arrives in its territory. According to O.Keefe, in the context of criminal law, the distinction between legislative and adjudicatory jurisdiction is generally unnecessary because 'the application of a state's criminal law is simply the exercise of actualisation of prescription: both amount to an assertion that the law in question is applicable to the relevant conduct.'[46]

---

[43] See article 2 of the Drugs Convention 1988; For comparable provisions, see article 4 the UN Convention against Corruption 2003; article 4 the Organised Crime Convention 2000 and article 20 the Terrorism Financing Convention 1999

[44] See article 2 (3) the Drugs Convention 1988

[45] O'Keefe (n 19) 736; See also Colangelo (n 11) 123; Joseph J. Lambert, *Terrorism and Hostages in International Law, A Commentary on Hostages Convention 1979* (Cambridge: Grotius Publications Limited 1990) 133

[46] See O'Keefe (n 19) 737; See also Colangelo (n 11) 126; See also *S.S. Lotus* (n 13) at Para 45-46

1.4) Rationale of having extraterritorial laws without power to enforce

The proponents of the view that extraterritorial jurisdiction includes the authority to enforce, challenge the logic of having extraterritoriality without the power to enforce. For instance, Shubber asks, what can be the purpose of requiring the enactment of laws having extraterritorial scope, when the parties would be lacking the authority to enforce them? [47]

To answer this question, one must look into the statements of purpose of various international conventions on terrorism and organised crime. Their most common theme is that the aim of the convention is to promote inter-state cooperation in law enforcement. For example, article 1(b) of the UN Convention against Corruption 2003 states that the purposes of the Convention are '[t]o promote, facilitate and support international cooperation and technical assistance in the prevention of and fight against corruption, including in asset recovery.'[48]

Similarly, the preamble of the Terrorism Financing Convention 1999 provides:

> *The States Parties to this Convention*...[b]eing convinced of the urgent need to enhance international cooperation among States in devising and adopting effective measures for the prevention of the financing of terrorism, as well as for its suppression through the prosecution and punishment of its perpetrators...*[h]ave agreed as follows*...[49]

Considering the explanation above, it is plain that the international conventions on terrorism and organised crime have been designed to facilitate state cooperation in law enforcement. For this purpose, they rely on law enforcement measures of extradition and mutual legal assistance.[50] The laws and treaties regulating these measures demand that requesting states have jurisdiction over the crime in respect of which surrender or

---

[47] Shubber (n 25) 707

[48] See article 1(b) the UN Convention against Corruption 2003; See also article 2(1) the Drugs Convention 1988 and article 1 the Organized Crime Convention 2000

[49] See Preamble of the Terrorism Financing Convention 1999; Similar statements can be seen in a majority of the treaties under consideration. For corresponding provisions of other treaties, see (n 4) Chapter 3 below.

[50] ibid; See also M. Cherif Bassiouni, 'Policy Considerations on Interstate Cooperation in Criminal Matters' 4 Pace Y.B. Int'l L. (1992) 123 at 127; Guymon (n 23) 87

interrogation is sought.[51] Since the conventions establish crimes which spread across national frontiers, the demand in relation to these crimes translates into extraterritorial jurisdiction or the competence of states to punish conduct taking place outside their territory.[52] This necessitates the enactment of laws having extraterritorial scope.[53]

It can be argued therefore that the obligation to establish extraterritorial jurisdiction under the international conventions on terrorism and organised crime is designed to enable the parties to meet jurisdictional requirements of extradition and mutual assistance laws with respect to crimes transcending national frontiers.[54]

Up to this point, the focus has been on the purpose of the obligation to establish extraterritorial jurisdiction under the international conventions on terrorism and organised crime. I have explained that the prosecution and punishment of the crimes established by these conventions call for state cooperation in extradition and mutual legal assistance and the laws and treaties regulating these measures demand extraterritorial reach of national laws. Hence, the obligation to establish extraterritorial jurisdiction under these conventions can be said to have been designed to facilitate extradition and interrogation of the offenders involved in cross-country crimes.

Section 2: Bases provided by the international counterterrorism and organised crime conventions to give extraterritorial effect to national laws and the impact of the obligation to implement those bases

2.1) Grounds customarily relied on by states to assert jurisdiction over crime

In 1935, the Harvard Research Draft was prepared by noted lawyers and scholars of international law.[55] This draft convention is not a legally binding instrument but is based on extensive research of international law,

---

[51] Bassiouni 'Theories of Jurisdiction' (n 25) 1,2; Blakesley in Bassiouni, *Multilateral & Bilateral Enforcement* (n 42) 86

[52] Boister 'Treaty Crimes' (n 10)

[53] ibid

[54] Christopher C. Joiner, 'Countering Nuclear Terrorism: A Conventional Response' 18 EJIL (2007) 225 at 236; See also Sproule (n 20) 276

[55] See Introductory Comment, 'Jurisdiction With Respect to Crime-Research in International Law' 29 AJIL (1935) Supp. 443, 445.

hence, is considered declaratory of customary international law.[56] It pointed out certain bases traditionally relied upon by states to claim jurisdiction over crime. The five bases identified by it are: territoriality, nationality, protection, passive personality and universality. The common denominator of the first four is that the state wishing to prosecute must have a substantial link with the event required to be regulated. The last one is grounded on the concept of universal condemnation of crimes.[57]

2.1.1) Territoriality

The territorial theory is based on the principle that every state has unrestricted authority to regulate the events occurring within its territorial boundaries.[58] According to Bassiouni, '[t]he power of a state to proscribe conduct within its territory... is concomitant to the principle of sovereignty and enjoys universal recognition.' [59] Hence, each state is vested with sovereign right to make punishable the crimes committed within its geographical limits by its nationals, residents, non-residents and legal entities.[60]

The theory has a number of extensions and applications including the principles of objective and subjective territoriality. By virtue of these, the territorial theory can be applied to assert jurisdiction over crimes taking place beyond state territory.[61] Whereas the subjective territoriality activates jurisdiction when a crime begins in state territory but culminates abroad, the objective territoriality triggers it when a crime originates abroad but ends in state territory.[62] Furthermore, it is usually advanced that aircrafts and ships carrying the flag of a state or registered in it [63] represent the floating pieces of that state's territory.[64] Hence, the crimes committed in these objects can be made punishable by giving wider interpretation to

---

[56] See Abamovsky (n 42) 123; Also see Christopher L. Blakesley, 'United States Jurisdiction over Extraterritorial Crime' 73 J. Crim. L. & Criminology (1982) 1109 at 1110

[57] O'Keefe (n 19) 738; R.I.R Abeyratne, 'Attempts at Ensuring Peace and Security in International Aviation' 24 Transp. L.J. (1996-1997) 27 at 38

[58] Introductory Comment (n 56) 445; See also Colangelo (n 11) 127

[59] Bissouni 'Theories of Jurisdiction' (n 25) 4

[60] ibid; see also Blakesley 'Wings of Talon' (n 11) 117

[61] See Vaughan Lowe in Malcom D Evans, *International law* (2ndedn Oxford University Press 2006) 343-344

[62] ibid; See also Bissouni 'Theories of Jurisdiction' (n 25) 12

[63] ibid

[64] Joyner (n 55) 234

territorial theory.[65] While the subjective territoriality and flag state principles are universally recognised, the application of the objective territoriality remains controversial. The controversy surrounds its conflicting interpretations at national level.[66]

2.1.2) The active personality or nationality theory

The nationality theory entails that every state has a right to prosecute and punish the crimes committed by its nationals, irrespective of the place of commission.[67] Its rationale is that nationals of a state enjoy the protection of its laws wherever they are. Hence, they have corresponding obligation to respect those laws within and outside state territory.[68] It has been argued that jurisdiction over nationals, like jurisdiction over territory, is corollary of state sovereignty.[69] Hence, the theory is not only universally recognised but is also declaratory of customary international law.[70]

2.1.3) The passive personality theory

The theory of passive personality enables a state to make punishable the crimes committed by aliens against its nationals in foreign territories.[71] Since the welfare of a state depends on the welfare of its citizens, a state is presumed to have ample interest in the prosecution of those who commit crimes against its nationals.[72] The theory is fraught with controversy and a major objection to it concerns its foundation on a very weak link between the proscribing state and the event.[73]

2.1.4) The Protective principle

The protective theory allows a state to criminalise the acts committed by foreigners outside state territory, when they are designed to threaten its

---

[65] ibid

[66] Bassiouni 'Theories of Jurisdiction' (n 25) 12,13; See also Blakesley 'US Jurisdiction over Extraterritorial Crime' (n 57) 1112

[67] Introductory Comment (n 56) 445

[68] Bissouni 'Theories of Jurisdiction' (n 25) 41

[69] ibid at 40; See also Boister 'Treaty Crimes' (n 10) 342

[70] See Shubber (n 25) 708; See also Blakesley 'Wings of Telon' (n 11) 119

[71] Bruce Zagaris and Jay Rosenthal, 'United States Jurisdictional Consideration in International Criminal Law' 15 California Western International Law Journal (1985) 303 at 310

[72] Bissouni ‘Theories of Jurisdiction’ (n 25) 44

[73] Robert Jennings, 'Extraterritorial Jurisdiction and the United States Antitrust Laws' 33 BYBIL (1957) 146 at 155

vital national interests.[74] The theory has traditionally been applied to assert jurisdiction over a range of extraterritorial acts impacting the national security and diplomatic relations of the state concerned.[75] Although it enjoys widespread recognition, it is deserving of criticism if it is interpreted broadly, that it covers almost every event with only a remote effect on the interests of the proscribing state.[76]

2.1.5) The Universality Principle

All the above theories require a link between the proscribing state and the event, offender or the victim. There are however certain offences, which due to their seriousness, are deemed to affect the interests of all states, even if committed at a specific place or against a given victim or interest.[77] For prosecution of these crimes, no territorial or nationality link is required because the offender is considered to be enemy of the entire human race.[78] Thus, any state that apprehends the offender may prosecute and punish him under the universality theory which is designed to protect the universal values and interests of mankind.[79] Although the theory has been applied to assert jurisdiction over a range of crimes including, slave trade, genocide, torture and hijacking, most common and least controversial application relates to the crime of piracy.[80] Hence, its recognition depends on the crime in relation to which it is applied.

In the light of above, it is clear that the territoriality (subjective and flag state) and nationality theories have universal recognition, the protective and universality theories are recognised in a more limited way and the passive personality and objective territoriality theories are most controversial.[81]

---

[74] Zagaris (n 72) 307
[75] ibid
[76] Bissouni 'Theories of Jurisdiction' (n 25) 50; See also Jonathan O.Hafen, 'International Extradition: Issues arising under Dual Criminality Requirement' Brigham Young University Law Review (1992) 191 at 215
[77] ibid
[78] Zagaris (n 72) 310
[79] Bissouni 'Theories of Jurisdiction' (n 25) at 51; Blakesley 'Wings of Telon' (n 11) 132
[80] See Bassiouni ibid; See also Blakesley ibid at 133
[81] Bissouni 'Theories of Jurisdiction' (n 25)

2.2) Bases of jurisdiction under the international conventions on terrorism and organised crime

The international counterterrorism and organised crime conventions require the parties to give extraterritorial effect to their laws on a variety of jurisdictional grounds. These can broadly be classified into primary and secondary groupings. Primary bases refer to the grounds which enable the parties to make punishable an extraterritorial crime, right from its beginning; the secondary bases allow them to regulate the crime, once the offender is found in their territory after the commission of his crime.[82] Primary bases can be further sub-divided into mandatory and permissive categories. The mandatory bases embody universally recognised theories of jurisdiction; the permissive bases represent less-recognised or controversial theories. In other words, the mandatory bases concern the states directly affected by crime;[83] the permissive bases involve the states less directly affected.[84]

2.2.1) Primary bases of jurisdiction provided by the counterterrorism conventions

2.2.1.1) The Hague Convention 1970

Article 4 of the Convention obliges a state party to make punishable the offences set forth by it: (i) when they are committed on board an aircraft registered in that state[85] (ii) when the aircraft in respect of which the crime is committed lands in its territory with the offender still on board [86] and (iii) when the aircraft in which the crime is committed is leased to a lessee and the lessee has his principal place of business or permanent residence in that state.[87] The obligation of the state of registration is based on flag state principle,[88] the obligation of the state of the charterer's residence represents

---

[82] See Abeyratne (n 58) 38-39; See also AB Green; 'Convention on the Prevention and Punishment of Crimes against Internationally Protected Persons, including Diplomatic Agents: An analysis' 14 Virginia Journal of International Law (1973-74) 703 at 715-716

[83] See Lambert (n 46) 133

[84] Abeyratne (n 58) 38, 39

[85] See article 4(1)(a) the Hague Convention 1970

[86] See article 4(1)(b) ibid

[87] See article 4(1)(c) ibid

[88] Gary N. Horlick, 'The Developing Law of Air Hijacking' 12 Harv.Int'l. L. J. (1971) 33 at 36

an extension of the territorial theory[89] and the obligation of state of landing embodies the universality theory.[90]

2.2.1.2) The Montreal Convention 1971

In addition to reproducing the bases supplied by the Hague Convention 1970, article 5 of the Montreal Convention obliges a party to establish jurisdiction when the crime takes place in its territory.[91]

2.2.1.3) The Protection of Diplomats Convention 1973

Article 3 of the Convention obliges a party to make punishable the offences proscribed by it: (i) when they are committed in its territory or on board an aircraft registered in it[92] (ii) when the offender is a national of that state[93] and (iii) when the victim is a national of that state.[94] The first two bases reflect the application of the territoriality and nationality theories; the third embodies the passive personality theory.[95]

2.2.1.4) The Hostages Convention 1979

Article 5 of the Convention provides two kinds of primary bases, mandatory and permissive. The mandatory bases comprise the territoriality[96] and nationality theories.[97] Furthermore, a new mandatory basis obliges a party which has been the subject of coercion to make punishable the act of hostage taking, regardless of the place of its commission.[98] It demonstrates an application of the protective theory.[99] Under the permissive bases, a

---

[89] See Abeyratne (n 58) 50; See also Shubber (n 25) 710-711

[90] Commonwealth Implementation kits for the International Counter Terrorism Conventions at 51
<http://www.thecommonwealth.org/internal/38061/documents/>
[Date accessed 21/03/23]

[91] See article 5(1)(a) the Montreal Convention 1971

[92] See article 3(1)(a) the Protection of Diplomats Convention 1973

[93] See article 3(1)(b) ibid

[94] See article 3(1)(c) ibid

[95] Interestingly, the Protection of Diplomats Convention 1973 represents the only transnational treaty under consideration, which sets forth mandatory obligation to establish jurisdiction on this basis.

[96] See article 5(1)(a) the Hostages Convention 1979

[97] See article 5(1)(b) ibid

[98] See article 5(1)(c) ibid

[99] The argument that right of the state which is being coerced, to establish jurisdiction, represents an application of protective theory finds support from Lambert's work on the Hostages Convention 1979. According to Lambert, in the

party is recommended to establish jurisdiction when the offence is committed against its nationals[100] or by a person habitually residing in its territory.[101] The former exemplifies passive personality and the latter a less-recognised extension of the nationality theory.[102]

2.2.1.5) The Nuclear Materials Convention 1980

Article 8 of the Convention obliges a party to make punishable the offences, when they are committed: (i) in its territory[103] (ii) on board a ship or aircraft registered to it[104] and (iii) by its national.[105] Clearly, the Convention does not go beyond the universally recognised links of territoriality and nationality.

2.2.1.6) The Rome Convention 1988

Article 6 of the Convention obliges a party to establish jurisdiction, when the offence is committed: (i) on board a ship flying its flag[106] (ii) within its territory including territorial sea [107] and (iii) by its national.[108] In addition, the Convention authorises the criminalisation of the offences by a state: (i) when they are committed by an offender habitually residing in its territory[109] (ii) when the victim is a national[110] and (iii) when the offences are committed to compel to do or abstain from doing something.[111] The

---

Achillo Lauro incident, Israel was being compelled to release certain terrorists imprisoned in its national detention centres as a condition for the release of hostages. Since the demand was likely to affect Israel's national security or vital national interests, Israel was within its right to assert extraterritorial jurisdiction under the protective principle. See Lambert (n 46) 150

[100] See article 5(1)(d) the Hostages Convention 1979

[101] See article 5(1)(b) ibid

[102] Michael Akehurst, 'Jurisdiction in International Law' 46 BYBIL (1972-73) 145 at 157

[103] See article 8(1)(a) the Nuclear Materials Convention 1980

[104] ibid

[105] See article 8(1)(b) ibid

[106] See article 6(1)(a) the Rome Convention 1988

[107] See article 6(1) (b) ibid; keeping in view the possibility of the crime occurring in a ship found in coastal area, the makers of the Rome Convention have widened the jurisdiction of territorial / coastal state by adding the words territorial sea while requiring establishment of jurisdiction on territorial basis.

[108] See article 6(1)(c) the Rome Convention 1988

[109] See article 6(2)(a) ibid

[110] See article 6(2)(b) ibid

[111] See article 6(2)(c) ibid

Convention takes the standard approach of obliging the parties only when the link between the proscribing state and the event is direct and universally recognised.

2.2.1.7) The Terrorist Bombing Convention 1997

Article 6 of the Convention obliges a party to make punishable the offences, when they are committed (i) in its territory[112] (ii) on board a vessel or aircraft registered in it[113] and (iii) by its national.[114] Moreover, the Convention authorises the criminalisation of the offences by a state: (i) when the victim is a national[115] (ii) when the offences are committed to compel it to do or abstain from doing something [116] (iii) when the offences are committed on board an aircraft operated by its government[117] (iv) when they are committed against its facility abroad including its diplomatic premises[118] and (v) when they are committed by a stateless person having his habitual residence on the territory of that state.[119] Again, the mandatory bases represent the universally agreed links of territoriality and nationality whereas the permissive bases embody less recognised links such as a victim's nationality and state security. The right of the state whose buildings or infrastructure abroad has been targeted to establish jurisdiction can be said to reflect the application of the protective theory.[120]

2.2.1.8) The Terrorism Financing Convention 1999

Article 7 of the Convention obliges a state party to establish jurisdiction when the act of financing is committed: (i) in its territory[121] (ii) on board a vessel or aircraft registered to it[122] and (iii) by its national.[123] Since the offences covered by the Convention are victimless, it could not possibly have duplicated the jurisdictional bases provided by the other counterterrorism

---

[112] See article 6(1)(a) the Terrorist Bombings Convention 1997
[113] See article 6(1)(b) ibid
[114] See article 6(1)(c) ibid
[115] See article 6(2)(a) the Terrorist Bombings Convention 1997
[116] See article 6(2)(d) ibid
[117] See article 6(2)(e) ibid
[118] See article 6(2)(b) ibid
[119] See article 6(2)(c) ibid
[120] Samuel M. Witten, 'International Convention for the Suppression of Terrorist Bombings' 92 AJIL (1998) 774 at 778
[121] See article 7(1)(a) Terrorism Financing Convention 1999
[122] See article 7(1)(b) ibid
[123] See article 7(1)(c) ibid

treaties.[124] It therefore adopts an innovative approach while providing permissive bases. Accordingly, it authorises a state party to criminalise the offence of financing, wherever committed, when it is directed towards carrying out a terrorist attack: (i) in the territory or against a national of the state concerned[125] (ii) against its governmental facility abroad including diplomatic premises[126] (iii) in order to compel the state to do or refrain from doing something[127] (iv) by a stateless person who has his or her habitual residence in the territory of that State[128] and (v) on board an aircraft which is operated by the government of that state.[129] Evidently, the mandatory bases are characterized by universally recognised links whereas permissive bases comprise both less recognised and controversial links. Thus, even the indirect approach adopted by the Convention takes into account the traditional theories of jurisdiction.[130]

2.2.1.9) The Nuclear Terrorism Convention 2005

Article 9 of the Convention obliges a state to make punishable the offences, when they are committed: (i) in its territory[131] (ii) on board an aircraft or vessel registered to it[132] and (iii) by its nationals.[133] Furthermore, it authorises a state party to criminalise the offences when they are committed: (i) against a national of that state[134] (ii) against a government facility abroad, including diplomatic premises[135] (iii) by a person having his habitual residence on that state's territory[136] (iv) in order to compel that state to do or to refrain from doing something[137] and (v) on board an aircraft operated by the government of that state.[138]

---

124 See Roberto Lavelle, 'The International Convention for the Suppression of Financing of Terrorism' 60 Heidelberg Journal of International law (2000) 492 at 506
125 See article 7(2)(a) the Terrorism Financing Convention 1999
126 See article 7(2)(b) ibid
127 See article 7(2)(c) ibid
128 See article 7(2)(d) ibid
129 See article 7(2)(e) ibid
130 Lavelle (n 125)
131 See article 9(1)(a) the Nuclear Terrorism Convention 2005
132 See article 9(1)(b) ibid
133 See article 9(1)(c) ibid
134 See article 9(2)(a) ibid
135 See article 9(2)(b) ibid
136 See article 9(2)(c) ibid
137 See article 9(2)(d) ibid
138 See article 9(2)(e) ibid

2.2.1.10) The Beijing Convention 2010

Article 8 of the Convention obliges a state party to establish jurisdiction, when the offences are committed: (i) on its territory[139] (ii) on board an aircraft registered in that state[140] (iii) by its nationals[141] (iv) in the territory of charterer's place of residence or place of business[142] and (v) when the aircraft lands in its territory with the offender still on board.[143] Furthermore, it authorises the criminalisation of the offences by a state party when they are committed (i) against its national[144] and (ii) by a person habitually residing there.[145]

2.2.2) Primary bases of Jurisdiction under the organised crime conventions

2.2.2.1) The Drugs Convention 1988

Article 4 of the Convention obliges a state party to make punishable the offences set forth by it when they are committed (i) in its territory[146] and (ii) on board an aircraft or vessel registered in that state.[147] Moreover, it authorises a party to criminalise offences when they are committed (i) by its national[148] or (ii) by a person habitually residing in that state.[149] Additionally, it lays down two previously unknown permissive bases. According to the first, a party is allowed to establish jurisdiction when the offences are committed on board a vessel in relation to which it has an agreement with the state whose flag the vessel is bearing, to inspect it and to be on board.[150] Secondly, the convention recommends that parties criminalise extraterritorial conspiracies designed to commit drug trafficking or money laundering crimes within state territory.[151] The former is based

139 See article 8(1)(a) the Beijing Convention 2010
140 See article 8(1)(b) ibid
141 See article 8(1)(e) ibid
142 See article 8(1)(d) ibid
143 See article 8(1)(c) ibid
144 See article 8(2)(a) ibid
145 See article 8(2)(b) ibid
146 See article 4(1)(a)(i) the Drugs Convention 1988
147 See article 4(1)(a)(ii) ibid
148 See article 4(1)(b)(i) ibid
149 ibid
150 See article 4(1)(b)(ii) & (iii) ibid
151 See article 4(1)(b)(iii) ibid; In the words of Clarke, 'this is an attempt to prevent narcotics importation by asserting jurisdiction over thwarted conspiracies

on the agreement between states parties and the latter typifies the objective territoriality theory.[152]

2.2.2.2) The Organised Crime Convention 2000

Article 15 of the Convention obliges a state party to criminalise the offences set forth by it, when they are committed: (i) in its territory[153] and (ii) on board a vessel or aircraft registered in that state.[154] Moreover, it authorises the establishment of jurisdiction by a state party, when the offences are committed: (i) by its national[155] (ii) against its national [156] or (iii) by a person habitually residing in that state.[157] Additionally, the Convention recommends that parties make punishable the extraterritorial acts of planning or conspiracy designed to commit a serious crime within state territory.[158] Furthermore, the parties are allowed to criminalise extraterritorial conspiracies intended to carry out money laundering crimes within state territory.[159] The former represents the application of the protective theory; latter, the objective territoriality theory.[160]

2.2.2.3) UN Convention against Corruption 2000

Article 42 of the Convention provides bases of jurisdiction identical to the Organized Crime Convention 2000.[161]

2.2.3) Secondary basis

Apart from primary bases, each convention under consideration obliges a party to make punishable the crimes committed abroad by an offender who may subsequently be found in its territory.[162] It illustrates the application

---

occurring beyond national borders' See Clarke (n 23) 169; See also Sproule (n 20) 276

[152] See Clarke ibid at 179 foot note 85

[153] See article 15(1)(a) the Organized Crime Convention 2000

[154] See article 15(1)(b) ibid

[155] See article 15(2)(a) ibid

[156] See article 15(2)(b) ibid

[157] ibid

[158] See article 15(2)(c)(i) ibid

[159] See article 15(2)(c)(ii) ibid

[160] See Blakesley 'US Jurisdiction over Extraterritorial Crime' (n 57) 1111, 1112

[161] See article 42 of the UN Convention against Corruption 2003

[162] See article 4(2) the Hague Convention 1970, article 5(2) the Montreal Convention 1971, article 3(2) the Protection of Diplomats Convention 1973, article 5(2) the Hostages Convention 1979, article 8(2) the Nuclear Materials Convention

of universality theory which enables any state apprehending the offender to prosecute him without any territorial or nationality link.[163] Its purpose is to ensure that the offender may not find refuge in the territory of any state party to the relevant convention.[164] Although it is described as secondary basis, its secondary status by no means renders it inferior to the other bases because there is no inter se priority among the bases provided by the conventions.[165]

2.3) Mandatory bases - a move towards uniformity

The above overview reveals that the international conventions on terrorism and organised crime impose a duty to establish jurisdiction only when there is a universally recognised, territorial or nationality link between the prosecuting state and the event or the offender. On the rare occasions when they do oblige the parties to make punishable the offences in the absence of such links, it is precisely because the nature of the offence so demands. For example, in the Protection of Diplomats Convention 1973, it was necessary to oblige the state of the victim's nationality to establish jurisdiction otherwise the offender could have escaped punishment due to the disinterest of other states.[166] Similarly, in cases involving hostage taking, the state which is being coerced is likely to have greater interest in the prosecution of the offender than the territorial or nationality state, because the purpose of the crime is to get something done by that state.[167] Accordingly, the Hostages Convention 1979 sets forth a mandatory obligation to establish jurisdiction on this basis. Likewise, in the Hague 1970, the Montreal 1971 and the Beijing 2010 Conventions, it was considered desirable to oblige the state of landing to make the offence

---

1980, article 6(4) the Rome Convention 1988, article 6(4) the Terrorist Bombing Convention 1997, article 7(4) the Terrorism Financing Convention 1999, article 9(4) the Nuclear Materials Convention 2005, article 4(2) the Drugs Convention 1988, article 15(4) the Organized Crime Convention 2000, article 42(3) the UN Convention against Corruption 2003 and article 8(3) the Beijing Convention 2010.

163 Abraham Abramovsky, 'Multilateral Conventions for Suppression of Unlawful Seizure and Interference with Aircraft Part 1: Hague Convention' 13 Colum. J. Transnat'l L.(1974) 381 at 397

164 Shubber (n 25) 713; See also Commonwealth Implementation Kits (n 91) 52

165 Omer Y. Elegab, 'The Hague as the Seat of Lockerbie Trial: Some Constraints' 34 The International Lawyer (2000) 289 at 296

166 See Lambert (n 46) at 153; See also UN Doc. A/8710/Rev.1 at p.311; Report of the ILC on the work of its 24th session < www.un.org/law/ilc/index/htm> [Date accessed 21/03/23]

167 See Lambert ibid at 150

punishable because the landing state represents the most appropriate forum of trial, in view of the presence of the offender and availability of witnesses and evidence.[168]

Apart from these exceptions, nowhere do the conventions appear to oblige the parties to establish jurisdiction in the absence of a universally recognised link. The instances of departure being rare and justifiable, it can be argued that the makers of the conventions did not want to go beyond the sacrosanct principles of jurisdiction while imposing the duty to establish jurisdiction.[169] This can be seen as a move towards harmonising national laws, which, it will be explained later, marks an attempt at facilitating state cooperation in extradition and mutual legal assistance.[170] For present purposes, suffice it to refer to the observation made by the Dutch representative during the drafting of the Hague Convention 1970, 'states with mandatory bases at least bear a moral responsibility to seek extradition of offenders'.[171]

2.4) Permissive bases - A move towards diversity

The approach adopted by the makers of the conventions in providing permissive bases, stands in stark contrast to the one taken in the listing of mandatory bases. As opposed to relying on direct links between the proscribing state and the event or offender, the makers have introduced rules grounded on less direct or remote links such as the victim's nationality, state security, universality and objective territoriality.

The listing of several permissive bases founded on less recognised theories of jurisdiction is likely to produce disharmony in national theories of jurisdiction, in particular when their implementation is optional. Since there is no priority between mandatory or optional bases, the unifying influence of the mandatory bases can be said to have been effectively counter-balanced by the permissive bases.[172] It will be suggested in section IV below that this arrangement is ill-suited to the aim of facilitating state cooperation in extradition and mutual legal assistance, which on account

---

[168] Commonwealth Implementation Kits (n 91) 51

[169] Sproule (n 20) 278

[170] Legislative Guide for implementing the Organized Crime Convention 2000 (n 26) at 130 paragraph 261

[171] See UN GAOR, 34th Sess. (13th mtg.) p.9, para 40, UN Doc A/C.6/SR.13 (1979); See also Lambert (n 46) at 143

[172] Elegab (n 166) 296

of its reciprocal nature, demands similarity in the national theories of jurisdiction.

In view of the above, it is evident that the international conventions on terrorism and organised crime oblige the parties involved to make punishable the acts proscribed by them on several bases of extraterritoriality. Some of these bases reflect universally agreed theories of jurisdiction; the others represent less recognised or controversial theories. The purpose of the obligation is to expand the extraterritorial reach of national laws to make them conducive to the requirements of extradition and mutual legal assistance, with a view to bringing to justice transnational offenders. I shall now analyse the counterterrorism and organised crime laws of the US, the UK, Pakistan and India to see the extent to which they have been impacted by the obligation.

2.5) Impact of the obligation to establish extraterritorial jurisdiction on national laws

2.5.1) Laws of Pakistan and India on terrorism and organised crime

National laws have witnessed a surge towards extraterritoriality since 1970 when the first international convention[173] regulating transnational crimes, namely the Hague Convention 1970, came into force. The analysis of the domestic laws of the four states of Pakistan, India, the US and UK reveal that all four have widened the net of their criminal laws to cover offences occurring outside their territory. For example, the penal codes of both India and Pakistan now apply to crimes occurring beyond their territory.[174] The extraterritorial reach of these laws, however, remains confined to the principles of nationality and flag state.[175]

---

[173] Under consideration

[174] See Sc.3 of the Indian Penal Code 1860, Act No.45 of 1860 [hereinafter the Indian Penal Code 1860]:

Punishment for offences committed beyond but which may by law may be tried within India: Any person liable, by any 7*[Indian law], to be tried for an offence committed beyond 5*[India] shall be dealt with according to the provisions of this Code for any act committed beyond 5*[India] in the same manner as if such act had been committed within 5*[India].

See also Sc. 3 of Pakistan Penal Code, Act XLV of 1860 [hereinafter Pakistan Penal Code 1860]

[175] See Sc. 4 of the Indian Penal Code 1860:

Extension of Code to Extraterritorial Offences: The provisions of this code apply also to offences committed by (1) any citizen of India in any place without and

This is not however the case as regards their laws implementing the international conventions on terrorism and organised crime. These laws have been made applicable to extraterritorial crimes on such broad theories of jurisdiction as national security, objective territoriality and universality. For example, Pakistan's law on drug trafficking criminalises the attempt and conspiracy to import narcotics into Pakistan from a place outside Pakistan.[176] It exemplifies the application of objective territoriality theory as contained in the Drugs Convention 1988.[177] Similarly, the Indian anti-terrorism law makes extraterritorial conduct punishable when it is designed to threaten the security, integrity and sovereignty of India by means of damaging Indian property located abroad or by compelling India to do or refrain from doing something through injuring or threatening to injure its nationals.[178] It manifests the application of protective theory conjoined with passive personality as contained in the Terrorist Bombings and Financing Conventions.[179] Likewise, the Indian anti-hijacking law makes punishable the crimes committed abroad by a person who may

---

beyond India, (2) any person on any ship or aircraft registered in India wherever it may be.

See also Sc. 4 Pakistan Penal Code 1860:

Extension of Code to Extra-Territorial Offences: The provisions of this Code apply also to any offence committed by:-1[(1) any citizen of Pakistan or any person in the service of Pakistan in any place without and beyond Pakistan;] (4) any person on any ship or aircraft registered in Pakistan wherever it may be.

[176] See Sc. 14 Control of Narcotics Substances Act (CNSA) 1997, Act No. XXV of 1997 [hereinafter the Control of Narcotics Substances Act 1997 of Pakistan] 'No one shall within or outside Pakistan, participate in, associate or conspire to commit, attempt to commit, aid, abet, facilitate, incite, induce or counsel the commission of an offence under this Act.' For prohibition on the import, export and transport of Narcotics, see Sc.7 Control of Narcotics Substances Act 1997 of Pakistan. Also see Sc. 8 of the corresponding law of India, the Narcotics Drugs and Psychotropic Substances Act 1985, Act No.61 of 1985 [hereinafter the Narcotics Drugs and Psychotropic Substances Act 1985 of India]

[177] See article 4(1)(b)(iii) the Drugs Convention 1988

[178] See Sc. 15 of the Unlawful Activities (Prevention) Act 1967, Act No.37 of 1967 as amended in 2008 [hereinafter the Unlawful Activities (Prevention) Act 1967 of India]

[179] See Report of the ILC on the work of its 24th session, UN Doc. A/8710/Rev.1 at 311 <www.un.org/law/ilc/index/htm> [Date accessed 21/03/23]; See also FA Mann quoted in Lambert (n 46) 152 foot note 78; See also article 6(2)(a)(b)(d) the Terrorist Bombings Convention 1997 and article 7(2)(a)(b)(c) the Terrorism Financing Convention 1999

subsequently be found in India.[180] It provides an example of universality theory as embodied in each convention under consideration.[181] Additionally, the law regulates crimes committed in an aircraft leased to a lessee having his permanent place of business or residence in India, as well as crimes committed in aircraft landing in India with the offender still on board.[182] The two provisions incorporate the extended territoriality and universality theories respectively as laid down by the Conventions relating to aircraft terrorism.[183] Apart from these, the anti-money-laundering laws of India and Pakistan apply to the offences made criminal under the foreign enactments.[184] These can be said to reflect the application of the objective territoriality theory as contained in the Organised Crime Convention 2000 and UN Convention against Corruption 2003.[185]

2.5.2) US laws on terrorism and organised crime

The US law on transnational terrorism makes punishable the extraterritorial acts of killing, injuring or kidnapping a person who is a member of the US armed forces or an official or employee of its legislature, executive or judiciary.[186] It exemplifies the application of passive personality theory as contained in a majority of the conventions under consideration.[187] The enactment further criminalises the extraterritorial acts of terrorism directed

---

[180] See Sc. 6 of the Anti- Hijacking Act 1982, Act 65 of 1982 [hereinafter the Anti-Hijacking Act 1982 of India]

[181] See, for instance, article 4(2) of the Hague Convention 1970, article 5(2) of the Montreal Convention and article 8(3) of the Beijing Convention 2010

[182] ibid

[183] See article 4(1)(b)&(c) the Hague Convention 1970, article 5(1)(c)&(d) the Montreal Convention 1971and article 8(1)(d)&(c) the Beijing Convention 2010

[184] See Sc. 8 Narcotics Drugs and Psychotropic Substances Act 1985; See also Sc. 2(I) Anti-Money Laundering Act 2010, Act No. VII of 2010 [hereinafter Anti-Money Laundering Act 2010 of Pakistan]

[185] See article 42(2)(c) the UN Convention against Corruption 2003 and article 15(2)(c)(ii) the Organized Crime Convention 2000

[186] See United States Code, Title 18 - Crimes and Criminal Procedure [hereinafter 18 U.S.C.], Chapter 113B-Terrorism, Sc.2332b, Acts of Terrorism Transcending National Borders; For a different version of passive personality under US law see Sc. 2332 f- (Bombing of places).

[187] See article 3(1)(c) the Protection of Diplomats Convention 1973, article 5(1)(d) the Hostages Convention 1979, article 6 (2)(b) the Rome Convention 1988, article 7(2)(a) the Terrorism Financing Convention 1999, article 9(2)(a) the Nuclear Terrorism Convention 2005, article 15(2)(b) the Organized Crime Convention 2000, article 42(2)(a) the UN Convention against Corruption 2003 and article 8(2)(a) the Beijing Convention 2010

against the buildings and superstructure leased to the US in foreign territories.[188] It represents the application of protective theory as contained in the modern counterterrorism conventions.[189] Additionally, the law regulates conspiracies hatched abroad to commit terrorist crimes within the US territory.[190] It implements the protective theory as contained in the Organised Crime Convention 2000.[191] In like manner, the US law on financing of terrorism applies to the extraterritorial acts of terrorist funding, when the act is committed by its nationals, a habitual resident or by a person found on US territory.[192] It illustrates the application of nationality, extended nationality and universality theories as embodied in the Terrorism Financing Convention 1999. The enactment further outlaws the acts of financing, wherever committed, with a view to committing terrorist crimes, involving the destruction of buildings and superstructure leased to the US in a foreign state or to compel the US to do or abstain from doing something.[193] It manifests the application of protective theory as expressed in the Financing Convention 1999.[194] Likewise, the US law on drug trafficking makes punishable conspiracies hatched abroad to import narcotics into the US.[195] It implements the objective territoriality theory as laid down in the Drugs Convention 1988.[196]

---

[188] See 18 U.S.C. Sc.2332b, Acts of Terrorism Transcending National Borders

[189] See the Conventions on Terrorist Bombing 1997, Nuclear Terrorism 2005 and Terrorism Financing 1999

[190] See 18 U.S.C.Sc.2332b, Acts of Terrorism Transcending National Borders

[191] The conspiracy to commit terrorist offences differs from conspiracy to import drugs or to carry out money laundering. The former poses a threat to state security and sovereignty; hence, it qualifies to be placed under the protective theory of jurisdiction. On the other hand, as the importation of drugs or laundering of crime proceeds cannot be said to challenge state security, jurisdiction over conspiracies to commit these crimes arises under the objective territoriality theory. Taking into account this distinction, the Organized Crime Convention 2000 contains separate provisions on each type of conspiracy; See article 15(2)(c)(i) &(ii) of the Organized Crime Convention 2000; See also Blakesley' US Jurisdiction over Extraterritorial Crime' (n 57) 1111,1112

[192] 18 U.S.C. Sc. 2339A, Providing Material Support to Terrorists; See also 18 U.S.C. Sc. 1203, Hostage Taking

[193] 18 U.S.C Sc. 2339A, Providing Material Support to Terrorists

[194] See article 7(2) the Terrorism Financing Convention 1999

[195] 21 U.S.C. Ss.846 & 963, The Controlled Substances Act

[196] See article 4(1)(b)(iii) of the Drugs Convention 1988

2.5.3) Laws of the UK on terrorism and organised crime

The English anti-terrorism laws create extra-territorial offences based both on the nationality of the offenders and the nationality of the victims.[197] Moreover, its Aviation Security Act 1982 applies to offences occurring in aircrafts registered in the UK as well as to offences occurring in any aircraft flying over the airspace of the UK.[198] In the same way, the UK's Proceeds of Crime Act 2002 makes punishable any extraterritorial act, whether only a part of which takes place in the UK or although no part occurs there at all, if it relates to a crime having taken place or liable to be prosecuted in the UK.[199] It demonstrates the application of the objective territorial theory as contained in the conventions relating to organised crime.[200] Likewise, its anti-bribery law makes punishable the crime when the offender is one of its nationals or the commission of the offence involves the participation of a legal entity registered in the UK.[201] It implements the nationality theory as embodied in the UN Convention against Corruption 2003.[202]

Clearly the international conventions on terrorism and organised crime have significantly impacted national laws in terms of expanding their extraterritorial reach. As argued earlier, the extraterritoriality required by the conventions is directed towards facilitating state cooperation in extradition and mutual legal assistance. It is thus appropriate now to focus to the conditions of extradition and mutual legal assistance sought to be fulfilled by the international conventions through the obligation to establish extraterritorial jurisdiction. In section III, the conditions of legality and crime having occurred on state territory will be discussed and in section IV the condition of special use of double criminality will be

---

[197] See Explosive Substances Act 1883, 46 Vict. Ch.13 [hereinafter the Explosive Substances Act 1883 of UK]; Sc. 62, 63 c Terrorism Act 2000, 2000 Chapter 11 [hereinafter Terrorism Act 2000 of UK] , Sc.1 Taking of Hostages Act 1982, 1982 Chapter 28 [hereinafter Taking of Hostages Act 1982 of UK]

[198] Aviation Security Act 1982, 1982 Chapter 36 [hereinafter Aviation Security Act 1982 of UK]

[199] See Sc. 340(2)(b) Proceeds of Crime Act (POCA) 2002, 2002 Chapter 29 [hereinafter Proceeds of Crime Act 2002 of UK]

[200] See article 4(1)(b)(iii) Drugs Convention 1988, article 15(2)(c)(ii) Organized Crime Convention 2000 and article 42(2)(c) UN Convention against Corruption 2003

[201] See Sc.12 The Bribery Act 2010, 2010 Chapter 23 [hereinafter The Bribery Act 2010 of UK]

[202] See article 42(2)(b) & 26 UN Convention against Corruption 2003

considered. It will be suggested that the obligation to establish extraterritorial jurisdiction under the international conventions does facilitate the fulfilment of the former conditions, however, it provides little support with respect to the fulfilment of the latter. The reason is that the conditions of legality and crime having occurred on state territory only require extraterritorial reach of national laws while the condition of special use of double criminality also requires harmony in national theories of jurisdiction. However, the obligation to establish extraterritorial jurisdiction allows diversity in national theories of jurisdiction.

Section 3: Fulfilment of legality principle and the condition of crime having occurred on state territory through the obligation to establish extraterritorial jurisdiction

3.1) Principle of Legality

The principle of legality is based on the ancient maxim of *nullum crimen sine lege* which means 'no crime without a previous law.'[203] It means punishability of an act depends on there being a previous legal provision declaring it to be a penal offense, subject to the jurisdiction of the national courts of the proscribing state.[204] Hence, the principle not only requires the existence of a law proscribing the crime but also competence of the national courts to punish it.[205] Its object is to give timely notice to the accused of the law he will be subjecting himself to by committing his crime.[206]

---

[203] Christopher L. Blakesley, 'A Conceptual Framework for Extradition and Jurisdiction over Extraterritorial Crime' 1984 Utah Law Review (1984) 685 at 739

[204] See for instance, article 22(1) of the Rome Statute of the ICC 1998, 'A person shall not be criminally responsible under this Statute unless the conduct in question constitutes, at the time it takes place, a crime within the jurisdiction of the Court.' Likewise, Sc. 1 of Strafgesetzbuch, StGB 1998 [hereinafter German Criminal Code] provides, 'An act may only be punished if its punishability was determined by law before the act was committed.' <http://www.gesetze-im-internet.de/englisch_stgb/german_criminal_code.pdf> [date accessed 21/03/23]. The rule also finds expression under article 111-3 of Code Penal 1810 [hereinafter French Penal Code] <http://www.equalrightstrust.org/ertdocumentbank/french_penal_code_33.pdf> [date accessed 21/03/23]

[205] See Colangelo (n 11) 126

[206] ibid at 167

Applying the principle to extraterritorial crimes, it is required that national laws proscribing the relevant conduct must be given extraterritorial effect at the time of its commission and not afterwards. In the words of O'Keefe:

> The exercise of prescriptive jurisdiction on the basis of a jurisdictional nexus established subsequent to the commission of the offence is a form of ex post facto criminalisation and, therefore, repugnant ...[207]

In the context of extradition and mutual legal assistance, legality demands that jurisdiction of the requesting state to punish the crime in respect of which inter-state assistance is sought, must exist at the time of its commission.[208] If it is established subsequent thereto, the surrender or interrogation will amount to violation of the prohibition against non-retroactivity of criminal laws.

The principle is widely applied in the laws and treaties on extradition and mutual legal assistance. For instance, article II (1) of Canada-Spain Extradition Treaty 1989 provides:

> For the purpose of this treaty, extradition shall be granted for conduct which is punishable under the laws of both contracting States, both at the time of the commission of the offence and at the time of the extradition request…[209]

The significance of extraterritorial jurisdiction can hardly be over-emphasised as regards the fulfilment of legality in extradition and mutual assistance proceedings involving transnational crimes. The rule of legality demands that the requesting state must have criminalised the act in respect of which surrender or interrogation is sought, right from its beginning. When the act constitutes an extraterritorial crime, legality further demands that the law making it punishable must have been given extraterritorial effect at the time of its commission. Since the acts of transnational terrorism and organised crimes essentially involve the element of extraterritoriality, the international conventions regulating these crimes oblige the parties to make them punishable on several grounds of extraterritoriality. Thus, the obligation to criminalise offences on grounds such as nationality, state security and passive personality enables the requesting state to fulfil the legality condition of the requested state's law while obtaining the extradition or interrogation of transnational offenders.

---

[207] O'Keefe (n 19) 743

[208] Colangelo (n 11) 165

[209] See Article II (1) of Spain and Canada Treaty of Extradition. Signed at Madrid on 31 May 1989 [hereinafter Canada-Spain Extradition Treaty 1989]

3.2) Requirement of crime having occurred in the territory of the requesting state

Another requirement of extradition proceedings is that the crime in respect of which surrender is being sought must have occurred in the 'territory' of the requesting state. For instance, article 1 of the India-Nepal Extradition Treaty 1953 provides:

> The two Governments hereby engage on a basis of strict reciprocity to deliver up to each other those persons, who, being accused, or convicted, of a 'crime committed in the territory' of one Government, shall be found within the territory of the other Government...[210]

Some bilateral treaties use the word 'jurisdiction' instead of 'territory'. For example, Hong Kong, Singapore-China Extradition Treaty 1997 provides that the surrender shall be granted for crimes committed within the 'jurisdiction' of the requesting state.[211] Apparently, this formulation increases the possibility of surrender because it makes all those crimes extraditable which fall within jurisdiction of the requesting state.

However, a number of extradition rulings indicate that the term 'jurisdiction' has been interpreted by some national courts to mean 'territory'. For instance, *In re Stupp*, Germany requested from the US, extradition of its national who had committed murder and robbery in Belgium. The extradition proceedings between the two states were governed by the treaty between the United States and the Kingdom of Prussia of June 16, 1852 which provided that extradition should be allowed for crimes committed within the 'jurisdiction' of the requesting party. Germany asserted jurisdiction on the basis of the active nationality principle. The US District Court held that the words committed within 'jurisdiction' in the extradition treaty implied 'territory' of the requesting state.[212] Consequently,

---

[210] See article 1, Treaty of Extradition Between the Government of India and the Government of Nepal signed at Kathmandu on 2 October 1953 [hereinafter India-Nepal Extradition Treaty 1953]

[211] See article 1, Agreement between the Government of the Hong Kong Special Administrative Region of the People's Republic of China and the Government of the Republic of Singapore for the Surrender of Fugitive offenders. Signed at Hong Kong 11 November 1997 [hereinafter Hong Kong, China- Singapore Extradition Treaty 1997]

[212] *In re Stupp* 23 F.Cas.281 (C.C.S.D.N.Y.1873) (No.13562)

the extradition was rejected for the crime in question not having taken place on German territory.[213]

Obviously, the condition creates difficulties in situations where the commission of crime involves more than one state and the requesting state claims jurisdiction on a theory other than territoriality. The makers of the international conventions on terrorism and organised crime have attempted to facilitate the fulfilment of this condition by employing a legal fiction.[214] According to this fiction, the crime must not only be considered to have taken place in the territory of the state where it actually occurs, but also in the territory of each state having established jurisdiction under any of the bases provided by the conventions. For example, article 13 (4) of the Nuclear Terrorism Convention 2005 reads:

> If necessary, the offences set forth in article 2 shall be treated, for the purposes of extradition between States Parties, as if they had been committed not only in the place in which they occurred but also in the territory of the States that have established jurisdiction in accordance with article 9, paragraphs 1 and 2.[215]

According to Abramovsky, the provision is designed to increase the number of states qualified to be requesting states, so that if the requested state is unwilling to surrender the fugitive to a territorial state, it may have other options to fall back upon.[216] For example, in the current political situation, Iran might not be willing to surrender a fugitive to the US. However, if the condition of territoriality does not stand in its way and some other state such as Russia is equally competent to demand surrender, Iran might be willing to accede to the request, in order to fulfil its

---

[213] Similarly, *In re Lo Dolce*, a Sergeant of the US Army was found involved in the murder one of his fellow soldiers during World War II in German-occupied Italy. After the war, *Lo Dolce* returned to the US where he could not be charged because at that time, the US did not rely on any other theory of jurisdiction except territoriality, whereas, the crime had taken place outside its territory. When Italy requested extradition of *Lo Dolce* pursuant to the US-Italian Extradition Treaty of 1859, the same was denied on the ground that Italy had no dominion or control over the 'territory' where the crime was committed. See *In re La Dolce* 106 F. Supp. 455 (W.D.N.Y. 1952)

[214] See Lambert (n 46) at 243

[215] See article 13(4) the Nuclear Terrorism Convention 2005

[216] See Abramovsky, 'Multilateral Conventions Hague Part I (n 164) 404

convention obligations.[217] It can thus be argued that this legal fiction has optimised the chances of surrender of transnational fugitive offenders.[218]

In the light of above, it can be argued that the obligation to establish extraterritorial jurisdiction under the international counterterrorism and organised crime conventions appears effective to the extent of facilitating the compliance of those conditions of extradition and mutual assistance proceedings which require the extraterritorial reach of national laws. Now we shall analyse the effectiveness of the obligation in relation to that condition which requires harmony in national theories of jurisdiction. The condition is known as special use of double criminality and is widely applied in extradition and mutual assistance laws. It will be suggested that the obligation to establish extraterritorial jurisdiction is unlikely to produce a level of harmony sufficient to satisfy special use condition. The reason is that the bases of jurisdiction outlined by the international conventions are non-exhaustive and are open to multiple interpretations. Accordingly, when they are implemented domestically, they reflect the diversity of national legal systems of states parties. In view of this, the better way to facilitate law enforcement cooperation is to relax the application of special use condition.

Section 4: Fulfilment of special use of double criminality through the obligation to establish extraterritorial jurisdiction

4.1) Special use of double criminality

The rule of double criminality represents one of the most widely applied conditions of extradition and mutual legal assistance laws.[219] It requires that the act in respect of which surrender or interrogation is sought must constitute a crime under the laws of both the requesting and the requested state.[220] Over the years, in view of the specific nature of multi-jurisdictional

[217] ibid

[218] Abraham Abramovsky, 'Multilateral Conventions for the Suppression of Unlawful Seizure and Interference with the Aircraft Part II- The Montreal Convention' 14 Colum. J. Transnat'l L. (1975) 268 at 297,298; See also Abramovsky 'Multilateral Conventions Hague Part 1' (164) 404

[219] Blakesley 'A Conceptual Framework for Extradition' (n 204) 743

[220] See for instance Sc.2 of Extradition Act, Chapter 103, Original Enactment: Act 14 of 1968, Revised Edition 2000 [hereinafter Singapore Extradition Act 2000] <http://statutes.agc.gov.sg/aol/search/display/view.w3p;page=0;query=DocId%3A%226a7ef250-75a5-4da8-ad13-07d2b2cd6e01%22%20Status%3Ainforce%20Depth%3A0;rec=0> [date accessed 21/03/23]

crimes, a special use of double criminality has evolved.[221] It stipulates that when the request relates to an extraterritorial crime, in addition to the usual requirement of the act constituting a crime under the laws of two states, the theory applied by the requesting state to give extraterritorial effect to its law must be accepted or correspond to the national legal principles of the requested state.[222] This means that the requesting state must present a mutually acceptable jurisdictional theory in order to satisfy dual criminality requirement.[223]

Although, unlike double criminality, its special use has not yet acquired the status of customary law,[224] it is nonetheless frequently applied in the laws and treaties on extradition and is considered to be one of the major hurdles in the surrender of fugitives involved in transnational crimes.[225] For instance, Article IV (5) of the 1989 Extradition Treaty between Canada and Spain provides that extradition may be refused:

> when the offence was committed outside the territory of requesting state and the law of requested state does not in corresponding circumstances provide for the same jurisdiction. [226]

Likewise, article 2(4) of US-South Africa extradition treaty 1999 provides that with regard to offences committed outside the territory of the requesting state, extradition shall be granted where the laws in the requested state provide for punishment of an offence committed outside its territory in similar circumstances.[227]

---

[221] Hafen (n 77) 215

[222] Hafen ibid at 219

[223] ibid

[224] See M. Plachta, *The Role of Double Criminality in International Cooperation in Penal Matters* in N. Jareborg, ed., Double Criminality. Studies in International Criminal Law (Uppsala, 1989) 111.

[225] Blakesley 'A Conceptual Framework for Extradition' (n 204) 745; See also Hafen (n 77) 215

[226] See article IV (5) Canada-Spain Extradition Treaty 1989

[227] See article 2(4) Extradition Treaty Between the Government of the United States and the Government of the Republic of South Africa, Signed at Washington on September 16,1999 (1999 U.T.S. Lexis 158) [hereinafter US-South Africa Extradition Treaty 1999]; See also article 2(4) of Extradition Treaty Between Australia and the Republic of India signed at Canberra on 23 June 2008 (2008 ATNIF 9) [hereinafter India-Australia Extradition Treaty 2008] and article 6(2) of France and Canada Extradition Treaty. Signed at Ottawa on 17 November 1988 [hereinafter Canada-France Extradition Treaty 1988

In the same way, article 7(2) of the European Convention on Extradition 1957 reads:

> When the offence for which extradition is requested has been committed outside the territory of the requesting Party, extradition may only be refused if the law of the requested Party does not allow prosecution for the same category of offence when committed outside the latter Party's territory or does not allow extradition for the offence concerned.[228]

Significantly, the principle also finds expression under the UN Model Treaty on Extradition which provides that extradition may be refused:

> If the offence for which extradition is requested has been committed outside the territory of either Party and the law of the requested State does not provide for jurisdiction over such an offence committed outside its territory in comparable circumstances...[229]

The special use condition, like all other conditions derived from the principle of reciprocity, seeks to ensure that, if circumstances are reversed and the requested state steps into the shoes of the requesting state, it must be entitled to obtain similar assistance in respect of the act in question. Another purpose could be to ensure that if extradition becomes impracticable and the requested state decides to prosecute the offender pursuant to *aut dedere aut judicare* rule, it must have jurisdiction to conduct the trial of the crime in question.[230]

Scholarly opinion varies with respect to the rationale of special use condition. For example, one scholar notes that the condition protects the offender from being extradited for an act not made criminal by, or not subject to the jurisdiction of, the requested state.[231] According to Wise, it serves the dual purposes of safeguarding the offender's rights and ensuring that the criminal justice system of the requested state prevails in matters of

---

[228] See article 7(2) the European Convention on Extradition 1957. Signed at Paris on 13.XII.1957 [hereinafter the European Convention on Extradition 1957]

[229] See article 4(e) UN Model Treaty on Extradition 1990 G.A. Res 116, U.N. GAOR,45th Sess., Annex, at 211-15, U.N. Doc. A/Res/45/116 (1990) [hereinafter the UN Model Treaty on Extradition 1990]

[230] Edward M. Wise, 'Some Problems of Extradition' 15 Wayne State Law Review (1968-69) 709 at 716

[231] See Sharon A Williams 'The Double Criminality Rule and Extradition: A Comparative Analysis' 15 Nova Law Review (1991) 581 at 589. See also Blakesley 'A Conceptual Framework for Extradition' (n 204) 739

state cooperation.[232] Williams suggests that the special use condition is a product of reciprocity which demands that extradition must be viewed as an exchange of comparable favours based on the shared opinion of the community of states about acts of certain kinds.[233] If the requested state is convinced that the act should not be punished, the extradition ought to be denied.[234] Considering the fact that many extradition laws and treaties explicitly state that their underlying basis is reciprocity, this view appears most convincing.

Besides its recognition in extradition treaties, the theory has also been applied in certain landmark court decisions. For example, *In Re Ryat* the surrender of the fugitives was requested by Canada of the UK in connection with the planting of a bomb on board a Canadian airliner which resulted in two Japanese baggage handlers being killed while the aircraft was in Japan.[235] In order to obtain the surrender, the Canadian government had to prove not only that its courts were competent to prosecute the offenders for deaths in Japan, but also, that if the UK were substituted for Canada, the fugitive would be subject to English jurisdiction for their extraterritorial crimes.[236] In the same way, the principle was applied by the House of Lords in *Pinochet 3*.[237] In this case the Extradition Act 1989 of the UK was held to require that the offence must not only constitute a crime under the law of the UK but the basis of jurisdiction applied by the requesting state to give extraterritorial effect to its law must also be accepted or correspond to British national legal principles.[238] The extradition of General Pinochet was requested by Spain on the basis of

[232] See Edward Wise (n 231) 711; Hafen (n 77) 230; Lech Gardocki, 'Double Criminality in Extradition Law' 27 Isr. L. Rev (1993) 288 at 290; Christopher L. Blakesley, 'The Autumn of the Patriarch: The Pinochet Extradition Debacle and Beyond - Human Rights Clauses Compared to Traditional Derivative Protections Such as Double Criminality' 91 Journal of Criminal Law and Criminology (200-2001) 1 at 4, 5

[233] Williams (n 232) 582; Gardocki (n 233) 256; Bruce Zagaris, 'US International Cooperation against Transnational Organised Crime' 44 Wayne State L. Rev. (1998-1999) 1401 at1422; Wise (n 251) at 713

[234] Gardocki (n 233) 296; Wise (n 231) at 711; Boister 'Treaty Crimes' (n 10) 354

[235] *In re Ryat* Unreported, QDB,1989; See also Gilbert (n 3) 425-426 & foot note 73

[236] ibid

[237] *R. v. Bow Street Metropolitan Stipendiary Magistrate exparte Pinochet Urgate* (Amnesty International and others intervening) (No.3), 2 ENG. Rep 97,170 (H.L 1999) [1999] 2 WLR 827

[238] ibid

universality theory for acts of torture committed in Chile. Torture was subjected to universal jurisdiction under article 5(2) of the Convention against Torture and Other Cruel, Inhuman or Degrading Treatment or Punishment (CAT) 1984.[239] The UK did not recognise torture as a crime subject to universal jurisdiction until 1988 when it implemented CAT into its domestic law through the enactment of Criminal Justice Act 1988. On account of the non-existence of a corresponding theory of jurisdiction under the UK law on the relevant date, the House held that extradition could only be granted for crimes committed subsequent to 1988.[240]

4.1.1) Lack of harmony in national theories of jurisdiction and its implications for state cooperation in law enforcement

As noted by Blakesley, bases of jurisdiction are essential concepts for the purposes of state cooperation in law enforcement.[241] The decision to deny or grant extradition often depends on the theory of jurisdiction applied by the requesting state and its recognition under the laws of the requested state.[242] Thus, confusion over these bases risks disagreement and denial of extradition for non-fulfilment of the special use of double criminality.

Since the aim of the international conventions on terrorism and organised crime is to facilitate state cooperation in law enforcement, their rules should be directed towards harmonising national theories of jurisdiction, so that no occasion arises for the requested state to block surrender or interrogation due to the incompatibility of jurisdictional theories. It is pertinent, however, to note that the national laws implementing the international conventions reflect significant variation in the interpretation and application of the bases provided by the conventions

We shall now analyse some of these inconsistencies in order to advance the argument that the obligation under the international counterterrorism and organised crime conventions to establish extraterritorial jurisdiction is ill-suited for facilitating the fulfilment of the special use of double criminality condition under extradition law. The analysis will focus mainly on the rules relating to objective territoriality, active nationality and passive

---

[239] See article 5(2) Convention Against Torture and Other Cruel, Inhuman or Degrading Treatment or Punishment 1984,1465 UNTS 85/ [1989] ATS 21 [hereinafter the UN Convention against Torture1984]

[240] *R. v. Bow Street* (n 238)

[241] Blakesley ' A Conceptual Framework for Extradition' (n 204) 685

[242] ibid

personality because majority of the disputes concerning non- fulfilment of the special use condition revolve around these theories.

4.1.1.1) Objective territoriality basis

The objective territoriality rule enables states to make punishable an offence which, though entirely consummated abroad, has had its effects in the proscribing state's territory or which was intended to have such effect.[243] The rule appears in three organised crime conventions which authorise the parties to criminalise conspiracies hatched abroad to commit money laundering, drug trafficking or corruption or other organised crimes within their territory.[244]

The national laws implementing the counterterrorism and organised crime conventions reflect telling discrepancies in the interpretation and application of the objective territoriality rule. For example, France gives extraterritorial effect to its laws on the basis of territoriality and its variants when at least a part of the crime occurs in French territory.[245] On the other hand, the UK asserts jurisdiction on this basis when, although the offence entirely takes place abroad, it relates to a crime liable to be prosecuted in the UK or having already taken place in its territory.[246] A few states, such as India, Pakistan and the US, go even further and assert jurisdiction when the crime neither partially occurs nor relates to a prosecutable crime, but was only 'intended' to produce effects in state territory.[247] Some examples of situations where conflicting interpretations of objective territoriality led to complications in extradition proceedings are given immediately below.

---

[243] See Lowe in Evans (n 62); Bassiouni 'Theories of Jurisdiction' (n 25) 12

[244] See article 4(1)(b)(iii) the Drugs Convention 1988; article 15(2)(c)(ii) the Organized Crime Convention 2000 and article 42(2)(c) the UN Convention against Corruption 2003

[245] See article 113-2 French Penal Code:

French Criminal law is applicable to all offences committed within the territory of the French Republic. An offence is deemed to have been committed within the territory of the French Republic where one of its constituent elements was committed within that territory.

[246] See Sc.12 The Bribery Act 2010 of UK; see also Sc. 340(2)(b) Proceeds of Crime Act 2002 of UK

[247] See Sc. 14 Control of Narcotics Substances Act 1997 of Pakistan; Sc. 8 the Narcotics Drugs and Psychotropic Substances Act 1985 of India; Sc. 2(I) Anti-Money Laundering Act 2010 of Pakistan; article 2(a) the Extradition Act 1962, Act No.34 of 1962 [hereinafter the Indian Extradition Act 1962] and 21 U.S.C. Ss.846 & 963, the Controlled Substances Act

a) *Kirk W. Munroe* extradition case[248] between the US and Canada

In 1996, the US requested from Canada the extradition of a suspect on the charges of a failed money laundering sting which occurred entirely in Canada.[249] Although the offender was a Canadian national, had never travelled to the US and had never collected any money there-from, the US demanded his extradition for violating a local narcotics law which criminalised extraterritorial money laundering conspiracies, entirely thwarted abroad but intended to produce effects in the US territory.[250] The concerned court rejected the request because Canadian law did not make punishable conspiracies that were entirely thwarted abroad, while the relevant extradition treaty demanded compatibility in the theories of jurisdiction applied by the requesting and requested state.[251] Subsequently, the Canadian Supreme Court granted extradition by treating the act in question as an 'attempt', which did constitute a crime under Canadian national law and subject to extraterritorial jurisdiction.[252] It can however be argued that the Supreme Court had to satisfy the requirement of double criminality by altering the nature of the offence.

b) *The NatWest Three* Case

In this case, the US requested extradition of suspects from the UK on charges of fraud in violation of its national law.[253] The only link between the US and the crime was that the alleged fraud impacted its financial market by causing the collapse of an energy company based in the US.[254] The extradition was, however, granted despite every part of the crime

---

[248] *Kirk W. Munroe*, 'Canadian Appeals Court refuses to Extradite for US Money Laundering Sting' 12 Int'l Enforcement L. Rep (1996) 138-139

[249] ibid

[250] 21 U.S.C S.846 & 963, the Controlled Substances Act

[251] *Kirk W. Munroe* (n 249)

[252] ibid

[253] *R. (on the application of Bermingham) v Director of the Serious Fraud Office and Bermingham and others v the Government of the United States of America and the Secretary of State for the Home Department* [2006] E.W.H.C. 200 (Admin); [2007] Q.B. 727; [2007] 2 W.L.R. 635

[254] G. Davies, 'Extradition post the NatWest Three' 156 NLJ (2006) 1542; See also Obinna H.C. Onyeneke, 'Extradition: International Law and Domestic Law: Gary McKinnon v. Natwest Three' SSRN (December 4, 2009) <http://ssrn.com/abstract=1589502 or http://dx.doi.org/10.2139/ssrn.1589502> [Date accessed 21/03/23]

having taken place in the UK and the offenders holding UK nationality and working for a bank based in the UK.[255]

The decision sparked countrywide protests by human rights groups based in the UK.[256] The protesters demanded urgent re-negotiation of US-UK extradition arrangements.[257] This resulted in promulgation of the 'forum bar law' according to which, when the majority of the acts constituting a crime take place in the UK, the crime must be tried by its national courts. The law was never put into force.[258] The episode nonetheless makes it clear that if the theory of jurisdiction has no recognition under the laws of the requested state, even if extradition is granted, it causes public resentment and creates difficulties for future extraditions.

4.1.1.2) Passive personality principle

The rule of passive personality allows a state to make punishable an offence when the victim happens to be its national, irrespective of the place of commission or nationality of the offender.[259] The rule appears in all counterterrorism treaties apart from those concerning aircraft terrorism.[260] Furthermore, it finds expression in each organised crime treaty under consideration except the Drugs Convention 1988.[261]

Despite its inclusion in majority of the counterterrorism and organised crime conventions, its implementation at national level remains far from consistent. For example, Indian law gives recognition to passive personality when it converges with the protective principle. Thus, a terrorist attack against civilians abroad will be subjected to Indian jurisdiction only if it is directed to compel India or any other state to do or

---

255 The NatWest Three/ Norris <http://www.simmons simmons.com/docs/feb_06_the_natwest_three_norris.pdf> [Date accessed 21/03/23]

256 The Telegraph, 'Christopher Tappin: A History of Extradition Cases' The Telegraph (24/02/12) <http://www.telegraph.co.uk/news/uknews/law-and-order/9102825/Christopher-Tappin-a-0history-of-extradition-cases.html> [Date accessed 21/03/23]

257 ibid

258 ibid

259 See Bassiouni 'Theories of Jurisdiction' (n 25) 45-47

260 Beijing Convention is an exception to aircraft terrorism treaties as it recommends the parties to establish jurisdiction on passive personality basis. See article 8(2)(a) Beijing Convention 2010

261 For provisions of transnational treaties requiring the establishment of jurisdiction on passive personality basis, see (n 188) above

abstain from doing something.[262] To the contrary, the US law attaches no such condition regarding the application of passive personality,[263] while, the principle has no recognition under the counterterrorism and organised crime laws of Pakistan.[264]

a) *Abu Daoud* Case

An example of the refusal of extradition on the grounds of dissimilar national approaches towards passive personality is *Abu Daoud case* of 1977.[265] According to its facts, Israel requested from France the extradition of Abu Daoud, an alien, who was found to have been involved in the murder of Israeli nationals on German territory, during the Munich Olympic massacre. The French court refused to grant extradition because the relevant bilateral treaty demanded compatible theories of jurisdiction and the theory applied by Israel to make punishable the crime was not recognised by France.[266] The only link between Israel and the crime was the murder of its nationals by some aliens in German territory.[267] French law had no identical basis of jurisdiction at the time of the commission of the offence. Thus, the court ruled that the arrest of Abu Daoud, upon Israel's extradition request would be tantamount to punishing the offender for an act not made criminal under the national law of France.[268] Although, after the offences in question, passive personality was made a basis of jurisdiction under French law, this was not relied upon by the Court

[262] See Sc. 15 The Unlawful Activities (Prevention) Act 1967 of India

[263] See 18 U.S.C. Sc.2332 b, Acts of Terrorism Transcending National Borders; for a different version of passive personality under US law see Sc. 2332 f, Bombing of places.

[264] See Anti-Terrorism Act (ATA), Act No. XXVII of 1997 [hereinafter, the Anti Terrorism Act 1997 of Pakistan] the Control of Narcotics Substances Act 1997 of Pakistan and the Anti-Money Laundering Act 2010 of Pakistan

[265] *Abu Daud case,* judgement of Jan.11, 1977, Chambre d' Accusation De La Cour D'appel Paris; See also Jeffery B. Gaynes, 'Bringing the Terrorist to Justice: A Domestic Law Approach' 11 Cornell Int'l L.J (1978) 71; See also Blakesley 'A Conceptual Framework for Extradition' (n 204) 702; Thomas E. Carbonneau, 'Terrorist Acts - Crimes or Political infractions? An Appraisal of Recent French Extradition Cases' 3 Hastings International and Comparative Law Review (1980) 265 at 284; The Abu Daoud Affair, 'The Note' 11 J.Int'l L.& Econ (1977) 539 at 540-545

[266] Article 2 of Extradition Treaty Between Israel and France signed in 1958, ratified by France in 1971 [hereinafter Israel-France Extradition Treaty 1971]

[267] *Abu Daoud* case (n 266)

[268] ibid

because to do so would have violated prohibition against non-retroactivity of criminal laws.[269]

4.1.1.3) Nationality principle

According to the nationality principle, a state is entitled to make punishable the acts committed by its nationals regardless of the place of their commission. This principle appears in nearly all counterterrorism and organised crime conventions under consideration.[270] Counterterrorism conventions set forth mandatory obligation to establish jurisdiction on this basis, whereas organised crime treaties only recommend the parties to do so.[271]

Similar to objective territoriality and passive personality, a request for extradition based on active nationality theory is fraught with difficulties when put to the test regarding the special use of double criminality. The reason is that several states, including those belonging to continental Europe, do not allow the extradition of their nationals.[272] States not permitting extradition of nationals generally assert much wider jurisdiction over crimes committed by their nationals.[273] For example, French Extradition law of 1927 prohibits the extradition of nationals.[274] Accordingly, its Penal Code asserts jurisdiction over crimes committed abroad by French nationals on widest possible bases. For instance, it asserts jurisdiction even if nationality was acquired subsequent to the commission of crime.[275] Moreover, the Code applies to crimes committed anywhere by

---

[269] ibid; See also text to (n 204-210) above

[270] See article 3(1)(b) the Protection of Diplomats Convention 1973, article 5(1)(b) the Hostages Convention 1979, article 8(1)(b) the Nuclear Materials Convention 1980, article 6(1)(c) the Rome Convention 1988, article 6(1)(c) the Terrorist Bombing Convention 1997, article 7(1)(c) the Terrorism Financing Convention 1999, article 9(1)(c) the Nuclear Terrorism Convention 2005 and article 8(1)(e) the Beijing Convention 2010

[271] See article 4 the Drugs Convention 1988, article 15 the Organized Crime Convention 2000 and article 42 the UN Convention against Corruption 2003; In the words of Sproule, '…refusal [of states] to support this [nationality theory] as a mandatory ground was largely a response to civil law states' adamant refusal to accept any provision requiring the extradition of nationals.' See Sproule (n 20) 275

[272] See article 6(1)(a) of European Convention on Extradition 1957 and article3(1) Canada-France Extradition Treaty 1988

[273] Blakesley 'A Conceptual Framework of Extradition' (n 204) 709

[274] See article 1, Law of 10 March 1927 [hereinafter French Extradition Law of 1927]

[275] See article 113-6 of French Penal Code:

French citizens including those occurring in the territory of states with which France has no extradition treaty.[276] This may be compared with the US law which does not allow such broad interpretation of nationality principle except in cases involving threats to national security.[277] Nonetheless, the extradition treaty to which both the US and France are parties provides that extradition shall only be granted for offences committed outside the territory of the requesting state, when the law of the requested state makes the offence punishable in similar circumstances.[278] Keeping in view the different versions of nationality theory applied by the two states, the French request to the US for extradition of a French national who obtained French nationality subsequent to the commission of crime or who committed his crime in a non-party state, remains under the threat of being refused.

Other discrepancies in national laws concerning the application of nationality theory include regulation by some states of crimes committed by habitual residents and legal entities under this theory. For example, the US law on terrorism makes punishable crimes committed by stateless persons, habitually residing in the US.[279] Similarly, the anti-bribery law of the UK interprets the term 'nationals' to include legal entities and corporations.[280] However, the corresponding laws of India and Pakistan do not permit such broad interpretations of nationality.[281] In the words of Sproule and Dennis, 'habitual residence also lends itself to varied interpretations that could well lead to disputes between the requesting and requested state.'[282]

French criminal law is applicable to any felony committed by a French national outside the territory of the French Republic. The present article applies even if the offender has acquired French nationality after the commission of the offence of which he is accused.

[276] ibid

[277] See 18 U.S.C. Chapter 209 – Extradition, Ss. 3181 to3184; See also Blakesley 'A Conceptual Framework of Extradition' (n 204) 712

[278] See article I, Extradition Treaty between the United States of America and France. Signed at Paris on April 23, 1996 [hereinafter US- France Extradition Treaty 1996]

[279] See also 18 U.S.C. Sc. 2332f (Bombing of places); 18 U.S.C. Sc. 2339B, Providing Material Support or Resources to Designated Foreign Terrorist Organizations;18 U.S.C. Sc. 2339A, Providing Material Support to Terrorists

[280] See article 12(4)(iv) of The Bribery Act 2010 of UK

[281] the Unlawful Activities (Prevention) Act 1967 of India and the Anti-Terrorism Act 1997 of Pakistan

[282] See Sproule (n 20) 276

4.1.1.4) Inconsistencies with respect to other bases of Jurisdiction

The US and Indian counterterrorism laws make punishable attacks against buildings and infrastructure located abroad, under the theory of state security or protection. However, this jurisdictional theory has no equivalent in the corresponding law of Pakistan.[283] Significantly, all three states have ratified Terrorist Bombings and Financing Conventions which recommend that parties establish this basis of jurisdiction.[284]

Similar discrepancies can be viewed in national interpretations of secondary basis of jurisdiction, as found in each counterterrorism and organised crime convention under consideration.[285] For example, Indian law makes punishable the acts committed abroad by an offender who is subsequently found in India if the offender is an Indian national or when the crime is committed in an aircraft or vessel registered in India.[286] By contrast, the US law regulates such crimes regardless of any territorial or nationality link.[287] Furthermore, it proscribes these crimes even if the offender was 'brought' to the US.[288] For example, the US law on Providing Material Support to Designated Terrorists makes punishable the acts committed abroad by an offender subsequently 'brought' to the US.[289] In the same way, Indian hijacking law criminalises acts committed on board an aircraft landing in India, under the theory of universality as found in the conventions relating to aircraft terrorism. This theory has no application in the parallel legislation of Pakistan.[290]

---

[283] See Sc. 15 the Unlawful Activities (Prevention) Act 1967 of India; 18 U.S.C. 2339A, Providing Material Support to Terrorists; 18 U.S.C. Sc. 2332f Bombing of Places and the Anti-Terrorism Act 1997 of Pakistan

[284] See for current ratification status, United Nations Treaty Collection <http://treaties.un.org/Pages/ViewDetailsIII.aspx?&src=IND&mtdsg_no=XVIII~15&chapter=18&Temp=mtdsg3&lang=en.>[Date accessed 21/03/2013]

[285] See text to(n 163-166) above

[286] See sc.6 The Anti-Hijacking Act 1982 of India

[287] 18 U.S.C. Sc 1203, Hostage Taking Act

[288] as opposed to 'found'

[289] 18 U.S.C. Sc. 2339B: Providing Material Support or Resources to Designated Foreign Terrorist Organizations

[290] See Sc.6 The Anti-Hijacking Act 1982 of India; See Sc. 402-A to C Pakistan Penal Code 1860

4.1.2) Inconsistent theories of jurisdiction- A contradiction of the aim of facilitating state cooperation in law enforcement

Clearly, national approaches towards the bases of extraterritorial jurisdiction provided by the international counterterrorism and organised crime conventions reflect disunity and disharmony. While this appears to be in accord with the observation made in the *Lotus* judgement that no rule of international law prohibits states from applying their laws to extraterritorial events,[291] it may however lead to complications in law enforcement cooperation due to the non-fulfilment of special use of double criminality.[292]

The dissimilarity in the national theories of jurisdiction affords opportunity to the requested state to refuse extradition for non-fulfilment of special use of double criminality. Although extradition may still be granted in spite of dissimilar theories, the same will depend on discretion of the requested state, likely to be exercised in view of political and diplomatic considerations.[293] This denies the objective of facilitating state cooperation in bringing to justice transnational offenders.[294] Following this approach multilateral cooperation vis a vis transnational crimes remains as discretionary as bilateral cooperation concerning ordinary crimes.[295]

In bilateral cooperation, states tend to raise or lower the barriers of extradition depending on their political and diplomatic relations with the requesting state.[296] For example, the French court's judgement in *Abu Daoud* case was criticised for having political flavouring.[297] According to *Carbonneau*, the fugitive had strong connection with certain Middle-Eastern states and the France government did not want to annoy them by extraditing him to Israel.[298] Therefore, the Court raised the barrier of

---

[291] *S.S. Lotus* (n 13) paragraph 73
[292] Sproule (n 20) 276
[293] Bassiouni 'Policy Consideration' (n 51) 135-136; Hafen (n 77) 191
[294] Bassiouni ibid
[295] ibid; See also Kathleen A. Basso, 'The 1985 US-UK Supplementary Extradition Treaty: A Superfluous Effort' 12 Boston College International and Comparative Law Review (1989) 301 at 315-316; Cherif Bassiouni, 'The Political Offence Exception Revisited: Extradition between the US and UK- A Choice between Friendly Cooperation among Allies'15 Denv. J. Int'l L. & Pol'y (1986-1987) 255 at 224-225; Blakesley 'Autumn of the Patriarch' (n 233) 15
[296] Hafen (n 77) 202-203; Bassiouni 'Policy Considerations' (n 51) 135-136; Bassiouni 'The 1985 US-UK Supplementary Extradition Treaty' (n 296)
[297] Carbonneau (n 266) at 284,286
[298] ibid

double criminality to block extradition.[299] Similarly, the UK's extradition arrangements with the US are often seen with disapproval for carrying lesser safeguards for the offenders to be extradited from the UK to US as compare to those to be extradited from the latter.[300]

4.1.3) Flexibilities in the obligation to establish extraterritorial jurisdiction

4.1.3.1) Permissive nature of the new bases introduced by the conventions

The international counterterrorism and organised crime conventions recommend that parties give extraterritorial effect to their laws on several grounds previously unknown to many of them.[301] All these grounds are derived from less recognised or controversial theories of jurisdiction such as national security, universality and objective territoriality. In view of their non-consensual nature, reliance on them is permitted under the laws of some states only. Therefore, uniformity with respect to their application could have been brought only by imposing mandatory obligations. This would have forced the parties to amend their laws. However, the conventions have merely recommended the parties to implement these bases. Consequently, the new bases are likely to be adopted only by those states whose existing legal systems allow them to do so.

4.1.3.2) Savings Clause

Each counterterrorism and organised crime convention under consideration includes a residual provision which provides that the bases of jurisdiction laid down by these conventions in no way supersede the other bases recognised by the domestic law of state parties.[302] This implies that any

---

[299] ibid

[300] See text to (n 173)

[301] These include crimes committed by the habitual residents, crimes perpetrated in aircrafts landing in state territory, crimes directed at destruction of the buildings and infrastructure located abroad, act of conspiracies, planning and financing committed abroad to carry out principle crimes within state territory, conspiracies hatched abroad to commit money laundering and drug trafficking crimes within state territory and the acts committed abroad to compel the state to do or abstain from doing something

[302] See article 4(3) the Hague Convention 1970, article 5(3) the Montreal Convention 1971, article 3(3) the Protection of Diplomats Convention 1973, article 5(3) the Hostages Convention 1979, article 8(3) the Nuclear Materials Convention 2005, article 6(5) the Rome Convention 1988, article 6(5) the Terrorist Bombings

basis of jurisdiction set forth by the domestic law shall be acceptable and preserved. The clause can be invoked to justify the existence in domestic law of the less-familiar interpretations of the traditional theories of jurisdiction.

For example, in the *Babar Ahmad* case, the extradition of the offender was sought by the US from the UK on the ground that he used a web-server based in the US to seek funding for Jihadist activities in Chechnya.[303] Similarly, in *Gary McKinnon*, extradition was requested for the crime of hacking the computer system of the US Military, while operating from the UK.[304] In both these cases, the US gave the broadest interpretations to the objective territoriality and protective theories. They cannot, however, be considered repugnant to the international counterterrorism and organised crime conventions because their savings clause indemnifies any theory recognised by national law.[305]

4.1.3.3) Offences to be defined in accordance with national law

The organised crime conventions explicitly provide that the offences are to be defined in accordance with national legal principles.[306] This authorisation

---

Convention 1997, article 7(6) the Terrorism Financing Convention 1999, article 9(5) the Nuclear Terrorism Convention 2005, article 8(4) the Beijing Convention 2010, article 4(3) the Drugs Convention 1988, article 15(6) the Organized Crime Convention 2000 and article 42(6) the UN Convention against Corruption 2003

303 *Case of Babar Ahmad and Others v. the United Kingdom* (Applications nos. 24027/07, 11949/08, 36742/08, 66911/09 and 67354/09) ECtHR (Fourth Section) Admissibility decision of 6 July 2010

304 *McKinnon v United States* (2007) EWHC 762 (Admin); (2007) 157 N.L.J. 554; *McKinnon v United States* (2007) EWHC 762 (Admin); (2007) 157 N.L.J. 554; *McKinnon v Government of the USA*, [2008] U.K.H.L. 59

305 Some of the more recent treaties do clarify that the bases protected under the savings clause are those which are in accord with customary international law. However, since there is no universal interpretation of customary law theories, the clarification does little to harmonize national laws. See article 7(6) the Terrorist Financing Convention 1999, article 15(6) the Organized Crime Convention 2000 and article 42(6) the UN Convention against Corruption 2003

306 See article 30(9) UN Convention against Corruption 2003 and article 11(6) Organized Crime Convention 2000:

Nothing contained in this Convention shall affect the principle that the description of offences and of the applicable legal defences or other legal principles controlling the lawfulness of conduct is reserved to the domestic law of a state party and that such offences shall be prosecuted and punished in accordance with that law.

See also article 3(11) the Drugs Convention 1988,

is implicit in counterterrorism conventions.[307] Since extraterritorial jurisdiction entails the competence to enact laws with extraterritorial scope, the ability to define offences locally also includes the authorisation to give them extraterritorial effect. Therefore, by defining offences in a specific manner, states can give extraterritorial effect to their laws on any ground chosen by them, whether or not the same corresponds to the bases provided by the conventions.

For example, one of the elements of the definition of the crime of 'transnational terrorism' under the US law is that the act in question involves the utilization of the US mail or any facility of inter-state commerce.[308] The enactment extends the operation of the US law abroad on the grounds of the offender having used local mail or transportation facilities. Although the definition underlies two unusual theories of jurisdiction, it cannot be said to have contravened the international counterterrorism and organised crime conventions in view of the right given to the parties to define offences domestically. Therefore, inherent in the permissibility to define offences locally is the authorisation to give them extraterritorial effect on any grounds permissible under national laws. The argument finds support in a report entitled 'the Barker Report' and presented to the UK's Home Secretary on the review of the US-UK extradition arrangements. In this report it was observed that the offences of wire fraud, mail usage and extraterritorial bribery have been defined under the US law in such a way that the US can prosecute even if its link to the crime is very remote.[309]

As such, it is quite plain to see that the international conventions on terrorism and organised crime impose no restriction on the parties with respect to giving extraterritorial effect to their national laws under any theory of jurisdiction. To justify this approach, it can be argued that jurisdictional rules of the conventions are derived from customary

---

[307] For example, Fletcher suggests that treaty crimes are parochial and they are subject to moral and legal order within a state, because they threaten its parochial self- interests. See Fletcher quoted in Boister 'Treaty Crimes' (n 10) 346 at 352

[308] See 18 U.S.C. Sc. 2332B, Acts of Terrorism Transcending National Boundaries; See also 18 U.S.C. Sc. 2339B, Providing Material Support or Resources to Designated Foreign Terrorist Organizations

[309] A Review of the United Kingdom's Extradition Arrangements (following Written Ministerial Statement by the Secretary of State for the Home Department of 8 September 2010). Presented to the Home Secretary on 30 September 2011 <http://www.homeoffice.gov.uk/publications/police/operational-policing/extradition-review?view=Binary> [Date accessed 21/03/23]

international law and since custom imposes no restraint on extraterritoriality of national laws, the rules derived there from may not either. The argument however discounts the fact that the makers of the conventions have already adopted a non-traditional approach in establishing mandatory obligations.[310] The oft-quoted justification of these obligations is that states are required to surrender a portion of their sovereignty to combat 'collectively' the phenomenon of borderless crimes.[311] Arguably, therefore, states could, through treaty law, have evolved consensual interpretations of traditional theories of jurisdiction to be effective amongst the parties to conventions only.[312]

The celebrated case of *Strassheim v. Daily* provides an excellent example of a domestic court establishing the parameters of an otherwise open-ended objective territoriality rule. In this case, it was held that assertion of jurisdiction will be enforced as proper in either state and extradition will be approved pursuant to either state's theory of jurisdiction so long as the offence itself, its results or effects or any of the constituent elements actually occur within the territory of requesting state. The relevant part of the judgement reads:

> Acts done outside a jurisdiction, but intended to produce and producing detrimental effects within it, justify a state in punishing the cause of the harm as if he had been present at the effect if the state should succeed in getting him within its power.[313]

The wording ‘and producing detrimental effects’ effectively excludes controversial theories like 'intended effects' from the scope of the objective territoriality rule.

4.2) Alternatives to Uniformity

It has been argued that the international conventions have allowed inconsistent interpretations of the bases of jurisdiction provided by them in order to preserve the diversity of national legal systems and with a view to obtain the maximum number of ratifications.[314] This argument calls into question the technique of facilitating law enforcement cooperation by

---

[310] Lambert (n 46) 101
[311] See for instance, Guymon (n 23) 89
[312] Colangelo (n 11) 132
[313] *Strassheim v. Daily*, 221 U.S. 280 (1911) at 285 <http://supreme.justia.com/us/221/280/> [Date accessed 21/03/23]
[314] See Legislative Guide for implementing the Organized Crime Convention 2000 (n 26) at 130

imposing mandatory obligations. If preserving diversity was the objective, then imposing mandatory obligations appears futile because mandatory obligations are directed towards harmonising national legal systems to make them conducive to demands of extradition and mutual legal assistance.

Nonetheless, it is possible to reconcile desire to preserve diversity with the aim of facilitating law enforcement cooperation. This would require a shifting of focus from the harmonising national theories of jurisdiction to the regulating of the special use of double criminality condition. According to Bassiouni, facilitation of state cooperation calls for international regulation of the double conditions associated with the principle of reciprocity which tend to hinder extradition and mutual legal assistance on account of the disparity between national legal systems.[315]

The regulation of the special use condition is not something alien to states. Rather, it has been done in some bilateral treaties and domestic court cases. The condition is usually expressed in these words:

> When the offence has been committed outside the territory of the Requesting State, the Requested State shall grant extradition according to the provisions of this Treaty if its laws would provide for the punishment of such an offence committed in similar circumstances.[316]

Some of the modern extradition treaties modify this requirement with the effect of clarifying that refusal of extradition on this ground is optional and discretion vests with the executive authorities of the requested state to grant extradition in spite of its law not making punishable the offence in similar circumstances. For example, article 2(4) of the US-UK Extradition Treaty 2003 provides:

> …If the laws in the Requested State do not provide for the punishment of such conduct committed outside of its territory in similar circumstances,

---

[315] See Cherif Bassiouni, 'The "Political Offence Exception" Revisited: Extradition between the US and the UK- A Choice between Friendly Cooperation among Allies and Sound Law and Policy' 15 Denv. J. Int'l L. Pol'y (1986-1987) 255 at 260; See also Bassiouni 'Policy Considerations' (n 51) 128, 143, 144; Gardocki (n 233) at 288; Bassiouni 'Theories of Jurisdiction' (n 25) 3

[316] See article 1(2) of Treaty Between Australia and Federal Republic of Germany Concerning Extradition. Signed on 1/04/1987 [hereinafter Australia-Germany Extradition Treaty 1988]

> the executive authority of the Requested State, in its discretion, may grant extradition provided that all other requirements of this Treaty are met.[317]

Similarly, in the *Assarsson* case involving the US and Sweden, a US court held that extradition can be granted, regardless of the dissimilar theories of jurisdiction, if the language of the extradition treaty is *permissive* as regards the expression of double criminality.[318] According to the Court, when the relevant treaty uses words like extradition *need not* to be granted, it should be considered permissive. If the treaty includes expression such as extradition *shall not* be granted, the fulfilment of double criminality should be deemed essential.

A more radical way of regulating special use condition is to make it inapplicable altogether. For example, article 2(4) of the US-India Extradition Treaty 1997 provides, '[e]xtradition shall be granted for an extraditable offense regardless of where the act or acts constituting the offense were committed.'[319] According to this provision, the requested state shall be bound to grant extradition if the offence is 'extraditable'. It would be irrelevant which theory of jurisdiction has been applied by the requesting state to make the offence punishable.[320]

Conclusions

The international conventions on terrorism and organised crime set forth offences which spread across national frontiers, the prosecution of which demands the extraterritorial reach of national laws. Hence, the conventions oblige the parties to enact laws which have extraterritorial scope. At the same time, the conventions prohibit states from enforcing those laws in foreign territories without the approval of territorial sovereign. Accordingly, if the offender is found outside state territory, or the evidence of his crime is located abroad, the parties, despite having extraterritorial laws, are left

---

[317] See article 2(4), Extradition Treaty between the Government of the United Kingdom of Great Britain and Northern Ireland and the Government of the United States of America. Signed at Washington 31 March 2003 [hereinafter US-UK Extradition Treaty 2003]

[318] *Assarsson* case, 635 F.2d 1237 (7th Cir 1979); See also Blakesley 'A Conceptual Framework of Extradition' (n 204) 748

[319] See article 2(4) of Extradition Treaty between United States of America and India. Signed at Washington on June 25,1997 [hereinafter US-India Extradition Treaty 1997]

[320] An Extraditable offence has been defined under article 2(1) of the US-India Extradition Treaty 1997 as an offence punishable under the laws of two states with deprivation of liberty of one year or longer.

with no option but to wait for the offender to return voluntarily or to request his extradition or interrogation. Since the aim of the conventions is to promote state cooperation in law enforcement, it is safe to assume that the obligation set forth by them to establish extraterritorial jurisdiction is meant to facilitate extradition and mutual assistance proceedings.

Extradition and mutual legal assistance are carried out in accordance with national laws and bilateral treaties. These laws and treaties lay down certain conditions with respect to jurisdiction. The foremost amongst them are legality, special use of double criminality and the crime having occurred in the requesting state's territory. The obligation to establish extraterritorial jurisdiction under the international conventions clearly facilitates the fulfilment of the first and the last of these conditions. As regards the second condition, i.e. special use of dual criminality, the obligation provides little support. The reason for this is that while the conditions of legality and crime having occurred on state territory require the extraterritorial reach of national laws, special use of double criminality also demands similarity in national theories of jurisdiction. However, the obligation under the international conventions to establish extraterritorial jurisdiction produces diversity in national theories of jurisdiction. Although extradition may still be granted in spite of dissimilar theories of jurisdiction, the same will depend upon the discretion of the requested state, likely to be exercised in view of diplomatic and political consideration. This contradicts the scholarly assertion that the international conventions on terrorism and organised crime evidence the emergence of a new treaty regime which is aimed at promoting state cooperation in the specific context of transnational crimes. Following this approach state cooperation in regard to transnational crimes remains as discretionary as cooperation concerning ordinary crimes

In order to facilitate the fulfilment of the special use of double criminality condition, two courses might be adopted. Firstly, national theories of jurisdiction could be harmonised by providing universal interpretation of the traditional theories of jurisdiction and then obliging the parties to implement them without exception. Alternatively, the condition of special use of double criminality can be relaxed in the extradition and mutual legal assistance proceedings involving transnational crimes, with a view to accommodating the inherently extraterritorial nature of these crimes.

The adoption of the first option might be impracticable in view of the fact that international law imposes no limit on the right of states to apply their laws extraterritorially. Hence, it is suggested that makers of the international conventions on terrorism and organised crime should focus on the second option. This technique has been used in bilateral and regional treaties and strikes a balance between the aim of facilitating law enforcement cooperation and the constraint of preserving diversity of national legal systems.

CHAPTER 3

PROMOTING LAW ENFORCEMENT COOPERATION THROUGH THE OBLIGATION TO LEGISLATE AGAINST UNIVERSAL DEFINITIONS OF CRIME

Introduction

Modern international conventions on terrorism and organised crime impose the duty on states to legislate against universal definitions of crimes. The aim of the conventions is to facilitate state cooperation in extradition and mutual legal assistance. Both these measures require similarity in the national coverage of crimes. In other words, they demand that the act in respect of which surrender or interrogation is sought must constitute a crime under the laws of both the requesting and requested states. The requirement is known as 'double criminality' and is almost universally found in the laws and treaties on extradition and mutual legal assistance.

On several occasions, the non-fulfilment of double criminality by the requesting state either led to extradition having been blocked or trial of the accused being restricted. For example, when the US requested Switzerland to extradite Adnan Khashoggi for the crime of racketeering and conspiracy to racket, obstruction of justice and mail fraud, Switzerland had to impose a restriction on the trial of Khashoggi because the acts of racketeering and conspiracy to racket did not constitute crimes under Swiss national law. When the offender was subsequently tried in the US, the US had to drop the charges with respect to which Switzerland had imposed restriction. Since the remaining offences of mail fraud and obstruction of justice were only remotely linked to the US, the offender had to be acquitted. Similarly, in *Riley v. Commonwealth*, the defendant raised objection against his extradition from Australia to the US on the ground that the act of Continued Criminal Enterprise (CCE) for which his extradition was requested by the US did not constitute a crime under Australian national law.

Since the crimes established by modern counterterrorism and organised crime conventions had no domestic law parallels, without establishing an international duty to implement their exact definitions, it would have been difficult for the parties to satisfy the double criminality condition in extradition and mutual legal assistance proceedings involving these crimes. Therefore, to enable the parties to negotiate double criminality in their cooperative endeavors, the conventions imposed a duty upon states to legislate the exact definitions of the crimes. The rationale of the duty is to ensure that there remains no disparity in the national laws that might allow the requested state to refuse surrender or interrogation due to non-fulfillment of double criminality or non-existence of the crime under its national law. This chapter looks into the question of the extent to which the duty represents an effective technique of promoting state cooperation in extradition and mutual legal assistance.

It will be argued that the implementation of the duty is subject to several qualifications and safeguards. The reason for this is that makers of the conventions wanted to preserve the diversity of national legal systems in order to gain maximum ratifications. As long as an unconditional obligation is not established, a requested state can always claim that the act in respect of which surrender or interrogation is sought does not constitute a crime under its national law. It is more likely in the case of crimes established by recent counterterrorism and organised crime conventions because a majority of these crimes consist of several parts and, in view of the discretion afforded to states in the matter of implementation, national laws are likely to diverge in the coverage of one or more of their elements. Resultantly, despite imposing the duty to legislate, a request for extradition or interrogation remains under the threat of being refused due to disparity in national coverage of crimes.

Since it is unlikely that the consensus may evolve amongst states with respect to accepting an unqualified obligation to legislate, the way forward is to shift the focus from harmonising the definitions of crimes to regulating the use of double criminality. Through this method, states can be encouraged to collectively relax the application of double criminality considering the inherently complex nature of crimes established by modern counterterrorism and organised crime conventions. It provides a much better technique of facilitating extradition and mutual legal assistance as compared to inconclusive obligations to implement the exact definitions of the crimes.

The paper has been divided into four sections. Section 1 will discuss the crimes established by the international conventions on terrorism and organised crime, the object of their international criminalisation and the relevance of dual criminality for their suppression. Section 2 will consider the duty to legislate, the conventions establishing that duty and the complications arising in state cooperation as a result of dissimilar definitions of crime. Section 3 will analyse the impact of the duty to legislate on domestic laws on counterterrorism and organised crime as well as bilateral treaties on extradition and mutual legal assistance. Section 4 will look into the controlled use of dual criminality as a substitute to the duty to legislate.

Section 1: Crimes established by the international conventions on terrorism and organised crime, the object of their international criminalisation and relevance of dual criminality for their suppression

1.1) Acts criminalised under the international conventions on terrorism and organised crime

Historically, international law has been less concerned with crimes committed by non-state actors.[1] For example, non-state sponsored terrorism involving violence by individuals against civilian populations had formerly remained the exclusive domain of national law.[2] However, when non-state actors operating in one state started to threaten peace and security of other states, international law had to intervene. The Charter of the UN, one of the primary sources of international law, focuses on the perseveration of international peace and security.[3] Accordingly, non-state sponsored crimes spreading across national frontiers were subjected to UN sponsored multilateral suppression conventions, the object of which was to promote state cooperation in criminal law enforcement.[4]

---

[1] Christian Walter, Salja Voneky et al, *Terrorism as a Challenge for National and International Law: Security versus Liberty* (Max-Planck Germany-2004) 791

[2] ibid

[3] ibid; See also Article 38(1)(a) of the Statute of International Court of Justice; Article 1, Chapter 1 of the UN Charter 1945.

[4] The purpose of promoting state cooperation has been reiterated in each transnational treaty under consideration apart from the Hague Convention 1970 and the Montreal Convention 1971. See for instance, preamble to the Terrorism Financing Convention 1999:

With respect to counterterrorism, the impetus for international criminalisation came from the growing number of incidents of hijacking and their adverse effect on the international civil aviation industry.[5] In relation to organised crime, trafficking in narcotic drugs and its negative fallout on state economies was the reason for bringing these crimes subject to international control. [6]

1.1.1) Principal crimes under the counterterrorism conventions

Principal crimes under counterterrorism conventions can be classified into three broad groups: (1) attacks against civilian populations (2) crimes against specific targets and (3) crimes involving the means to commit acts of terrorism. The first group includes crimes of terrorist bombing [7] and nuclear terrorism.[8] The second group comprises attacks against internationally protected persons,[9] the taking of hostages,[10] attacks against ships,[11] the hijacking of aircrafts,[12] crimes against the safety of civil aviation[13] and the

---

BEING CONVINCED OF the urgent need to enhance international cooperation among States in devising and adopting effective measures for the prevention of the financing of terrorism, as well as for its suppression through the prosecution and punishment of its perpetrators...

See also article 1(b) the UN Convention against Corruption 2000. The object of the Convention is '[t]o promote, facilitate and support international cooperation and technical assistance in the prevention of and fight against corruption, including in asset recovery.'

For corresponding provisions, see article 2(1) the Drugs Convention 1988 and article 1 the Organized Crime Convention 2000. See also preambles of the Beijing Convention 2010, the Nuclear Terrorism Convention 2005, the Terrorist Bombing Convention 1997, the Rome Convention 1988, the Protection of Diplomats Convention 1973, the Nuclear Materials Convention 1980 and the Hostages Convention 1979.

[5] Abraham Abramovsky, 'Multilateral Conventions for Suppression of Unlawful Seizure and Interference with Aircraft part 1: Hague Convention' 13 Colum. J. Transnat'l L. (1974) 381

[6] D.W Sproule and Paul St-Denis, 'The UN Drug Trafficking Convention: An Ambitious Step' 27 Canadian Yearbook of International Law (1989) 263 at 264

[7] See article 2, the Terrorist Bombings Convention 1997

[8] See article 2, the Nuclear Terrorism Convention 2005

[9] See article 2(1), the Protection of Diplomats Convention 1973

[10] See article 1, the Hostages Convention 1979

[11] See article 3, the Rome Convention 1988

[12] See article 1, the Hague Convention 1970

[13] See article 1, the Montreal Convention 1971; See also article 1, the Beijing Convention 2010

theft of nuclear materials.[14] The third group contains the crime of financing terrorism which includes financing of all acts of terrorism as mentioned in the other two groups.[15] Features common to all these crimes include the involvement of more than one state in their perpetration or impact[16] and the achievement of a political goal as the motivation behind their commission.[17]

1.1.2) Principal crimes under the organised crime conventions

The principal crimes under organised crime conventions can be classified into two categories: specific and ancillary crimes. Specific crimes include drug trafficking,[18] migrant smuggling,[19] human trafficking,[20] weapons trafficking [21] and corruption.[22] Ancillary crimes consist of participation in

---

[14] See article 7(1), the Nuclear Materials Convention 1980

[15] See article 2, the Terrorism Financing Convention 1999

[16] See for example, article 3 Terrorist Bombing Convention 1997:
This Convention shall not apply where the offence is committed within a single State, the alleged offender and the victims are nationals of that State, the alleged offender is found in the territory of that State and no other State has a basis under article 6, paragraph 1 or paragraph 2, of this Convention to exercise jurisdiction, except that the provisions of articles 10 to 15 shall, as appropriate, apply in those cases.
Identical provisions can be seen in almost all transnational treaties. See (n 22) Chapter 2 above

[17] M. Cherif Bassiouni, 'Effective National and International Action against Organised Crime and Terrorist Criminal Activities' 4 Emory Intl L. Review (1990) 9 at 10

[18] See article 3, the Drugs Convention 1988

[19] See article 6, 2006 Protocol against the Smuggling of Migrant by Land, Sea and Air, supplementing the United Nations Convention against Transnational Organised Crime; 40 ILM 384 (2001) / UN Doc. A55/383(Annex III P.62) / [2004] ATS 11 [hereinafter the Migrant Smuggling Protocol to the Organized Crime Convention 2000]

[20] See article 3, 2000 Protocol to Prevent, Suppress and Punish Trafficking in Persons, Especially Women and Children, supplementing the United Nations Convention against Transnational Organised Crime; 40 ILM 335(2001)/ UN Doc. A/55/383 (Annex II, p.53) / [2005] ATS 27 [hereinafter the Human Trafficking Protocol to the Organized Crime Convention 2000]

[21] See article 5, 2001 Protocol against the Illicit Manufacturing of and Trafficking in Firearms, their Parts and Components and Ammunition, supplementing the United Nations Convention against Transnational Organised Crime; 40 ILM 335 (2001) / [2202] ATNIF 7 [hereinafter the Weapons Trafficking Protocol to the Organized Crime Convention 2000]

an organised criminal group,[23] money laundering [24] and the obstruction of justice.[25] Their common features include transnationality,[26] involvement of an organised criminal group and the motive of profit maximization.[27]

1.2) The object of international criminalisation

Offenders involved in terrorism and organised crime spread their operations in more than one state in order to defeat territorially restricted national laws.[28] Hence, their prosecution and punishment call for state cooperation in law enforcement. Although organised crime and terrorism significantly differ with respect to their nature and motivation,[29] the means adopted by the offenders to carry out these crimes are more or less the same. According to Guymon, means adopted by organised criminals to carry out drug trafficking are similar to those adopted by terrorists in

---

[22] See articles 7, 12, 15, 16, 18, 20 and 22 of the UN Convention against Corruption 2003

[23] See article 5, the Organized Crime Convention 2000

[24] See article 3, the Drugs Convention 1988; See also article 6, the Organized Crime Convention 2000 and article 23, the UN Convention against Corruption 2003

[25] See article 6, the Organized Crime Convention 2000 & article 23, UN Convention against Corruption 2003

[26] Transnationality has been defined under article 3(2) of the Organized Crime Convention 2000 in these words:

This Convention shall apply, except as otherwise stated herein, to the prevention, investigation and prosecution of: (a) The offences established in accordance with articles 5, 6, 8 and 23 of this Convention; and(b) Serious crime as defined in article 2 of this Convention; where the offence is transnational in nature and involves an organised criminal group. 2. For the purpose of paragraph 1 of this article, an offence is transnational in nature if: (a) It is committed in more than one State; (b) It is committed in one State but a substantial part of its preparation, planning, direction or control takes place in another State; (c) It is committed in one State but involves an organised criminal group that engages in criminal activities in more than one State; or (d) It is committed in one State but has substantial effects in another State.

[27] Bassiouni (n 17) 10

[28] M. Sornarajah, 'Extraterritorial Criminal Jurisdiction' 2 Singapore Journal of International and Comparative Law (1998)1 at 1, 4

[29] According to Bassiouni, what essentially distinguishes organised crime from terrorism is the 'motive' of the actor. While organised crime is characterized by 'profit motive', terrorism is typified by an ideological motive. See Bassiouni (n 17) 10

committing nuclear smuggling.[30] In view of this, similar law enforcement measures are used to prevent, suppress and control terrorism and organised crime.[31] In order to coordinate national and international efforts in the application of these measures, the acts of cross -border terrorism and organised crime have been subjected to international treaty regimes.

In the past, state cooperation was carried out on bilateral and regional basis. Since the acts of transnational terrorism and organized crime involve more than one state which may or may not be having bilateral treaties, this approach of state cooperation started to prove ineffective. Hence, the rationale of subjecting these crimes to international treaty regimes was to facilitate cooperation among all states affected by them.[32]. This prompted some scholars to collectively label these crime as 'transnational crimes' indicating a kind of criminality that requires coordination of efforts at international and transnational rather than bilateral level.[33]

Besides transnationality, another reason for laying emphasis on state cooperation was the growing nexus between organised criminals and terrorist offenders. Several scholars are of the view that organised criminals and terrorists share the common goal of paralyzing national justice systems to ensure the non-enforcement of law.[34] Significantly, this

---

[30] See Carrie Lyn Donigan Guymon, 'International Legal Mechanism for combating Transnational Organised Crime' 18 Berkley Journal of International Law (2000) 53 at 87; See also M. Cherif Bassiouni, 'Policy Considerations on Interstate Cooperation in Criminal Matters' 4 Pace Y.B.Int'l L. (1992) 123 at 127

[31] Bassiouni, 'Effective National and International Action' (n 17) 13

[32] See for instance, article 1 of the Organised Crime Convention 2000. 'The purpose of this Convention is to promote cooperation to prevent and combat transnational organised crime more effectively.' For Corresponding provisions of other transnational treaties, see (n 4) above

[33] See Kofi A Annan, Foreword to the Organized Crime Convention 2000 at p.iii; Neil Boister, 'Transnational Criminal Law', 14 EJIL (2003) 953 at 953; Guymon (n 30) 86-87; Sproule (n 6) at 266; UNODC's Technical Assistance Guide 2009 for implementing UN Convention against Corruption 2003 at 133

[34] Louise Shelley, 'The Unholy Trinity: Transnational Crime, Corruption and Terrorism' 11 Brown J. World Aff. (2004-2005) 101; See also Patricia Bibes, 'Transnational Organised Crime and Terrorism - Columbia a Case Study' 17 Journal of Contemporary Criminal Justice (2001) 243 at 244; Louis Shelly, 'The Nexus of Organised Crime and Terrorism: Two Case Studies in Cigarette Smuggling' 32 International Journal of Comparative and Applied Criminal Justice (2008) 1 at 15; John Rollins & Liana Sun Wyley, 'International Terrorism and

commonality has also been recognised by the UN Security Council which notes with concern in paragraph 4 of its resolution 1373 (2001) a growing connection between international terrorism and organised crime.[35] Similarly, resolution 1817 (2008) of the Security Council calls upon states to coordinate their efforts to respond to the threat posed by linkage between terrorism and organized crime. The relevant paragraph is reproduced below:

> Noting with concern the existing links between international security, terrorism and transnational organised crime, money-laundering, trafficking in illicit drugs and illegal arms, and in this regard *emphasizing* the need to enhance coordination of efforts on national, sub-regional, regional and international levels in order to strengthen a global response to this serious challenge.[36]

Likewise, the UN General Assembly in its Global Counterterrorism Strategy 2006 also emphasizes the need for closer cooperation between states with respect to the crimes that might be connected with terrorism, including drug trafficking and arms smuggling.[37]

It is thus clear that the element of transnationality and growing nexus between the offenders, motivated the international community to subject the acts of cross border terrorism and organised crime to international treaty regimes, so that state cooperation may be promoted in regard to their suppression, at international rather than bilateral level.

1.2.1) Measures of state cooperation are to be enforced subject to the Requesting state fulfilling the demands of principle of reciprocity

To effectuate state cooperation, the international conventions on terrorism and organised crime rely on the enforcement modalities of extradition and mutual legal assistance. Both these measures being admixture of national and international law demand the fulfilment of certain traditional conditions, for their employment.[38] In other words, the application of these measures requires the requesting state to fulfil certain conditions which are

---

Transnational Crime, Security threats, US Policy & Considerations for Congress' <www.fas.org/sgp/crs/terror/R41004.pdf> [Date accessed 21/03/23]

[35] See S/RES/1373 (2001)

[36] S/RES/1817(2008) Adopted by the Security Council at its 5907th meeting, on 11 June 2008 [hereinafter S/RES/1817 (2008)]

[37] Plan of Action annexed to Global Counter-Terrorism Strategy (2006),paragraphs 5 & 6 on Measures to Prevent and Combat Terrorism. A/Res/60/288

[38] Abramovsky (n 5) 400

found, either in the domestic law of the requested state pertaining to extradition or mutual legal assistance or under the bilateral treaty to which both the requesting and requested states are parties. The international conventions on terrorism and organised crime do not supersede these bilateral treaties and domestic laws rather they aim to make national legal systems responsive to their demands through establishing harmony.[39]

Laws and treaties on extradition and mutual legal assistance are based on the principle of reciprocity or exchange of comparable favours. According to this principle, the cooperating states must share equivalent concepts of justice or similar legal principles with respect to the act concerning which extradition or mutual legal assistance is sought. The rationale of the principle is to ensure that legal systems of cooperating states are similar enough to allow them to assist each other on reciprocal basis. In other words, the principle seeks to ensure that if circumstances are reversed and the requested state steps into the shoes of requesting state, it must be entitled to obtain similar assistance as regards the act in question. Thus, the principle lays down a set of double condition which are needed to be fulfilled by a requesting state in order to obtain surrender or interrogation.

One traditional condition derived from the principle of reciprocity is the fulfilment of double criminality. According to this condition, the act in respect of which extradition or mutual legal assistance is sought must constitute a crime under the laws of both the requesting and requested state.[40] To facilitate the fulfilment of this condition, the international conventions on terrorism and organised crime oblige the parties to legislate exact definition of crimes, so that surrender or interrogation may not be refused for non-existence of crime under the law of the requested state.[41] I shall now discuss in detail the double criminality condition and its relevance for suppression of crimes set forth by the international conventions on terrorism and organised crime.

---

[39] See Sproule (n 6) 266; Technical Guide to UN Convention against Corruption (n 33)

[40] M. Cherif Bassiouni, *International Criminal Law, Volume II: Multilateral and Bilateral Enforcement Mechanisms* (3rd edn, Martinus Nijhoff, Netherlands, 2008) 324

[41] ibid

1.3) Relevance of double criminality for suppression of crimes established by the international conventions on terrorism and organised crime

One of the most widely applied conditions in the domestic laws and bilateral treaties on extradition and mutual legal assistance is the double criminality requirement.[42] According to Williams, 'dual criminality rule is the one that is more or less uniformly applied in extradition law and process on a worldwide basis.' [43] It stipulates that a state, when seeking extradition or mutual legal assistance, must establish that the act in respect of which assistance is sought constitutes a crime under the laws of both the requesting as well as requested state. Scholarly opinion is divided about the purpose of dual criminality. While some argue that dual criminality is meant to protect the human rights of the offenders,[44] others maintain that it is designed to safeguard the sovereign interests of the requested state.[45] Still others claim that dual criminality is directed towards establishing reciprocal obligations between states.[46]

According to the first view, the justification for dual criminality lies in the principle of legality or *nullum crimen* which applies to all criminal proceedings including extradition and mutual assistance.[47] As discussed in Chapter 2, the principle requires that there can be no punishment without a prior violation of law.[48] Since extradition and some forms of mutual legal assistance are steps towards punishment,[49] no person could be subjected to them unless his deed is a crime under the law of both the requesting and requested state.[50] The second view entails that states are the only subjects of international law and all individual rights are derivative of state

---

[42] See Edward M. Wise, 'Some Problems of Extradition' 15 Wayne State Law Review (1968-69) 709 at 716

[43] Sharon A Williams, 'The Double Criminality Rule and Extradition: A Comparative Analysis' 15 Nova Law Review (1991) 623 at 581

[44] Williams (n 43) 582

[45] Wise (n 42) 710-711; See also Christopher L. Blakesley, 'The Autumn of the Patriarch: The Pinochet Extradition Debacle and Beyond - Human Rights Clauses Compared to Traditional Derivative Protections Such as Double Criminality' 91 Journal of Criminal Law and Criminology (200-2001) 1 at 5

[46] Lech Gardocki, 'Double Criminality in Extradition Law' 27 Isr. L. Rev (1993) 287 at 289

[47] Williams (n 43) 582

[48] See (n 204-207) Chapter 2 above

[49] Williams (n 43) 582

[50] ibid

sovereignty. Therefore, conditions such as dual criminality are limits that states impose on the requesting parties to insist on protection of their nationals.[51] The third view implies that dual criminality is meant to give assurance to the requested state that it could obtain the cooperation of the requesting state as regards the offence in question if their roles were reversed.[52] According to this view, double criminality condition represents an off shoot of principle of reciprocity which customarily governs extradition and mutual assistance proceedings. Since there is no rule of general international law that compels a state to extradite an offender or to provide legal assistance with respect to his crime in the absence of a treaty, such proceedings are carried out traditionally on reciprocal basis. Double criminality ensures reciprocity by requiring states to provide assistance in respect of those crimes only, concerning which they can demand assistance in future.

The status of the principle of dual criminality under international law is also disputed. Some commentators claim that dual criminality enjoys the status of customary international law; [53] others maintain that it is a product of treaty and does not bind a state automatically.[54] In *Factor v. Laubenheimer*, the US Supreme Court held that that the principle is based not on custom but treaty.[55] Hence, a fugitive cannot raise the dual criminality question as a bar to extradition if the applicable treaty or statute is silent.[56] There is a growing consensus that fulfilment of dual criminality is necessary only when the requesting state proposes to take a coercive action against the offender.[57]

Two methods are generally used to reflect dual criminality in bilateral treaties and domestic laws on extradition and mutual assistance. The first is based on a listing of offences. According to this method, offences in respect of which state cooperation can be sought are specifically listed in

---

[51] Blakesley (n 45) 3; See also Wise (n 42) 711

[52] Gardocki (n 46) 289

[53] M. Plachta, *The Role of Double Criminality in International Cooperation in Penal Matters* in N. Jareborg, ed., Double Criminality. Studies in International Criminal Law (Uppsala, 1989) 111

[54] Williams (n 43) 582

[55] *Factor v. Laubenheimer* 90 U.S. 276 (1933) <http://supreme.justia.com/cases/federal/us/290/276/case.html> [Date accessed 21/03/23]

[56] ibid

[57] Guy Stessens, *Money Laundering a New International Law Enforcement Model* (UK Cambridge University Press 2004) 291

the relevant treaty or law. For instance, article 1 of the Australia-Indonesia Mutual Assistance Treaty 1995 provides, 'parties shall grant to each other assistance in investigations or proceedings in respect of crimes listed in the Annex to the treaty'. The Annex includes offences such as human trafficking, hijacking, drug trafficking, or aiding, abetting, counselling or procuring the commission of, being an accessory to, attempting or conspiring to commit these offences.[58]

The second way of expressing dual criminality is to state it plainly that an offence shall be extraditable only if it is punishable under the laws of both the requesting and requested states.[59] Accordingly, article II (1) of the US-Italy Extradition Treaty 1983 provides '[a]n offence, however denominated, shall be extraditable only if it is punishable under the laws of both contracting parties by deprivation of liberty for more than one year or by a more severe penalty.' [60]

In view of the above, it is clear that dual criminality necessitates the congruence of offences in the requesting and requested states to allow them to cooperate. To harmonise national laws with respect to coverage of crimes, modern international conventions on terrorism and organised crime oblige the parties involved to legislate exact definitions of crimes established by them. The nature, scope and purpose of the duty to legislate under these conventions and the extent to which it enables states to satisfy dual criminality, will be discussed below.

Section 2 Duty to legislate under modern international conventions on terrorism and organised crime

2.1) Significance of the duty to legislate

Modern international conventions on terrorism and organised crime impose a duty on states to legislate against universal definitions of crimes established by them. Its rationale is to ensure the exact fulfilment of the obligation, so that there remains no discrepancy in the laws of cooperating states leading to refusal of law enforcement cooperation based upon the

---

[58] See article 1 & Annex of Treaty between Australia and the Republic of Indonesia on Mutual Assistance in Criminal Matters. Signed at Jakarta on 7 October 1995 [hereinafter Australia-Indonesia Mutual Assistance Treaty]; See also article 2 Hong-Kong, China-Singapore Extradition Treaty 1997

[59] Wise (n 42) 716

[60] See United States of America and Italy Extradition Treaty. Signed at Rome on 13 October 1983 [hereinafter US-Italy Extradition Treaty 1983]

non-satisfaction of dual criminality condition.[61] It can be argued, therefore, that the duty is meant to circumscribe the discretion available to the requested state to block extradition or mutual legal assistance under the rule of double criminality.

According to Bassiouni, state cooperation is necessary in order to combat crimes that involve border crossing as an essential element of criminal activity.[62] To encourage cooperation, it is essential that national laws must exhibit a certain degree of uniformity.[63] Uniformity provides a legal basis for detection, prevention and repression of crimes through state cooperation in mutual legal assistance and extradition.[64] To bring about uniformity, imposition of a duty to legislate represents an effective technique.[65]

Extradition signifies an area where uniformity of national laws plays a crucial role. A majority of states apply the principle of double criminality in their extradition laws, which requires identical definitions of crime under the laws of both the requesting and the requested state for the purposes of surrender.[66] Duty to legislate under the international counterterrorism and organised crime conventions facilitates the fulfilment of double criminality by requiring each party to establish identical definitions of crimes.[67] In the same way, the duty enables the parties to

---

[61] Bassiouni 'Policy Considerations' (n 30) 125-126; See also Bruce Zagaris, 'US Cooperation Against Transnational Organised Crime' 44 Wayne State Law Review (1998-1999) 1401 at 1425

[62] Bassiouni, 'Effective Action' (n 17) at 33 & 36

[63] UNODC's Legislative Guide For Implementation of the Human Trafficking Protocol to the UN Convention against Transnational Organized Crime 2000 at 269 paragraph 35 <http://www.unodc.org/pdf/crime/legislative_guides/Legislative%20guides_Full%20version.pdf> [date accessed 21/03/23]

[64] UNODC's Legislative Guide for Implementation of the Organized Crime Convention 2000 at 39 <http://www.unodc.org/pdf/crime/legislative_guides/Legislative%20guides_Full%20version.pdf> [date accessed 21/03/23]

[65] ibid

[66] UNODC's Legislative Guide to the Universal Anti-terrorism Conventions & Protocols (2003) at 8 paragraph 18 <http://www.unodc.org/pdf/crime/terrorism/explanatory_english2.pdf> [date accessed 21/03/23]

[67] AB Green, Convention on the Prevention and Punishment of Crimes against Diplomatic Agents and Other Internationally Protected Persons: An Analysis' 14 Virginia Journal of International Law (1973-1974) 703 at 714

satisfy double criminality in cross-border investigation of crimes, which is a key to success in global fight against transnational criminality.[68]

Another important function of the duty is to prevent the states from failing to cooperate. If laws are available domestically, states cannot show their inability to cooperate due to the absence of enabling laws. It should be noted that in the early phases of the formation of ICTY, the Federal Republic of Yugoslavia (FRY) expressed its inability to cooperate on account of the absence of enabling national laws.[69]

The international conventions on terrorism and organised crime by imposing a duty to legislate, promise to redefine the role of international law which thus far has been limited to laying down general obligations.[70] General obligations refer to those provisions of multilateral treaties which do not require the parties to legislate in order to perform their international obligations.[71] They rather leave the parties free to choose ways and means of performing their international obligations.[72] Their purpose is to provide guidelines to legislators to ensure that national systems are capable enough to carry out treaty obligations;[73] hence they are akin to statements of policy.[74] According to Lambert, general obligations are based on the premise that 'international law imposes obligation not of way but of result.'[75] On the contrary, the duty to legislate establishes binding obligations whose non-compliance could entail state responsibility.[76]

---

[68] Olympia Beku, 'A Case For the Review of Article 88 of the ICC Statute: Strengthening a Forgotten Provision' 12 New Criminal Law Review (2009) 468 at 482

[69] Fourth Annual Report of the International Tribunal for the Prosecution of Persons Responsible for Serious Violations of International Humanitarian Law Committed in the Territory of Former Yugoslavia Since 1991, 150 U.N. Doc A/52/375-S/ 1997/729 (Sept. 18 1997); See also Beku (68) 470

[70] Stefano Betti, 'Duty to Bring Terrorists to Justice and Discretionary Prosecution' 4 Journal of International Criminal Justice (2006) 1104 at 1110

[71] Beku (68) 475

[72] ibid

[73] ibid

[74] See Vaughan Lowe, *International Law* (New York: Oxford University Press 2007) at 119

[75] Joseph J Lambert, *Terrorism and Hostages in International Law, A Commentary on Hostages Convention 1979* (Cambridge: Grotius Publications Limited 1990) at 101

[76] Lowe (74)

2.2) Evolution of the duty to legislate in the international conventions on terrorism and organised crime

The duty to legislate has gradually emerged in the international conventions on terrorism and organised crime. The older counterterrorism conventions merely define these crimes and require the parties to make them punishable under their national laws. However, modern conventions specifically oblige the parties to legislate them in their national laws. The duty to make a crime punishable is distinguishable from the duty to legislate as the former does not require the adoption of the exact definitions of crimes: states can comply with their obligation by making punishable domestic law counterparts of these crimes.[77] For instance, if national law makes punishable the acts of abduction, illegal confinement and coercion, the concerned state will be deemed to be in compliance with its obligation to penalise hostage-taking as per the requirements of the UN Convention against Taking of Hostages.[78] According to Lambert, the reason for not imposing the duty to legislate in earlier treaties was the relatively simple nature of the crimes which rarely caused problems of dual criminality in extradition and mutual assistance proceedings.[79]

However, when it was realised that criminalisation of domestic law equivalents was not sufficient to satisfy dual criminality requirement as regards complex aggregate crimes, the duty to make the offences punishable gave way to the duty to legislate. For instance, offences such as terror financing and money laundering represent an aggregate of several specialized offences; as such, either their domestic law counterparts did not exist or their constituent elements varied from one state to another.[80] It was thus difficult for states to fulfil the dual criminality condition in extradition or interrogation proceedings without having legislated similar definitions of crime.[81]

---

[77] Lambert (n 75); See also Betti (70)

[78] See article 2 the Hostages Convention 1979. 'Each state party shall make the offences set forth in article 1 punishable by appropriate penalties which take into account the grave nature of those offences.' See also Lambert (n 75) at 77, 101

[79] Lambert (n 75)

[80] Roberto Lavelle, 'The International Convention for the Suppression of Financing of Terrorism' 60 Heidelberg Journal of International law (2000) 492 at 507

[81] Zagaris (n 61)

2.2.1) Analysis of definitions of crimes under the older and modern counterterrorism conventions

A comparative analysis of the crimes set forth by the Hague Convention 1970 and the Terrorist Bombing Convention 1997 provides useful insights into the distinction between the duty to legislate and the duty to make offences punishable. It also sheds light on the reasons that compelled the drafters to impose a duty to legislate with respect to the offences set forth by the latter Conventions. Article 2 of the Hague Convention 1970 provides 'Each Contracting State undertakes to make the offence punishable by severe penalties.'[82] This may be compared to article 4 of the Terrorist Bombing Convention 1997 which provides:

> Each state party shall adopt such measures as may be necessary: (a) To establish as criminal offences under its domestic law the offences set forth in article 2 of this Convention; (b) To make those offences punishable by appropriate penalties which take into account the grave nature of those offences.[83]

Clearly, the Hague Convention 1970 simply requires that the offences be made punishable under national laws. By contrast, the Terrorist Bombing Convention 1997, in addition to requiring penalisation of offences, further obliges the parties to establish them as criminal offences under their national laws.

Article 1 of the Hague Convention 1970 provides the following definition of the crime:

> any person who (a) on board an aircraft in flight unlawfully, by force seizes, or exercises control of, that aircraft (b) is an accomplice of a person who performs or attempts to perform any such act commits an offence... [84]

Conversely, article 2 of the Terrorist Bombings Convention 1997 defines the offence as follows:

> 1. Any person commits an offence within the meaning of this Convention if that person unlawfully and intentionally delivers, places, discharges or detonates an explosive or other lethal device in, into or against a place of public use, a state or government facility, a public transportation system or an infrastructure facility: a) with the intent to cause death or serious bodily injury or b) with the intent to cause extensive destruction of such a place,

---

[82] See article 2 the Hague Convention 1970

[83] See article 4 the Terrorist Bombing Convention 1997

[84] See article 1 the Hague Convention 1970

> facility or system, where such destruction results in or is likely to result in major economic loss.
>
> 2. Any person also commits an offence if that person attempts to commit an offence as set forth in paragraph 1 of the present article.
>
> 3. Any person also commits an offence if that person: a) Participates as an accomplice in an offence as set forth in paragraph 1 or 2 of the present article; or b) Organises or directs others to commit an offence as set forth in paragraph 1 or 2 of the present article; or c) In any other way contributes to the commission of one or more offences as set forth in paragraph 1 or 2 of the present article by a group of persons acting with a common purpose; such contribution shall be intentional and either be made with the aim of furthering the general criminal activity or purpose of the group or be made in the knowledge of the intention of the group to commit the offence or offences concerned.[85]

Evidently, the definition of terrorist bombing under the 1997 Convention is much more complex as compared to the definition of hijacking under the 1970 Convention. While the latter only deals with the act of hijacking on board aircrafts, the former takes into its fold destruction of public places, transportation system, infrastructure facility and governmental facility. Moreover, the 1970 Convention provides only two inchoate offences, i.e. attempt and participation as an accomplice, whereas the 1997 Convention establishes a wide range of inchoate offences, including organisation, direction and contribution.

The international criminalisation of these offences underlies the assumption that it will facilitate the extradition and interrogation of the offenders involved in borderless crimes. However, the non-existence of any of the elements of crimes under the national law of the requested state allows it to refuse cooperation due to a failure of the requesting state to fulfil the double criminality condition of its extradition or mutual legal assistance law. Since this possibility was always present in extradition and interrogation proceedings involving complex crimes, the modern international conventions on terrorism and organised crime imposed a duty to legislate against their universal definitions with a view to bringing similarity in the national coverage of crimes.

In a nutshell, it was felt that state cooperation in extradition and mutual legal assistance concerning complex crimes might not be facilitated merely by defining the offences at international level and requiring the

[85] See article 4 the Terrorist Bombing Convention 1997

parties to criminalise their domestic law counterparts. This realisation led to imposition of an international duty to implement exact definitions of crimes. Some instances of complications arising in law enforcement cooperation as a result of diverse national definitions of complex crimes are discussed immediately below.

2.3) Complications arising in law enforcement cooperation as a result of diverse national definitions of crimes

2.3.1) *Adnan Khashoggi* case

Several extradition cases demonstrate the necessity of imposing the duty to legislate in modern complex crimes. One of them is the 1989 case of *Adnan Khashoggi* between the US and Switzerland.[86] Here, the US demanded extradition of Adnan Khashoggi, an international arms smuggler, from Switzerland on the charges of conspiracy and racketeering as well as obstruction of justice and mail fraud.[87] The first two charges were based on the alleged violations of a US law, Racketeer Influenced Corrupt Organizations Act (RICO).[88] The domestic law counterpart of this enactment was not available under the Swiss legal system.[89] Therefore, in order to satisfy the condition of dual criminality, the US had to drop these charges from its extradition request.[90]

When the accused was subsequently tried in the US, the rule of 'specialty' prevented it from adding further charges.[91] The rule requires correspondence between the facts presented in the extradition request and charges brought against an offender once he is extradited.[92] In other words, according to this rule, an extradited fugitive can be prosecuted for those offences only

---

[86] *US V. Khashoggi* 717 F. Supp.1048 (1989)

[87] ibid; see also James Barron, 'Swiss Extradite Khashoggi to US' (July 20, 1989) *The New York Times*<http://www.nytimes.com/1989/07/20/world/swiss-extradite-khashoggi-to-us.html> [Date accessed 21/03/23]

[88] 18 USCA Sc.1961-1968, RICO ACT

[89] *US V. Khashoggi* (n 86); See also Zagaris (n 61)

[90] Zagaris ibid

[91] *US V. Khashoggi* (n 86); See also Barron (n 87)

[92] SZ Feller, 'Reflections on the nature of the Specialty Principle in Extradition Relations' 12 Isr .L. Rev (1977) 466; See also article 14(1) European Convention on Extradition 1957:

> A person who has been extradited shall not be proceeded against, sentenced or detained with a view to the carrying out of a sentence or detention order for any offence committed prior to his surrender other than that for which he was extradited...

for which he was surrendered.[93] If further charges are to be introduced after the extradition, the requesting state is obliged to seek permission of the requested state.[94] The rule is universally applied in extradition and mutual legal assistance laws and treaties and is considered to represent customary international law.[95]

In its bid to obtain the surrender of Khashoggi, the US agreed to drop the complex charges of conspiracy and racketeering from its extradition request. Since the remaining offences of mail fraud and obstruction of justice were only remotely linked to the US, the ensuing trial culminated in the acquittal of the accused.[96] According to a news report, the jurors had doubts whether the remaining charges fell within the jurisdiction of the US courts.[97] Arguably, in this case, the disparity of national laws resulting from the complexity of modern transnational crimes led to the acquittal of the offender.

To forestall the recurrence of such happenings, article 5 of the Organised Crime Convention 2000 obliges the parties to legislate against universal definitions of conspiracy, planning and participation in the activities of an organised criminal group, and the act of simply being a member of such group.[98] The obligation effectively covers the charges of racketeering and conspiracy to racket.

2.3.2) *Ross v Israel*

Another case relates to the US request for extradition of Ross, an Israeli national.[99] In this case, the US demanded the extradition of Ross from Israel on charges of inter-state transportation of humans. It was alleged

---

[93] Zagaris (n 61) 1433; See also Roberto Iraola, 'The Doctrine of Speciality and Federal Criminal Prosecutions' 83 Valparaiso University Law Review (2008) 89

[94] See article 14 European Convention on Extradition 1957

[95] Feller (n 92); See for instance, article 14 European Convention on Extradition 1957, article 18 Canada-France Extradition Treaty 1988 and article 67 Federal Act on International Mutual Assistance in Criminal Matters, Mutual Assistance Act, IMAC of 20 March 1981 [hereinafter Swiss Federal Law on Mutual Legal Assistance 1981] <http://www.admin.ch/ch/e/rs/3/351.1.en.pdf> [date accessed 21/03/23]

[96] *US V. Khashoggi* (n 86)

[97] Newsmax.com, 'Marcos Juror Among Stewart Jury Finalists' (25 January 2004) <http://archive.newsmax.com/archives/articles/2004/1/25/74621.shtml> [Date accessed 21/03/23]

[98] See article 5 the Organised Crime Convention 2000

[99] *Steven Ivan Ross v. State of Israel* (1973) (II) 27 P.D. 365

that the offender abducted a US national from its territory and then transported him abroad. The offender contended that the offence of inter-state transportation of humans was not covered by the US-Israel Extradition Treaty 1962.[100] Moreover, he argued that, given that the crime did not exist under Israel's penal law, the condition of dual criminality as required by its extradition law was not met.[101] The Court however found that the extradition treaty between the US and Israel included the offence of abduction which if seen in the international context could be interpreted to embrace the interstate transportation of humans. According to its reasoning, the US law defined abduction to include the act of transportation. Since the US definition of a crime listed in the bilateral treaty was as binding on Israel as its own, Israel could not have construed the offence restrictively.[102] As noted by Feller, the judgment was unconvincing because the definition of abduction under the relevant extradition treaty clearly fell short of covering the crime of inter-state transportation.[103] Under this judgement, an unusual approach was adopted to determine the fulfilment of double criminality, i.e. considering one party's definition of crime relevant for the purposes of interpreting an offence listed in the extradition treaty.[104] To avoid such complications in the extradition and interrogation of offenders, the Organised Crime Convention 2000 has now imposed a duty on states to legislate against universal definitions of inter-state human trafficking and human smuggling which covers the act of inter-state transportation of human.[105]

2.3.3) *Riley v. the Commonwealth*

A similar situation arose in the famous Australian case of *Riley v. the Commonwealth.*[106] In this case, the custody of fugitives was sought by the US for the offence of Continuing Criminal Enterprise (CCE) under 21

---

[100] See Convention on Extradition Between the Government of United States and the Government of the State of Israel. Signed at Washington on December 10, 1962 (18 U.S.T. 1707) [hereinafter US-Israel Extradition Treaty 1962]

[101] L.S.I 144 - Israel's Extradition Law of 1954

[102] *Ross v. Israel* (n 99) 369-70

[103] S.Z Feller, 'The Significance of the Requirement of Double Criminality in the Law of Extradition' 10 Isr L.Rev (1975) 51 at 55, 57

[104] ibid

[105] See article 5, Human Trafficking Protocol to the Organised Crime Convention 2000; See also article 6, Migrant Smuggling Protocol to the Organised Crime Convention 2000

[106] *Riley and Butler v.the Commonwealth* 260 ALR 106 (Austrl. 1985) ; See also Williams (n 43) 614

USC 848. The fugitives were involved in a series of offences regarding the import of drugs, making them liable to be prosecuted in the US under the cumulative charge of CCE. The schedule of the offences appended with the relevant Extradition Treaty had no CCE offence.[107] However, the court opted for a test of double criminality which was based on the assessment of whether the acts comprising CCE would be considered criminal in Australia if committed there.[108] Although CCE had no exact parallel in Australian law, the acts of the accused taken individually did constitute crimes under it, albeit with different names and elements. Hence, the extradition was granted on the ground that the conduct in question would have been criminal, if committed in Australia.[109] To paraphrase the words of Gobert, this kind of liberal approach towards application of dual criminality could be fairly useful in the extradition of offenders involved in complex crimes.[110]

The offence of Continuing Criminal Enterprise (CCE) now stands criminalised under the UN Convention against Transnational Organised Crime 2000 [111] and each state party is bound to legislate it under its national law. It is thus expected that the parties should be able to negotiate dual criminality in their cooperative efforts involving this crime.

The above analysis indicates that national courts tend to take different approaches while interpreting the dual criminality requirement. Whereas some courts interpret it to mean exact similarity of offences,[112] others are of the view that it is sufficient that elements of the offence should be a crime in two states.[113] A few maintain that offences need only be substantially similar.[114] However, there appears to be a broad consensus that the non-existence of the crime in relation to which the extradition is sought under the national law of either state means the offender may raise dual criminality objection and the requested state is under no obligation to

---

[107] See Treaty on Extradition between Australia and United States of America. Signed at Washington on 14 May1974, entered into force 1976 [hereinafter US-Australia Extradition Treaty 1976]

[108] James Gobert & Maurice Punch, *Rethinking Corporate Crimes* (UK Butterworth's 2003) 158

[109] *Riley v.the Commonwealth* (n 106)

[110] Gobert (n 108)

[111] See article 5 the Organized Crime Convention 2000

[112] *US V. Khashoggi* (n 86)

[113] *Factor v. Laubenheimer* (n 55)

[114] *Canada v. Aronson* [1989] 2 All E.R. 1025

extradite. Thus, it was observed by the Canadian Supreme Court in *R v. Parisien*:

> Most [extradition] treaties are limited to crimes therein listed. This ensures that a state to which a request to surrender a person is made is not obliged to surrender its citizens and other persons within its allegiance and protection for prosecution in the requesting state for behaviour not considered criminal in the requested state.[115]

Since modern complex crimes never really existed under the national laws of a majority of states, it was difficult to satisfy even the minimum threshold of dual criminality, i.e. that the offence be a crime under the national law of both, the requesting and requested states. Hence, it can be argued that the duty to legislate was imposed in response to the complexity of modern transnational crimes, the non-availability of whose domestic law parallels caused complications of dual criminality in extradition and mutual assistance proceedings. The conventions establishing duty to legislate and specific features of the crimes set forth by them will be analysed below.

2.4) The international conventions establishing duty to legislate

2.4.1) Counterterrorism Conventions

2.4.1.1) The Terrorism Financing Convention 1999

The Convention establishes the crime of providing funds to commit terrorist offences with the intention and knowledge that the funds will be so used.[116] Article 4 provides that 'Each State Party shall adopt such measures as may be necessary:(*a*)[t]o establish as criminal offences under its national law the offences set forth in article 2.'

2.4.1.2) The Terrorist Bombing Convention 1997

The Convention establishes the crime of using explosives and other lethal devices in public places with intent to kill or cause injury or destruction of

---

[115] *R. v. Parisien* [1988] 1 S.C.R. 950 at 957 <http://scc.lexum.org/en/1988/1988scr1-950/1988scr1-950.html> [Date accessed 21/03/23]

[116] See articles 2, the Terrorism Financing Convention 1999

public places.[117] Article 4(a) obliges a party to establish as criminal offences under its national law the offences set forth by the Convention.

2.4.1.3) The Nuclear Terrorism Convention 2005

The Convention proscribes the act of possessing or using radioactive material or a device producing radioactivity, with intent to cause death, injury, damage to property or the environment, in order to compel a state to do or to refrain from doing an act.[118] Article 5 provides that 'Each State Party shall adopt such measures as may be necessary: (*a*)[t]o establish as criminal offences under its national law the offences set forth in article 2.'

2.4.2) Organised Crime Conventions

2.4.2.1) The Drugs Convention 1988

The Convention proscribes the acts of manufacture, production, sale, transportation and cultivation of narcotics drugs.[119] Article 3(1) obliges each state party to establish as criminal offences under its national law the offences set forth by the Convention.

2.4.2.2) The UN Convention against Corruption 2003

The Convention establishes the crimes of bribery in both public[120] and private[121] sectors as well as bribery involving national and foreign public officials and officials of international organizations.[122] It further criminalises solicitation and acceptance of bribe[123] as well as embezzlement,[124] trading in influence,[125] illicit enrichment and associated inchoate offences. Articles 15 to 27 oblige each state party to take such legislative and other measures as may be necessary to make the offences set forth in the Convention criminal offences under its national laws.

---

[117] See article 2, the Terrorist Bombings Convention 1997
[118] See article 2, the Nuclear Terrorism Convention 2005
[119] See article 3(1)(a) & (b) the Drugs Convention 1988
[120] See article 7 the UN Convention against Corruption 2003
[121] See article 12 ibid
[122] See article 15, 16 ibid
[123] ibid
[124] See article 22 ibid
[125] See article 18 ibid

2.4.2.3) The Organised Crime Convention 2000

Article 5 of the Convention requires that each State Party shall adopt such legislative and other measures as may be necessary to establish as a criminal offence the act of being member of an organised criminal group regardless of the nature of its activities.[126] Three of its protocols require the criminalisation of human trafficking,[127] migrant smuggling[128] and weapon trafficking.[129]

2.5) Distinguishing features of the conventions establishing duty to legislate

Features that distinguish the counterterrorism and organised crime conventions establishing duty to legislate from their older counter-parts include their specific focus on inchoate offences and ancillary crimes.

2.5.1) Inchoate offences

The initial focus of the counterterrorism and organised crime conventions was to criminalise principal acts only. Hence, the older conventions such as the Hague,[130] the Montreal,[131] the Protection of Diplomats,[132] and the Hostages[133] Conventions did not define any inchoate offence besides attempt and participation as an accomplice. However, modern conventions such as the Terrorism Financing and the Drugs Conventions establish a wide range of inchoate offences encompassing acts such as conspiracy, planning, financing, directing and organising.[134] These are preparatory-type offenses, the criminalisation of which is directed towards facilitating

---

[126] See article 2 the Organized Crime Convention 2000

[127] See article 3, Human Trafficking Protocol to the Organized Crime Convention 2000

[128] See article 6, Migrant Smuggling Protocol to the Organized Crime Convention 2000

[129] See article 5, Weapons Trafficking Protocol to the Organized Crime Convention 2000

[130] See article 1 the Hague Convention 1970

[131] See article 1 the Montreal Convention 1971

[132] See article 2 the Protection of Diplomats Convention 1973; article 2(1)(c) includes a new inchoate offence of threat to commit

[133] See article 1 the Hostages Convention 1979

[134] See for instance article 2(2) the Terrorist Bombings Convention 1997, article 2(4) the Terrorism Financing Convention 1999, article 2(2) the Nuclear Terrorism Convention 2005, article 3 the Drugs Convention 1988

law enforcement cooperation at planning stages of the crimes.[135] The impetus for their criminalisation came from new forms of terrorism, such as suicide bombing.[136] As the offenders involved in these crimes were ideologically motivated, they were unlikely to be deterred by a fear of punishment. Discouraging such crimes was thus possible only by taking effective action at the planning stages.[137]

Since these crimes were new to many states, with a view to bringing similarity in national laws in regard to their coverage, recent counterterrorism and organised crime conventions imposed a duty on states to legislate against their universal definitions. Significantly, legislation of these crimes has also been required by Security Council Resolution 1373 (2001).[138] Subsequent resolutions of the Council further expanded the range of inchoate offences against which states were required to legislate, including acts such as incitement to terrorism.[139] Now efforts are underway to criminalise religious indoctrination.[140] All these international efforts are directed towards bringing harmony to national laws in order to facilitate state cooperation in law enforcement.

2.5.2) Ancillary crimes

In addition to inchoate offences, recent counterterrorism and organised crime conventions also establish ancillary crimes. Ancillary crimes refer to the acts which make it possible for the offenders to carry out principal crimes. These are: obstruction of justice, money laundering, corruption and membership of an organized criminal group. Through obstruction of justice and corruption, the offenders seek to paralyse national justice systems to ensure non-enforcement of law and through money laundering and joining organised criminal groups they contribute to continuation of criminal enterprises. Like inchoate offences, these crimes were also either non-existent or their constituent elements varied in national laws. To bring about harmony in national laws and thereby to facilitate law enforcement cooperation, modern counterterrorism and organised crime conventions

---

[135] UNODC's Legislative Guide to the Universal Legal Regime against Terrorism 2008 <www.unodc.org/unodc/en/treaties/CAC/legislative-guide.html> [Date accessed 21/03/23]
[136] ibid
[137] ibid
[138] S/RES/1373 (2001)
[139] S/RES/1624 (2005), Adopted by the Security Council at its 5261st meeting, on 14 September 2005
[140] Legislative Guide to Counter-Terrorism Regime (n 135)

imposed a duty on states to legislate against these crimes. A brief introduction to two ancillary crimes is given below.

2.5.2.1) Participation in an organised criminal group

Article 5 of the Organized Crime Convention 2000 obliges the parties to criminalise the act of agreeing with one or more persons to commit a serious crime for the purposes of obtaining a material benefit. In other words, it refers to the act of being a member of an organised criminal group regardless of the nature of its activities.[141] One commentator has described the crime as 'umbrella criminality' because it applies to participation in a group formed to carry out any type of criminal activity.[142]

2.5.2.2) Money Laundering

Another common feature of modern counterterrorism and organised crime conventions is that they require the criminalisation of money laundering. This was first required by the UN Convention against Drugs 1988, followed by the Terrorism Financing Convention 1999, the Organised Crime Convention 2000 and the UN Convention against Corruption 2003.[143] The requirement is directed towards depriving an offender of the benefit of his criminal activity.[144]

Money laundering refers to an activity by which source and ownership of criminally derived wealth is changed to confer on it a perception of legitimacy.[145] It is therefore not a single crime but a criminal process, the suppression of which calls for criminalisation of three inter-related acts.[146] Firstly, it requires the criminalisation of the concealment and disguise of the ownership and location of the proceeds of crime. Secondly, it demands

---

[141] See article 5 the Organized Crime Convention 2000

[142] Alexandra V. Orlova & James W. Moore, 'Umbrellas or Building Blocks? Defining International Terrorism and Transnational Organised Crime in International Law' 27 Houston Journal of International Law (2004-2005) 268

[143] See article 6 the Organized Crime Convention 2000, article 23 the UN Convention against Corruption 2003, article 3(1)(b)&(c) the Drugs Convention 1988 and article 8 the Terrorism Financing Convention 1999

[144] Cherif Bassiouni, 'Effective Action' (n 17) at 21; See also Legislative Guide to the Organized Crime Convention (n 64) at 136

[145] Money Laundering and the Financing of Terrorism, 19th Report of the House of Lords on its 2008-09 Session at p. 7, published 22 July 2009 <http://www.coe.int/t/dghl/monitoring/moneyval/activities/UK_Parlrep.pdf> [Date accessed 21/03/23]

[146] ibid

criminalisation of predicate offences or acts through which the illicit proceeds are generated. Thirdly, it necessitates the criminalisation of the offences involving the participation of legal entities. Since these offences were previously unknown to a majority of states, which had only the conventions to define them, national laws might have diverged with respect to their implementation. Accordingly, mandatory obligations were imposed by modern counterterrorism and organised crime conventions to establish these acts as criminal offences under national law.[147]

In the light of above, it is evident that modern counterterrorism and organised crime conventions are distinguishable from their older counterparts on account of the complex nature of the crimes set forth by them. Since these crimes were non-existent under national laws, it was difficult for states parties to satisfy dual criminality conditions in extradition and mutual assistance proceedings involving these crimes. Thus, the duty to legislate was imposed under these conventions to facilitate state cooperation in law enforcement with respect to complex aggregate crimes. However, the duty is not without its limitations.

2.6) Limitations of Duty to Legislate

To accommodate divergent national interests, the duty to legislate has been subjected to several exceptions and safeguards that authorise states to depart from definitions of crimes as laid down by the conventions. The said exceptions will be analysed below in order to establish that, despite the mandatory wording of the duty, its implementation remains a prerogative of the states.

2.6.1) Offences are to be defined in accordance with national law of the states parties

All organised crime conventions under consideration contain a common provision suggesting that notwithstanding the duty to legislate crimes, their exact definitions shall be determined in accordance with the national laws of states parties.[148] The purpose of the provision is to allow the

---

[147] See (n 143)

[148] See article 30(9) the UN Convention against Corruption 2003 and article 11(6) the Organized Crime Convention 2000. The provision lays down in unambiguous terms that:

Nothing contained in this Convention shall affect the principle that the description of offences established in accordance with this Convention and of the applicable legal defences or other legal principles controlling the lawfulness of conduct is

parties to criminalise the acts proscribed by the conventions in accordance with the fundamental principles of their national justice systems.[149]

2.6.2) Safeguard clauses

Safeguard clauses[150] were introduced to address the concerns of some states that criminalisation of a number of offences set forth by the conventions would be inconsistent with the basic concepts of their national justice systems.[151] Thus, with a view to secure consensus, several offences set forth by the conventions such as possession and purchase of drugs,[152] participation as an accomplice in the crime of human trafficking[153] and possession and use of property derived through proceeds of crime, were subjected to the principles of national laws and constitutions.[154]

---

reserved to the domestic law of state parties and that such offences shall be prosecuted and punished in accordance with that law.
See also article 3(11) the Drugs Convention 1988

[149] Sproule (n 6) 270

[150] The phrase ‘safeguards clause’ has been used in the UNODC’s Legislative Guide for implementing the UN Convention against Corruption 2003 at p. 4 para 13 www.unodc.org/.../LegislativeGuide/UNCAC_Legislative_Guide_A.pdf [Date accessed 21/03/23]

[151] Sproule (n 6) 270

[152] Article 3(2) of the Drugs Convention 1988 provides:
Subject to its constitutional principles and the basic concepts of its legal system, each party shall adopt such measures as may be necessary to establish as a criminal offence under its domestic law, when committed intentionally, the possession, purchase or cultivation of narcotic drugs or psychotropic substances for personal consumption contrary to the provisions of the 1961 Convention, the 1961 Convention as amended or the 1971 Convention.

[153] Article 5(2) of 2000 Human Trafficking Protocol to the Organized Crime Convention 2000 provides:
Each State Party shall also adopt such legislative and other measures as may be necessary to establish as criminal offences:(a) Subject to the basic concepts of its legal system, attempting to commit an offence established in accordance with paragraph 1 of this article; (b) Participating as an accomplice in an offence established in accordance with paragraph 1 of this article; and (c) Organizing or directing other persons to commit an offence established in accordance with paragraph 1 of this article .

[154] See for instance article 3(1)(c)(i) the Drugs Convention 1988

2.6.3) Reservations

All counterterrorism and organised crime conventions authorise the parties to make reservations.[155] A state making a reservation is not bound as regards the provisions concerning which the reservation has been effected. Relying on a reservation clause, many states have shown their inability to consider as crimes the acts of terrorism committed in the course of freedom movements.[156]

2.6.4) Use of the words 'unlawful' and 'intentional' in definitions of offences

Both counterterrorism and organised crime conventions stipulate that the conduct proscribed by them is required to be criminalised only when it is

---

[155] See for instance, article 23(2) the Nuclear Terrorism Convention 2005:

Each State may, at the time of signature, ratification, acceptance or approval of this Convention or accession thereto, declare that it does not consider itself bound by paragraph 1 of the present article. The other States Parties shall not be bound by paragraph 1 with respect to any State Party which has made such a reservation.

Corresponding provisions can be found in all transnational crime treaties under consideration.

For Corresponding provisions, see article 12(2) the Hague Convention 1970, article 14(2) the Montreal Convention 1971, article 13(2) the Protection of Diplomats Convention 1973, article 17(3) the Nuclear Materials Convention, article 16(2) the Hostages Convention 1979, article 16(2) the Rome Convention 1988, article 20(2) the Terrorist Bombings Convention 1997, article 24(2) the Terrorism Financing Convention 1999, article 32 (4) the Drugs Convention 1988, article 35(3) the Organized Crime Convention 2000, article 66(3) the UN Convention against Corruption 2000 and article 20(2) the Beijing Convention 2010.

[156] For instance, while ratifying Terrorist Bombing Convention 1997, government of Pakistan recorded its reservation that nothing in this Convention shall be applicable to acts committed in the course of exercising right of self-determination (Government of Pakistan's declaration dated 13 August 2002 to Terrorist Bombings convention 1997). Similarly, Egypt recorded its reservation with respect to Terrorist Financing Convention 1999 that it does not consider that act of national resistance in all its forms constitute acts of terrorism within the meanings of article 2(1)(b) of the Convention(Egypt's declaration to Terrorist Financing convention 1999 dated 1 march 2005).Likewise, Syria observed in its reservation that the acts of resistance to foreign occupation are not included under acts of terrorism (Syria's declaration to Terrorist Financing convention 1999 dated 24th April 2005). See problematic reservations and declarations to counterterrorism conventions <www.unodc.org> [date accessed 21/0313]

unlawful and intentional.[157] Nevertheless, the terms 'unlawful' and 'intentional' have not been defined by the conventions. Hence, their inclusion in the definitions of crimes makes it possible for states to introduce exceptions and defences.[158]

2.6.5) Discretion in the matter of establishing predicate crimes

As suggested above, predicate crimes are the acts through which the proceeds of crime are generated. In order to forfeit assets upon foreign request, it is not sufficient that the requested state makes punishable the act of laundering.[159] It further necessitates the criminalisation of the acts through which the illicit proceeds are generated. The fulfilment of double criminality in forfeiture proceedings demands correspondence in the predicate crimes set forth by the requesting and requested states. In other words, it requires that the act through which illicit proceeds are generated must constitute a crime under the laws of both the requesting and requested state. Therefore, along with establishing the obligation to criminalise money laundering, the counterterrorism and organised crime conventions further oblige the parties to establish as criminal offences under their national laws, the acts proscribed by them as predicate crimes.[160]

The Drug Convention 1988, which represents the forerunner of the conventions establishing money laundering provisions, requires the

---

[157] Words 'unlawfully' and 'intentionally' appear in almost all transnational treaties. See for instance, article 3(1)(a) of the Rome Convention 1988 'Any person commits an offence if that person unlawfully and intentionally: (a) seizes or exercises control over a ship by force or threat thereof or any other form of intimidation.' See also article 2 (1) the Terrorist Bombing Convention 1997:

> Any person commits an offence within the meaning of this Convention if that person unlawfully and intentionally delivers, places, discharges or detonates an explosive or other lethal device in, into or against a place of public use, a State or government facility, a public transportation system or an infrastructure facility…

[158] Lavalle (n 80) 500

[159] See text to (n 145-147) above

[160] See article 6(2)(b) of the Organized Crime Convention 2000 '[e]ach State Party shall include as predicate offences all serious crime as defined in article 2 of this Convention and the offences established in accordance with articles 5, 8 and 23 of this Convention.' Articles 5, 8 and 23 establish the crimes of money laundering, obstruction of justice and corruption whereas article 2 defines the term serious crime as any criminal activity punishable with maximum deprivation of liberty of four years or more. See also article 23(2)(b) of the UN Convention against Corruption 2003

criminalisation of only one offence as predicate crime, i.e. drug trafficking.[161] This model is replicated in the Terrorism Financing Convention 1999.[162] A state following this approach can only assist another in the forfeiture of proceeds, if the proceeds are derived by committing the designated crime. Fortunately, this approach has been revisited in modern conventions like the Organized Crime Convention 2000 and the UN Convention against Corruption 2003. Under these Conventions, states are required to apply their money laundering laws to the widest range of predicate crimes.[163] However, both conventions restrict the obligation to legislate, to the offences expressly set forth by them.[164] In relation to other crimes, they merely recommend the parties establish them as predicate crimes.[165] Even the so-called obligation to legislate is subject to the fundamental principles of domestic law of state parties.[166] Furthermore, the obligation is subject to the rule that the description of offences is exclusively reserved to the domestic law of the state parties.[167] Additionally, the obligation is governed by the general provision that the conventions are required to be implemented to the extent permissible under national law.[168] Consequently, the duty to legislate predicate crimes is unlikely to have the desired harmonising impact on national laws.

In the light of the above, it is evident that the duty to legislate crimes is not absolute and is subject to a number of exceptions and safeguards. Several

---

[161] Article 3(1)(b)&(c) the Drugs Convention 1988

[162] See article 8 the Terrorism Financing Convention 1999; According to this provision, the funds can be seized when they are directed towards financing the acts of terrorism or have been derived as a result of an act of terrorism.

[163] For instance, the Organized Crime Convention 2000 enjoins the parties to establish as predicate offence any serious crime of organised nature involving the element of border crossing or transnationality. Moreover, both the Organized Crime Convention 2000 and the UN Convention against Corruption 2003 recommend the parties to consider applying their money laundering laws to the widest range of predicate offences. See article 6(2)(a) & (b) the Organized Crime Convention 2000 and article 23(2)(a) & (c) the UN Convention against Corruption 2003.

[164] See article 6(2)(b) the Organized Crime Convention 2000. See also article 23(2)(b) the UN Convention against Corruption 2003

[165] See article 6(2)(a) the Organized Crime Convention 2000; See also article 23(2)(a) the UN Convention against Corruption 2003

[166] See article 6(1) the Organized Crime Convention 2000

[167] See article 11(6) the Organized Crime Convention and article 30(9) the UN Convention against Corruption 2003

[168] See article 65 the UN Convention against Corruption 2003 and article 11(6) the Organized Crime Convention 2000

scholars are of the view that these exceptions have rendered the duty hortatory or recommendatory.[169] The purpose of imposing a duty to legislate was to facilitate state cooperation in law enforcement with respect to complex aggregate crimes having no parallels in national laws. However, the above exceptions point to the fact that states are entitled to implement the duty to the extent permissible under their national laws.[170] This arrangement is likely to produce disharmony in domestic coverage of crimes.

According to the rule of double criminality, the advancement of state cooperation in law enforcement depends upon the existence and recognition of the crime in the national law of the requested state, with respect to which cooperation is sought. Pursuant to above exceptions, states are competent to adopt so much of the definitions of crimes as are permissible under their national law. The resultant disharmony ensures that the leverage available to the requested state to block surrender or interrogation due to the non-fulfilment of double criminality remains intact. The discretion of the requested state could have been circumscribed through establishing unqualified obligations to legislate under the counterterrorism and organised crime conventions. However, this course was avoided in order to gain maximum ratifications.[171]

Section 3: Impact of duty to legislate

The duty to legislate under the international conventions on terrorism and organised crime is aimed at bringing harmony in national definitions of crimes in order to facilitate extradition and mutual legal assistance

---

[169] For instance, Sproule remarks that he ‘fails to understand’ the purpose of these concessions in the treaties which are supposed to be establishing binding obligations. See Sproule (n 6) 272; Bassiouni takes the view that if states are allowed to have their own definitions, they are likely to create exceptions blurring the distinction between international and domestic crimes. See Bassiouni, ‘Effective Action’ (n 17) 9, 19; Mark Peith states that exceptions can be used to introduce selective legislation sparing certain individuals or groups, the legislators want to protect. See Mark Pieth, ‘Criminalizing the Financing of Terrorism’ 4 Journal of International Criminal Justice (2006) 1074 at 1080. Philipa Webb notes that exceptions are being used as a convenient means to avoid international obligations with impunity. See Philipa Webb, ‘The UN Convention against Corruption: Global achievement or missed opportunity’ 8 Journal of International Economic Law (2005) 191 at 206.

[170] Sproule (n 6)

[171] Legislative Guide for implementing Organized Crime Convention 2000 (n 64) at 130

proceedings involving these crimes.[172] The acts proscribed by the conventions are criminalised under national laws on terrorism and organised crime. Additionally, they are also listed in bilateral treaties on extradition and mutual legal assistance.[173] Thus, the impact of the duty to legislate will be analysed at the level of both, national laws on terrorism and organised crime and bilateral treaties on extradition and mutual legal assistance.

3.1) Impact of duty to legislate on national counterterrorism and organised crime laws

3.1.1) counterterrorism laws

The counterterrorism conventions establishing duty to legislate include the Terrorist Bombing Convention 1997, the Terrorism Financing Convention 1999 and the Nuclear Terrorism Convention 2005. In response to legislative obligations imposed by them, Pakistan enacted the Anti-Terrorism Act 1997.[174] India has enacted the Unlawful Activities (Prevention) Act 1967 as amended in 2008.[175] Both Acts provide definitions of terrorist activities and make them punishable with severe penalties.[176]

---

172 See (n 228) below

173 See for example Sc. 2 of Israel's Extradition Law 1954 http://www.mfa.gov.il/MFA/Archive/Communiques/1995/EXTRADITION%20IN%20ISRAEL

174 See Anti-Terrorism Act 1997 of Pakistan; For full citation see (n 265) Chapter 2 above

175 The Unlawful Activities (Prevention) Act 1967 of India; For full citation see (n 179) Chapter 2 above

176 See section 6, the Anti-Terrorism Act 1997 of Pakistan:
Whoever, to strike in the people, or any section of the people, or to alienate any section of the people or adversely affect harmony among different sections of the people, does any act or thing by using bombs, dynamite or other explosive or inflammable substances, or fire-arms, or other lethal weapons or poisons or noxious gases or chemicals or other substances of a hazardous nature in such a manner as to cause, or to be likely to cause the death of, or injury to, any person or persons, or damage to or destruction of, property or disruption of any supplies of services, essential to the life of the community or displays fire-arms, or threatens with the use of force public servants in order to prevent them from discharging their lawful duties commits a terrorist act.
See also section 7, the Anti-Terrorism Act 1997 of Pakistan:
Whoever commits a terrorist act shall— (1) if such act has resulted in the death of any person be punished with death; and (ii) in any other case be punishable with

The two enactments, however, do not include separate provisions for each criminal activity prohibited by the conventions. The Indian definition adequately covers all three activities subjected to duty to legislate, i.e. financing, bombing and nuclear terrorism. By contrast, Pakistan's definition falls short of covering nuclear terrorism and financing of terrorism. Pakistan, nonetheless, claims to have covered financing of terrorism under its money laundering law which establishes the crime of generating the proceeds of crime through terrorist activities.[177]

---

imprisonment for a term which shall not be less than seven years but may extend to life imprisonment, and shall also be liable to fine.

See also Section 15, the Unlawful activities (Prevention) Act 1967 of India:

Whoever does any act with intent to threaten or likely to threaten the unity, integrity, security or sovereignty of India or with intent to strike terror or likely to strike terror in the people or any section of the people in India or in any foreign country (a) by using bombs, dynamite or other explosive substances or inflammable substances or firearms or other lethal weapons or poisonous or noxious gases or other chemicals or by any other substances (whether biological, radioactive, nuclear or otherwise) of a hazardous nature or by any other means of whatever nature to cause or likely to cause (i) death of, or injuries to, any person or persons; or (ii) loss of, or damage to, or destruction of, property; or (iii) disruption of any supplies or services essential to the life of the community in India or in any foreign country; or (iv) damage or destruction of any property in India or in a foreign country used or intended to be used for the defence of India or in connection with any other purposes of the Government of India, any State Government or any of their agencies; or (b) overawes by means of criminal force or the show of criminal force or attempts to do so or causes death of any public functionary or attempts to cause death of any public functionary; or (c) detains, kidnaps or abducts any person and threatens to kill or injure such person or does any other act in order to compel the Government of India, any State Government or the Government of a foreign country or any other person to do or abstain from doing any act, commits a terrorist act.

See also section 16, the Unlawful Activities (Prevention) Act 1967 of India:

(1) Whoever commits a terrorist act shall (a) if such act has resulted in the death of any person, be punishable with death or imprisonment for life, and shall also be liable to fine; (b) in any other case, be punishable with imprisonment for a term which shall not be less than five years but which may extend to imprisonment for life, and shall also be liable to fine.

[177] See preamble of the Anti-Money Laundering Act 2010 of Pakistan:

Whereas it is expedient to provide for prevention of money laundering, combating financing of terrorism and forfeiture of property derived from or involved in money laundering or financing of terrorism and for matters connected therewith and incidental thereto.

According to the House of Lords, this approach blurs the distinction between money laundering and terror financing.[178] While the former is concerned with the concealment of proceeds of crime, the latter involves making the funds available to terrorists.[179] To maintain this distinction, Indian law created the two separate offences of holding proceeds of terrorism[180] and raising funds for terrorist acts.[181] Moreover, Indian legislation makes a clear distinction between international and domestic terrorism, whereas Pakistan's law makes no such distinction.[182]

The anti-terrorism laws of the US[183] and New Zealand[184] include separate provisions on each terrorist activity prohibited by the counterterrorism conventions. Furthermore, these laws make a clear distinction between

---

See also section (ix) of the schedule to Anti-Money Laundering Act 2010 of Pakistan which includes all offences proscribed under Anti-terrorism Act 1997 of Pakistan as predicate offences to terrorism.

[178] See 19th Report of the House of Lords (n 145)

[179] ibid

[180] See section 21 The Unlawful activities (Prevention) Act 1967 of India:
Whoever knowingly holds any property derived or obtained from commission of any terrorist act or acquired through the terrorist fund shall be punishable with imprisonment for a term which may extend to imprisonment for life, and shall also be liable to fine.

[181] See section 17 The Unlawful Activities (Prevention) Act 1967 of India:
Whoever, in India or in a foreign country, directly or indirectly, raises or collects funds or provides funds to any person or persons or attempts to provide funds to any person or persons, knowing that such funds are likely to be used by such person or persons to commit a terrorist act, notwithstanding whether such funds were actually used or not for commission of such act, shall be punishable with imprisonment for a term which shall not be less than five years but which may extend to imprisonment for life, and shall also be liable to fine.

[182] See section 15 The Unlawful Activities (Prevention) Act 1967 of India: 'Whoever does any act… in India or in any foreign country'. See also section 6 the Anti-Terrorism Act 1997 which makes no reference to terrorist acts involving foreign countries.

[183] The US law on counter terrorism (18 U.S.C Chapter 113-B) criminalizes terrorist bombing under section 2332-f, the use of radioactive dispersal devices under section 2332-a and financing of terrorism under section 2332-d. It includes a separate provision i.e. section 2332-b on the acts of terrorism transcending national boundaries.

[184] See Terrorism Suppression Act 2002, Act No. 34 of 2002 [hereinafter Terrorism Suppression Act 2002 of New Zealand]. The Act establishes the crimes of terrorist bombing under section 7, terrorist financing under section 8 and nuclear terrorism under section 13 E. Moreover, it makes itself applicable to extraterritorial crimes under sections 14 to 19.

international and local terrorism, and specifically criminalise the financing of terrorism.[185]

These variations illustrate two distinct approaches at a national level for implementing counterterrorism conventions. The first approach focuses on the enactment of separate provisions on each terrorist activity prohibited under the conventions. The second approach is based on enacting a single provision purportedly covering all terrorist activities for which states have a duty to legislate. The latter approach has the disadvantage of omitting certain crimes which may lead to difficulties in the fulfilment of the double criminality condition. Nevertheless, states following this approach cannot be said to have violated their duty to legislate because they are entitled to implement the conventions to the extent permissible under their national laws.

In any case, the above analysis reveals that states are largely in compliance with their duty to implement the crimes set forth by counterterrorism conventions. However, the compliance appears to be more a result of binding resolutions of the Security Council than the duty to legislate.[186] This argument finds support from the fact that a number of states have submitted their reports to the Security Council concerning the enactment of implementing laws pursuant to SCR 1373.[187] Furthermore, domestic

---

185 See 18 USC Chapter 113-B Sc. 2332- d; See also section 8 of the Terrorism Suppression Act 2002 of New Zealand

186 Binding resolution 1373 of the Security Council calls upon states to implement Universal Counter-Terrorism Conventions. See S/RES/1373(2001). Besides it, the United Nations Global Counter-Terrorism Strategy 2006 also encourages the UN member states to adopt Universal Counter-Terrorism Conventions. See A/RES/60/288. The International Community's seriousness in combating terrorism can be ascertained from the fact that terrorism finds place in ILC's Draft Code of Crimes against Peace and Security of Mankind. See article 20(f) (iii) & (iv) Draft Code of Crimes against Peace and Security of Mankind 1996. See U.N. GAOR, 51ST Sess., Supp. No.10, at 9 U.N. Doc. A/ 51/10 (1996).

187 See for example Letter dated 19 December 2001 from the Permanent Representative of the United Kingdom of Great Britain and Northern Ireland to the United Nations addressed to the Chairman of the Committee established pursuant to resolution 1373 (2001) concerning Counter-Terrorism. The letter suggests that pursuant to SCR 1373(2001) the UK has implemented Anti-Terrorism, Crime and Security Act 2001. See S/2001/1232
<http://www.refworld.org/pdfid/46d571150.pdf> [Date accessed 21/03/12].
See also Supplementary Report of the Republic of Cyprus to the Counter-Terrorism Committee (CTC) established pursuant to the Security Council

laws of some state expressly state that the purpose of their enactment is to implement SCR 1373. For example, the Unlawful Activities (Prevention) Act 1967 of India as amended in 2008 contains a provision to this effect.[188]

3.1.2) organised crime laws

Instances of departure from definitions of crimes provided by the conventions are more visible in the national laws on organised crime. For example, the UN Convention against Corruption 2003 requires criminalisation of active and passive bribery[189] as well as private sector corruption.[190] The term active bribery refers to the act of giving a bribe, whereas passive bribery means acceptance of a bribe by a public official. Both these crimes have been duly legislated against under national law of the UK.[191] However, India and Pakistan do not criminalise active bribery

---

Resolution 1373 (2001) concerning Counter-Terrorism, in reply to the letter dated 1 April 2002 from the Chairman of the CTC. See S/2002/689 <http://www.mfa.gov.cy/mfa/mfa2006.nsf/All/F91E0D83B87C299CC22571D3002497CB/$file/Terrorism%20Report%202.pdf> [Date accessed 21/03/12]

188 See preamble of the Unlawful Activities (Prevention) Act 1967 of India as amended in 2008:

[w]hereas the Security Council of the United Nations in its 4385 meeting adopted Resolution 1373 (2001) on 28 September, 2001, under Chapter VII of the Charter of the United Nations requiring all the States to take measures to combat international terrorism...And whereas the central government in exercise of powers conferred by section 2 of the United Nations (Security Council) Act, 1947,has made the prevention and suppression of terrorism (Implementation of Security Council Resolutions) Order, 2007.

189 See article 15 of the UN Convention against Corruption 2003:

Each State Party shall adopt such legislative and other measures as may be necessary to establish as criminal offences, when committed intentionally: (a) The promise, offering or giving, to a public official, directly or indirectly, of an undue advantage, for the official himself or herself or another person or entity, in order that the official act or refrain from acting in the exercise of his or her official duties; (b) The solicitation or acceptance by a public official, directly or indirectly, of an undue advantage, for the official himself or herself or another person or entity, in order that the official act or refrain from acting in the exercise of his or her official duties.

190 See article 12 the UN Convention against Corruption 2003. 'Each State Party shall take measures, in accordance with the fundamental principles of its domestic law, to prevent corruption involving the private sector…'

191 See sections 1 & 2 of the Bribery Act 2010 of UK on active and passive bribery; See also section 7 on private sector corruption.

and private sector corruption.[192] Since both of these states apply the dual criminality principle in their laws on extradition, a request for extradition from the UK to Pakistan or India involving these offences remains under the threat of being rejected.[193]

Similarly, article 5 of the Organised Crime Convention 2000 requires criminalisation of the act of simply being a member of an organised criminal group.[194] Nonetheless, a majority of states consider it a crime only when a step is taken in furtherance of the objectives of the gang. For instance, the human trafficking law of Pakistan provides enhanced punishment if the offence is committed by an organised criminal group.[195]

---

[192] The criminalization provisions of Indian Anti-Corruption law are found in Ss. 7-13 of the Prevention of Corruption Act 1988, Act No.49 of 1988 [hereinafter the Prevention of Corruption Act 1988 of India]. Those of Pakistan's Ant-Corruption law are found in Sc. 9 of the National Accountability Bureau (NAB) Ordinance 1999, Act XVIII of 1999 as modified on 26-03-2010 [hereinafter National Accountability Bureau Ordinance 1999 of Pakistan]. Neither these laws criminalize active bribery nor private sector corruption. Significantly, both Pakistan and India have signed and ratified the UN Convention on Corruption 2003; See Signatories to the UN Convention against Corruption 2003
<www.unodc.org/unodc/en/treaties/CAC/signatories.html>
[Date accessed 21/03/23]

[193] See Sc. 2(1) (a) of the Extradition Act, 1972, Act No. XXI of 1972 [hereinafter the Extradition Act 1972 of Pakistan]; See also section 2(3)(c) Indian Extradition Act 1962

[194] See article 5 of the Organized Crime Convention 2000:
1. Each State Party shall adopt such legislative and other measures as may be necessary to establish as criminal offences, when committed intentionally: (a) Either or both of the following as criminal offences distinct from those involving the attempt or completion of the criminal activity: (i) Agreeing with one or more other persons to commit a serious crime for a purpose relating directly or indirectly to the obtaining of a financial or other material benefit and, where required by domestic law, involving an act undertaken by one of the participants in furtherance of the agreement or involving an organised criminal group; (ii) Conduct by a person who, with knowledge of either the aim and general criminal activity of an organised criminal group or its intention to commit the crimes in question, takes an active part in: (a) Criminal activities of the organised criminal group; b) Other activities of the organised criminal group in the knowledge that his or her participation will contribute to the achievement of the above-described criminal aim…

[195] See Sc. 4 Prevention and Control of Human Trafficking Ordinance, 2002 [hereinafter Human Trafficking Ordinance 2002]:
Offences committed by organised criminal groups. —Where an organised criminal group is guilty of any offence under clauses (i), (ii), (iii) or (iv) of section 3, the

However, it does not penalise the act of simply being a member of such a group.[196] On the other hand, the RICO (Racketeer-Influenced and Corrupt Organizations) Act[197] of the US symbolises one of the rare domestic law parallels of the Organised Crime Convention 2000 as it does criminalise the membership of an organised criminal group.[198] According to Wise, due to the absence of RICO's equivalents in other legal systems, the US has successively faced difficulties in extraditing fugitives involved in this crime.[199]

Likewise, all organised crime conventions require the parties to criminalise predicate offences.[200] However, apart from drug trafficking, national laws do not reflect uniformity in the coverage of other predicate crimes.[201] For example, the Canadian law on money laundering applies to all types of enterprise crimes through which proceeds can be generated.[202] Similarly, the Australian[203] and UK laws make punishable all indictable offences as predicate crimes.[204] Likewise, the US law on money laundering applies to a broad range of offences including sexual exploitation of children, terror financing, corruption, drug trafficking and racketeering activities.[205] Conversely, Pakistan's law on money laundering does not cover the predicate crimes of conspiracy to commit drug trafficking, active bribery,

---

term of imprisonment for each member of such group involved in the commission of such offence shall not be less than ten years imprisonment and may extend to fourteen years where the purpose of trafficking of a victim is exploitative entertainment and shall also be liable to fine.

[196] ibid

[197] See 18 USC Sc.1961-68

[198] Edward W. Wise, 'Rico and its Analogues: Some Comparative Considerations' 27 Syracuse J. Int'l L. & com (2000) 303 at 321

[199] ibid at 303

[200] See article 6 the Organized Crime Convention 2000, article 23 the UN Convention against Corruption 2003, article 3(1)(b)&(c) the Drugs Convention 1988 and article 8 the UN Convention against Financing of Terrorism 1999

[201] Wise 'Rico & its Analogues' (n 198) at 305

[202] See Sc.462.3, Part XII.2, Criminal Code, RSC 1985, cC-46 [hereinafter the Criminal Code of Canada 1985]

[203] Sc.4(1),14(1) Proceeds of Crimes Act 1987 (CWLTH), Act No.87 of 1978 as amended on 3 march 2005 [hereinafter Australian Proceeds of Crime Act 1987]

[204] Sc.71 (a) (c) & Sched. 4, 12 Criminal Justice Act of 1988, 1988 Chapter 33 Halsbury's Stat.1154, 1183 (1989 Reissue); Criminal Justice (International Cooperation Act) of 1990, 1990 Chapter 5 and Sc. 13 of the Prevention of Terrorism (Temporary Provisions) Act of 1989 F1 (Repealed) 1989 Chapter 4

[205] 18 U.S.C Chapter 46 Forfeiture Sc. 981(1991) Civil Forfeiture, 31 U.S.C Ss.5316,5317 (1991) Search and Forfeiture of Monetary Instruments

human trafficking, nuclear theft and terrorism, attacks against diplomats and enterprise crime.[206] In the same way, the Indian law does not cover the predicate crimes of active bribery and private sector corruption.[207] These dissimilarities in the national coverage of predicate crimes lead to difficulties in satisfying the double criminality condition in forfeiture proceedings.

To counter these difficulties, some states, such as the US, apply a civil forfeiture mechanism which enables a state to forfeit assets even in the absence of any predicate crime.[208] This concept is, as yet, alien to a majority of states.[209] Hence, on several occasions, the US requests for civil forfeiture have had to remain unsatisfied due to non-existence of the corresponding law in the requested states.[210]

It is thus clear that national laws evidence a great deal of variation as regards implementation of the crimes set forth by the organised crime conventions. Drug trafficking represents the only exception concerning which national laws reflect a considerable amount of uniformity.[211] As noted by Bassiouni, the prevalence of organised crimes in a society depends on its tolerance towards a particular criminal activity which is viewed by its members as a provider of employment and earner of bread.[212] It is therefore perplexing that instead of targeting greater harmony in respect of these crimes, the organised crime conventions give wider latitude to the parties as regards their implementation. This is obvious from a common provision of the organised crime conventions which stipulates that the description of the offences is reserved for the domestic law of states parties.[213]

---

[206] See Anti-Money Laundering Act 2010 of Pakistan

[207] See Sc.5 & 8(6), the Prevention of Money Laundering Act 2002, Act 15 of 2003 [hereinafter the Prevention of Money Laundering Act 2002 of India]

[208] See 21 USC Sc.881 (1991): Forfeitures

[209] Bruce Zagaris, 'Asset Forfeiture International and Foreign Law-An Emerging Regime' 5 Emory International Law Review (1991) 445 at 481

[210] ibid

[211] Accordingly, the laws of Pakistan, India, the US and UK closely follow the UN Convention on Drug Trafficking 1988. See Control of Narcotics Substances Act 1997 of Pakistan, The Narcotics Drugs and Psychotropic Substances Act 1985 of India, 21 U.S.C Chapter 13 s.801 (The Controlled Substances Act) and Drugs Act 2005 of the UK

[212] Bassiouni, 'Effective Action' (n 17) 20

[213] See (n 148) above

This approach has resulted in the enactment of inconsistent crime definitions which may lead to increased complications of dual criminality in the extradition and forfeiture proceedings involving these crimes. According to Bassiouni, even the limited uniformity discernible with respect to drug trafficking owes more to the customary status of the prohibition rather than to the duty to legislate under the counterterrorism and organised crime conventions.[214]

3.2) Impact of the duty to legislate on bilateral treaties

The international counterterrorism and organised crime conventions imposing a duty to legislate include a common provision suggesting that all existing and future bilateral treaties between state parties shall stand modified to include the offences set forth by them.[215] This provision has the effect of making all crimes established by the conventions extraditable and subject to mutual legal assistance.

Bilateral treaties take two different approaches to the implementation of this obligation. The first approach calls for a general declaration that the treaty shall apply to all those offences which have been proscribed by the international conventions and to which the *aut dedere aut judicare* obligation applies. The US-Italy Extradition Treaty 1983 represents this approach.[216] The second approach envisages the inclusion of a list of offences within the treaty in respect of which extradition and mutual assistance can be provided. For instance, the Mutual Assistance Treaty between Australia and Indonesia of 1995 includes offences such as human trafficking, hijacking, civil aviation and drug trafficking as well as aiding, abetting, counselling, procuring, attempting and conspiring to commit these crimes.[217]

---

214 Bassiouni includes Drug Trafficking amongst potential *Jus Cogens* crimes. See Cherif Bassiouni, *International Criminal Law Vol 1: Sources, Subjects and Contents* (3rd edn, Martinus Nijhoff-Netherlands 2008) 139.

215 See for instance, article 16(3) of the Organized Crime Convention 2000. For Corresponding provisions, see (n 87) Chapter 4 below.

216 See article V (2) Italy-US Extradition Treaty 1983; See also article 3(1) (c) of 2004 Treaty on Mutual Legal Assistance in Criminal Matters. Signed on 29 November 2004 in Kuala Lampur, Malaysia [hereinafter 2004 Mutual Assistance Treaty among eight far-eastern states]

217 See Annex to Australia- Indonesia Mutual Legal Assistance Treaty 1995; See also article 2(1) Hong Kong, China-Singapore Extradition Treaty 1997

However, bilateral treaties are meant to list only those offences which are already crimes under the national laws of states parties. According to Wise, the listing approach duplicates the offences under the national law because an offence is not likely to appear in a bilateral treaty unless it is found in the national laws of both parties.[218] Thus, some recent extradition treaties categorically declare that surrender shall be granted for any offence listed in the treaties, provided that the offence is punishable under the national law of state parties. The 1997 Extradition Treaty between Hong Kong, China and Singapore adopts this approach.[219]

This implies that the inclusion of the offence in a bilateral treaty does not guarantee surrender of fugitives. The same further requires that the offence in question must constitute a crime under the national law of both the requesting and requested states. If this view is taken as correct, the declaration under the counterterrorism and organised crime conventions with respect to the modification of the existing bilateral treaties becomes meaningless because notwithstanding the inclusion of the new offences in bilateral treaties, the grant or refusal of extradition would rest on the recognition of the crime under the national laws of the parties concerned. Arguably, therefore, the international counterterrorism and organised crime conventions are in need of clarification with respect to a situation when the bilateral treaty has been modified as a result of the entry into force of a new international convention but the national laws are yet to reflect the offences set forth by it.

The issue of a crime having been included in the national law but not finding place in a bilateral treaty arose in the *Mega upload* Extradition Case (2012).[220] In this case, the offender was charged by the US with the crimes of racketeering and conspiracy to commit copy-right infringement.[221]

---

[218] Wise 'Some Problems of Extradition' (n 42) 716

[219] See article 2(1) of Hong Kong, China -Singapore Extradition Treaty 1997

[220] *Kim Dotcom, et al., v. United States of America* Judgement of 29 May 2012 in the District Court at North Shore in the matter of a request by the Government of United States of America for the surrender of persons in New Zealand <http://www.scribd.com/doc/95215045/Torrent-Freak-Mega-Extra> [date accessed 21/03/23]

[221] *United States of America v. Kim Dotcom, et al.*, Criminal no. 1:12 CR 3 US District Court Alexandra Virginia, Indictment 5 January, 2012 <http://www.scribd.com/doc/78786408/Mega-Indictment> [date accessed 21/03/23]

The US-New Zealand Extradition Treaty did not contain this offence.[222] When the defence counsel requested bail for the accused based upon the non-existence of the crime under the relevant bilateral treaty, the prosecutor opposed it by relying on the extradition law of New Zealand. He argued that the Extradition Act of New Zealand allows extradition for each crime set forth by the Organised Crime Convention 2000, which covers under its article 5, racketeering and conspiracy to commit any organised crime including copy- right violations.[223] The Court however granted bail on the ground that the offender posed no risk of flight as his assets had been frozen.[224] The episode indicates that the inclusion of a crime in a bilateral treaty will be of little consequence if the crime does not appear in domestic laws of state parties.

Section 4 Controlled use of dual criminality as an alternative to duty to legislate

Gardocki remarks that uniformity of national definitions of crimes is relevant only for the purposes of comparing the penal provisions of two legal systems in order to come to conclusion that scope of criminalisation differs.[225] In reality, there can never be a uniform national criminal code.[226] Clarke supports this view by stating that there is a limit on how far harmonisation of domestic legal systems must go.[227] The argument questions the technique of promoting law enforcement cooperation by establishing the duty to legislate against universal definitions of crimes.

The above analysis makes it clear that national definitions continue to reflect disharmony despite the imposition of the duty to legislate under the

---

[222] See Treaty on Extradition Between the United States of America and New Zealand. Signed at Washington on January 12, 1970 [hereinafter US-New Zealand Extradition Treaty 1970]

[223] *Kim Dotcom, et al., v. United States of America* (n 200); See also Michael Foreman (2012, February 13) 'US Cites United Nations Treaty in Mega upload case' *International Extradition Lawyers*. <http://internationalextraditionblog.com/2012/02/13/us-cites-united-nations-treaty-in-megaupload-case/> [Date accessed 21/03/23]

[224] *Kim Dotcom, et al., v. United States of America* (n 200); See also the Guardian UK (February 22, 2012) 'Kim Dotcom Granted Bail in Mega upload case' <http://www.guardian.co.uk/technology/2012/feb/22/kim-dotcom-granted-bail-megaupload> [Date accessed 21/03/23]

[225] Lech Gardocki (n 46) 289

[226] ibid

[227] Roger Clarke, 'The UN Convention against Transnational Organised Crime' 50 Wayne State Law Review (2004) 161 at 177

international counterterrorism and organised crime conventions, and dual criminality remains as significant a hurdle in extradition and mutual legal assistance proceedings as it was before the imposition of the duty. Whatever harmony is achieved owes more to extraneous reasons such as Security Council resolutions and customary international law, rather than duty to legislate. Therefore, it is clear that the technique of facilitating law enforcement cooperation through establishing mandatory obligations under the international conventions needs to be revisited.

The current approach is focused on harmonising definitions of crimes only, without giving necessary attention to conditions of state cooperation such as dual criminality. Accordingly, when the conventions provide that the conditions of extradition and mutual assistance shall be determined in accordance with the national law of the requested state,[228] such a state may apply any version or interpretation of dual criminality for the purposes of providing inter-state assistance in law enforcement. It may choose to apply a flexible version, ignoring minor discrepancies to accommodate the request of a friendly state or may insist upon the exact similarity of offences. Therefore, under the current scheme of the conventions, advancement of state cooperation depends on the discretion of the requested state. This contradicts the scholarly claim that the international conventions on terrorism and organised crime have established a new

---

[228] See for example, article 44(8) the UN Convention against Corruption 2003:
Extradition shall be subject to the conditions provided for by the domestic law of the requested State Party or by applicable extradition treaties, including, inter alia, conditions in relation to the minimum penalty requirement for extradition and the grounds upon which the requested State Party may refuse extradition.
See also article 46(2) the UN Convention against Corruption 2003:
A request [for Mutual Legal Assistance] shall be executed in accordance with the domestic law of the requested State Party and, to the extent not contrary to the domestic law of the requested State Party and where possible, in accordance with the procedures specified in the request
For Corresponding provisions, see articles 8(2) & 10(1) the Hague Convention 1970, articles 8(2) & 11(1) the Montreal Convention 1971, article 8(2) & 10(2) the Protection of Diplomats Convention 1973, articles 10(2) & 11(2) the Hostages Convention 1979, articles 11(2) & 13(2) the Convention on Physical Protection of Nuclear Materials 1980, articles 11(2) & 12(2) the Rome Convention 1988, articles 9(2) & 10(2) the Terrorist Bombings Convention 1988, articles 11(2) & 12(5) the Terrorism Financing Convention 1999, articles 13(2) & 14(2) the Nuclear Terrorism Convention 2005, articles 6(5) & 7(12) the Drugs Convention 1988, articles 16(7), 18(6) &(17) of the Organised Crime Convention 2000 and articles 12 (2) & 17 of the Beijing Convention 2010.

regime of state cooperation subordinating sovereign discretion to collective law enforcement.

This technique of facilitating state cooperation may have worked if the duty to legislate was accepted by states without any exception or qualification. Only then would national definitions of crime have been harmonious enough to satisfy any use of, or interpretation of, double criminality. However, the concessions and safeguards afforded to the states in the matter of implementation effectively precluded this possibility. Under these circumstances, the international regulation of double criminality condition provides the best route to facilitate state cooperation in law enforcement.[229] Examples of some bilateral treaties which regulate the use of double criminality are discussed below.

4.1) Totality of the acts shall be considered for satisfaction of dual criminality

Article II (3) of the Canada-Spain Extradition Treaty 1989 provides:

> For the purposes of this article, in determining whether an offence is an offence against the laws of both Contracting States, the totality of the acts or omissions alleged against the person whose extradition is requested shall be taken into account without reference to the elements of the offence prescribed by the law of the Requesting State.[230]

This provision implies that it is not essential for extradition that each act alleged against the fugitive should constitute a crime under the laws of the requesting and requested states. It is sufficient if the totality of his acts is criminal under the laws of two states.

4.2) An offence to be extraditable irrespective of different terminology used by the cooperating states with respect to its expression

Article 2(2) of the Australia-Germany Extradition Treaty 1988 provides:

> For the purpose of this Article it shall not matter whether the laws of the Contracting Parties place the acts or omissions constituting the offence

---

[229] Cherif Bassiouni, 'The "Political Offence Exception" Revisited: Extradition between the US and the UK- A Choice between Friendly Cooperation among Allies and Sound Law and Policy' 15 Denv. J. Int'l L. Pol'y (1986-1987) 255 at 260

[230] See Article II (3) of Canada-Spain Extradition Treaty 1989; See also article 2(3) of Hong Kong, China- Singapore Extradition Treaty 1997

> within the same category of offence or denominate the offence by the same or similar terminology.[231]

The provision clarifies that extradition shall not be refused on the ground that the laws of contracting states describe the offence with different terminology.[232]

4.3) Where an offence is extraditable, attempt, conspiracy, planning and abetment are also extraditable

Article 2(2) of the US-UK Extradition Treaty 2003 provides:

> An offense shall also be an extraditable offense if it consists of an attempt or a conspiracy to commit, participation in the commission of, aiding or abetting, counselling or procuring the commission of, or being an accessory before or after the fact to any offense described in paragraph 1 of this Article.[233]

Article 2(1) defines an extraditable offence as an offence punishable with deprivation of liberty of one year or more under the laws of both the requesting and requested state.[234] Accordingly, the provision implies that extradition of a person involved in an attempt, conspiracy or abetment of an extraditable crime cannot be refused on the grounds of these crimes not having been made independently punishable under the laws of the requested state. They shall be deemed to be extraditable by virtue of this provision.

4.4) Non-Application of dual criminality in mutual legal assistance

There is a growing consensus among states that dual criminality should be applied in those matters only where the requesting state proposes to take coercive action against the offender.[235] If the object of dual criminality is to protect the human rights of offenders, it should only be invoked when

---

[231] See article 2(2) Australia-Germany Extradition Treaty 1988

[232] For Corresponding provisions see article II (2) Canada-Spain Extradition Treaty 1989; article 2(3)(a) US-UK Extradition Treaty 2003; article II (1) US-Italy Extradition Treaty 1983; article 2(2) of the UN Model Treaty on Extradition 1990; article 2(2) Treaty on Extradition between the Republic of Korea and the People's Republic of China. Signed at Seoul October 18, 2000 [hereinafter China-Korea Extradition Treaty 2002]; article 2(2) Australia-India Extradition Treaty 2008 and article 2(3) US-India Extradition Treaty 1997

[233] See article 2(2) US-UK Extradition Treaty 2003

[234] See article 2(1) US-UK Extradition Treaty 2003

[235] Stessens (n 57)

proposed action is likely to affect those rights. For example, extradition, confiscation and enforcement of foreign penal judgments are steps towards punishment. Hence, state cooperation in all these matters should be subject to the satisfaction of dual criminality.[236] On the other hand, because measures such as asset freezing and information sharing are investigatory in nature and do not involve infliction of punishment as such, they should be exempted from a requirement of dual criminality.[237] Thus, several bilateral treaties and regional Conventions on mutual legal assistance exempt certain measures from the application of dual criminality. For instance, the European Convention on Mutual Legal Assistance 1959 does not require dual criminality. However, it clarifies that the Convention does not apply to extradition and enforcement of foreign penal judgements.[238] Similarly, the US-France Mutual Assistance Treaty 1998 does not include a dual criminality condition. Nonetheless, it makes clear that the treaty does not apply to requests for provisional arrests and enforcement of criminal judgements.[239] By contrast, the international counterterrorism and organised crime conventions make no such distinction between coercive and non-coercive measures and include a general provision to the effect that mutual legal assistance might be declined for non-fulfilment of dual criminality.[240] According to Stessens, a requirement to establish congruence of offences with respect to measures having no bearing on the rights of the offenders, amounts to needlessly burdening the requesting state.[241]

4.5) Making non- Retroactivity less relevant

Some uses of double criminality require that the act in respect of which surrender or interrogation is sought must not only be a crime under the laws of the requesting and requested states at the time when the request for inter-state assistance is made, but also at the time of its commission.[242] In other words, the crime must not have been created subsequent to commission of the act, otherwise it will violate the prohibition against non-retroactivity of criminal laws. For example, in the *Pinochet case* the

---

[236] ibid at 292

[237] ibid

[238] See article 1(2) European Convention on Mutual Legal Assistance 1959

[239] US-France Mutual Assistance Treaty 1998; See also article 1 of 2004 Mutual Legal Assistance among eight far-eastern states.

[240] See for instance, article 18(9) of the Organised Crime Convention 2000

[241] Stessens (n 57)

[242] ibid at 291-292; See also Christopher L. Blakesley, 'A Conceptual Framework For Extradition and Jurisdiction over Extraterritorial Crime' 1984 Utah Law Review (1984) 685 at 739

House of Lords observed that the principle of dual criminality could not be satisfied with respect to the acts Pinochet committed prior to 29 September 1988, when the Criminal Justice Act 1988 was enforced in the UK incorporating the crime of torture in respect of which his extradition was sought.[243] This application of double criminality prevents the requested state from extraditing a fugitive whose acts were made crimes under its national law subsequent to their commission. It is rooted in the ancient maxim of *nullum crimen sine lege* which means 'no crime without a previous law.' The maxim denotes that punishability of an act depends on there being a previous legal provision declaring it to be a penal offense, subject to the jurisdiction of the national courts of the proscribing state.[244]

Several bilateral treaties remove this hurdle by declaring that states may grant extradition even if the relevant act was made a crime at the time the request for extradition was received. For example, article 2(4) of the Hong Kong, China- Singapore Extradition Treaty 1997 provides that an offence shall be an offence according to the laws of the requested state if the act constituting the offence was committed at the time a request for surrender was made. This provision gives another example of the facilitation of law enforcement cooperation through relaxed application of dual criminality.

In view of the above, it can be argued that the approach of controlling the use of double criminality appears far more effective in facilitating law enforcement cooperation, as compared to the imposition of an inconclusive duty to legislate. Nonetheless, it can only be made to have global effect by introducing it under the international conventions regulating transnational crimes.

---

243 *Regina v. Bartle and the Commissioner of Police for the Metropolis and Others Ex Parte Pinochet & Regina v. Evans and Another and the Commissioner of Police for the Metropolis and Others Ex Parte Pinochet* (On Appeal from a Divisional Court of the Queen's Bench Division) <http://www.publications.parliament.uk/pa/ld199899/ldjudgmt/jd990324/pino1.htm> [Date accessed 21/03/23]

244 See for instance, article 22(1) of the Rome Statute of the ICC 1998, 2187 UNTS 90/37 ILM 1002 (1998) / [2002] ATS [hereinafter the Rome Statute of the ICC 1998]:

'A person shall not be criminally responsible under this Statute unless the conduct in question constitutes, at the time it takes place, a crime within the jurisdiction of the Court.'

Conclusions

The duty to legislate represents a technique employed by modern counterterrorism and organised crime conventions to facilitate state cooperation in extradition and mutual legal assistance. As the crimes set forth by these conventions are complex and had been less well-known, either their domestic law parallels are non-existent or the definitions of their several parts differ from state to state. The non-existence of the crimes, or the variation with respect to their constituent elements affords opportunity to the requested state to block surrender or interrogation for non- fulfilment of double criminality condition or non- existence of crimes under its national law. A number of extradition requests have had to remain unsatisfied when the act in issue constituted a complex crime, and the requested state did not have its counter-part under its national law.

To establish harmony in the national coverage of crimes, the counterterrorism and organised crime conventions imposed a duty on states to legislate exact definitions of crimes set forth by them. Along with imposing the duty, the conventions gave several concessions to the states authorising them to modify crime definitions in accordance with their domestic requirements. As a result, the national implementation of these crimes does not reflect the legislative harmony for which the duty was imposed.

Consequently, the discretion available to the requested state to refuse surrender or interrogation based upon non-fulfilment of double criminality remains intact. This contradicts the objective of the conventions to promote state cooperation in bringing to justice transnational offenders. Following this approach, law enforcement cooperation concerning transnational crimes remains as unregulated and as discretionary as cooperation in relation to ordinary crimes. It also refutes the scholarly assertion that the international counterterrorism and organised crime conventions are meant to promote consensual sharing of authority at the expense of sovereign discretion. It rather reaffirms the view that the authority of states in the matter of providing inter-state assistance in law enforcement is subject to no restraint. Significantly, the duty has been abolished in some recent counterterrorism and organised crime conventions such as the Beijing Convention 2010 and replaced with the old methodology of defining the crimes internationally and authorising the parties to make punishable their domestic law equivalents.[245]

---

[245] See article 3, the Beijing Convention 2010 'Each State Party undertakes to make the offences set forth in Article 1 punishable by severe penalties.' The

As an alternative strategy, some bilateral treaties pay attention to relaxing the application of the double criminality in extradition and mutual legal assistance proceedings. This technique does away with the requirement of having an exact similarity of offences. It thus offers the twin advantage of circumscribing the discretion available the requested state while preserving the diversity of national legal systems. The adoption of this strategy requires a shift of focus from harmony in the definitions of crimes to collective lowering of the barriers to law enforcement cooperation. The growing number of the bilateral treaties subscribing to this methodology provides evidence of its acceptability amongst states. Nonetheless, to give it an international impact, it is necessary that the technique be tested in the international counterterrorism and organised crime conventions. Significantly, an attempt has been made in the UN Convention against Corruption 2003 to encourage the parties to relax the double criminality condition in extradition proceedings.[246] However, it loses its essence in view of the use of qualifiers such as 'a state party whose law so permits'.[247] Needless to say, if counterterrorism and organised crime conventions are to be more productive in facilitating law enforcement cooperation, their makers will have to abandon the approach of leaving the conditions of extradition and mutual legal assistance entirely up to state parties.

---

reversion to previous formulation is perplexing in view of the fact that the Beijing Convention sets forth as complex crimes as Cyber Terrorism and Biological Terrorism. See article 1(d)(g)(h)(i) of the Beijing Convention 2010

[246] See article 44 (2) of the UN Convention against Corruption 2003:

Notwithstanding the provisions of paragraph 1 of this article, a State Party whose law so permits may grant the extradition of a person for any of the offences covered by this Convention that are not punishable under its own domestic law.

[247] ibid

CHAPTER 4

PROMOTING LAW ENFORCEMENT COOPERATION THROUGH THE OBLIGATION TO PROVIDE FAIR TREATMENT

Introduction

The international counterterrorism and organised crime conventions aim to facilitate state cooperation in bringing to justice the offenders involved in borderless crimes. For this purpose, the conventions rely on enforcement measures of extradition and mutual legal assistance. Both these measures being amalgam of national and international law require for their application, the fulfilment of certain traditional conditions, which necessitate harmony in the justice systems of cooperating states.

One such condition is double punishability. It requires that the act in respect of which extradition or mutual legal assistance is sought must fulfil the standards of criminal responsibility of each cooperating state. In other words, the act must not be deemed non-punishable under the laws of either the requesting or requested state. The actual or anticipated violation of human rights represents one of the major grounds for considering a crime non-punishable under national constitutions and criminal codes. Correspondingly, human rights violations are applied as grounds for refusal of assistance in bilateral treaties and domestic laws on extradition and mutual legal assistance. Thus, possibility of human rights violations in the requesting state allows a requested state to refuse surrender or interrogation for non-fulfilment of double punishability.

Human rights violations have time and again led to surrender or interrogation having been blocked. For example, in *Abu Salem* Case, Portugal imposed a restriction on the extradition of the fugitive to India that he shall not be awarded death penalty. Subsequent to surrender, when the Indian government charged the fugitive with crime of terrorism which attracted death penalty under Indian national law, the concerned Portuguese Court cancelled the extradition order. Similarly, in *James Anderson's* case, the

US bid to obtain the extradition of a fugitive from Canada for the crime of murder remained unsuccessful because the offender pleaded that he committed the crime in the US to secure his release from slavery. Since escape from slavery constituted a valid defence against criminal liability in Canada, Canada showed its inability to surrender the fugitive for an act not constituting a crime under its national law.

Evidently, the absence of corresponding human rights safeguards in the legal systems of cooperating states result in refusal of extradition and mutual legal assistance. Since the purpose of counterterrorism and organised crime conventions is to facilitate state cooperation and disparity in national legal systems leads to its denial, the conventions adopt the strategy of harmonising national legal systems with respect to protection of human rights. The objective is to ensure that the requesting state's failure to guarantee these rights may not provide justification to the requested state to refuse surrender or interrogation. To establish harmony, the conventions oblige the parties to provide fair treatment to the relators.[1] This chapter looks into the question of the extent to which the obligation has led to harmonisation of national legal systems and facilitation of state cooperation in extradition and mutual legal assistance.

It will be argued that the technique of facilitating state cooperation through establishing harmony in national human rights protection overlooks the fact that human rights are applied in multiple ways as grounds for refusal of assistance under the laws and treaties on extradition and mutual legal assistance. The varying applications of these rights as grounds for refusal afford opportunity to a requested state to block extradition or mutual legal assistance on the basis of its laws demanding additional protection or not recognising the protection guaranteed by the requesting state. Hence, a general obligation to provide fair treatment under the international conventions is insufficient to produce the level of harmony needed to satisfy every application of human rights as grounds for refusal of assistance. As long as the use of human rights as grounds for refusal is not regulated, facilitation of state cooperation may not be actualised. While the omission to regulate their use as grounds for refusal may have little relevance for cooperative endeavours relating to ordinary crimes, it poses

[1]The term 'Relator' refers to an individual accused or convicted in the requesting state of an offence for which the requesting state is seeking his extradition or interrogation from the requested state. See M. Cherif Bassiouni, 'Ideologically Motivated Offences and Political Offence Exception in Extradition - A Proposed Juridical Standard for an Unruly Problem'19 DePaul L. Rev. (1969-1970) 217 at 221

a significant risk of the failure of state cooperation in transnational crimes, owing to their specific nature.

The Chapter will recommend that the makers of the international conventions replace or complement the obligation to provide fair treatment with the technique of controlling the use of human rights as grounds for refusal of assistance. The regulation of their use as grounds for refusal is not something alien to states rather it has been done in some bilateral treaties and domestic laws on extradition and mutual assistance. Nonetheless, to make this approach work at international level, it is desirable to introduce this technique in international conventions directed at promoting state cooperation in law enforcement.

The chapter has been divided into four sections. Section 1 will provide an over-view of the requirement of harmony for enforcing the measures of extradition and mutual legal assistance, the double punishability requirement and use of human rights violations as grounds for refusal of assistance. Section 2 will discuss the obligation to provide fair treatment under the international conventions, its interpretation and significance in the context of state cooperation in extradition and mutual legal assistance. Section 3 will analyse the unifying effect of the fair treatment obligation as regards protection of due process rights and its usefulness in facilitating the surrender or interrogation. Section 4 will consider the harmonising effect of the fair treatment obligation with respect to protection of fundamental human rights and its utility in facilitating surrender and interrogation.

Section 1: Requirement of harmony for extradition and mutual legal assistance and use of human rights violations as grounds for refusal of assistance

In the words of Piragoff and Kran, 'contemporary criminal activity knows no territorial boundaries and as a result sovereign states are increasingly obliged to cooperate in the criminal justice area.'[2] Since the acts of transnational terrorism and organised crime fall into this category of crimes, the object of the international conventions focusing these crimes is to facilitate state cooperation in law enforcement. For this purpose, the

---

[2] Donald K Piragoff & Marcia V.J Kran, 'The Impact of Human Rights Principles on Extradition from Canada and the US: Role of National Court' 3 Crim Law Forum (1992) 225 at 225

conventions adopt the technique of harmonising national legal systems through establishing mandatory obligations.[3]

Harmony is needed owing to the fact that laws and treaties on state cooperation are based on the principle of *reciprocity* or mutuality of obligations necessitating the adoption of common legal principles by states wishing to cooperate.[4] The principle is explained by Williams in these words, 'When a state enters into an extradition treaty, based on reciprocity with another state, this seems to imply an understanding that the parties have more or less equivalent conceptions of the fundamentals of criminal justice.'[5] The rationale of the principle is to ensure that cooperating states must be in a position to provide assistance to each other on reciprocal basis. This means, if circumstances are reversed and the requested state steps into the shoes of the requesting state, it must be entitled to obtain similar assistance in relation to the crime in question. Since there is no rule of general international law that compels a state to provide law enforcement cooperation in the absence of a treaty, such assistance is provided traditionally on the basis of bilateral treaties premised on the principle of reciprocity. For example, Chinese extradition law provides, '[t]he People's Republic of China cooperates with foreign states in extradition on the basis of equality and reciprocity.'[6]

With a view to enabling the parties to fulfil the demands of reciprocity in state cooperation proceedings, the international conventions on terrorism and organised crime establish mandatory obligations. Thus, UNODC's legislative guide to the Organised Crime Convention 2000 provides that the aim of establishing universal obligations under this convention is to harmonise national legal systems with respect to criminalisation, jurisdiction, prosecution and treatment of offenders, in order to facilitate

---

[3] See (n 34) Chapter 3 above; also see (n15,75 & 83) Chapter 1 above

[4] Lech Gardocki, 'Double Criminality in Extradition Law' 27 Isr. L. Rev. (1993) 288

[5] Sharon A Williams, 'Human Rights Safeguards and International Cooperation in Extradition: Striking in Balance' 3 Criminal Law Forum (1992) 191 at 200

[6] See article 3 of Extradition Law of the People's Republic of China (Order of the President No.42 of 2000); See also Sec. 2, Israel's Extradition Regulations 1970 (Law Procedures and Rules of Evidence in Petitions) 5731 <https://www.imolin.org/doc/amlid/Israel/Israel_Extradition_Law_1954.pdf> [Date accessed 21/03/23]

the coordination of the national and international efforts to combat transnational criminality.[7]

Although the crimes established by the conventions differ significantly with respect to their nature and the motivation of the individual committing them,[8] owing to their shared feature of transnationality, the conventions provide identical modalities of law enforcement for their suppression.[9] These are extradition and mutual legal assistance.[10] Laws and treaties governing these measures require states to fulfil a range of double conditions to enforce them.[11] These include double criminality, double possibility of criminal proceedings, double penal policy standards and double punishability.[12] All these conditions are derived from principle

---

[7] See UNODC's Legislative Guide 2004 for implementing the Organized Crime Convention 2000 at 130 <http://www.unodc.org/pdf/crime/legislative_guides/Legislative%20guides_Full%20version.pdf> [Date accessed 21/03/23]

[8] See M. Cherif Bassiouni, 'Effective National and International Action against Organised Crime and Terrorist Criminal Activities' 4 Emory Intl L. Review (1990) 9 at 10

[9] Typically, international law instruments deal with any of the six mechanisms to combat criminality at the international level. These are (1) Recognition of foreign penal judgements (2) transfer of penal proceedings (3) extradition (4) mutual legal assistance in criminal matters (5) transfer of prisoners and (6) seizure and forfeiture of illicit proceeds of crime. Out of these, extradition, mutual legal assistance and forfeiture are the very essence of enforcement and without them, international, transnational, and even national crimes would be deprived of international enforcement methods. See M. Cherif Bassiouni, 'Policy Considerations on Interstate Cooperation in Criminal Matters' 4 Pace Y.B.Int'l L. (1992) 123 at 126-127

[10] The enforcement modalities of Extradition and Mutual Legal Assistance appear in the following Conventions on transnational crime: The Hague convention 1970 (articles 9 & 10), the Montreal Convention 1971 (articles 8 &11), the Protection of Diplomats Convention 1973 (articles 8 & 10), the Hostages Convention 1979 (articles 10 & 11), the Nuclear Materials Convention 1980 (articles 11 & 13), the Rome Convention 1988 (articles 11 &12), the Terrorist Bombing Convention 1997 (articles 9&10), the Terrorism Financing Convention 1999 (articles 11 &12), the Nuclear Terrorism Convention 2005 (articles 13 &14), the Drugs Convention 1988 (articles 6 &7), the Organized Crime Convention 2000 (articles 16 &18), the UN Convention against Corruption 2003 (articles 44&46) and the Beijing Convention (articles 12 &17).

[11] See Edward M Wise, 'Some Problems of Extradition' 15 Wayne L. Rev. (1968-1969) 709 at 713; See also Gardocki (n 4) 288

[12] Gardocki ibid; See also SZ Fellar, 'The Significance of the requirement of Double Criminality in the Law of Extradition' 10 Isr. L. Rev. (1975) 51 at 71-75

of reciprocity, and their purpose is to ensure that cooperating states share a certain set of values and legal prescriptions about the act in respect of which surrender or interrogation is sought.[13] The international conventions do not purport to abolish these conditions; rather they aim to make national legal systems responsive to their demands through establishing harmony.

1.1) Double punishability condition

One traditional condition entrenched in the principle of reciprocity or mutuality of obligation is the double punishability requirement.[14] It stipulates that the act in respect of which extradition or mutual legal assistance is sought must fulfil the standards of criminal responsibility of each cooperating state.[15] In other words, the act must not be deemed non-punishable under the laws of either the requesting or requested state.

John Anderson's case of 1860-61 provides a classic example of the application double punishability in extradition proceedings.[16] Here, the extradition of the fugitive was requested by the US from Canada, on charges of stabbing and killing a US citizen Diggs in Massiouri. Although murder was an extraditable crime as per the terms of the applicable bilateral treaty,[17] the fugitive claimed that he had committed the crime in order to secure his release from slavery.[18] The applicable bilateral treaty stipulated that sufficient evidence of criminality existed such that according to the laws of the requested state the apprehension and trial of the fugitive would be warranted, had the crime been committed there.[19] Since slavery was prohibited in Canada, the criminal liability of the offender was deemed to have been excluded under the Canadian law.[20]

---

[13] Gardocki ibid

[14] Gardocki ibid; See also Fellar (n 12)

[15] Gardocki ibid

[16] *In re John Anderson*, 20 U.C.Q.B.R. 124 (1860); See also Paul Finkelman, 'International Extradition and Fugitive Slaves: The John Anderson Case' 18 Brook. J. Int'l L. (1992) 765

[17] A treaty to settle and define the boundaries of the US and the possessions of Her Britannic Majesty in North America for final suppression of African slave trade and for giving up criminals, fugitives from justice in certain cases, Aug 9, 1842, US-UK, article X, 8 Stat.572,12 Bevans 82 [hereinafter Webster Ashburton Treaty 1842]

[18] *In re John Anderson* (n 16) at Para 124, 145-150, 174 & 186 (1860); See also Finkelman (n 16) 787,778,766

[19] See article X Webster Ashburton Treaty 1842

[20] *In re John Anderson* (n 16); See also Finkelman (n 16) 787

The court held that although Anderson did stab and kill Diggs, it would be an insufficient statement in an indictment for murder in any of the Canadian courts.[21] The requirement that there must be such evidence of crime as would justify the trial of a fugitive in the requested state represents the dual punishability principle.[22]

1.2) Use of human rights violations as grounds for refusal of assistance

A major ground for making an offence non-punishable or excluding criminal responsibility is the actual or anticipated violation of human rights of the offender.[23] Human rights violations as circumstances excluding criminal responsibility or making an offence non-punishable are generally reflected amongst defences to criminal liability in national constitutions and criminal codes. Correspondingly, they are applied as grounds for refusal of assistance in domestic laws and bilateral treaties on extradition and mutual legal assistance. For instance, UN Model Treaty on Extradition 1990 requires the parties to refuse surrender when there are grounds for believing that the person whose extradition is sought would be subjected in the requesting state to torture, cruel, inhuman or degrading treatment or punishment.[24] Similarly, the 1995 Mutual Assistance Treaty between Australia and Indonesia obliges the parties to refuse cooperation when the request for assistance appears to be motivated by a desire to prosecute or punish the offender on account of his racial, religious, ethnic or political affiliations.[25]

Both these provisions illustrate the application of 'fundamental human rights' as ground for refusal of assistance. According to Plachta, the concept of fundamental human rights is based on the understanding that, out of all human rights a group has been recognised as non-derogable in all universal and regional instruments and, therefore, has to be protected regardless of distinction between trial, extradition and mutual legal assistance proceedings.[26]

---

[21] ibid

[22] Gardocki (n 4); Fellar (n 12)

[23] J. Dugard and Christine Van den Wyngaert, 'Reconciling Extradition with Human Rights' 92 AJIL (1998) 187 at 188

[24] See 3(f) UN Model Treaty on Extradition 1990

[25] See article 4(1)(c) of the 1995 Mutual Assistance Treaty between Australia and Indonesia

[26] M. Plachta, 'Contemporary Problems of Extradition: Human Rights, Grounds for Refusal and Principle of Aut dedere' 114th International Training Course

Apart from these, laws and treaties on extradition and mutual legal assistance apply rights relating to trial proceedings or 'due process rights' as grounds for refusal of assistance. These rights are connected with the proceeding that has led to conviction or sentencing of the offender in the requesting state, on the basis of which extradition or mutual legal assistance is requested.[27] The actual or potential violation of these rights allows a requested state to refuse surrender or interrogation. For example, US-Italy Extradition Treaty of 1983 obliges the parties to refuse surrender when the person sought has been convicted or acquitted or pardoned or has served his sentence for the same acts for which extradition is requested.[28] The provision exemplifies the application of double jeopardy or successive punishments as a ground for refusal of assistance. In the same way, the European Convention on Extradition 1957 obliges the parties to refuse extradition when the person claimed has become immune from prosecution due to the amount of time that has elapsed between the act and prosecution or punishment.[29] The provision characterises the use of prescription or time barred prosecution as a ground for refusal of assistance. The term prescription denotes a statute of limitation that restricts the time within which legal proceedings may be brought against an offender.[30] Once the limitation has expired, the court lacks jurisdiction to try or punish an offender.[31]

Since rights relating to trial proceedings or due process rights are not considered non-derogable, some commentators maintain that it is optional for states to apply them in extradition and mutual legal assistance proceedings.[32]

In view of the above, it is clear that principle of double punishability applicable to extradition and mutual legal proceedings requires that the act in respect of which the surrender or interrogation is sought must fulfil the standards of criminal responsibility of each cooperating state. In other words, the act in question must not be considered non- punishable under

Visiting Experts Papers at 65 <www.or.jp/english/pdf/PDF_rms/no57/57-16pdf> [Date accessed 21/03/23]

[27] ibid at 66

[28] See article VI US-Italy Extradition Treaty of 1983

[29] See article 10, the European Convention on Extradition 1957

[30] See the Free Dictionary by Farlex <http://legal dictionary.thefreedictionary.com/Period+of+prescription> [Date accessed 21/03/23]

[31] ibid

[32] Plachta 'Contemporary Problems of Extradition' (n 26) 66

the laws of either the requesting or requested state. National constitutions and criminal codes identify certain human rights whose actual or anticipated violation makes an offence non-punishable. Correspondingly, theses rights are applied as grounds for refusal of assistance in laws and treaties on extradition and mutual legal assistance. It is therefore important that harmony should exist in national legal systems with respect to giving protection against violations of these rights, so that the requesting state's omission to guarantee a right may not allow the requested state to block surrender or interrogation. To bring about harmony, the international conventions establish the obligation to provide fair treatment.

Section 2: Obligation to provide fair treatment, its interpretation and significance in the context of state cooperation in extradition and mutual legal assistance

2.1) Introduction to Fair Treatment Obligation

A provision common to a majority of the international conventions on terrorism and organised crime requires that parties provide fair treatment to the offenders. The counterterrorism conventions containing the obligation comprise the Hostages Convention 1979,[33] the Protection of Diplomats Convention1973,[34] the Nuclear Materials Convention 1980,[35] the Rome Convention 1988, the Terrorist Bombings Convention 1997,[36] the Terrorism Financing Convention 1999,[37] the Nuclear Terrorism Convention 2005[38] and the Beijing Convention 2010.[39] The organised crime conventions establishing the obligation include the UN Convention against Corruption 2003 and the Organised Crime Convention 2000.[40]

Earlier conventions, such as the Protection of Diplomats Convention 1973 and the Nuclear Materials Convention 1980, feature a shorter version of the provision, leaving it unclear as to what kind of fair treatment is

[33] See article 8(2) the Hostages Convention 1979

[34] See article 9 the Protection of Diplomats Convention 1973

[35] See article 12 the Nuclear Materials Convention 1980

[36] See article 10 (2) of the Rome Convention 1988 and article 14 the Terrorist Bombings Convention 1997

[37] See article 17 the Terrorist Financing Convention 1999

[38] See article 12 the Nuclear Terrorism Convention 2005

[39] See article 11 the Beijing Convention 2010

[40] See article16 (13) the Organised Crime Convention 2000 and 44(14) the UN Convention against Corruption 2003

required to be provided to the relators.[41] For example, article 12 of the Nuclear Materials Convention 1973 reads:

> Any person regarding whom proceedings are being carried out in connection with any of the offences set forth in article 7 shall be guaranteed fair treatment at all stages of the proceedings.[42]

By contrast, modern conventions such as the Terrorism Financing Convention 1999, the Terrorist Bombing Convention 1997, the Nuclear Terrorism Convention 2005 and the Beijing Convention 2010 lay down fuller versions of the provision explaining plainly that parties are required to provide all those rights to the relators which are guaranteed under national and international law, including human rights law. For example, article 17 of the Terrorism Financing Convention 1999 reads:

> Any person who is taken into custody or regarding whom any other measures are taken or proceedings are carried out pursuant to this Convention shall be guaranteed fair treatment, including enjoyment of all rights and guarantees in conformity with the law of the State in the territory of which that person is present and applicable provisions of international law, including international human rights law.[43]

2.1.1) Interpretation of the obligation

According to the Commonwealth Implementation Kits of the UN counterterrorism conventions, the obligation to provide fair treatment has no particular significance as it does nothing more than reaffirm the rights already protected under international human rights instruments and national constitutions.[44] A closer look at the provision, however, reveals that it lays down a ground-breaking rule which may have significant

---

[41] AB Green, 'Convention on Protection and Punishment of Diplomatic Agents and Other Internationally Protected Persons: An Analysis' 14 Virginia Journal of international law (1973-1974) 703 at 721

[42] See article 12 the Nuclear Materials Convention 1980; See also article 9 the Protection of Diplomats Convention 1973

[43] See article 17 the Terrorism Financing Convention 1997; See also article 14 the Terrorist Bombing Convention 1997, article 12 the Nuclear Terrorism Convention 2005, article 11 the Beijing Convention 2010, article 8(2) the Hostages Convention 1979 and article 10(2) the Rome Convention 1988.

[44] Commonwealth Implementation Kits of the UN Counter-Terrorism Conventions at 144 <http://www.thecommonwealth.org/shared_asp_files/uploadedfiles/%7B8AE4DB15-88A5-46F2-8037-357DFF7D3EC1%7D_Implementation%20Kits%20for%20Counter-Terrorism.pdf> [Date accessed 21/03/23]

impact on extradition and interrogation of the offenders involved in transnational crimes.[45] The obligation has three important elements, i.e. 'any proceedings', 'fair treatment' and 'in accordance with national and international, including human rights law'. Each of these will be discussed below in order to determine the nature of the obligation.

2.1.1.1) 'any proceedings'

In the first place, the provision declares that offenders facing 'any proceedings' under these conventions shall be guaranteed fair treatment in accordance with national and international law, including human rights law. The phrase 'any proceeding' presumably refers to extradition, mutual legal assistance and prosecution in lieu of extradition, because the enforcement mechanism of all conventions under consideration revolves around these three measures. Accordingly, each convention establishes mandatory obligation to extradite or prosecute the offenders and to provide mutual legal assistance with respect to their crimes.[46] Owing to this, the conventions are sometimes referred to as 'international agreements establishing the obligation to extradite or prosecute' or 'universal mutual assistance and extradition agreements'.[47]

---

[45] According to Rozaqis, the provision sets forth a very vital obligation since it makes the parties accountable for possible misuses of their jurisdictional authority. See Christos L Rozaqis, 'Terrorism and the Internationally Protected Persons in the Light of ILC's Draft Articles' 23 ICLQ (1974) 32 at 61

[46] For provisions of the treaties on extradition and mutual legal assistance, see (n 10) above. The obligation to prosecute in lieu of extradition refers to the duty to extradite or prosecute. See for instance, article 7 of the Protection of Diplomats Convention 1973:

The State Party in whose territory the alleged offender is present shall, if it does not extradite him, submit, without exception whatsoever and without undue delay, the case to its competent authorities for the purpose of prosecution, through proceedings in accordance with the laws of that State.

See also article 7 the Hague Convention 1970, article 7 the Montreal Convention 1971, article 8 the Hostages Convention 1979, article 10 the Nuclear Materials Convention 1980, article 10 the Rome Convention 1988, article 8 the Terrorist Bombing Convention 1997, article 10 the Terrorism Financing Convention 1999, article 11 the Nuclear Terrorism Convention 2005, article 10 the Beijing Convention 2010, article 6(9) the Drugs Convention 1988, article 16(10) the Organized Crime Convention 2000 and article 44(11) the UN Convention against Corruption 2003.

[47] See article III (1)(b) Canada-Spain Extradition Treaty 1989; See also Carrie Lyn Donigan Guymon, 'International Legal Mechanisms for Combating Transnational

It is thus clear that when the conventions oblige the parties to provide fair treatment to offenders in 'any proceedings', they refer to extradition, trial and mutual assistance proceedings. The argument lends credence from the observation of Lambert concerning the rationale of the obligation in the Hostages Convention 1979:

> The proceedings during which fair treatment must be guaranteed would presumably include all measures which may be taken with respect to the alleged offender, including preliminary custody, extradition hearings, trial and sentencing.[48]

2.1.1.2) 'fair treatment'

The term 'fair treatment' has been used as a substitute for 'fair trial' in order to bring within the ambit of the obligation not only trial proceedings but also other proceedings mandated by the conventions such as extradition and mutual legal assistance.[49] Had the makers of the conventions used the expression 'fair trial' instead of 'treatment', the parties may have considered that guaranteeing of rights is essential only when the offender is facing trial proceedings. The argument draws support from the commentary of International Law Commission (ILC) on the Protection of Diplomats Convention 1973:

> The expression 'fair treatment' was preferred because of its generality, to more usual expressions such as due process, fair hearing or fair trial which might be interpreted in a narrow technical sense…[50]

2.1.1.3) 'in accordance with national and international, including human rights law'

The wording 'in accordance with national and international including human rights law' implies that the conventions require the parties to provide all those rights to the offenders which have been recognised under national constitutions, statutory law, bilateral treaties and international

---

Organised Crime: The Need for a Multilateral Convention' 18 Berkeley J. Int'l L (2000) 53 at 55; Bassiouni, 'Effective Action' (n 7) 33

[48] Joseph J Lambert, *Terrorism and Hostages in International Law, A Commentary on Hostages Convention 1979* (Cambridge: Grotius Publications Limited 1990) at 206

[49] See Plachta 'Contemporary Problems of Extradition' (n 26) 66

[50] 1972 Yearbook of the International Law Commission (YBILC) Vol. II at 320

human rights instruments.[51] On account of this, the ILC noted in its commentary to the Protection of Diplomats Convention 1973:

> The expression 'fair treatment' is intended to incorporate all the guarantees generally recognised to a detained or accused person. An example of such guarantees is found in article 14 of the International Covenant on Civil and Political Rights.[52]

Considering the explanation above, it is clear that the obligation to provide fair treatment requires the parties to comply with standards of human rights and justice as established by national and international law in all proceedings under the conventions including extradition and mutual legal assistance.[53]

2.2) Significance of the obligation

National approaches can be classified in two opposing camps with respect to guaranteeing human rights to persons facing extradition and mutual assistance proceedings.[54] The first camp represents cooperation-centred states such as Canada and the US. According to their view, extradition and mutual legal assistance, unlike domestic trials, are treaty matters creating rights and obligation for states only.[55] Hence, individual rights ought to have restricted application in these matters.[56] The second camp consists of human rights-oriented states. These include states parties to the European Convention on Human Rights (ECHR) 1950.[57] To them, international law is no longer concerned with states alone. After the dramatic development of human rights law, international law recognizes the capacity of individuals to acquire rights and obligations under it. Therefore, individual rights should be as effectively protected in extradition and mutual assistance proceedings as constitutional rights in domestic trials.[58]

By establishing the obligation to provide fair treatment, the makers of the international conventions have rejected the argument that extradition and

---

[51] William (n 5) 198
[52] YBILC (n 50)
[53]Rozakis (n 45) 61
[54] Williams (n 5) at 194
[55] ibid
[56] ibid at 198-199
[57] See European Convention on Human Rights (ECHR) 1950; the UK is excluded from the category of states following human rights approach to state cooperation. See Williams ibid at 193, 199
[58] Williams (n 5) 223

mutual assistance proceedings are not identical to trials and that persons facing these proceedings are not entitled to the rights available to suspects under trial. They have made it abundantly clear that, for the purposes of providing human rights, there exists no difference between a suspect facing trial and a person facing extradition or mutual assistance proceedings.

Section 3: Effectiveness of the fair treatment obligation in facilitating the fulfilment of due process rights as grounds for refusal of assistance

As explained above, the obligation to provide fair treatment requires that parties provide two kinds of rights to the offenders: rights relating to due process and fundamental human rights.'[59] This section concerns the former category of rights.

3.1) Right to be protected against double jeopardy

The principle of double jeopardy is derived from the Latin maxim *nemo debet bis vexari* which means no one shall be prosecuted or punished more than once for the same conduct.[60] It affords protection to the offenders against successive punishments or prosecutions.[61] Being embedded in national constitutions, bilateral treaties and international human rights treaties, the principle has two uses, domestic as well as international.[62] At domestic level, it gives protection to a person facing trial, against violation of his constitutional right to be immune from successive punishments or prosecutions.[63] At international level, it enables a person facing extradition or mutual legal assistance to resist these proceedings by claiming that they will expose him to double punishment or prosecution in the requesting state.[64] Due to its widespread application in extradition and mutual

---

[59] See Plachta 'Contemporary Problems of Extradition' (n 26) 66

[60] James A Ballentine, *A Law Dictionary of words, terms, abbreviations and phrases* (New Jersey: The Law book exchange Ltd 2005) 325

[61] ibid

[62] Christine van den Wyngaert and Guy Steesens, 'The International Non Bis In Idem Principle: Resolving Some of the Unanswered Questions' 48 ICLQ (1999) 779 at 780

[63] See for instance article 13 (a) The Constitution of Islamic Republic of Pakistan, 12th April 1973 [hereinafter the Constitution of Pakistan 1973]. 'Protection against Double Punishment and Self Incrimination. No person:- shall be prosecuted or punished for the same offence more than once…'

[64] Wyngaert & Stessens (n 62) 781; See also article 12 of Extradition Act 2003, 2003 Chapter 41 [hereinafter Extradition Act 2003 of UK]:

assistance laws, it is considered to be one of the foremost grounds for refusal of inter-state assistance in law enforcement.[65] Therefore, harmony is needed in national systems with respect to giving protection against it, so that the requesting state's failure to guarantee that right may not give justification to the requested state to block surrender or interrogation.

To harmonise national legal systems, the international conventions on terrorism and organised crime establish the obligation to provide fair treatment to the offenders facing 'any proceedings' under the treaties. Since the obligation requires that parties provide all those rights which are available under national, international and human rights law, right to be protected against successive punishments or prosecutions, which has the status of a general principle of law, naturally finds its place under it.[66] The hope is that with all states guaranteeing protection, there will be no occasion for the requested state to refuse surrender or interrogation for breach of the rule against double jeopardy.[67]

This approach however disregards the fact that there are several applications of double jeopardy as a ground for refusal of assistance under the laws and treaties on extradition and mutual legal assistance. It is thus possible that the requested state's way of applying it as a ground for refusal may not accord with the requesting state's manner of giving protection against its violation. This may lead to refusal of surrender or interrogation notwithstanding the requesting state having guaranteed protection as required by the obligation to provide fair treatment under the international counterterrorism and organised crime conventions.[68] To illustrate this

---

Rule against double jeopardy - A person's extradition to a category 1 territory is barred by reason of the rule against double jeopardy if (and only if) it appears that he would be entitled to be discharged under any rule of law relating to previous acquittal or conviction on the assumption — (a) that the conduct constituting the extradition offence constituted an offence in the part of the United Kingdom where the judge exercises jurisdiction; (b) that the person was charged with the extradition offence in that part of the United Kingdom.

[65] See Wyngaert & Stessens (n 62) at 779

[66] See Wyngaert & Stessens (n 62) 780. Double jeopardy is acknowledged as a 'general principle of law'.

[67] See Abdullah Y. Shehu, 'International Initiatives against Corruption and Money Laundering: An Overview' 12 Journal of Financial crime (2005) 221 at 231.

[68] See Bassiouni, 'Ideologically Motivated Offences' (n 1) 260; Also see Bassiouni, Policy Considerations' (n 9) 132,144; Christopher L. Blakesley, 'The Autumn of the Patriarch: The Pinochet Extradition Debacle and Beyond - Human Rights Clauses Compared to Traditional Derivative Protections Such as Double Criminality' 91 Journal of Criminal Law and Criminology (200-2001) 1

point, three aspects of the double jeopardy rule will be discussed concerning which the national approaches diverge. The divergence necessitates international regulation of the manner in which double jeopardy is used as a ground for refusal under bilateral treaties and domestic laws on extradition and mutual legal assistance.

3.1.1) Dissimilarities in national approaches concerning the use of double jeopardy as a ground for refusal of assistance

3.1.1.1) Recognition of the principle in extradition and mutual legal assistance proceedings

The disagreement begins with the recognition of double jeopardy in extradition and mutual assistance proceedings. Double jeopardy blocks extradition or mutual legal assistance when the requested state comes to know that the offender has previously been convicted or acquitted for the conduct concerning which the request for assistance has been made.[69] On a number of occasions, national courts refused to consider previous conviction relevant for the purposes of extradition and mutual legal assistance. For example, in *Schmidst v. Canada,* the Canadian Supreme Court observed that protection against double jeopardy in Canada is derived from the Canadian Charter of Rights and Freedoms, which only applies to trials held in Canada.[70] In extradition, since the violation of double jeopardy take places in a foreign country, i.e. the requesting state, it cannot be raised as a ground to resist extradition proceedings held in Canada because the Canadian Charter of Rights and Freedoms has no extraterritorial application.[71] In other words, extradition proceedings are not identical to trials and the rule of double jeopardy blocks trials, not the extradition of suspects.[72] A different approach is taken under Extradition Act 2003 of the UK. Section 12 of the Act requires the Judge conducting an extradition hearing to reject extradition if the offender, had he been tried in the UK, would have been immune from prosecution under the rule of double jeopardy.[73]

---

[69] See for instance article 6 of Extradition Treaty between the Government of United States of America and the Government of the Republic of South Africa, Signed at Washington on September 16,1999 [hereinafter US-South Africa Extradition Treaty 1999]

[70] See *Canada v. Schmidt* [1987] 1 S.C.R 500 AT 501-502 (CAN)

[71] ibid

[72] See Williams (n 5) at 215

[73] See article 12 Extradition Act 2003 of UK (n 64)

It is thus clear that national approaches differ with respect to recognition of double jeopardy in extradition and mutual legal assistance proceedings. The international conventions on terrorism and organised crime attempt to bring harmony in national approaches by clarifying that offenders facing 'any proceedings', including extradition and interrogation, are entitled to *fair treatment* which brings into the fold protection against double jeopardy. Nevertheless, the conventions are only meant to supplement and not override national laws and bilateral treaties.[74] Hence, it cannot be said that by establishing the obligation to provide fair treatment, the international conventions have harmonised national approaches with respect to recognition of double jeopardy in extradition and mutual legal assistance proceedings.

3.1.1.2) Forum of previous conviction

Another dissimilarity in national approaches concerning the use of double jeopardy as a ground for refusal of assistance relates to the forum of previous conviction. National laws and bilateral treaties on extradition and mutual legal assistance are divided as regards the state where previous conviction should have occurred for the purposes of blocking surrender or interrogation under the rule of double jeopardy.[75] Some states require that previous conviction occurs in the requested state, others stipulate that occurrence of previous conviction in either the requesting or requested state operates as a bar, while a few provide that previous conviction in any state precludes extradition or interrogation under the rule of double jeopardy. For instance, the China-Korea Extradition Treaty 2002 obliges the parties to refuse extradition if the surrender is sought in respect of an offence concerning which judgement of acquittal or conviction has been passed in the 'requested state'.[76] By contrast, the 2004 Mutual Assistance treaty among eight far-eastern states obliges the parties to compulsorily refuse assistance if the previous conviction or acquittal occurred in the 'requesting and requested state'.[77] This may be compared with Singapore's extradition law, which provides that a person shall not be surrendered to a

[74] See (n 228) Chapter 3 above
[75] See Wyngaert & Stessens (n 62) 783
[76] See article 3(2) of China-Korea Extradition Treaty 2002
[77] See article 3(1) (d) of Treaty on Mutual Legal Assistance in Criminal Matters. Signed on 29 November 2004 in Kuala Lampur, Malaysia [hereinafter 2004 Mutual Legal Assistance treaty among eight far-eastern states]

foreign state in respect of an offence if he has been convicted, acquitted or pardoned by a competent tribunal or authority in 'any country'.[78]

It has been argued that states following the first approach, i.e. barring extradition only if a previous conviction occurs in the requested state, give preference to state cooperation over human rights because the smaller the number of states whose conviction is likely to bar subsequent prosecution, the smoother the surrender of suspects from one state to another will be.[79] The *Joseph Aumeier* case from 1980 provides an example of how extradition can be facilitated by considering a previous conviction to be a ground of refusal only when it took place in the 'requested state'.[80] In this case, the offender was convicted and sentenced to a one year custodial sentence by a Dutch court for the offence of drug trafficking across the border of Germany and the Netherlands. His extradition was requested by Germany but was rejected by the Netherlands on the ground that Dutch law prohibited extradition of suspects who had previously been convicted for the same offence by the requested state.[81] Subsequently, the offender went to Belgium, where his extradition was again requested by Germany for the offence in respect of which he had been convicted earlier by the Netherlands. This time the extradition was granted because Belgian law only precluded extradition if the previous conviction took place in Belgium. Since the previous conviction had occurred in the Netherlands, Belgium was under no obligation to consider it an obstacle to extradition under the double jeopardy rule.[82]

Notwithstanding its suitability for bringing to justice transnational offenders, the policy of restricting the protection against double jeopardy to those instances only where previous conviction occurs in the requested state has been criticized by a number of scholars advocating a human rights approach to state cooperation. For instance, Wyngaert and Stessens maintain that restricting double jeopardy protection to those instances only where previous conviction occurs in the requested state, amounts to depriving the offender of his right to be immune from extradition in respect of conduct concerning which at least one state may have

[78] See article 7(4) of Singapore' Extradition Act 1968 (Act 14 of 1968 as amended in 2000)

[79] See Wyngaert & Stessens (n 62) 783

[80] *Joseph Aumeier's* case of 1980 involving Belgium and Germany (Laatste Nieuws, 5 Nov. 1990) cited in Wyngaert & Stessens (n 62) at 785

[81] Wyngaert & Stessens ibid

[82] ibid

previously rendered its judgement.[83] Similarly, Williams states that 'double jeopardy safeguard should be broadened to encompass acquittals and convictions in the requested, requesting or third states…' [84]

In light of foregoing, it is plain that national approaches diverge concerning the use of double jeopardy as a ground of refusal, in terms of the forum of the previous conviction. According to Wyngaert and Stessens, since the domestic laws of many states do not always recognise the res-judicata effect of foreign criminal judgments, efforts are needed to create an international double jeopardy system.[85]

The international conventions on terrorism and organised crime were expected to harmonise national approaches by providing a universal formula as regards the forum, the previous judgement of which may operate as a bar to extradition or mutual legal assistance. Two reasons gave rise to this expectation. Firstly, the conventions gave jurisdictional competence over the crimes set forth by them to more than one state. This made it more likely in transnational crimes, as compared to ordinary crimes, that the offence charged in the extradition or interrogation request may have previously been adjudicated upon by one or more parties involved.[86] Secondly, the conventions purport to establish a cooperative network amongst states following distinct legal systems which may or may not have bilateral treaties with each other.[87] To synchronise their

---

[83] ibid at 786 & 803

[84] Williams (n 5) at 216

[85] See Wyngaert & Stessens (n 62) 786 & 803

[86] See for instance article 6 of the Terrorist Bombing Convention 1997. It contains a non-exhaustive list of states competent to exercise jurisdiction over the offences including states of active and passive nationality, territoriality and state of registration of the ship or aircraft. Identical provisions can be seen in all transnational treaties under consideration. See also Chapter 2 above.

[87] See for instance, article 44 the UN Convention against Corruption 2003. The article binds only those states which do not make extradition conditional on the existence of bilateral treaties, whereas states making extradition conditional on such treaties are only recommended to consider the Convention as legal basis of extradition. For corresponding provisions, see article 9 the Hague Convention 1970, article 8 the Montreal Convention 1971, article 8 the Protection of Diplomats Convention 1973, article 10 the Hostages Convention 1979, article 11 the Nuclear Materials Convention 1980, article 11 the Rome Convention 1988, article 9 the Terrorist Bombing Convention 1997, article 11 the Terrorism Financing Convention 1999, article 13 the Nuclear Terrorism Convention 2005, article 6 the UN Convention against Drugs 1988, article 16 the Organised Crime Convention 2000 and article 12 the Beijing Convention 2010.

approaches, it was necessary to provide a consensual rule with respect to the forum of previous conviction. However, the conventions fell short of the expectation, as they left it entirely up to the requested state to determine the conditions of surrender or interrogation, including the application of double jeopardy as a ground for refusal of assistance and hence determination as to the suitability of the previous forum.[88]

Interestingly, the Extradition Treaty between France and Canada 1988 provides a workable solution to the controversy surrounding the forum, the previous judgements of which may operate as a bar to extradition or interrogation. According to that treaty, if a previous conviction occurs in the requested state, it constitutes a mandatory ground for refusal. On the other hand, if it takes place in the requesting or a third state, it represents an optional ground for refusal.[89] The approach centres on controlling the use of double jeopardy as a ground for refusal and appears far more effective in facilitating state cooperation in extradition and mutual legal assistance as compared to the general obligation to provide fair treatment.

3.1.1.3) Offences or facts

Another controversy surrounding the use of double jeopardy as a ground for refusal, relates to the scope of the previous judgement.[90] It raises the issue whether surrender or interrogation should be barred only when the offender has previously been tried for precisely the 'same offence' to which the request for extradition or mutual legal assistance relates or should it also be precluded if the request relates to a different charge but arises out of the 'same transaction.'[91] Put differently, can a person found guilty of theft in country A, be subsequently extradited to country B under the aggravated charge of robbery arising out of the same conduct which led to his earlier conviction or acquittal.[92]

National approaches are again at odds concerning this aspect of the double jeopardy rule. For instance, the UK-UAE Extradition Treaty 2008 obliges the parties to refuse extradition when the request relates to an ‘offence’ for which the accused has previously been convicted or acquitted.[93] This may be contrasted to 1997 Extradition Treaty between China and Singapore

[88] See (n 228) Chapter 3 above
[89] See Article 4 & 5 Canada-France Extradition Treaty 1988
[90] Wyngaert & Stessens (n 62) 789
[91] ibid
[92] ibid at 779
[93] See article III (3) UK-UAE Extradition Treaty 2008

which obliges the parties to refuse extradition if the offender has previously been tried for the offence to which request for extradition relates or for 'any other offence constituted by the same act'.[94] The latter approach reflects prioritization of human rights over state cooperation because it blocks extradition for every offence arising out of the conduct which led to previous judgement.[95]

The disagreement surrounding the application of double jeopardy to facts or specific crimes poses a considerable challenge in bringing to justice transnational offenders because many of these offences constitute complex aggregate crimes.[96] The features of complexity and aggregation imply that either several individual facts form part of one scheme or the criminal situation continues to develop.[97] For example, a person involved in drug trafficking across the border of two states can be charged with export of narcotics in one state and their import in the other. Furthermore, he may as well be charged with inter-state transportation of narcotics and their unauthorised possession by either of the two states.[98] Thus, four different offences can be carved out of a single transaction. Suppose he is convicted for the minor offence of unauthorised possession [99] and his extradition is

---

[94] See article 5(2) of Hong-Kong, China-Singapore Extradition Treaty 1997. See also article 7(4) of Singapore Extradition Act 1968:

> A person shall not be liable to be surrendered to a foreign State in respect of an offence if he has been acquitted or pardoned by a competent tribunal or authority in any country, or has undergone the punishment provided by the law of, or of a part of, any country, in respect of that offence or of another offence constituted by the same act or omission as that offence.

< http://www.oecd.org/dataoecd/4/44/39368700.pdf> [Date accessed 21/03/23]

[95] Williams (n 5) 213

[96] Bruce Zagaris, 'US Cooperation against Transnational Organised Crime' 44 Wayne State Law Review (1998-1999) 1401 at 1425-1426

[97] ibid

[98] The Drugs Convention requires the criminalization of all four offences of import, export, transportation and possession of Drugs. See article 3(1)(a)(i) and (c)(i) of the UN Drugs Convention 1988

[99] The Drugs Convention provides that the offence of possession can be criminalized subject to national Constitutions and basic legal principles. See article 3(1)(C)(i) of the Drugs Convention 1988; According to Taylor, this provision can be interpreted to mean, states are entitled to provide minor punishments for possession, particularly when its purpose is consumption. See David R. Bewley-Taylor, 'Challenging the UN Drug Control Conventions: Problems and Possibilities' 14 International Journal of Drug Policy (2003) 171 at 171. A number of states while implementing this provision make the act of possession punishable with lesser penalties such as simple fine. For example, article 9(a) of Control of

later requested for the aggregate crime of inter-state transportation.[100] If the requested state applies double jeopardy to the entire transaction, the extradition will have to be refused resulting in impunity for more serious offences.

Similarly, the crime of human trafficking includes the offences of abduction and transportation of individuals beyond national borders for commercial exploitation.[101] When these crimes are committed by organised criminal groups, different tasks are usually assigned to individual members of the group. Let us assume that some members are entrusted with the task of abduction and transportation in one state and the others with the commercial exploitation in another. The conviction of the former for abduction alone may preclude their extradition or interrogation for the aggregate crime of human trafficking, provided the requested state applies double jeopardy to entire criminal transaction in its extradition and mutual assistance laws.

Accordingly, it has been argued that application of double jeopardy to specific offences, rather than to the entire transaction, appears desirable in cases involving transnational crimes. If the rule is applied to the entire transaction, the offender may avoid punishment for more serious crimes which might be discovered subsequently and relate to the same transaction.[102] However, the international conventions on terrorism and organised crime provide no such guideline, in spite of the fact that crimes proscribed by them are prone to aggregation and complication.

Obviously, the criterion of states applying double jeopardy to facts differs from those applying it to specific offences. In case, extradition or mutual

---

Narcotics Substances Act 1997 of Pakistan provides two years maximum imprisonment for possession and simple fine as minimum punishment.

[100] Transportation of Drugs is generally considered much serious offence as compare to possession or consumption. For example, Pakistan's Law on drug trafficking provides death sentence as maximum punishment for transportation of drugs and 14 years imprisonment as minimum punishment. See article 9(c) of Control of Narcotics Substances Act 1997

[101] See article 3(a) Human Trafficking Protocol to the Organized Crime Convention 2000:

> Trafficking in persons shall mean the recruitment, transportation, transfer, harbouring or receipt of persons, by means of the threat or use of force or other forms of coercion, of abduction, of fraud, of deception, of the abuse of power or of a position of vulnerability or of the giving or receiving of payments or benefits to achieve the consent of a person having control over another person, for the purpose of exploitation...

[102] Wyngaert & Stessens (n 62) 792

legal assistance is to take place between states following these two conflicting approaches, surrender or interrogation will be deemed barred in one state but not in the other. This leaves the matter effectively into the hands of requested state, the subordination of whose discretion is said to be the primary aim of the regime set forth by the international counterterrorism and organised crime conventions.

3.2) Right to be protected against time-barred prosecutions

The principle of prescription or time-barred prosecutions constitutes another ground for making an offence non-punishable or excluding criminal responsibility. It protects an offender from long delayed prosecutions that may prejudice his human rights.[103] In the words of Doyle, 'the purpose of a statute of limitation in a criminal case is to ensure the prompt prosecution of criminal charges and thereby spare the accused of the burden of having to defend against stale charges after memories may have faded or evidence is lost'.[104]

Lapse of time bars prosecution under the national statutes of limitation that set a maximum time after an event within which legal proceedings based on that event must be brought.[105] For instance, US federal law provides a limitation of eight years for bringing criminal proceedings against non-violent violations of terrorism-associated statutes.[106] However, no limitation is provided for bringing action against violent violations.[107] In general, limitation periods are longer for more serious offenses.[108]

The principle at domestic level prevents an accused from trial for time barred charges. At international level, it precludes a requested state from extraditing a fugitive or providing legal assistance with respect to his crime, if the prosecution of the crime has become barred by lapse of time. For example, article 5 of the US-Switzerland Extradition Treaty 1990 obliges the parties to refuse extradition when the prosecution of the person

---

103 Sharon A William (n 5) 216

104 Charles Doyle, 'Statutes of Limitation in Federal Criminal Cases: An Overview' CRS Report for Congress (April 9, 2007) <http://www.fas.org/sgp/crs/misc/RL31253.pdf> [Date accessed 21/03/23]

105 Doyle (n 104)

106 See 18 U.S.C. 3286 (a) Extension of Statutes of Limitation for certain Terrorism Offences

107 ibid

108 Doyle (n 104)

sought would be barred by lapse of time under the domestic law of the Requesting Party.[109]

Although the principle is not universally applied in criminal proceedings, it is widely applied in bilateral treaties and domestic laws on extradition and mutual legal assistance as a ground for refusal of assistance. For instance, the principle appears in article 10 of the European Convention on Extradition 1957, article 8(6) of the Chinese Extradition Law 2000 and article 4(1)(c) of the Australia-Indonesia Mutual Assistance Treaty of 1995. Notably, it also finds expression under article 3(f) of the UN Model Treaty on Extradition 1990. Therefore, harmony is needed in national systems with respect to giving protection against time-barred prosecutions, so that the requesting state's failure to guarantee that right may not give opportunity to the requested state to block surrender or interrogation.

To bring harmony, the international conventions on terrorism and organised crime oblige the parties to provide fair treatment to the offenders in accordance with national, international and human rights law. Since the right to be protected against time-barred prosecutions enjoys widespread recognition in national constitutions and criminal codes, the right may be said to be implied in the obligation to provide fair treatment.[110] This view draws support from several provisions of the conventions which recommend that parties provide longer statutes of limitation for crimes established by the conventions.[111]

The fair treatment obligation is directed towards making national justice systems harmonious with respect to the provision of human rights to offenders. However, the potential for conflict lies in the application of these rights as grounds for refusal of assistance in extradition and mutual assistance proceedings. Thus, even if each party guarantees protection

---

[109] See article 5 of the Extradition Treaty between the Government of United States of America and the Government of Swiss Confederation. Signed at Washington on November 14, 1990 [hereinafter US-Switzerland Extradition Treaty 1990]

[110] YBILC (n 50); See also Rozakis (n 45); Plachta, 'Contemporary Problems of Extradition' (n 26)

[111] See for instance, article 11(5) of the Organised Crime Convention 2000:

Each State Party shall, where appropriate, establish under its domestic law a long statute of limitations period in which to commence proceedings for any offence covered by this Convention and a longer period where the alleged offender has evaded the administration of justice.

For corresponding provisions, see article 29 of the UN Convention against Corruption 2003 and article 3(8) the Drugs Convention 1988

against time-barred prosecutions, surrender or interrogation can still be refused where the requested state applies the right differently as a ground for refusal under its extradition and mutual assistance laws, from the way of its protection is guaranteed by the requesting state.

3.2.1) Dissimilarities in national approaches concerning the use of time-barred prosecution as a ground for refusal of assistance

States-Parties to the international conventions on terrorism and organised crime can be classified into two distinct groups: states relying on bilateral treaties for the provision of assistance and states depending on international conventions themselves.[112] It will be argued, in relation to both of these groups, the obligation, under the international conventions, to provide fair treatment, falls short of producing enough harmony in national rules on human rights protection, as to enable the parties to satisfy multiple applications of time barred prosecutions as a ground for refusal of assistance. As a result, complications arise in bringing to justice transnational offenders.

3.2.1.1) Disparity with respect to applicable limitation law

The rule against time barred prosecutions excludes criminal responsibility or makes an offence non-punishable, if prosecution for the offense charged, or enforcement of the penalty, has become barred by lapse of time under the applicable limitation law.[113] Bilateral treaties diverge as regards the law deemed relevant for blocking surrender or interrogation on the ground of time barred prosecutions. In some treaties the applicable limitation law is that of the requested state; in others it is that of the requesting state. Under a few treaties, either state's statute of limitations is deemed relevant for the purposes of blocking extradition or mutual legal assistance. For example, China-Korea Extradition Treaty 2002 provides that extradition shall be refused when the person sought has, under the law of 'either party', become immune to prosecution by lapse of time.[114] Conversely, India-Australia Extradition Treaty 2008 precludes extradition if the prosecution has become time barred under the law of the 'Requesting State'.[115] On the other hand, Canada-Spain Extradition Treaty 1989 obliges

---

[112] See (n 87) above

[113] Charles Doyle (n 104)

[114] See article 3(3) of China-Korea Extradition Treaty 2002; See also article 10 of the European Convention on Extradition 1957; See also article 3(e) UN Model Treaty on Extradition 1990

[115] See article 4(1)(b) of India-Australia Extradition Treaty 2008

the parties to refuse extradition when the prosecution is time barred under the 'Requested State's' statute of limitation.[116]

In 1980, Australia requested extradition of *Kamrin* from the US on charges of fraud committed in 1974. Under US law, the offence committed in Australia was time- barred for the purposes of prosecution. The offender challenged his extradition on this ground. The 9th Circuit Court rejected the objection by observing that according to the applicable bilateral treaty it was the requesting state's law (Australia's) that was relevant for the purposes of blocking extradition under the rule against time barred prosecutions.[117] Since Australian law did not attach any time limitation for prosecution of the crime in question, extradition was granted.[118] This case provides an example of a requesting state's limitation law being deemed relevant for the purposes of barring extradition under the rule of time barred prosecutions.

The *Kamrin* case reveals that conflicting national approaches towards 'applicable limitation law' pose no real difficulties in situations where state cooperation is to take place between two states, having a single bilateral treaty between them. However, in transnational crimes where the crime spreads across national frontiers, in terms of its perpetration or nationality or location of the victim or offender, it is possible that that the crime takes place in one state, the evidence is located somewhere else and the offender is found in yet another state. For example, in money laundering cases, the crime through which illegal proceeds are generated is committed in one state, the conversion of unlawful wealth takes place in another, while the offender might be found somewhere else.[119] In such cases, more than one bilateral treaty might be in operation with respect to a single crime. Each bilateral treaty could provide different rule for blocking state cooperation on the basis of time barred prosecutions. The situation obviously leads to difficulties in securing the surrender of fugitives or obtaining evidence with respect to a fugitive's crime.

For example, the Australia-India Extradition Treaty 2008 mandates the refusal of extradition when the prosecution or punishment is barred under

[116] See article III (4) of Canada-Spain Extradition Treaty 1989
[117] *Jeffrey Phillip Kamrin v. United States of America*, 725 F.2d 1225, Decided by United States Court of Appeals Ninth Circuit on Feb 14, 1984
[118] ibid
[119] For definition of Money Laundering, see article 3(b) of the Drugs Convention 1988

the law of the 'requesting state'.[120] Conversely, the Australia-Indonesia Mutual Legal Assistance Treaty 1995 provides that assistance shall be refused where it is barred by lapse of time under the law of the 'requested state'.[121] If Australia claims extradition of a fugitive from India, it is Australian limitation law which will be deemed relevant for the purposes of limitation. However, in case the evidence of his crime is located in Indonesia, Australia will have to comply with the Indonesian limitation law for the purposes of mutual legal assistance. Supposing prosecution is time- barred under Indonesian law, the fugitive will have to be set free for the want of evidence.

The above complications have led some states to adopt a different approach, according to which neither state's limitation law, should be deemed relevant for the purposes of blocking extradition or mutual legal assistance on the ground of time barred prosecutions. For example, Article 6 of the Extradition Treaty between the UK and US 2003 provides, '[t]he decision by the Requested State whether to grant the request for extradition shall be made without regard to any statute of limitations in either State.'[122] This approach underlies the advancement of state cooperation at the expense of human rights.[123] Accordingly, the treaty was subjected to severe criticism in view of its disregard for human rights.[124] For example, the cross-party joint committee on human rights of the UK called for the urgent renegotiation of the treaty.[125]

3.2.1.2) States not applying statutes of limitation to criminal proceedings

The International Conventions on terrorism and organised crime purport to establish a cooperative network among a variety of national justice systems. Some of these systems do not even apply statutes of limitation to criminal proceedings, yet they are required to observe the limitation laws of their treaty partners in extradition and mutual assistance proceedings. The reason is that the conventions conclusively declare that conditions of state cooperation, including grounds of refusal, shall be determined in

---

[120] See article 4(1)(b) India-Australia Extradition Treaty 2008
[121] See article 4(1)(c) Australia-Indonesia Mutual Assistance Treaty 1995
[122] See section 6 of the Extradition Treaty between the UK and US 2003
[123] Bruce Zagaris, *International White Collar Crime: Cases and materials* (New York: Cambridge University Press 2010) at 325
[124] 'Call for Over-haul of UK Extradition Rules' *BBC News UK* (June 22, 2011) <http://www.bbc.co.uk/news/uk-politics-13867921> [Date accessed 21/03/23]
[125] ibid

accordance with the national law of the requested state.[126] For example, the Limitation Act 1908 of Pakistan does not apply to criminal proceedings.[127] In the same way, the Limitation Act 1980 of the UK only relates to civil claims.[128] If either of the two states seeks extradition or mutual legal assistance from France, assuming both Pakistan and UK have no bilateral treaty with France, the requesting state will have to abide by the limitation law of France because the latter duly applies limitation to criminal proceedings.[129]

It is thus obvious that states relying on the international conventions as legal basis for cooperation are obliged to observe the limitation statutes of the requested state regardless of the dictates of their own law. Consequently, if the requested state does not apply such statutes to crime, the due process rights of the offender will be compromised,[130] and if it does but the requesting state does not, the interests of the requesting state will suffer.[131]

The mutual assistance efforts between Pakistan and Switzerland in relation to the recovery of the former's embezzled wealth, provides but one example of how the interests of the requesting state could be imperilled if it does not apply statutes of limitation to criminal proceedings but the requested state does.

In 1997, Pakistan sought assistance from Switzerland for the return of $60 million frozen by the Swiss government on charge of money laundering.[132]

---

126 See (n 228) Chapter 3 above

127 See the Limitation Act 1908, Act No. IX of 1908 [hereinafter the Limitation Act 1908 of Pakistan]

128 See Limitation Act 1980, 1980 Chapter 58 [hereinafter Limitation Act 1980 of UK]

129 For the application of Limitation to Criminal Offences in France, see article 112-2 (4) of the French Penal Code 1994 <http://www.legifrance.gouv.fr/content/download/1957/13715/version/4/file/Code_33.pdf> [Date accessed 21/03/23]

130 Williams (n 5) 217

131 ibid

132 Mohammed Rizwan 'Switzerland Ready to Cooperate in Zardari Graft Cases'.*The Express Tribune* (*January 18th, 2012*) <http://tribune.com.pk/story/323226/switzerland-ready-to-cooperate-in-zardari-graft-cases/> [Date accessed 21/03/23]; See also Umar Cheema 'Experts Confused at Swiss Time Bar' *The News Pakistan* (January 20, 2012)

The money was frozen in compliance with a judgement delivered by a Swiss local court holding that the money was derived from the crime of corruption involving two Swiss companies, the late Prime Minister of Pakistan, Benazir Bhutto and her husband.[133] Since Pakistan had no mutual assistance treaty with Switzerland, assistance was sought in 1997 through diplomatic channels.[134] In 2007, then President Pervez Musharraf of Pakistan promulgated an amnesty law entitled National Reconciliation Ordinance (NRO) 2007 withdrawing all criminal charges against the late Prime Minister and her husband, including the asset recovery proceedings in Switzerland.[135] Consequently, the government of Pakistan filed a petition before the relevant Swiss court requesting the withdrawal of the application regarding the asset recovery proceedings.[136]

In 2008, the husband of the late Prime Minister Bhutto, Asif Ali Zardari, became the President of Pakistan and, as such, was vested with sovereign immunity against all criminal proceedings by virtue of article 248 of the Constitution of Pakistan 1973.[137] In 2010, the Supreme Court of Pakistan, after declaring the controversial amnesty law (NRO) unconstitutional, directed the government to write a letter to Swiss authorities requesting the revival of asset recovery proceedings.[138] The government however claimed it was unable to comply with this direction on the ground that the applicable treaty between Pakistan and Switzerland, the UN Convention against Corruption 2003, required the requesting party under article 61 to

---

<http://www.thenews.com.pk/Todays-News-2-88577-Experts-confused-at-Swiss-time-bar> [Date accessed 21/03/23]; Terence J Sigamony 'Will Swiss Cases Follow Zardari When He Leaves Office?' *The Nation Pakistan* (June 27 2012) <http://www.nation.com.pk/pakistan-news-newspaper-daily-english-online/national/27-Jun-2012/will-swiss-cases-follow-zardari-when-he-leaves-office> [Date accessed 21/03/23]

133 Judgment of Swiss Magistrate in *SGS, Cotecna* case <http://www.assetrecovery.org/kc/node/2fb39f42-5114-11de-bacd-a7d8a60b2a36.8> [date accessed 21/03/23]

134 *Pakistan v. Zardari et al*, [2006] EWHC 2411 (Comm) <http://www.bailii.org/ew/cases/EWHC/Comm/2006/2411.html Noorani A.G.> [date accessed 21/03/23]

135 The National Reconciliation Ordinance (NRO), October 5 2007, Declared null and void by the Supreme Court of Pakistan on December 16,2009 [hereinafter the National Reconciliation Ordinance 2007 of Pakistan]

136 Mohammed Rizwan (n 132)

137 See article 248 of the Constitution of Pakistan 1973

138 *Dr Mobashir Hassan etc v. Federation of Pakistan etc* (PLD 2010 SC 265) <http://www.supremecourt.gov.pk/web/user_files/File/NRO_Judgment.pdf> [Date accessed 21/03/23]

obtain a domestic judgement as regards the predicate offence before seeking the assistance of a foreign state for recovery of assets.[139] Since domestic proceedings were barred under the constitutional immunity enjoyed by the President, this pre-requisite could not be met.[140] In other words, the government claimed that proceedings for recovery of assets could not be initiated in Switzerland so long as Pakistan itself did not render criminal judgement concerning the offence through which proceeds were generated.

Pakistani courts were, however, precluded from delivering such judgement until October 2013, when the constitutional immunity of the President would come to an end along with his term in office.[141]

Because section 97 of the Swiss criminal code provided a fifteen year time limit for bringing asset recovery proceedings[142] and since Pakistan originally approached Switzerland in 1997, the Swiss time limit was considered to have elapsed in September 2012, well in advance of the President losing his immunity.[143]

The position taken by the government did not satisfy the Supreme Court of Pakistan, which held the government guilty of contempt and disqualified then- Prime Minister, Yousuf Raza Gilani as punishment for wilful disobedience of its order.[144] Subsequently, the government wrote a letter to Swiss authorities calling for the reopening of the asset recovery cases.[145] In reply, the Attorney- General, of Geneva, Switzerland stated that the money laundering cases against President Zardari could not be reopened,

---

[139] See Mohammed Rizwan (n132)

[140] ibid

[141] Umar Cheema (n 132)

[142] See article 97(1) (b) of Swiss Criminal Code of 21 December 1937, SR 311.0 (Status as of January 2013) [hereinafter Swiss Criminal Code 1937]. The article provides 15 year time limit for bringing criminal proceedings if the offence is punishable by a custodial sentence of more than 3 years

[143] See Mohammed Rizwan (n 132)

[144] *Muhammad Azhar Siddique vs. Federation of Pakistan etc.* Judgement of the Supreme Court of Pakistan dated 19th June, 2012 passed in Constitution Petition No. 40/2012; See also *Federation of Pakistan v. Dr. Mubashir Hassan* (PLD 2012 SC 106)

[145] *The News Pakistan* (June 19, 2012) Graft Cases against President Zardari cannot be reopened: Swiss authorities <http://www.pakistantoday.com.pk/2013/06/18/news/national/graft-cases-against-president-zardari-cannot-be-reopened-swiss-authorities> [date accessed 21/03/23]

on the ground that the statutory limitation period of fifteen years had expired and no new evidence or facts had been revealed.[146]

It is therefore clear that although Pakistan did not apply statutes of limitation to criminal proceedings, it was obliged to observe Swiss limitation law in regard to asset recovery proceedings. This was so because the UN Convention against Corruption 2003, which constituted the legal basis of cooperation between the two states, stipulated that *conditions* and *procedures* of state cooperation shall be determined in accordance with the domestic law of the requested state.[147] Obviously, this arrangement disregards the interest of the requesting state which happens to be the actual victim of the crime in the case in hand.

To safeguard the interests of the requesting states, the international conventions on terrorism and organised crime could have borrowed a provision from domestic statutes of limitation suggesting that time limitation shall not apply where delay is caused by the offender's own misconduct.[148] Such a provision would have addressed the concerns of both, states applying statutes of limitation to crime and states not applying them. However, no such middle ground can be found in the conventions.

It is thus apparent that fair treatment obligation may fail to address the complications arising in extradition and mutual legal assistance pursuant to multiple applications of time-barred prosecutions as grounds for refusal of assistance. As regards states relying on bilateral treaties, the obligation is found deficient with respect to providing any consensual rule concerning the limitation law deemed relevant for applying time barred prosecutions as a ground of refusal. In relation to states depending on the international conventions, the obligation fails to provide any mechanism to safeguard the interests of a requesting state which does not apply statutes of limitation to crime. Hence, the establishment of only a general obligation to provide fair treatment can hardly be expected to make national legal systems harmonious enough to overcome the hurdle of time barred prosecutions. As a result, the discretion of the requested state to refuse state cooperation remains intact. This denies the scholarly claim

---

[146] Hasnaat Malik, *Daily Times Pakistan* (Wednesday, June 19, 2013) Swiss money laundering case buried once and for all <http://www.dailytimes.com.pk/default.asp?page=2013%5C06%5C19%5Cstory_19-6-2013_pg1_2.> [date accessed 21/03/23]

[147] See section 46 of the UN Convention against Corruption 2003

[148] See for instance section 5 of the Limitation Act 1908 of Pakistan

that the mandatory obligations evidence the emergence of a new treaty regime subjecting sovereign discretion to collective law enforcement.

Up to this point, the effectiveness of fair treatment obligation in harmonising national approaches towards provision of due process rights has been discussed. In the next section, I shall discuss the usefulness of the obligation in unifying national approaches towards provision of fundamental human rights and its impact on facilitating state cooperation in extradition and mutual legal assistance.

Section 4) Effectiveness of the fair treatment obligation in facilitating the fulfilment fundamental human rights as grounds for refusal of assistance

4.1) Right to be protected against torture

Right to be protected against torture safeguards an offender from being subjected to physical distress. At domestic level, evidence obtained through torture vitiates the trial, at international level, possibility of torture allows a requested state to block extradition or mutual legal assistance, when it has reason to believe that if surrendered or allowed to be interrogated, the suspect would be tortured in the requesting state. Therefore, harmony is needed in national justice systems with respect to giving protection against torture, so that the requesting state's failure to guarantee that right may not give justification to the requested state to refuse cooperation.

To harmonise national systems, international convention on terrorism and organised crime impose mandatory obligation upon the parties to provide fair treatment to persons facing any proceedings under the treaties. Since the obligation requires the parties to provide all those rights which are guaranteed by national and international law including human rights law, the right to be protected against torture, having the status of *jus cogens*, naturally finds its place under it. For example, it was held by the ICJ in *Belgium v. Senegal*, '[i]n the Court's opinion, the prohibition of torture is part of customary international law and it has become a peremptory norm *(jus cogens)*.'[149]

Whereas rights such as protection against double jeopardy and time-barred prosecutions arise from statutory laws and bilateral treaties,

[149] See *Questions relating to the Obligation to Prosecute or Extradite (Belgium v. Senegal)*, ICJ Reports 2012, p. 422. Judgement of July 20, 2012 at para 99

prohibition against torture derives from international human rights law.[150] For instance, article 3 of the European Convention on Human Rights (ECHR) provides, 'No one shall be subjected to torture or to inhuman or degrading treatment or punishment'.[151] Similarly, article 7 of the International Covenant on Civil and Political Rights (ICCPR) states, 'No one shall be subjected to torture or cruel, inhuman or degrading treatment or punishment...'[152]

As an off-shoot of this prohibition, article 3(1) of the UN Convention against Torture 1984 provides, 'No State Party shall expel, return ("refouler") or extradite a person to another State where there are substantial grounds for believing that he would be in danger of being subjected to torture.'[153] The principle also finds its expression as a mandatory ground of refusal under article 3(f) of the UN Model Treaty on Extradition 1990.[154]

Scholarly opinion is near unanimous concerning the *jus cogens* status of prohibition against torture.[155] In the words of Dugard and Wyngaert, 'If any human rights norm enjoys the status of *Jus Cogens*, it is prohibition on torture'.[156] Likewise, it has been suggested that a restriction on the extradition of a fugitive likely to face torture in the requesting state also represents a peremptory norm of international law.[157] For example, Plachta maintains, in the context of extradition and mutual legal assistance, there are only a few human rights which are non-derogable, these include prohibition against torture.[158] This has led some commentators to observe that, even if the possibility of torture is not included as a ground for refusal under the relevant bilateral treaty or statutory law, an offender can still raise it as an objection to extradition under customary international law.[159]

---

[150] Plachta 'Contemporary Problems of Extradition' (n 26) 66

[151] See article 3 of the European Convention on Human Rights, signed at Rome on 4 November 1950 [hereinafter ECHR]

[152] See article 7 of the International Covenant on Civil and Political Rights, Adopted by the General Assembly of the United Nations with resolution 2200A (XXI) of 16 December 1966 [hereinafter ICCPR]

[153] See article 3(1) of the UN Convention against Torture 1984

[154] See article 3(f) of UN Model Treaty on Extradition 1990

[155] See Plachta 'Contemporary Problems of Extradition' (n 26) 65

[156] Dugard & Wyngaert (n 23) 198

[157] Aoife Duffy, 'Expulsion to face Torture? Non-Refoulment in International Law' 20 Int'l. J. of Refugee law (2008) 373 at 374

[158] See Plachta 'Contemporary Problems of Extradition' (n 26) 65

[159] See Duffy (n 157)

4.1.1) Need to reconcile the prohibition against torture with the severe punishment requirement of transnational criminality

Despite the clear import of the obligation to provide fair treatment and despite the fact that the right to be immune from torture forms part of it, it is difficult to suggest that the obligation has led to harmonisation of national justice systems and facilitation of state cooperation in law enforcement. Since the international conventions on terrorism and organised crime do not provide definition of torture, states at times find it difficult to reconcile the right not to be subject to such treatment with the severe punishment requirement of crimes set forth by these conventions. As a result, where the law of requesting state provides severe punishment for the crime in respect of which surrender or interrogation is sought, the requested state may refuse cooperation, notwithstanding, the requesting state having guaranteed protection in compliance with the obligation to provide fair treatment.

A number of states, while establishing prohibition against torture, clarify that the prohibition also applies to cruel punishments. For example, article 3 of the ECHR, in addition to establishing prohibition against 'cruel treatment', also outlaws 'cruel punishment'.[160] In the same way, Chinese extradition law provides as mandatory ground of refusal, the possibility of the fugitive being subjected to 'cruel punishment' in the requesting state.[161] Likewise, Bulgaria's law of extradition requires the denial of extradition:

> if the person will be a subject of violence, torture or cruel, inhuman or humiliating penalty related with the prosecution and with the execution of the penalty as per the requirements of the international law in the applying country.[162]

It is thus clear that right to be protected against torture has been interpreted by some jurisdictions to include protection against cruel punishments. Significantly, the approach has been approved by the UN Model Treaty on Extradition 1990, which provides that extradition shall be refused where the person whose surrender is requested is likely to be subjected in the

---

160 See article 3 ECHR 1950

161 See article 8(7) of Chinese Extradition Law 2000

162 See article 7(5) of Extradition and European Arrest Warrant Act 2005, In force since 01/07/2005 [hereinafter Bulgarian Extradition Act 2005]

requesting state to torture or cruel, inhuman or degrading treatment or 'punishment'.[163]

Since many of the crimes established by the international conventions on terrorism and organised crime comprise serious offences such as hijacking and drug trafficking,[164] more often than not they are made punishable with severe punishments such as death or life imprisonment.[165] These punishments have been held to be cruel in some national court decisions.[166] Hence, their existence in the law of the requesting state provides the requested state with a ground for denial of assistance.

Since international conventions on terrorism and organised crime purport to establish a cooperative network amongst diverse legal systems, it is possible that some states might consider these punishments as cruel, while others might not. This leads to disharmony in the national grounds for refusal of assistance and possible failure of law enforcement cooperation. Therefore, further guidance is needed with respect to the application of the right to be immune from torture as a ground for refusal of assistance in the specific context of transnational crimes. However, instead of providing clear guidelines differentiating severe punishments from torture, the international conventions regulating the acts of transnational terrorism and organised crime impose a general obligation to provide fair treatment to the offenders. Obviously, the obligations is insufficient to facilitate the fulfilment of multiple applications of torture as a ground for refusal of assistance under extradition and mutual legal assistance laws.

---

[163] See article 3(f) UN Model Treaty on Extradition 1990

[164] The seriousness of these offences is evident from references to their gravity in preambles of all transnational treaties. For example, preamble of the Hostages Convention 1979 provides 'Considering that taking of Hostages is an offence of grave concern to the international community…' Similarly, preamble of the Nuclear Materials Convention 1980 states 'convinced that offences relating to nuclear material are a matter of grave concern …' Likewise, preamble of the Drugs Convention 1988 reads:

> Deeply concerned by the magnitude of and rising trend in the illicit production of, demand for and traffic in narcotic drugs and psychotropic substances which pose a serious threat to health and welfare of human beings and adversely affect economic, cultural and political foundations of society...

[165] See Anti-Terrorism Act 1997 of Pakistan, The Unlawful Activities (Prevention) Act 1967 of India as amended in 2008, The Control of Narcotics Substances Act 1997 of Pakistan and The Narcotic Drugs and Psychotropic Substances Act, 1985 of India

[166] See text to (n 168-178) below

As a result, complications arise in the extradition of suspects whose crimes are punishable with death or life imprisonment in the requesting state. For example, when the ECtHR blocked the extradition of Abu Qatada from UK to Jordan on account of the offender having been convicted on the basis of evidence derived through torturing the co-accused, the British government regarded it an interference with its national justice system.[167]

4.1.2) Dissimilar national and regional approaches with respect to considering severe punishments as torture

4.1.2.1) Regional courts and monitoring bodies

The jurisprudence of regional courts and human rights monitoring bodies provides valuable insights into the view that the right to be protected against torture, inhuman treatment and cruel punishment might be violated if the fugitive is surrendered to a state which makes the offences charged in the extradition request punishable with death or life imprisonment. In the opinion of these courts and bodies, the prospect of a death penalty does not in itself constitute violation of the prohibition.[168] However, if the manner of execution is degrading to the physical and mental integrity of the extraditee, the same may amount to a breach of the right to be protected against inhuman and cruel punishment. Thus, the ECtHR observed in its landmark judgement in *Soering v. UK* that if the fugitive is likely to be put on death row and made to wait for a prolonged period for his execution in harsh conditions with ever present and mounting anguish of awaiting death, prohibition against cruel and inhuman treatment will be violated in his extradition.[169] Similarly, the Human Rights Committee observed in *Ng v. Canada,* that Canada was in breach of its obligation under the ICCPR when it extradited Mr. Ng to a state which provided death by asphyxiation

---

[167] *Othman (Abu Qatada) v. the United Kingdom* – 8139/09 [2012] ECHR 56; See also ANI (23rd January, 2012) David Cameron to Confront Court over Extraditing Suspected Osman; Europe News.net
<http://www.europenews.net/story/202878694> [Date accessed 21/03/23]

[168] For instance, article 6(2) of the ICCPR provides that the countries applying death penalty should reserve it for most serious offences. This implies that the penalty is not altogether abolished but has been required to be used sparingly, though the death was prohibited under article 1 of the Second Optional Protocol to the ICCPR, adopted by the General Assembly with resolution 44/128 of 15 December 1989 [Second Optional Protocol to the ICCPR 1989]

[169] *Soering v. The United Kingdom,* 1/1989/161/217, Council of Europe: European Court of Human Rights, 7 July 1989
<http://www.unhcr.org/refworld/docid/3ae6b6fec.html> [Date accessed 21/03/23]

as a mode of punishment for the offence charged.[170] According to the Committee, execution by gas asphyxiation would not meet the test of 'least possible physical and mental suffering' and would constitute cruel and inhuman treatment, in violation of article 7 of the Covenant.[171]

In the same way, in *Kafkaris v. Cyprus,* the ECtHR held that the imposition of an irreducible life sentence may raise an issue under article 3 of the ECHR which establishes prohibition against torture, cruel, inhuman and degrading treatment or punishment.[172] Likewise, in *Babar Ahmad and others v. UK,* the extradition of five terror suspects including *Babar Ahmad* and *Abu Hamza* from the UK to US was halted by the ECtHR because the offence charged in the extradition request provided for life imprisonment in solitary confinement without the possibility of parole.[173] The Court later ruled that although the conditions of imprisonment might not violate article 3 of the ECHR, it was still desirable in the interest of proper conduct of proceedings that the applicants should not be extradited.[174] As per the Court's opinion, the imposition of an irreducible life sentence would not in itself constitute a breach of the right to be protected against torture unless it were grossly or clearly disproportionate to individual circumstances of the offender i.e. when further imprisonment would no longer be justified on any ground - whether for reasons of punishment, deterrence or public protection.[175]

---

[170] *Chitat Ng v. Canada*, Communication No. 469/1991 at para 16.4, U.N. Doc. CCPR/C/49/D/469/1991 (1994)

[171] ibid

[172] *Kafkaris v. Cyprus* [GC], no. 21906/04 ECHR 2008

[173] *Case of Babar Ahmad and Others v. the United Kingdom* (Applications nos. 24027/07, 11949/08, 36742/08, 66911/09 and 67354/09) ECtHR (Fourth Section) Admissibility Decision of 6 July 2010. See also Vikram Dodd 'Abu Hamza Can Be Extradited to US, Human Rights Court Rules' *The Guardian UK* (10/04/2012) <http://www.guardian.co.uk/uk/2012/apr/10/abu-hamza-extradited-us-court> [Date accessed 21/03/23].PA/Huffington Post UK 'Abu Hamza Extradition: Human Rights Judges Set To Rule Over Terrorist Charges' *The Huffington Post UK* (10/04/2012) <http://www.huffingtonpost.co.uk/2012/04/10/abu-hamza-extradition-america-terrorist-human-rights_n_1413907.html> [Date accessed 21/03/23]

[174] *Case of Babar Ahmad and Others v. the United Kingdom* ECtHR (Fourth Section) Strasbourg Judgment 10 April 2012

[175] ibid at para 70; See also *Kafkaris v. Cyprus* [GC], no. 21906/04 ECHR 2008 and *R (Wellington) v. Secretary of State for the Home Department* [2008] UKHL 72

Thus, according to regional courts and monitoring bodies entrusted with the task of ensuring state compliance with human rights treaties, the possibility of a death sentence or life imprisonment in the requesting state may provide a ground for refusal of extradition when the mode of punishment is cruel.

4.1.2.2) National approaches towards torture and severe punishment

The above rule is not applied in bilateral treaties and national laws on extradition, many of which allow the refusal of surrender merely for the possibility of death sentence in the requesting state regardless of the manner of execution. For example, article 5 of the India-China Extradition Treaty 1997 obliges the parties to refuse surrender when the offence for which extradition is requested is punishable by death in the requesting state but not under the laws of the requested state.[176] The principle has also been applied in some national court decisions concerning extradition of suspects involved in transnational crimes. For example, in the *Abu Salem* case, the Portuguese Supreme Court rejected an Indian request to add charges of terrorism against a suspect who was extradited to India for the crime of murder and whose extradition was subsequently cancelled by a Portuguese court for violation of speciality rule on the part of Indian government.[177] The reason for rejection of Indian request was the attraction of the death penalty under Indian counterterrorism laws.[178] Apparently, no consideration was given by the Portuguese Supreme Court

---

[176] See article 5 of the Agreement for the Surrender of Fugitive Offenders between the Government of Hong Kong and the Government of the Republic of India. Signed at Hong Kong on June 28, 1997 [hereinafter Hong Kong, China-India Extradition Treaty 1997]; See also article IX of Italy-US Extradition Treaty 1983 and article 11 of the European Convention on Extradition 1957

[177] PTI New Delhi 'Abu Salem's Extradition: Portugal's SC rejects CBI plea' *Daily News and Analysis India* (17/01/2012) <http://www.dnaindia.com/india/report_abu-salem-s-extradition-portugal-s-sc-rejects-cbi-plea_1638666 > [Date accessed 21/03/23].

The permission for adding charges subsequent to extradition is needed under the 'doctrine of Speciality' which provides that a requesting state is not entitled to prosecute or punish an offender for an offence for which his extradition was not granted by the requested state. See text to (n 90-93) Chapter no.3 above

[178] The Indian Express 'India Has No Locus Standi in Abu Salem Matter: Portugal Court' *The Indian Express* (10/07/12) <http://www.indianexpress.com/news/india-has-no-locus-standi-in-abu-salem-matter-portugal-court/972654/2> [Date accessed 21/03/23]

to the manner of execution, the possibility of the death penalty being considered sufficient to disallow the addition of the new charges.[179]

To bring about harmony in national approaches, it is desirable that the makers of international conventions on terrorism and organised crime should provide guidelines following the guidance of the ECtHR and the Human Rights Committee that extradition may only be refused when the mode of punishment is likely to be cruel and inhuman.

The inclusion of such an explanation seems all the more justified in view of the fact that many states provide exemplary punishments for crimes such as hijacking and drug trafficking in order to produce deterrent effect.[180] Interestingly, the legal sanction for providing these punishments comes from the international conventions themselves, which in some instances oblige the parties to make the offences punishable with severe penalties.[181] According to Lambert, the requirement of making offences punishable with 'severe penalties' under previous counterterrorism treaties was replaced in the Hostages Convention with 'appropriate penalties' because a number of delegates raised the objection that the use of the term 'severe' could lead to a misuse of the Convention to infringe upon human rights.[182] It shows that the conventions prior to the Hostages Convention 1979 require the states parties to make the offences established by them punishable with severe punishments.

In any case, the only inference that one can draw from the obligation to provide fair treatment is that the international conventions on terrorism and organised crime require the parties to provide protection to the offenders from the possibility of being subjected to torture, inhuman treatment and cruel punishment in the requesting state. What constitutes these factors for the purposes denying assistance, has been left to be determined by the requested state in accordance with its national law.[183]

---

[179] ibid

[180] See for instance, Anti-Terrorism Act 1997 of Pakistan; The Unlawful Activities (Prevention) Act 1967 of India as amended in 2008; The Control of Narcotics Substances Act (CNSA) 1997 of Pakistan and The Narcotic Drugs and Psychotropic Substances Act 1985 of India

[181] See article 2 the Hague Convention 1970; article 3 the Montreal Convention 1971 and article 3 the Beijing Convention 2010

[182] Lambert (n 48) 106

[183] See (n 228) chapter 3 above

4.1.3) Diplomatic assurance as an alternative

Counter to the international conventions on terrorism and organised crime, some bilateral and regional treaties on extradition and mutual legal assistance provide mechanisms better suited to balancing the right to be immune from torture with the severe punishment requirement of crimes established by these conventions. For example, article 6 of the UK-UAE Extradition Treaty 2008 allows the requested state to refuse extradition when the offence for which extradition is sought is punishable with death under the laws of the requesting state 'unless the requesting Party provides an assurance that the death penalty will not be imposed or, if imposed, will not be carried out.'[184] The mechanism of seeking diplomatic assurance is also present in the Australia-China Extradition Treaty 1993,[185] the UK-US Extradition Treaty 2003,[186] the European Convention on Extradition 1957[187] and many other bilateral treaties.

This technique has also been applied in some domestic and regional court decisions. For example, in *US v. Burns*, the Canadian Supreme Court held that it would be a violation of Canada's constitution to extradite an accused without assurances from the United States that the death penalty would not be imposed, or, if imposed, would not be carried out.[188]

Besides endorsing the rule of surrender subject to diplomatic assurance, some regional courts also lay down the mechanism of judicial scrutiny of a diplomatic assurance. For example, the ECtHR in 2008 case of *Saadi v. Italy* affirmed the principle that diplomatic assurances are subject to judicial review.[189] According to the Court, a diplomatic assurance in itself may not provide adequate safeguard against torture and the courts of the

---

[184] See article 6, Extradition Treaty between the United Kingdom of Great Britain and Northern Ireland and United Arab Emirates. Signed at London on 6 December 2006. Instruments of Ratification were exchanged on 3rd March 2008 and the Treaty entered into force on 2nd April 2008 [hereinafter UK-UAE Extradition Treaty 2008].

[185] See article 4, Agreement for the Surrender of Accused and the Convicted Persons between the Government of Australia and the Government of Hong-Kong. Signed at Hong Kong on 15 November 1993 [hereinafter Australia-China Extradition Treaty 1993]

[186] See article 7 US-UK Extradition Treaty 2003

[187] See article 11 the European Convention on Extradition 1957

[188] *United States v. Burns,* 2001 SCC 7, [2001] 1 SCR 283

[189] *Saadi v. Italy*, No. 32201/06, 128 (Eur.Ct. H.R. Feb 2, 2008) <http://www.echr.coe.int/>

requested state remain competent to declare it insufficient.[190] As per the facts of the case, Italy decided to deport Saadi to Tunisia, where he had been convicted in absentia for the crimes of being member of a terrorist organisation and incitement to terrorism.[191] Upon Italy's request, Tunisia provided diplomatic assurance that it would observe the standards of human rights as outlined by its national law and the international treaties to which it was a party.[192] Saadi challenged his deportation before the ECtHR. The court held that Tunisian diplomatic assurance was insufficient to ensure that the deportee would not be subjected to torture once surrendered.[193] The reasons advanced by the ECtHR for arriving at this conclusion were: formal nature of the assurance given by Tunisia, conviction of Saadi in absentia and Amnesty International and Human rights watch reports of Torture and ill treatment of terror suspects.[194] The judgement made it clear that while considering the adequacy of a diplomatic assurance, the courts of the requested state may look into the actions rather than words of the requesting state.[195]

In the same way, in the *Abu Qatada* case, the ECtHR identified the circumstances in which it could be lawful under the ECHR to extradite an individual to a state where the use of torture was prevalent. According to the Court, the arrangement entered into between the UK and Jordan requiring the latter to provide diplomatic assurance to guarantee human rights to deportees affords adequate safeguards against the violation of article 3 of the ECHR, which establishes prohibition against torture.[196] The Court held further that it did not consider that the general human rights situation in Jordan excluded the acceptance of diplomatic assurance from the Jordanian Government.[197]

---

[190] Ibid at para 147
[191] Ibid at para 29
[192] Ibid at para 54
[193] Ibid at para 54-55
[194] Ibid at para 143-148
[195] Alice Izumo, 'Diplomatic Assurances Against Torture & Ill treatment European Court of Human Rights Jurisprudence' 42 Columbia Human Rights Law Review (2010) 233 at 258
[196] See *Abu Qatada* Case (n 167) at para 187
[197] Despite these observations, the extradition of Abu Qatada was blocked for possible violation of article 6 of the ECHR which guaranteed fair trial to the accused. The court accepted defendant's claim that his extradition was requested on the basis of ex-parte convictions awarded by relying upon evidence obtained through torturing the co-accused and use of such evidence would violate his right

In the light of above, it is clear that the mechanism of obtaining diplomatic assurances represents an effective technique of facilitating the surrender or interrogation of an offender who is faced with the possibility of torture in the requesting state. Apparently, it addresses the concerns of both cooperation-centred and human rights oriented states. It therefore merits to be included in the international counterterrorism and organised crime conventions because the crimes set forth by them are prone to raise the issue of torture in extradition and mutual assistance proceedings.

4.2) Non Discrimination and freedom from persecution

Another important ground for refusal of state cooperation in law enforcement is the possibility of discrimination and persecution in the requesting state. Article 15 of the 1999 Terrorism Financing Convention elaborates it in these words:

> Nothing in this Convention shall be interpreted as imposing an obligation to extradite or to afford mutual legal assistance, if the requested State Party has substantial grounds for believing that the request for extradition for offences set forth in article 2 or for mutual legal assistance with respect to such offences has been made for the purpose of prosecuting or punishing a person on account of that person=s race, religion, nationality, ethnic origin or political opinion or that compliance with the request would cause prejudice to that person=s position for any of these reasons.[198]

This ground allows a requested state to refuse extradition or mutual legal assistance if it has reason to believe that in case of surrender or provision of assistance, the relator will be subjected to discrimination or persecution in the requesting state on racial, religious, ethnic or political grounds or his trial will be prejudiced because of any of these reasons.

Besides its recognition in international conventions on terrorism and organised crime, non-discrimination also frequently appears, as a ground for refusal in domestic laws and bilateral treaties on extradition and mutual legal assistance. For example, article 3(1) (b) of the Australia-Germany Extradition Treaty 1988 provides, the assistance shall be refused if:

---

to fair trial under the ECHR. See *Abu Qatada* case (n 167) at Para 193-194, 267, 268-291

[198] See article 15 the Terrorism Financing Convention 1999. See also article 44(15) the UN Convention against Corruption 2003, article14 Beijing Convention 2010, article 6(6) the Drugs Convention 1988 and article 16(14) the Organized Crime Convention 2000

> the Requested State has substantial grounds for believing that the request for extradition has been made for the purpose of prosecuting or punishing the person claimed on account of his race, religion, nationality or political opinions or that he might, if extradited, be prejudiced at his trial, or punished, detained or restricted in his personal liberty, by reason of his race, religion, nationality or political opinion.[199]

Similarly, article 5(2)(g) of the Extradition Act 1972 of Pakistan provides that no fugitive shall be surrendered if it is shown to the satisfaction of the court that 'he might if surrendered be prejudiced at his trial on racial, religious, national or political opinions'.[200]

Keeping in view the widespread application of discrimination as a ground for refusal of assistance, harmony is needed in national approaches with respect to giving protection against it, so that the requesting state's failure to guarantee that right may not allow the requested state to refuse extradition or mutual legal assistance. To establish harmony, the international conventions on terrorism and organised crime oblige the parties to provide fair treatment to the offenders. Since the obligation requires the parties to provide all those rights which are recognised by national and international law, including human rights law, the principle of non-discrimination, which is entrenched in human rights and extradition law, can be said to be implied.[201]

In spite of the clear inference that the obligation to provide fair treatment includes protection against discrimination, it is difficult to suggest that the same is likely to produce enough harmony in national legal systems as to facilitate extradition or mutual legal assistance. A major reason for this is the absence of any guidelines under the international conventions concerning the use of discrimination as a ground for refusal of extradition or mutual legal assistance. Consequently, states are free to give any interpretation to it as per the dictates of their national law. The ensuing disparity in national legal systems with respect to manner of giving protection against discrimination and the way of applying it as a ground for refusal may result in denial of surrender or interrogation.

---

[199] See 3(1)(b) of the Australia-Germany Extradition Treaty 1988

[200] See article 5(2)(g) the Extradition Act 1972 of Pakistan

[201] The principle of non-discrimination appears in article 3(2) of the European Convention on Extradition 1957, article 4(1)(c) of the UN Model Treaty on Mutual Legal Assistance 1990 and article 14(1) of the ICCPR

I shall now discuss one aspect of non-discrimination rule with respect to which national approaches diverge necessitating international regulation of the use of discrimination as a ground for refusal of assistance.

4.2.1 Absence of any universal standard to determine prejudice on account of political opinion

The rule of non-discrimination provides that a requested state shall not be bound to surrender a fugitive or to provide mutual assistance if it has grounds for believing that the request has been made for the purposes of prosecuting or punishing a relator on account of his race, religion nationality or political opinion. While discrimination on the basis of race, religion, nationality or ethnic origin can be ascertained from unfair national laws, it would be more difficult to agree upon the existence of political persecution in the requesting state.[202] For instance, when apartheid was practiced in South Africa, most states had severed their diplomatic ties with it, at the latter stages, at any rate. Since there was no extradition arrangement, questions of racial discrimination never even had to be raised.[203] However, when Libya showed its reluctance to extradite the Lockerbie suspects to either the US or UK, its argument on anticipated political persecution in the requesting states left the world court divided.[204]

The Libyan claim was based on the possible negative media publicity that would be associated with a trial in the requesting states and the existence of adverse statements of government officials, some of whom demanded that Libya pay compensation to the victims. As per the Libyan argument, on account of these factors, the Lockerbie suspects were unlikely to receive a fair trial in either of the requesting states.[205] While three judges in their separate and dissenting opinions concurred with the Libyan position, the rest did not.[206] A possible explanation for this divide could be

---

[202] Dugard & Wyngaert (n 23) 202

[203] Ibid

[204] *Questions of Interpretation and Application of the 1971 Montreal Convention arising from the Aerial Incident at Lockerbie (Libyan Arab Jamahiriya v. United Kingdom),* Provisional Measures,1992 ICJ 216 (Apr.14) Para 141,191 and148; See also Omer Y. Elegab, 'The Hague as a Seat of Lockerbie Trial: Some Constraints' 34 The International Lawyer (2000) 289 at 303

[205] ibid

[206] *Lockerbie* case ibid. Dissenting Judgements of Judges El-Khosheri and Ajibola and Separate opinions of Judge Shahabuddin and Bedjoui. See paragraphs 61-2, 141, 148 and 191; See also Elegab ibid

the founding of Libyan argument on abstract reasoning.[207] To make everyone agree to it, the argument had to be based on generally agreed principles. Evidently, therefore, in order to achieve a consistent approach towards application of discrimination as a ground for refusal of assistance, international guidance is needed with respect to the factors constituting political persecution.

The identification of these factors assumes greater significance in cooperative endeavours relating to terrorist offences because underlying all these offences is the motivation to achieve political aims.[208] Whereas some states consider those aims to be legitimate, others do not. If states are given the freedom to make their own judgements as to what constitutes political persecution, extradition and mutual assistance will be blocked every time the motivation behind a crime is deemed lawful by the requested state. The tendency to justify terrorist offences on political grounds is evident from the fact that a number of states while ratifying counterterrorism conventions made reservations to the effect that they did not consider the offences committed in the course of freedom struggles as terrorist offences.[209]

Against this backdrop, a general obligation to provide fair treatment can hardly be expected to bring enough harmony to enable the requesting states to satisfy every use of discrimination as a ground for refusal of assistance. Even if each party guarantees protection, extradition or mutual legal assistance could be denied by applying the right differently, as a ground for refusal. Evidently, therefore, as per the existing arrangement, the discretion of the requested states to block extradition or mutual legal assistance based upon likelihood of discrimination in the requesting state is subject to no outside restraint.

In view of this, it is important that the international conventions provide guidelines with respect to factors constituting political persecution. One commentator suggests that terrorist offenders can be classified into three categories: revolutionaries, self-determinist and anarchists.[210] The last category, which features indiscriminate acts of violence, without any defined motive, should be excluded from the protection afforded under the

---

207 Dugard & Wyngaert (n 23) 202; See also Gary N Horlick, 'The Developing Law of Air-Hijacking' 12 Harv. Int'l. L. J. (1971) 33 at 46

208 Bassiouni (n 8) 10

209 See (n 155-156) Chapter 3 above

210 Geoff Gilbert, 'Terrorism and Political Offence Exemption Reappraised' 34 ICLQ (1985) 695 at 706-707

rule of political persecution.[211] This technique underlies the regulation of the use of discrimination as a ground for refusal of assistance and appears far more effective in facilitating extradition and mutual legal assistance as compared to general obligation to provide fair treatment.

Conclusions

The international conventions on terrorism and organised crime aim to facilitate state cooperation in law enforcement through harmonisation of national justice systems. For this purpose, they adopt the technique of imposing mandatory obligations.

Harmony is needed to overcome certain traditional hurdles associated with the principle of reciprocity which governs the laws and treaties on state cooperation, i.e. extradition and mutual legal assistance. These hurdles necessitate similarity of legal prescriptions in the laws of the requesting and requested state concerning the act with respect to which surrender or interrogation is sought. One such hurdle is the double punishability condition. It requires that the act charged against the offender must not be deemed non- punishable under the laws of either the requesting or requested state.

Human rights violations constitute the primary grounds for making an offence non- punishable under national constitutions and criminal codes. Correspondingly, they are applied as grounds for refusal of assistance under domestic laws and bilateral treaties on extradition and mutual assistance. It is therefore important that national legal systems be harmonious with respect to giving protection against violations of these rights, so that the requesting state's failure to guarantee the right might not provide an opportunity to the requested state to refuse surrender or interrogation.

To establish harmony, the international conventions on terrorism and organised crime impose a mandatory obligation on the parties to provide fair treatment to persons facing 'any proceeding' under the conventions. The obligation is ground-breaking in the sense that for the first time it recognises that all human rights available to a suspect facing trial should be extended to persons facing extradition and mutual assistance proceedings. Nevertheless, it may not provide a level of harmony sufficient to enable the parties to satisfy every use or application of human

---

[211] Ibid

rights as a ground for refusal of assistance under extradition and mutual legal assistance laws and treaties.

The problem is explained by Dugard and Wyngaert in these words:

> [I]nternational criminal law enforcement is not well served by a system that tolerates the refusal of extradition in some cases where human rights of the fugitives are at risk in requesting state but fails to provide the decision makers of the requested state clear standards or guidelines by which to make such a decision.[212]

Since it is difficult to develop a universal standard of human rights protection, encompassing their every conceivable use as a ground for refusal of assistance, the makers of conventions may wish to consider revisiting their existing technique of facilitating law enforcement cooperation, i.e. imposition of mandatory obligations to harmonise national justice systems. One alternative could be to regulate the use of human rights as a ground for refusal of assistance. This strategy would focus on regulating traditional hurdles to extradition and mutual legal assistance such as double punishability rather than harmonising the entire national justice systems to make them conducive to their demands. Since the object of both techniques is the same, i.e. facilitation of law enforcement cooperation, the latter being apparently more feasible, merits consideration for inclusion in the international conventions regulating transnational crimes. It is significant to note that in the context of transnational crime states have indicated their willingness to collectively lower the traditional barriers to extradition and mutual legal assistance.

[212] See Dugard & Wyngaert (n 23) 187-188

Part Two

Mandatory Obligations to Implement the Enforcement Mechanisms of *Aut Dedere Aut Judicare* and Confiscation of the Proceeds of Crime

CHAPTER 5

PROMOTING LAW ENFORCEMENT COOPERATION THROUGH DUTY TO IMPLEMENT *AUT DEDERE AUT JUDICARE*

Introduction

Aut dedere aut judicare represents a law enforcement mechanism which has been specifically designed to deny safe heavens to the offenders. It requires a state, in the territory of which the offender is found, to either extradite or prosecute him. In this way, it envisages the adoption of alternative measures of law enforcement, so that if one fails, the other can be employed to offer inter-state assistance. Evidently, the mechanism aims at facilitating state cooperation in bringing to justice fugitive offenders.

The application of the mechanism necessitates harmony in the laws of the requesting and requested states. In the absence of harmony, a foreign request to extradite or to prosecute in lieu thereof could be denied due to the requested state lacking enabling procedural rules or the request not being consistent with its procedural law. To establish harmony, the international counterterrorism and organised crime conventions impose mandatory obligation upon the parties to implement the mechanism of *aut dedere aut judicare*. This chapter looks into the effectiveness of the obligation in harmonising national laws and thereby to facilitate the application of the mechanism.

It will be argued that the alternative measures underlying the mechanism are to be enforced subject to the requesting state fulfilling the procedural requirements of the requested state's law. If the laws of the two states substantially differ in regard to these requirements, neither of the two measures could be enforced, leading to impunity for the offenders. However, the international conventions on terrorism and organised crime divest themselves from regulating these requirements. Hence, the mandatory obligation to implement *aut dedere aut judicare* may only bring harmony to the extent of including the mechanism in national laws, which is insufficient to facilitate its application. To facilitate the application of *aut dedere aut judicare*, it is essential that the conventions regulate the procedures of extradition and prosecution.

The disparity in national procedures of extradition and prosecution frustrates the objective of denying safe heavens to the offenders. For example, in *Lockerbie* case, Libya refused to surrender the suspects to the US or the UK because its extradition law carried a prohibition against surrender of nationals. All three states involved, i.e. Libya, the US and the UK were parties to the Montreal Convention 1971 which provided the mechanism of *aut dedere aut judiare*, pursuant to which, if extradition becomes impossible, the parties should resort to the option of prosecution. However, the US and the UK refused to accept the option of prosecution in Libya. Libya could have surrendered the suspects by considering Montreal Convention 1971 instead of its domestic law as a legal basis of extradition, however, it chose not to do so, because the relevant provision of the Convention was non-mandatory. Consequently, a stalemate occurred in the application of the mechanism which ultimately led to Security Council's interventions. Hence, due to the deferral of the Montreal Convention's *aut dedere aut judicare* provision to national rules of extradition and prosecution, neither of the two alternative measures could be enforced, despite the Convention having established a mandatory obligation to implement the mechanism. Clearly, therefore, international regulation is needed with respect to procedure of enforcing *aut dedere aut judicare* with a view to make national legal systems conducive to its application.

Although the international counterterrorism and organised crime conventions establish some rules to regulate the procedure of extradition, they are insufficient to facilitate the application of *aut dedere aut judicare* as a whole, particularly, in the specific context of borderless criminality. Furthermore, the conventions include multiple versions of *aut dedere aut judicare* which differ with respect to matters such as the trigger mechanism, the non-extradition of nationals and the prosecution of foreigners. Since the parties are allowed to implement any of these versions, enforcement of *aut dedere aut judicar* may become problematic where it involves states following different formulas.

As opposed to the international conventions on terrorism and organised crime, some bilateral treaties and domestic laws focus on simplifying trial in lieu of extradition and modernising extradition procedures. For example, they recommend states to take measures such as allowing observers to witness the trial and adopting a rule of reasonableness. Similarly, they encourage states to create new powers such as provision of mutual legal assistance in extradition. These recommendations are designed to make trial in lieu of extradition more effective and bringing extradition procedures in conformity with the demands of multi-jurisdictional and financial crimes. Their inclusion in national laws minimises the possibility of a foreign request being refused due to the requested state lacking the enabling procedural rules or the request not being consistent with its national law. This technique not only represents a progressive development of the ancient mechanism of *aut dedere aut judicare,* but also exemplifies a more effective system of bringing transnational offenders to justice. It will be suggested that provisions patterned on those contained in such laws and treaties should be included in the international conventions on terrorism and organised crime in order to facilitate the application of *aut dedere aut judicare,* as opposed to merely expressing the maxim.

This chapter has been divided into four sections. Section 1 analyses the expression of *aut dedere aut judicare* in the international counterterrorism and organised crime conventions and in national laws and bilateral treaties on extradition. Section 2 considers the requirement to enforce the mechanism in accordance with the requested state's law. Section 3 examines the regulation of the procedure of extradition under the international conventions on terrorism and organised crime. Section 4 makes recommendations about simplifying trial in lieu of extradition and bringing extradition laws in conformity with demands of multi-jurisdictional and financial crimes.

Section 1: Expression of *aut dedere aut judicare* in the international conventions on terrorism and organised crime and its implementation in national laws and bilateral treaties on extradition

1.1) Evolution of *aut dedere aut judicare*

The maxim *aut dedere aut judicare* represents the modern adaptation of the ancient phrase *aut dedere aut punier* which was introduced by Dutch scholar, Grotius, in 1625.[1] According to Grotius, international law imposed a duty on the state, to the territory of which an alleged offender had escaped after committing his crime elsewhere, either to return him to

[1] See M. Cherif Bassiouni & Edward M Wise, *Aut dedere Aut Judicare: The Duty to Extradite or Prosecute in International Law* (Netherlands: Matinus Nijhoff Publishers 1995) 3

the state of commission, or to punish him according to its own law.[2] It therefore symbolises a measure of law enforcement to bring to justice fugitive offenders.[3]

The modern equivalent of Grotius's phrase replaces the verb '*punier*' with '*judicare'* to give recognition to the fact that the alleged offender may be found innocent, thereby restricting the scope of the obligation to prosecution rather than punishment.[4] Thus, in contemporary legal instruments, the maxim is denoted '*aut dedere aut judicare',* creating an obligation on a state in the territory of which an offender is found to either extradite or prosecute him.

As of 2010, the obligation found expression in over 70 international law instruments including multilateral conventions focusing on law enforcement cooperation, as well as resolutions of the General Assembly and Security Council of the United Nations.[5] Furthermore, it is widely applied in municipal laws on extradition.[6]

1.2) Meanings of the maxim

Aut dedere aut judicare mechanism as contained in the international conventions on terrorism and organised crime has two parts. The first part involves the verb *dedere.* It requires a state, in the territory of which the alleged offender is found, to extradite him to a state having jurisdiction over crime and willing to prosecute.[7] Extradition is a proceeding whereby one state surrenders to another an individual, accused or convicted of an

---

[2] M.Plachta, 'Aut Dedere Aut Judicare: An Overview of Modes of Implementation and Approaches' 6 Maastricht J. Eur. & Comp. L. (1991) 331

[3] Bassiouni & Wise (n 1) 3

[4] ibid at 4; See also Zdzislaw Galicki, 'Preliminary Report on the Obligation to Extradite or Prosecute presented in the 58th Session of the International Law Commission (ILC) held in Geneva,1 May-9 June and 3 July-11 August 2006'. A/CN.4/571 at 6

[5] Amnesty International's Report on the Obligation to Extradite or Prosecute 2009 <http://www.amnesty.org/ar/library/asset/IOR40/001/2009/en/a4761626-f20a-11dd-855f-392123cb5f06/ior400012009en.pdf> [Date accessed 21/03/23]

[6] ibid

[7] Bassiouni & Wise (n 1) 3, 4; See also Plachta (n 2)

offence for which the requesting state is seeking to subject him to trial or punishment.[8] In 1878, Cardaillac defined extradition as:

> the right for a state on the territory of which an accused or convicted person has taken refuge, to deliver him up to another state which has requisitioned his return and is competent to judge and punish him.[9]

The second part of the mechanism relates to the gerund *judicare* which demands prosecution of the offender.[10] This entails, if the extradition is not possible, a state in the territory of which the offender is found is required to prosecute him itself, in accordance with its own law.[11] The mechanism therefore sets forth two law enforcement modalities in the alternative, so that if one fails, the other can be employed to offer inter-state assistance.[12] According to Plachta, the obligation is meant to ensure that the offender is brought to justice, regardless of the place where his trial might take place.[13] It is thus directed towards ending impunity for persons involved in international crimes.[14]

The mechanism is now regarded as the world community's most effective weapon against transnational criminality. For example, Security Council's binding resolution on counterterrorism 1373 (2001) obliges states to deny safe heavens to terrorists.[15] According to the International Law Commission (ILC), the obligation can be carried out in the best and most effective way through duty to extradite or prosecute the offender.[16] The subsequent resolutions of the Security Council including 1456 (2003) and 1566 (2004) confirm this view by suggesting that the obligation to bring terrorists to

---

[8] Cherif Bassiouni, 'Ideologically Motivated Offenses and the Political Offenses Exception in Extradition- A Proposed Juridical Standard for an Unruly Problem' 19 DePaul L. Rev. (1969-1970) 217 at 221-222

[9] Blackesley, 'The Law of International Extradition: A Comparative Study' 62 Revue Internationale De Droit Penal (1991) 381

[10] Plachta (n 2)

[11] ibid

[12] Bassiouni & Wise (n 1) 3 & foot note 2

[13] ibid

[14] Bassiouni & Wise (n 1) 3

[15] See para 2(c) S/RES/1373 (2001)

[16] See Zdzislaw Galicki, '4th Report on the Obligation to Extradite or Prosecute submitted in the 63rd session of the ILC' A/CN.4/648 at 9

justice is to be carried out on the basis of the principle of extradite or prosecute.[17]

The effectiveness of the mechanism, however, depends to a great extent upon harmony in national laws. Harmony is needed because the alternative measures underlying the mechanism, i.e. extradition and prosecution are required to be enforced in accordance with procedural requirements of the requested state's law.[18] If the requested state lacks the enabling procedural rules or the request is not in conformity with its procedural requirements, both measures could be refused. To establish harmony, the international conventions on terrorism and organised crime impose mandatory obligation upon parties to implement the mechanism domestically.

1.3) Expression of *aut dedere aut judicare* in the counterterrorism and organised crime conventions

1.3.1) Counterterrorism Conventions

Counterterrorism conventions follow the so-called 'Hague formula' in establishing the obligation of *aut dedere aut judicare*.[19] The formula is said to represent a strict version of the obligation leaving little room for interpretation.[20] It was first used in the Hague Convention 1970 which provided in its article 7:

> [t]he Contracting State in the territory of which the alleged offender is found shall, if it does not extradite him, be obliged, without exception whatsoever and whether or not the offence was committed in its territory, to submit the case to its competent authorities for the purpose of prosecution. Those authorities shall take their decision in the same manner as in the case of any ordinary offence of a serious nature under the law of that State.[21]

The above formula, with slight modifications, was adopted in a series of subsequent counterterrorism conventions. These include the Montreal

---

[17] See para 3, S/RES/1456 (2003) adopted by the Security Council at its 4688th meeting, on 20 January 2003; See also para 2, S/RES/1566 (2004) adopted by the Security Council at its 5053rd meeting, on 8 October 2004

[18] See (n 228) Chapter 3 above. For the requirement to conduct *prosecution* in accordance with the requested state's law, see joint declaration of Judges Evensen, Tarassov, Guillaume and Aguilar Mawdsley in *Lockerbie* Case 1992 I.C.J 136 (Apr 14) para 2

[19] Bassiouni & Wise (n 1) 18

[20] ibid

[21] See article 7 the Hague Convention 1970

Convention 1971,[22] the Protection of Diplomats Convention 1973,[23] the Hostages Convention 1979,[24] the Nuclear Materials Convention 1980,[25] the Rome Convention 1988,[26] the Terrorist Bombings Convention 1997,[27] the Terrorism Financing Convention 1999,[28] the Nuclear Terrorism Convention 2005[29] and the Beijing Convention 2010.[30] For example, article 10(1) of the Rome Convention 1988 provides:

> The State Party in the territory of which the offender or the alleged offender is found shall, in cases to which article 6 applies, if it does not extradite him, be obliged, without exception whatsoever and whether or not the offence was committed in its territory, to submit the case without delay to its competent authorities for the purpose of prosecution, through proceedings in accordance with the laws of that State. Those authorities shall take their decision in the same manner as in the case of any other offence of a grave nature under the law of that State.[31]

The difference between the Hague and Rome Convention's formulas is that the Rome Convention requires a state in the territory of which the offender is found to submit the case 'without delay', whereas the Hague Convention makes no such demand. Moreover, in suggesting how the authorities shall make their decision with respect to prosecution, the former uses the word 'grave' instead of 'serious' to refer to the crime to be prosecuted. Additionally, the Rome Convention uses the term 'the offender or the alleged offender' in place of 'the alleged offender' as used by the Hague Convention. This is meant to clarify that the obligation applies not only to 'suspects' but also to 'convicts'.[32] Clearly all these

---

[22] See article 7 the Montreal Convention 1971

[23] See article 7 the Protection of Diplomats 1973

[24] See article 8 the Hostages Convention 1979

[25] See article 10 the Nuclear Materials Convention 1980

[26] See article 10 the Rome Convention 1988

[27] See article 8(1) the Terrorist Bombings Convention 1997

[28] See article 10(1) the Terrorism Financing Convention 1999

[29] See article 11(1) the Nuclear Terrorism Convention 2005

[30] See article 10 the Beijing Convention 2010

[31] See article 10(1) of the Rome Convention 1988

[32] For example, article 1 of 1990 UN Model Treaty on Extradition provides:
Each Party agrees to extradite to the other, upon request and subject to the provisions of the present Treaty, any person who is wanted in the requesting State for prosecution for an extraditable offence or for the imposition or enforcement of a sentence in respect of such an offence.
The provision makes it plain that extradition can be granted in respect of both, the person wanted for imposition of sentence and the one required for trial.

differences reflect improvements upon language rather than the substance of the obligation.

1.3.2) Organised Crime Conventions

Organised crime conventions under consideration include the Drugs Convention 1988,[33] the Organised Crime Convention 2000,[34] and the UN Convention against Corruption 2003.[35] These conventions follow the approach taken in the treaties entered into force prior to the Hague convention 1970 such as the UN Convention against Counterfeiting 1929 and the European Extradition Convention 1957 in establishing the obligation to implement *aut dedere aut judicare*.[36] For example, article 16(10) of the Organised Crime Convention 2000 provides:

> A State Party in whose territory an alleged offender is found, if it does not extradite such person in respect of an offence to which this article applies solely on the ground that he or she is one of its nationals, shall, at the request of the State Party seeking extradition, be obliged to submit the case without undue delay to its competent authorities for the purpose of prosecution. Those authorities shall take their decision and conduct their proceedings in the same manner as in the case of any other offence of a grave nature under the domestic law of that State Party. The States Parties concerned shall cooperate with each other, in particular on procedural and evidentiary aspects, to ensure the efficiency of such prosecution.[37]

The above provision has been reproduced word for word in the UN Convention against Corruption 2003.[38] While the Drugs Convention 1988 employs a different formula, the difference mainly relates to the language and not the substance of the obligation. Thus, article 6(9) of the Drugs Convention 1988 provides:

> Without prejudice to the exercise of any criminal jurisdiction established in accordance with its domestic law, a Party in whose territory an alleged offender is found shall:

---

[33] See (n 40) Chapter 1 above

[34] See (n 42) Chapter 1 above

[35] See (n 44) Chapter 1 above

[36] See article 6(2) of the European Convention on Extradition 1957 and articles 8 & 9 of the International Convention for the Suppression of Counterfeiting Currency, adopted in Geneva on 20 April 1929 [hereinafter the UN Counterfeiting Convention 1929]

[37] See article 16(10) the Organised Crime Convention 2000

[38] See article 44(11) the UN Convention against Corruption 2003

a) If it does not extradite him in respect of an offence established in accordance with article 3, paragraph l, on the grounds set forth in article 4, paragraph 2, subparagraph a), submit the case to its competent authorities for the purpose of prosecution, unless otherwise agreed with the requesting Party;

b) If it does not extradite him in respect of such an offence and has established its jurisdiction in relation to that offence in accordance with article 4, paragraph 2, subparagraph b) submit the case to its competent authorities for the purpose of prosecution, unless otherwise requested by the requesting Party for the purposes of preserving its legitimate jurisdiction.[39]

1.3.3) Dissimilarities in the *aut dedere aut judicare* formula as contained in the Hague Convention 1970 and three organised crime conventions

a) Obligation to prosecute triggers once a request for extradition is received and rejected

The first dissimilarity between the two formulas is that *aut dedere aut judicare* mechanism, as contained in the organised crime conventions, stipulates that the obligation of the requested state to prosecute the offender is activated only once a request for extradition has been made to it and rejected.[40] In other words, the requested state is not bound to prosecute merely because the offender is present in its territory. Similar provisions can be seen in the European Convention on Extradition 1957 and the UN Counterfeiting Convention 1929.[41] By contrast, the Hague Convention 1970 does not make prosecution conditional upon the denial.

---

[39] See article 6(9) of the Drugs Convention 1988

[40] See for instance article 16(10) of the Organised Crime Convention 2000; See also article 44(11) of the UN Convention against Corruption 2003:

A State Party in whose territory an alleged offender is found, if it does not extradite such person in respect of an offence to which this article applies solely on the ground that he or she is one of its nationals, shall, at the request of the State Party seeking extradition, be obliged to submit the case without undue delay to its competent authorities for the purpose of prosecution. Those authorities shall take their decision and conduct their proceedings in the same manner as in the case of any other offence of a grave nature under the domestic law of that State Party. The States Parties concerned shall cooperate with each other, in particular on procedural and evidentiary aspects, to ensure the efficiency of such prosecution.

[41] See article 9 the UN Counterfeiting Convention 1929:

b) Refusal of extradition on specific grounds activates duty to prosecute

The second difference is that, according to the organised crime conventions, prosecution is necessary only where extradition could not take place solely on the ground of nationality of the offender. Thus, article 15(3) of the Organised Crime Convention 2000 provides:

> For the purposes of article 16, paragraph 10, of this Convention, each State Party shall adopt such measures as may be necessary to establish its jurisdiction over the offences covered by this Convention when the alleged offender is present in its territory and it does not extradite such person solely on the ground that he or she is one of its nationals.[42]

The Drugs Convention 1988 enlarges the scope of this obligation by requiring prosecution not only when the extradition is refused due to the nationality of the offender but also when it is refused because of the offence having occurred in the territory of the requested state or on board an aircraft belonging to the requested state.[43] Corresponding provisions can be seen in the European Convention on Extradition 1957 and the UN Counterfeiting Convention 1929.[44] Conversely, the Hague Convention 1970 does not make obligation to prosecute conditional upon denial of extradition on any specific ground. It rather enjoins the parties to prosecute regardless of the ground of refusal of extradition.

c) Prosecution of non-nationals for crimes committed abroad

The third discrepancy lies in the organised crime conventions not requiring mandatory prosecution of non-nationals for crimes committed abroad. As per the language used in these conventions, states 'may' submit the case against non-nationals for crimes committed abroad.[45] According to

...The obligation to take proceedings is subject to the condition that extradition has been requested and that the country to which application is made cannot hand over the person accused for some reason which has no connection with the offence.
See also article 6(2) European Convention on Extradition 1957

[42] See article 15(3) of the Organised Crime Convention 2000; See also article 42(3) of the UN Convention against Corruption 2003

[43] See article 4(2)(a) of the Drugs Convention 1988

[44] See article 9 of the UN Counterfeiting Convention 1929 and article 6(2) of the European Convention on Extradition 1957

[45] On the other hand, the word 'shall' has been used in the provision establishing obligation to prosecute nationals. See for instance article 42(3) & (4) of the UN

Bassiouni and Wise, the use of word 'may' in the obligation to prosecute non-nationals, is meant to address a situation where the national law of the requested state does not cover the extraterritorial crimes committed by non-nationals.[46] This scenario is explicitly recognised by the UN Counterfeiting Convention 1929 and the European Convention on Extradition 1957.[47] By contrast, the Hague Convention 1970 makes no distinction between nationals and non-nationals while establishing the obligation to prosecute. It rather enjoins the parties to prosecute the offender found present in their territory irrespective of his nationality or the place of the commission of crime.

In view of the above, it is clear that at least three different versions of *aut dedere aut judicare* can be found in counterterrorism and the organised crime conventions. The versions differ with respect to matters such as trigger mechanism, extradition of nationals and prosecution of non-nationals. States are free to implement any of these versions in their national laws and bilateral treaties on extradition. Each measure underlying the maxim, i.e. extradition or prosecution, depend upon correspondence in the laws of the requesting and requested state. If cooperation is to take place between states following two different formulas, application of the mechanism becomes problematic. This contradicts the goal of facilitating law enforcement cooperation through harmonisation. Accordingly, in some circumstances, the obligation to implement *aut dedere aut judicare* may only bring harmony to the extent that state parties include the maxim in national laws, not in relation to its application.

Convention against Corruption 2003, article 15(3) & (4) of the Organised Crime Convention 2000 and article 4(2) (a) & (b) of the Drugs Convention 1988.

[46] Bassiouni & Wise (n 1) 20

[47] See article 9 UN Counterfeiting Convention 1929:

> Foreigners who have committed abroad any offence referred to in Article 3, and who are in the territory of a country whose internal legislation recognises as a general rule the principle of the prosecution of offences committed abroad, should be punishable in the same way as if the offence had been committed in the territory of that country…

This may be compared with article 7(2) of European Convention on Extradition 1957:

> When the offence for which extradition is requested has been committed outside the territory of the requesting Party, extradition may only be refused if the law of the requested Party does not allow prosecution for the same category of offence when committed outside the latter Party's territory or does not allow extradition for the offence concerned.

1.4) Expression of *aut dedere aut judicare* in domestic laws

In line with different formulas used by the international conventions on terrorism and organised crime to express *aut dedere aut judicare*, its expression in national laws also reflects variation. For example, the criminal code of Azerbijan applies the 'Hague formula'. It, therefore, neither requires any trigger mechanism, nor makes any distinction between nationals and non-nationals while imposing the obligation to extradite or prosecute.[48] This may be compared with the Australian Extradition Act 1988 which, besides making prosecution conditional upon the refusal of extradition,[49] stipulates that prosecution may only be conducted if extradition has been refused because of the offender's nationality.[50] Clearly, Australia applies the formula as contained in the organised crime conventions.

In view of this, if Azerbaijan seeks the prosecution of a suspect from Australia, it must first establish that it had made an extradition request which was denied because the offender was an Australian national. Furthermore, Azerbaijan cannot demand prosecution by Australia of an Azerbaijani national for crimes committed in Azerbaijan because Australian law does not cover crimes committed abroad by non-nationals.

Conversely, if Australia seeks prosecution from Azerbaijan, it does not need to prove that it had previously made an extradition request which was refused by Azerbaijan. Moreover, Australia can demand prosecution by Azerbaijan of an Australian national for crimes committed in Australia because Azerbaijan's law covers crimes committed abroad by non-nationals.

In the same way, Indian law adopts the formula as contained in the Drugs Convention 1988. Whereas the Indian Extradition Act requires the government to prosecute the offender regardless of the place of the commission of crime or nationality of the offender,[51] its penal code provides that Indian courts may only exercise extraterritorial jurisdiction when the commission of the crime involves an Indian national or the crime

---

48 See Articles 12 (3) and 13 (3) of Criminal Code of the Azerbaijan Republic 2005 <http://www.legislationline.org/download/action/download/id/1658/file/4b3ff87c005675cfd74058077132.htm/preview> [Date accessed 21/03/23]

49 See article 45(4)(a)&(b) of Extradition Act 1988, Act No.4 of 1988 [hereinafter Australian Extradition Act 1988]

50 See article 45(4)(c) & 45(5) Australian Extradition Act 1988

51 See article 34 A & 2*34 Indian Extradition Act 1962

has been committed on a vessel or aircraft owned or operated by India.[52] Thus, the option of prosecution in lieu of extradition is closed if the offender happens to be a non-national who committed his crime abroad or on a foreign aircraft or vessel. By contrast, the Penal Code of Panama makes no distinction between nationals and foreigners while imposing the obligation to extradite or prosecute.[53]

Due to the foregoing, it is plain that the expression of *aut dedere aut judicare* in national laws reflects discrepancies similar to those in counterterrorism and organised crime convention.

1.5) Expression of *aut dedere aut judicare* in bilateral and regional treaties on extradition

The extradition laws of a majority of states require the existence of a bilateral or regional treaty for the surrender of suspects or to prosecute them instead of surrender. For instance, Israel's extradition law provides that a person may only be extradited from Israel if 'there is an agreement between Israel and the requesting state on the extradition of offenders.'[54] Since these treaties enshrine national legal principles of states parties to them, they provide useful insights into the way *aut dedere aut judicare* rule is being implemented in different parts of the world.[55] A survey of selected bilateral and regional treaties reflects that multiple formulas are being used to express the rule.

For example article 3 of Canada-France Extradition treaty 1988 provides:

> 2. If the request for extradition is refused solely because the person sought has the nationality of the requested State, that State shall, at the request of the requesting State, refer the matter to its competent authorities for prosecution. For this purpose, the files, documents and exhibits relating to

---

[52] See article 4 Indian Penal Code 1860; See also section 6 of Anti- Hijacking Act 1982 of India

[53] Código Penal de Panamá, Ley No.14, of 18 May 2007 <www.gacetaoficial.gob.pa/pdfTemp/25796/4580.pdf> [Date accessed 21/03/23]

[54] See article 2a Extradition Law 5714-1954 and the Extradition Regulations of Israel (Law, Procedures and Rules of Evidence in Petitions) 5731-1970

[55] See Edward M. Wise, 'Some Problems of Extradition' 15 Wayne State Law Review (1968-69) 709 at 716

> the offence shall be transmitted to the requested State. That State shall inform the requesting State of the action taken on its request.[56]

Clearly, the provision follows the *aut dedere aut judicare* formula as contained in the organised crime conventions.[57] It stipulates that prosecution is necessary only if the extradition has been refused on the ground of nationality of the offender.[58]

This may be compared with the Australia-China Extradition Treaty 1993 which makes it optional for the requested state to submit the case for prosecution even if the extradition is refused on the ground of the nationality of the offender. The relevant provision reads:

> (1) The Government of Australia reserves the right to refuse the surrender of its nationals. The Government of Hong Kong reserves the right to refuse the surrender of nationals of the state whose Government is responsible for its foreign affairs.
>
> (2) Where the requested Party exercises this right, the requesting Party may request that the case be submitted to the competent authorities of the requested Party in order that proceedings for prosecution of the person may be considered.[59]

A slightly different version of *aut dedere aut judicare* can be seen in the UK-UAE Extradition Treaty 2008. According to it, duty to prosecute arises only if the extradition is refused on the ground of nationality and the act charged against the offender constitutes a criminal offence under the law of both the requesting and requested state.[60] This illustrates the application of double criminality in trial or extradition proceedings.

Another variation of the formula can be seen in the Thailand-China Extradition Treaty 1993. According to it, the obligation to prosecute arises only if the extradition is refused on the ground of nationality. However, the requested state shall not be bound to prosecute if it has no jurisdiction

---

[56] See article 3(2) of Canada-France Extradition Treaty 1988; For identical provisions see article IV(1) Canada-Spain Extradition Treaty 1989; article 6 European Convention on Extradition 1957; article 4 UN Model Treaty on Extradition 1990; article 5 China-Korea Extradition Treaty 2002

[57] See text to (n 37 & 39) above

[58] See article 3(2) of Canada-France Extradition Treaty 1988

[59] See article 3 Australia-China Extradition Treaty 1993

[60] See article 3 UK-UAE Extradition Treaty 2008

over the offence.[61] Pursuant to this provision, the requested party is neither required to extradite nor to prosecute if the internal law does not recognize the principle of nationality as a valid basis of exercising jurisdiction over extraterritorial crimes.[62]

Two further unusual expressions of *aut dedere aut judicare* can be seen in China-Korea Extradition Treaty 2002 and India-Australia Extradition Treaty 2008. According to the former, extradition may be refused where the offence has been committed in whole or in part in the territory of the requested state. If so refused, the requested state shall be bound to submit the case against the offender to its competent authorities to consider prosecution.[63] The latter, on the other hand, allows the refusal of extradition on the ground that the offence is prosecutable in the requested state. If so refused, the requested state shall be bound to submit the case against the offender.[64] These provisions illustrate the implementation of *aut dedere aut judicare* in accordance with the formula contained in the Drugs Convention 1988.[65]

These may be compared with article 7 of the European Convention on Extradition 1957. It allows the parties to refuse extradition on the ground of the offence having wholly or partly occurred in the requested state, but it does not impose the corresponding obligation to prosecute the offender. Under article 6(2) of the Convention, the duty to prosecute only arises if the extradition is refused on the ground of nationality of the offender.

In light of the above, it can be suggested that owing to the absence of any single formula of *aut dedere aut judicare* in the international conventions on terrorism and organised crime, its expression in bilateral treaties differs. These differences run counter to the objective of facilitating law enforcement cooperation through establishing a universal regime of *aut dedere aut judicare.*

---

[61] See article 5, Treaty between the Kingdom of Thailand and People's Republic of China on Extradition. Signed at Beijing on 26 August 1993 [hereinafter Thailand-China Extradition Treaty 1993].

[62] It is significant to note that none of the organised crime conventions obliges the parties to establish jurisdiction on the basis of nationality. See (n 162 & 180) Chapter 2 above and article 42(2)(b) of the UN Convention against Corruption 2003

[63] See article 4 China-Korea Extradition Treaty 2002

[64] See article 6 India-Australia Extradition Treaty 2008

[65] See article 16(9) of the Drugs Convention 1988

In the next section, I shall explain that, according to the existing scheme of the conventions, the conditions and procedure of both extradition and prosecution are to be determined in accordance with national law of the requested state. Since the conventions do not attempt to regulate national law, they can only bring harmony to the extent that they require states to include the maxim in national laws, which is insufficient to facilitate its application. To facilitate the application of *aut derere aut judicare*, it is essential that the conventions regulate the conditions and procedures of extradition and trial.

Section 2: Application of *aut dedere aut judicare* in accordance with national law

A key factor which facilitates the performance of an international obligation is its over-riding effect. If an international obligation supersedes the contrary provisions of national laws and bilateral treaties, its performance is likely to be consistent. For example, the European Convention on Extradition 1957 provides, '[t]his Convention shall, in respect of those countries to which it applies, supersede the provisions of any bilateral treaties, conventions or agreements governing extradition between any two Contracting Parties.'[66] The Convention facilitates the performance of its obligations by over-riding contrary provisions of national laws and bilateral treaties.[67]

The international conventions on terrorism and organised crime stand in stark contrast to the European Convention in this respect. According to them, conditions and procedure of extradition including grounds of refusal are to be determined in accordance with the national law of the requested state. In the same way, the conventions desist from regulating national rules on prosecution of the offenders. Since these rules differ, it cannot be said that the obligation to implement *aut dedere aut judicare* as contained in the conventions facilitates the application of the mechanism. I shall now explain discretion afforded to states as regards applying different components of the mechanism in accordance with national law.

---

[66] See article 28(1) the European Convention on Extradition 1957

[67] Nonetheless, the Convention makes allowance for reservation owing to which its implementation is unlikely to be consistent. See article 26 of the European Convention on Extradition 1957; Also see Bassiouni & Wise (n 1) 11

2.1) Duty to apprehend the suspect

2.1.1) Duty under the international conventions on terrorism and organised crime

According to the international conventions on terrorism and organised crime, the primary duty of a state in the territory of which the offender is found, is to take him into custody to ensure his presence for trial or extradition. This duty went through a process of evolution. In earlier conventions, such as the Protection of Diplomats Convention 1973, the duty was to take appropriate measures to ensure the presence of the offender.[68] The word 'custody' was deliberately avoided so that it would not be misinterpreted as permission to put the offender in distress.[69] However, from the Hostages Convention 1979 onwards, the use of the word custody has been persistent. Thus, article 7 of the Rome Convention 1988 sets forth the obligation in these words:

> Article 7
>
> 1. Upon being satisfied that the circumstances so warrant, any State Party in the territory of which the offender or the alleged offender is present shall, in accordance with its law, take him into custody or take other measures to ensure his presence for such time as is necessary to enable any criminal or extradition proceedings to be instituted.
>
> 2. Such State shall immediately make a preliminary inquiry into the facts, in accordance with its own legislation.
>
> 3. Any person regarding whom the measures referred to in paragraph 1 are being taken shall be entitled to:
>
> (a) communicate without delay with the nearest appropriate representative of the State of which he is a national or which is otherwise entitled to establish such communication or, if he is a stateless person, the State in the territory of which he has his habitual residence;
>
> (b) be visited by a representative of that State.

---

[68] See article 6, the Protection of Diplomats Convention 1973

[69] Abraham Abramovsky, 'Multilateral Conventions for the Suppression of Unlawful Seizure and Interference with Aircraft part-II: The Montreal Convention' 14 Colum. J. Trannsnat'l L. (1975) 268 at 291

4. The rights referred to in paragraph 3 shall be exercised in conformity with the laws and regulations of the State in the territory of which the offender or the alleged offender is present, subject to the proviso that the said laws and regulations must enable full effect to be given to the purposes for which the rights accorded under paragraph 3 are intended.

5. When a State Party, pursuant to this article, has taken a person into custody, it shall immediately notify the States which have established jurisdiction in accordance with article 6, paragraph 1 and, if it considers it advisable, any other interested States, of the fact that such person is in custody and of the circumstances which warrant his detention. The State which makes the preliminary inquiry contemplated in paragraph 2 of this article shall promptly report its findings to the said States and shall indicate whether it intends to exercise jurisdiction.

According to this provision, as soon as the offender steps into the territory of a state party, it automatically assumes the obligation to take him into custody to ensure his presence for trial or extradition. However, the obligation is to be performed in accordance with the domestic law of the requested state.[70]

2.1.2) Implementation of the duty in extradition treaties

The national implementation of the obligation reflects that a majority of the states are unwilling to accept an automatic obligation to arrest the suspect. For instance, article XII of the US-Italy Extradition Treaty 1983 provides:

ARTICLE XII

Provisional Arrest

1. In case of urgency, either Contracting Party may apply for the provisional arrest of any person charged or convicted of an extraditable offense. The application for provisional arrest shall be made either through the diplomatic channel or directly between the United States Department of Justice and the Italian Ministry of Grace and Justice, in which case the communication facilities of the International Criminal Police Organization (Interpol) may be used.

2. The application shall contain: a description of the person sought including, if available, the person's nationality; the probable location of that person; a brief statement of the facts of the case including, if possible the time and location of the offense and the available evidence; a statement

[70] See article 7(1) Rome Convention 1988

of the existence of a warrant of arrest, with the date it was issued and the name of the issuing court; a description of the type of offenses, a citation to the sections of law violated and the maximum penalty possible upon conviction, or a statement of the existence of a judgment of conviction against that person, with the date of conviction, the name of the sentencing court and the sentence imposed, if any; and a statement that a formal request for extradition of the person sought will follow.

3. On receipt of the application, the Requested Party shall take the appropriate steps to secure the arrest of the person sought. The Requesting Party shall be promptly notified of the result of its application.

4. Provisional arrest shall be terminated if, within a period of 45 days after the apprehension of the person sought, the Executive Authority of the Requested Party has not received a formal request for extradition and the supporting documents required by Article X.

5. The termination of provisional arrest pursuant to paragraph 4 of this Article shall not prejudice the re-arrest and extradition of the person sought if the extradition request and the supporting documents are delivered at a later date.[71]

Pursuant to this provision, there is no automatic duty to apprehend the suspect once he arrives in state territory; the obligation of the custodial state begins once a formal request is made to it for the arrest of the suspect. The request must be accompanied by documents relating to the offence such as the warrant of arrest and a copy of the judgment of conviction. The requesting party is further obliged to give undertaking that an extradition request will follow and to understand that the offender will be set free if the request is not received within a specified time. Additionally, the requested party is not bound to arrest, it is merely required to notify to the requesting state of the result of its request.

While the international conventions on terrorism and organised crime envisage an automatic duty to arrest, its implementation under US-Italy Extradition Treaty 1983 suggests that states may be unwilling to accept it. Nevertheless, the parties to such bilateral treaties cannot be held liable for breach of their international duty because the duty is required to be

---

[71] See article XII of US-Italy Extradition Treaty 1983. For corresponding provisions, see article 12 Australia-China Extradition Treaty 1993; article 12 Australia-Germany Extradition Treaty 1988; article 11 US-Israel Extradition Treaty 1962; article 11 UK-UAE Extradition Treaty 2008; article 11 UN Model Treaty on Extradition 1990; article 9 Thailand-China Extradition Treaty 1993 and article 9 China-Korea Extradition Treaty 2002

performed in accordance with the procedural requirements of the requested state's law or the bilateral treaties to which it is bound.[72] This implies that the duty can be tailored to suit the needs of national justice systems.

A different approach is taken under the UK-UAE Extradition Treaty 2008. This treaty establishes two obligations for the party in the territory of which the offender is found. The first obligation demands that the offender must be taken into custody when a request for his arrest is made by a state having jurisdiction over crime.[73] The obligation is entitled 'provisional arrest' and is to be carried out in cases of urgency only. The second obligation requires arrest of the offender in every case where a request for extradition is received, even though no separate application for arrest is made. The obligation is entitled 'remand' and is reproduced below:

> Upon receipt of the request for extradition, the Requested Party shall arrest the person sought in accordance with its domestic laws. The person shall be held on remand until the Requested Party decides on the request for extradition. If the request for extradition is granted, the remand period shall continue until the person sought is handed over to the authorities of the Requesting Party.[74]

The establishment of two separate obligations of 'remand' and 'provisional arrest' does not indicate the exact fulfilment of the automatic duty to arrest as intended by the makers of the international counterterrorism and organised crime conventions. However, it may facilitate the application of *aut dedere aut judicare* by simplifying the procedure of seeking arrest of the fugitive. For example, it relieves the requesting party of the additional burden to make a separate request for arrest and to wait for its decision. At the same, it makes allowance for immediate arrest in cases where extradition request cannot be made forthwith and there is a threat of the offender fleeing the territory of the requested state. Needless to say that the provision merits to be tested at international level.

---

[72] See for instance, article 7 of the Rome Convention 1988. See also (n 228) Chapter 3 above

[73] See article 11 UK-UAE Extradition Treaty 2008

[74] See article 10 UK-UAE Extradition Treaty 2008

2.2) *Judicare* part of the obligation

2.2.1) Duty to submit the case to competent authorities for consideration

According to Bassiouni and Wise, the use of the term *judicare* is improper because it means to 'judge' or to 'try' which implies full trial.[75] What the conventions require from states is to submit the case for prosecution to their competent national authorities for the purposes of prosecution.[76] The authorities shall take their decision in the same manner as in the case of any ordinary domestic law crime of a serious nature.[77] Thus, the authorities are not bound to prosecute but are equally competent to drop the proceeding if so required by their national law. Hence, the obligation is to take steps towards prosecution or to conduct an inquiry into the accusation which may result in prosecution or termination of proceedings.[78] This view is in accord with the language used by the international conventions on terrorism and organised crime to express the obligation. For instance, article 7 of the Hague Convention 1970 provides:

> The Contracting State in the territory of which the alleged offender is found shall, if it does not extradite him, be obliged, without exception whatsoever and whether or not the offence was committed in its territory, to submit the case to its competent authorities for the purpose of prosecution. Those authorities shall take their decision in the same manner as in the case of any ordinary offence of a serious nature under the law of that State.[79]

In the words of Abramovsky, the drafters of the conventions refrained from establishing an absolute obligation to prosecute, in order to preserve the discretion of national authorities to differentiate between offenders on the basis of individual circumstances and of political climate.[80] He noted further that article 7 of the Hague Convention 1970 substantially weakens the obligation by allowing states to fulfil their duty merely by submitting the case to their prosecuting authorities for final decision.[81] It can be argued therefore that the obligation to prosecute implies that the requested state, in case it chooses not to extradite, is only required to investigate the charges against the offender. The investigation may either lead to trial or

---

[75] Bassiouni & Wise (n 1) 4
[76] See article 7 the Hague Convention 1970
[77] ibid
[78] Bassiouni & Wise (n 1) 4
[79] See article 7 of the Hague Convention 1970
[80] Abramovsky (n 69) 294
[81] ibid

pre-trial discharge of the offender. In any case, a state in the territory of which the offender is found would be relived of its obligation, once the case is submitted for consideration of competent authorities to make a decision about prosecution. Significantly, during the drafting of the Montreal Convention 1971, a proposal was made by Israel for mandatory prosecution. However, this was rejected after having been put to vote.[82]

Some bilateral and regional treaties further clarify the discretion afforded to the requested state in the matter of conducting prosecution in lieu of extradition. For example, article 6(2) of the European Convention on Extradition 1957 provides:

> [i]f the requested Party does not extradite its national, it shall at the request of the requesting Party submit the case to its competent authorities in order that proceedings may be taken if they are considered appropriate...[83]

The expression 'if they are considered appropriate' indicates that the competent authorities are not bound to prosecute but are equally competent to drop or terminate the proceedings.

Similarly, article 4 (b) of the UN Model Treaty on Extradition 1990 provides that extradition may be refused:

> if the competent authorities of the requested state have decided not to institute or to terminate proceedings against the person whose extradition is requested.[84]

Likewise, article 6(3) of India-Australia Extradition Treaty 2008 provides, 'if the competent authorities decide not to prosecute, the request for extradition may reconsidered in accordance with this treaty.'[85]

Clearly, therefore, duty to prosecute in lieu of extradition is limited to submission of the case to competent authorities for consideration who shall make their decision whether or not to prosecute, in accordance with national law.

---

[82] ibid
[83] See article 6(2) of the European Convention on Extradition 1957
[84] See article 4 (b) of the UN Model Treaty on Extradition 1990
[85] See article 6(3) of India-Australia Extradition Treaty 2008

2.2.2) Prosecution to be governed by national rules on prosecution of offenders

In case, the competent authorities choose to prosecute rather than to extradite, prosecution shall be performed in accordance with national rules on the prosecution of offenders. Thus, it is provided under the Organised Crime Convention 2000:

> Nothing contained in this Convention shall affect the principle that the description of the offences established in accordance with this Convention and of the applicable legal defences or other legal principles controlling the lawfulness of conduct is reserved to the domestic law of a State Party and that such offences shall be prosecuted and punished in accordance with that law.[86]

The provision categorically states that the crimes established by the Convention shall be prosecuted and punished in accordance with national law of state parties. Similar provisions can be seen in the Drugs Convention 1988 [87] and the UN Convention against Corruption 2003.[88]

National rules on prosecution are usually found in domestic constitutions and criminal procedure codes. For example, Pakistan's Constitution, as well as its criminal procedure code, prohibits prosecutions in contravention of the double jeopardy rule.[89] Likewise, Swiss penal code precludes time-barred prosecutions[90] and prosecutions in contravention of the rule of legality or *nullum crimen*.[91] In the same way, the UK gives immunity from criminal prosecution to foreign heads of states and diplomats and their families and servants.[92] Since these laws and constitutions establish diverse conditions for trial, a case deemed prosecutable by one state will not necessarily be treated as such by the other.

---

[86] See article 11 (6) of the Organised Crime Convention 2000

[87] See article 3(11) of the Drugs Convention 1988

[88] See article 30(9) of the UN Convention against Corruption 2003

[89] See article 13 of the Constitution of Pakistan 1973 as amended in 2012; See also section 403 of the Code of Criminal Procedure, Act V of 1898 as amended by Act II of 1997 [hereinafter Code of Criminal Procedure of Pakistan 1898]

[90] See article 97 Swiss Criminal Code 1937

[91] See article 1 Swiss Criminal Code 1937: 'No one may be punished for an act unless it has been expressly declared to be an offence by the law.'

[92] See section 20 State Immunity Act 1978, 1978 Chapter 33 [hereinafter State Immunity Act 1978 of UK]; See also articles 31 and 37 of Diplomatic Privileges Act 1964, 1964 Chapter 81 [hereinafter Diplomatic Privileges Act 1964]

The enforcement of prosecution in lieu of extradition depends upon the requesting state fulfilling the domestic law conditions of the requested state pertaining to trial. In the case of these conditions not being met, the request for prosecution might be refused. Since prosecution is conducted in place of extradition, if it cannot be carried out, the offender may escape punishment for his crime, altogether.

2.3) *Dedere* part of the obligation

As explained above, *dedere* part of the obligation requires a state to extradite the offender found in its territory to a state having jurisdiction over crime and willing to prosecute.[93] Although it appears first in the scheme of the maxim, there is no priority between the two alternative obligations.[94] In other words, a state in the territory of which an alleged offender is found is not required to consider the option of extradition first.[95]

Each counterterrorism and organised crime convention under consideration lays down extensive provisions on extradition.[96] I shall now discuss some of these to establish the point that the obligation to extradite, just like the obligation to prosecute, is required to be performed subject to the requesting state fulfilling the domestic law conditions of the requested state governing the extradition of offenders.

2.3.1) Obligation to consider the crimes extraditable

In the first place, the international counterterrorism and organised crime conventions declare that the offences established by them shall be included in the existing and future extradition treaties between states parties. Thus, article 8(1) of the Montreal Convention 1971 provides:

---

[93] See text to (n 7)

[94] Plachta (n 2) 334

[95] ibid

[96] See article 8 the Hague Convention 1970, article 8 the Montreal Convention 1971, article 8 the Protection of Diplomats Convention 1973, article 10 the Hostages Convention 1979, article 11 the Nuclear Materials Convention 1980, article 11 the Rome Convention 1988, article 9 the Terrorist Bombings Convention 1997, article 11 the Terrorism Financing Convention 1999, article 13 the Nuclear Terrorism Convention 2005, article 12 the Beijing Convention 2010, article 6 the Drugs Convention 1988, article 16 the Organised Crime Convention 2000 and article 44 the UN Convention against Corruption 2003

> The offence shall be deemed to be included as an extraditable offence in any extradition treaty existing between Contracting States. Contracting States undertake to include the offence as an extraditable offence in every extradition treaty to be concluded between them.[97]

The provision is meant to ensure that the offences set forth by the conventions are deemed extraditable by state parties.[98]

Bilateral treaties adopt different methodologies to reflect their applicability to the crimes set forth by the international conventions. A majority of them indicate this by pronouncing that the political offence exception shall not be applicable to the offences set forth by the international conventions establishing the obligation to extradite or prosecute.[99] For instance, article 6(2) of the Australia-China Extradition Treaty 1993 provides:

> For the purposes of paragraph (1) an offence of a political character does not include any offence in respect of which both Parties have an obligation in accordance with a multilateral agreement either to surrender the person sought or to submit the case to their competent authorities for decision as to prosecution.[100]

Some of them signify it by stating that their provisions shall not affect the obligation of either contracting party under multilateral agreements to which it is a party. For instance, article 1(2) of Canada-France Extradition Treaty 1988 provides:

> The provisions of this Treaty shall not affect the obligations of either Contracting State under any multilateral agreements to which it is a party.[101]

Apparently, the obligation leaves the requested state with no choice but to grant extradition if requisitioned by another state party which has an extradition treaty with it. However, little can be gained from such a provision in situations where the cooperating states do not have any extradition treaty between them and the national law of the requested state

---

[97] See article 8(1) of the Montreal Convention 1971. Identical provision can be seen in all transnational treaties under consideration. For comparable provisions, see (n 87) Chapter 4 above

[98] Omer Y. Elegab, 'The Hague as the Seat of Lockerbie Trial: Some Constraints' 34 The International Lawyer (2000) 289 at 297

[99] See article 3 the European Convention on Extradition 1957

[100] See article 6(2) of Australia-China Extradition Treaty 1993

[101] See article 1(2) Canada-France Extradition Treaty 1988

demands one for the surrender of suspects.[102] This is not just a theoretical proposition: a majority of the counterterrorism and organised crime conventions are ratified by at least three-quarters of the UN members, not all of which have bilateral treaties with each other.[103] Accordingly, it was held by four Judges of the ICJ in their joint declaration in *Lockerbie* case that Libya was under no obligation to extradite pursuant to article 8(1) of the Montreal Convention 1971, since it had no extradition treaty with the US or the UK and its national law required such a treaty for the surrender of Libyan nationals.[104] The declaration makes it clear that despite the imposition of a mandatory obligation under an international convention to consider certain crimes extraditable, the requested state is, in fact, under no obligation to extradite where it has no extradition treaty with the requesting state and its national law requires one. Thus, the determining factor as to whether or not extradition takes place remains the fulfilment of the national law condition of the existence of an extradition treaty, not the offences having been made extraditable by the international conventions on terrorism and organised crime.

2.3.2) Obligation to consider the international conventions as a legal basis of surrender

Another common provision of the international counterterrorism and organised crime conventions stipulates that if a contracting party that makes extradition conditional on the existence of a treaty, receives a request for surrender from another contracting party with which it has no extradition treaty, it 'may', at its own option, consider the conventions as legal basis for surrender.[105] This implies that the international conventions

---

[102] For instance, the Extradition Law of Israel requires the existence of an extradition treaty for surrender of fugitives. See article 2A Extradition Law of Israel 5714-1954 and the Extradition Regulations (Law Procedures and Rules of Evidence in Petitions) 5731-1970

[103] M. Cherif Bassiouni, '*International Criminal Law, Volume II: Multilateral and Bilateral Enforcement Mechanisms*' (3[rd]edn, Martinus Nijhoff, Netherlands, 2008) 47

[104] See Joint declaration (n 18); See also Elegab (n 98)

[105] See article 8 (2) Montreal Convention 1971:

> If a Contracting State which makes extradition conditional on the existence of a treaty receives a request for extradition from another Contracting State with which it has no extradition treaty, it may at its option consider this Convention as the legal basis for extradition in respect of the offences. Extradition shall be subject to the other conditions provided by the law of the requested State.

For Corresponding provisions see (n 87) Chapter 4 above

may constitute temporary extradition treaties in certain situations.[106] The provision suggests further that states parties whose domestic law does not make extradition conditional on the existence of an extradition treaty, 'shall' recognise the offences as extraditable between themselves.[107] However, in each of the two cases, extradition shall be subject to the conditions laid down in the domestic law of the requested state, including any applicable grounds for refusal.[108]

According to Elegab, the provision reduces the complexities of extradition by eliminating the assertion that surrender may not be granted because the requesting and requested states do not have an extradition treaty between them.[109] It nonetheless suffers from two fundamental weaknesses.

Firstly, it merely gives an option to a party which makes extradition conditional on the existence of a treaty, to consider the international conventions as a legal basis for surrender.[110] Such a party is not bound to do so and may refuse extradition on the ground that the requirement in its domestic law of a bilateral treaty is in existence, has not been fulfilled. For instance, in the *Lockerbie* case, Libyan domestic law blocked the extradition of nationals in the absence of an extradition treaty with the requesting state. Libya still had the option to deliver the suspects by relying on the Montreal Convention 1971 as a legal basis of surrender; however, it chose not to do so.[111] According to the dissenting opinion of Judge Bedjaoui, Libya was fully entitled to refuse extradition because there was no rule of international law that had imposed a duty to extradite nationals in the absence an extradition treaty.[112] Notably, the judgement concerned the application and interpretation of the Montreal Convention

---

[106] Elegab (n 98)
[107] See for instance article 8 (3) Montreal Convention 1971:
Contracting States which do not make extradition conditional on the existence of a treaty shall recognize the offences as extraditable offences between themselves subject to the conditions provided by the law of the requested State.
For Corresponding provisions see (n 87) Chapter 4 above
[108] See article 8(2) & 8(3) Montreal Convention 1971; Corresponding provisions can be seen in each transnational treaty under consideration, see (n 228) Chapter 3 above.
[109] Elegab (n 98)
[110] ibid
[111] *Questions of Interpretation and Application of the 1971 Montreal Convention Arising from the Aerial Incident at Lockerbie (Libyan Arab Jamahiriya v. United Kingdom) Provisional Measures*, 1992 ICJ Reports 3 (Apr 14) para 12 at 148
[112] ibid

1971, which represents one of the counterterrorism conventions under consideration.[113] It therefore makes clear that considering an international convention as a legal basis of surrender is purely optional for states whose domestic law makes extradition conditional on the existence of an extradition treaty.

Secondly, the provision has blurred the distinction between the mandatory obligation of states not making extradition conditional and the optional undertaking of states making extradition conditional, by subjecting both obligations to domestic law.[114] Accordingly, whether or not a state makes extradition conditional upon the existence of an extradition treaty, the surrender shall take place in accordance with the conditions laid down in the national law of the requested state.[115] Needless to say, domestic law conditions such as double criminality, extraterritorial jurisdiction and fair treatment can all be used to refuse extradition in either of the two situations.[116]

In summary, it is apparent that the enforcement of the *dedere* part of the obligation is subject to the requesting state fulfilling the domestic law conditions of the requested state pertaining to extradition. Accordingly, notwithstanding the offences having been made extraditable by the international conventions, extradition might be refused if the national law of the requested state demands the existence of an extradition treaty and there is no such treaty between the requesting and requested state. Furthermore, even if an international convention is made the legal basis of surrender, the requesting state is not relieved from its obligation to satisfy domestic law conditions of the requested state pertaining to extradition.

On the top of all this, we have seen that where extradition is refused, prosecution does not necessarily follow. The non-fulfilment of domestic law conditions relating to prosecution provides an equally valid ground to refuse prosecution in lieu of extradition. Clearly, therefore, inclusion of the maxim in national laws alone does not necessarily facilitate its application; harmony in domestic rules pertaining to trial and extradition may yet be required.

---

[113] ibid

[114] Elegab (n 98) 298

[115] ibid

[116] See Chapters 1, 2 and 3 above

Section 3: Regulation of the procedure of extradition under the international conventions on terrorism and organised crime

To bring about harmony in national laws with respect to the *procedure* of extradition, the international conventions on terrorism and organised crime have already set forth certain rules. However, these rules appear to be insufficient to facilitate the application of *aut dedere aut judicare* as a whole, particularly, in the specific context of transnational criminality. In any case, they represent an important step towards synchronisation of domestic laws. Accordingly, it seems appropriate to first consider these rules and second their impact at national level.

3.1) The fiscal offence exception

Before the introduction of the international conventions on terrorism and organised crime, extradition could be refused on the ground that the crime charged constituted a fiscal crime under the law of the requesting state.[117] The rationale of this exception was the general reluctance of states to enforce the internal revenue laws of foreign countries.[118] However, the international conventions, in particular those establishing crimes having financial implications, oblige the parties not to apply a fiscal crime exception to the extradition of suspects. For instance, article 13 of the Terrorism Financing Convention 1999 provides:[119]

> None of the offences set forth in article 2 shall be regarded, for the purposes of extradition or mutual legal assistance, as a fiscal offence. Accordingly, States Parties may not refuse a request for extradition or for mutual legal assistance on the sole ground that it concerns a fiscal offence.

This provision has had a profound impact at the national level. For instance, article II (4) of the Canada-Spain Extradition Treaty 1989 provides, 'An offence of a fiscal character is an extraditable offence.'[120] Similarly, article 5 of the European Convention on Extradition 1957 provides, '[e]xtradition shall be granted… for offences in connection with taxes, duties, customs and exchange only if contracting parties have so decided in respect of any such offence or category of offences.'[121]

---

[117] Satya Deva Bedi, *Extradition: A Treatise on the Laws Relevant to the Fugitive Offenders* (2002-USA) 433

[118] ibid

[119] See also article 16 (15) the Organised Crime Convention 2000 & article 44(16) the UN Convention against Corruption 2003

[120] See article II (4) of Canada-Spain Extradition Treaty 1989

[121] See article 5 the European Convention on Extradition 1957

Likewise, article 2(3) of the UN Model Treaty on Extradition 1990 provides, 'where extradition of a person is sought for an offence against a law relating to taxation, custom duties, exchange control or other revenue matters, extradition may not be refused on the ground that law of the requested state does not impose the same kind of tax, custom duty or exchange regulations of the same kind as law of the requesting state.'[122]

All these provisions illustrate the international regulation of fiscal crime exception to extradition. The harmonisation of national laws with respect to non-application of this requirement makes it easier for the requesting state to obtain extradition of the offenders involved in the acts of transnational terrorism and organised crime.

3.2) The political offence exception

In the past, a number of terrorist acts went unaccounted for because the requested states refused to surrender fugitives on the basis that the crimes charged against them were political. For example, the US has on a number of occasions refused to extradite IRA fugitives to Britain on this basis.[123] Similarly, Kuwait refused to extradite Arab suspects involved in the 1973 hijackings of PanAm and Lufthansa aircrafts which resulted in the deaths of scores of passengers.[124] The reason for world community's silence over these decisions was the existence of a political offence exception in extradition law. While there was no universally agreed definition of what constituted a political crime, it was widely believed that such an exception existed when the offence constituted a political crime under the national law of the requested state.[125]

According to Abramovsky, domestic laws give recognition to two kinds of political offenders: those who resort to a crime in an attempt to escape oppressive political system and those who seek international recognition of their cause by employing methods such as political blackmail and the

---

[122] See article 2(3) UN Model Treaty on Extradition 1990
[123] Bassiouni 'Political Offence Exception' (n 8) 264
[124] Thomas E Carbonneau, 'The Political Offence Exception to Extradition and Transnational Terrorists: Old Doctrine Reformulated and New Norms Created' 1 ASILS Int'l L.J (1977)1 at 33
[125] Charles L. Cantrell, 'The Political Offense Exemption in International Extradition' 60 Marquette Law Review (1977) 777 at 778

destruction of aircraft.[126] The limits of the exception were set out in the landmark British case of *In re Castioni*.[127] Here, it was held that political offences were acts that were incidental to and formed part of a political disturbance in which the offender was taking part.[128] Thus, to claim the political offence exception, an offender must establish that the act for which his extradition was sought had been committed in the course of on-going civil strife involving rival parties competing for power in a state.[129]

The traditional justification for the exception has been the presumption that the surrender of political enemies to the requesting state would result in their trial being influenced by political considerations.[130] The rule frequently appears in national laws and bilateral treaties on extradition as a mandatory ground for refusal. For example, article 5(2) (a) of Pakistan's Extradition Act 1972 provides '[n]o fugitive shall be surrendered: (a) if the offence in respect of which his surrender is sought is of a political character...'[131]

However, the makers of the international conventions on terrorism and organised crime have rejected this exception by declaring that offences established by these conventions shall not be regarded as political for the purposes of extradition or mutual legal assistance. For example, article 11 of Terrorist Bombings Convention 1997 provides:

> None of the offences set forth in article 2 shall be regarded, for the purposes of extradition or mutual legal assistance, as a political offence or as an offence connected with a political offence or as an offence inspired by political motives. Accordingly, a request for extradition or for mutual legal assistance based on such an offence may not be refused on the sole

---

[126] Abraham Abramovsky, 'Multilateral Convention For Suppression of Unlawful Seizure and Interference with Aircraft Part 1: The Hague Convention' 13 Colum. J. Transnat'l L. (1974) 381 at 382-384

[127] *In re Castioni* [1891] 1 QB 149, UK Court of Appeal (England and Wales) 10 Nov, 1890, available at <www. unhcr.org/refworld/docid/489abd.html> [date viewed 21/03/13]

[128] ibid at Para 159, 166

[129] ibid

[130] Geoff Gilbert, 'Terrorism and Political Offence Exemption Reappraised' 34 ICLQ (1984)695 at 695; See alsoCharles L. Cantrell (n 125) at 782

[131] See article 5(2)(a) of Pakistan's Extradition Act 1972; See also article 5, Australian Extradition Act 1988 and article 8(3) of Chinese Extradition Law 2000

> ground that it concerns a political offence or an offence connected with a political offence or an offence inspired by political motives.[132]

This provision has had a significant impact at a national level. For example, article III (1) of the Canada-Spain Extradition Treaty 1989 provides:

> Extradition shall not be granted in any of the following circumstances:
>
> [W]hen the offence for which extradition is requested is considered by the Requested State as a political offence. For the purpose of this paragraph, political offence shall not include ... (b) an offence for which each Contracting State has the obligation pursuant to a multilateral international agreement to extradite the person sought or to submit the case to its competent authorities for the purpose of prosecution...[133]

Similarly, article 6(2) of Australia-China extradition treaty 1993 provides,

> ... an offence of political character does not include any offence in respect of which both parties have an obligation in accordance with a multilateral agreement either to surrender the person sought or to submit the case to their competent authorities for decision as to prosecution.

In the same way, article V of the US-Italy Extradition treaty 1983 provides that extradition shall not be granted for a political offence; however:

> an offence with respect to which both contracting parties have the obligation to submit for prosecution or to grant extradition pursuant to a multilateral international agreement ...will be presumed to have the predominant character of a common crime...

The above provisions reflect that, although the political offence exception still remains intact in bilateral treaties and national laws on extradition, it has been made inapplicable to the offences set forth by the international conventions establishing the *aut dedere aut judicare* obligation. Since all counterterrorism and organised conventions under consideration include this obligation, the crimes established by them are automatically excluded from the operation of the political offence exception. Because transnational crimes, and in particular terrorist crimes, are prone to be regarded as

---

[132] See article 11 Terrorist Bombings Convention 1997. For corresponding provisions, see article 13 the Terrorism Financing Convention 1999, article 13 the Beijing Convention 2010, article 44(4) the UN Convention against Corruption 2003 and article 15 the Nuclear Terrorism Convention 2005

[133] See also article 3 the European Convention on Extradition 1957; article 6 India-China Extradition Treaty 1997 and article 4 the US-India Extradition Treaty 1997

political crimes,[134] the non-applicability of the political offence exception greatly facilitates the extradition and interrogation of suspects involved in these crimes.

However, in spite of the political offence exception having been made inapplicable to transnational crimes, a number of provisions contained in the international conventions regulating these crimes indicate that political crimes can still be treated differently. For example, the provisions on treaties of asylum[135] and principle of non -discrimination[136] suggest that certain concessions can be given to the offenders involved in political crimes.

3.3) Temporary Surrender

Modern international conventions on terrorism and organised crime provide that where a state is required by its domestic law to extradite its nationals subject to the condition only that, if convicted, he will be returned to the requested state to serve his sentence, such conditional extradition shall be considered sufficient discharge of its duty under *aut dedere aut judicare* rule. Thus, article 16 (11) of the Organised Crime Convention 2000 provides:

> Whenever a State Party is permitted under its domestic law to extradite or otherwise surrender one of its nationals only upon the condition that the person will be returned to that State Party to serve the sentence imposed as a result of the trial or proceedings for which the extradition or surrender of the person was sought and that State Party and the State Party seeking the extradition of the person agree with this option and other terms that they may deem appropriate, such conditional extradition or surrender shall be sufficient to discharge the obligation set forth in paragraph 10 of this article.[137]

---

[134] See (n 156) Chapter 3 above

[135] For example article 15 of Hostages Convention reads:

> The provisions of this Convention shall not affect the application of the Treaties on Asylum, in force at the date of the adoption of this Convention, as between the States which are parties to those Treaties; but a State Party to this convention may not invoke those Treaties with respect to another State Party to this Convention which is not a party to those treaties.

[136] See text to (n 191-194) Chapter 4 above

[137] See article 16(11) UN Convention against Transnational Organized Crime; See also article 44(12) UN Convention against Corruption 2003

According to Plachta, this provision has tremendous potential to facilitate extradition because it overcomes the traditional barrier of non-extradition of nationals.[138] This view however appears simplistic because only those states whose national law allows temporary surrender of nationals may benefit from it. States whose national laws impose an absolute prohibition against such extraditions will not be in a position to utilise it. Nevertheless, it represents a definite improvement upon the usual extradition provisions of the counterterrorism and organised crime conventions and could be further refined in future conventions.

The provision has been applied in some bilateral and regional treaties. For example, article 5 of the UK-UAE Extradition Treaty 2008 provides:

> the provisions of article 4(2)(b) shall not preclude the possibility of temporary surrender of the person sought for trial in the requesting state in accordance with conditions to be determined by mutual agreement. The requesting party shall return the person to the requested party after the conclusion of proceedings against that person. The requested party may seek further assurances in any individual case.[139]

Similarly, article 19 of the European Convention on Extradition 1957 provides,

> … the requested state may, instead of postponing surrender, temporarily surrender the person claimed to the requesting state in accordance with conditions to be determined by the mutual agreement between the parties.[140]

In the light of above, it is apparent that the international conventions on terrorism and organised crime have laid down certain rules to simplify and harmonise domestic procedures of extradition. The rules are however insufficient to facilitate the application of *aut dedere aut judicare* as a whole in the specific context of transnational crimes. For example, no attempt has been made under these rules to regulate trial instead of extradition. Furthermore, none of these rules, apart from the one concerning fiscal offence exception, deals with the technicalities of extradition, peculiar to multi-jurisdictional and financial crimes. To address these, further regulation is needed. In this respect, significant advances have been made in some bilateral treaties and domestic laws on extradition. A few of

---

[138] M. Plachta, 'The Lockerbie Case: The Role of Security Council in Enforcing the Principle of Aut Dedere aut Judicare' 12 EJIL (2001) 125 at 137
[139] See article 5 of UK-UAE Extradition Treaty 2008
[140] See article 19 of the European Convention on Extradition 1957

these will be analysed below, resulting in the suggestion that rules modelled after these should be included in the international conventions on terrorism and organised crime in order to facilitate the application of *aut dedere aut judicare* as a whole in the specific context of transnational criminality.

Section 4: Facilitating the application *of aut dedere aut judicare* as a whole in the specific context of transnational crimes

4.1) Facilitating the application of trial option of *aut dedere aut judicare*

To paraphrase the words of Plachta, if *aut dedere aut judicare* is to emerge as an effective tool of state cooperation in law enforcement, trial in lieu of extradition will have to be made more meaningful.[141] This alternative suffers from a number of weaknesses; as such it is generally viewed as a second class form of criminal proceeding.[142] These may include the absence of extraterritorial jurisdiction on the part of the requested state to prosecute crimes committed abroad by non-nationals and general lack of trust upon credibility of trial as a substitute to extradition.

4.1.1) Lack of extraterritorial jurisdiction to prosecute crimes committed abroad by non-national offenders

One of the major difficulties in conducting trial in lieu of extradition is the inability of many states to prosecute non- nationals for crimes committed abroad, on account of their laws not having been made applicable to extraterritorial conduct.[143] This result may lead to impunity.

Some commentators suggest that the Hague Convention 1970 and the conventions modelled after it have resolved this issue by obliging every party in the territory of which the offender is found to establish jurisdiction, regardless of his nationality or the place of the commission of crime.[144] According to Scharf, this represents the principle of *treaty based universality* which is meant to ensure that the offender may not find refuge in the territory of any state party.[145] The overriding effect of the obligation has

---

[141] Plachta 'Aut Dedere Aut Judicare' (n 2) 332
[142] ibid at 337
[143] See text to (n 45-47) above
[144] Bassiouni & Wise (n 1) 16
[145] M P. Scharf, 'Application of Treaty Based Universal Jurisdiction to Nationals of Non-Party States'35 New Eng. L. Rev. (2000-2001) 363 at 373

been confirmed by the ICJ in *Belgium v. Senegal*. In this case, it was held that the establishment of universal jurisdiction represents an integral part of the duty to prosecute as contained in the UN Convention against Torture (UNCAT) 1984 and the party failing to do so would entail international responsibility.[146] At the same time, however, the judgement clarified that it related to crime of torture only which entails customary law obligations superseding the contrary provisions of national law.[147]

The argument that the Hague Convention 1970 gives rise to an overriding duty to establish jurisdiction on the basis of offender's presence disregards the flexible nature of the duty. As explained in chapter 2, states are fairly autonomous in the matter of defining and applying the bases of jurisdiction set out in the international conventions on terrorism and organised crime, including the Hague Convention 1970.[148] In view of this, domestic laws vary as regards implementation of those bases.[149] For example, some states such as Pakistan, have not implemented the jurisdictional basis of offender's presence; others, such as India apply it in a restrictive manner. Yet other states such as the US give it a broad interpretation.[150] Interestingly, this practise has been endorsed by the implementation kits of some counterterrorism and organised crime conventions. For example, the technical assistance guide of the UN Convention against Corruption 2003 provides, 'states may wish to note that there is no single model of implementation.'[151]

Furthermore, while commenting upon the nature of the extradite or prosecute obligation under the Montreal Convention 1971, four judges of the ICJ held that '...in general international law, there is no obligation to prosecute in default of extradition'.[152] Thus, the obligation cannot be viewed as independent of national law. If this view is taken as correct, a state not establishing jurisdiction on the basis of the offender's presence may not be held responsible for violating its international obligation. If

[146] *Questions Relating to the Obligation to Prosecute or Extradite* (*Belgium v. Senegal*), ICJ Judgement July 20, 2012 at para 91
[147] ibid at Para 99 & 75
[148] See flexibilities in the obligation to establish extraterritorial jurisdiction (n 302-313) Part IV Chapter 2 above
[149] For domestic law variation in the implementation of the basis of offender's presence, see text to (n 286-290) Chapter 2 above
[150] ibid
[151] UNODC's Technical Assistance Guide 2009 for the implementation of the UN Convention against Corruption 2003 at 133
[152] Joint Declaration (n 18)

prosecution is non-mandatory, so must be the obligation to establish jurisdiction or to make the offence punishable under any specific theory of jurisdiction. Emphasising this point, Plachta notes, the alternative of prosecution in lieu of extradition 'is meaningful only to the extent that courts of the custodial state have the necessary jurisdiction over the crimes set out in the particular instrument…'[153]

In the light of above, the argument that, pursuant to the Hague Convention 1970, the parties have assumed an overriding duty to establish jurisdiction appears idealistic. Since the rules of the Convention concerning jurisdiction and prosecution are subject to national law, whether or not a state implements any specific basis of jurisdiction would depend upon authorisation under its national law. Accordingly, a state does not automatically become bound to prosecute a non- national offender found present in its territory for crimes committed abroad, simply because an international convention to which it is a party requires it to do so. For such obligation to arise national law must explicitly provide for this basis of jurisdiction or else the prosecution will be deemed violative of the principle of legality or *nullum crimen*. The conclusion draws support from Abelson's observation that '*aut dedere aut judicare* treaties operate in tandem with the law on extradition and extraterritorial jurisdiction'.[154]

Hence, it is clear that the option of trial in lieu of extradition still suffers from the problem of states lacking jurisdiction to prosecute crimes committed abroad by non-nationals. The Hague Convention 1970 and the conventions modelled after it cannot be said to have resolved this problem because their rules pertaining to extraterritorial jurisdiction are subservient to national law.

4.1.2) General lack of trust upon credibility of trial as an alternative to extradition

Another important limitation of the reliance upon trial as an alternative to extradition is general lack of trust among states as regards credibility of trials held abroad.[155] The credibility of a trial will suffer when questions are raised about its fairness or efficiency. Fairness becomes doubtful when a state in the territory of which the offender is found is suspected of being

---

[153] Plachta 'Aut Dedere Aut Judicare' (n 2) 358

[154] Adam Abelson, 'The Prosecute / Extradite Dilemma: Concurrent Criminal Jurisdiction and Global Governance' 16 University of California, Davis (2010) 102 at 124

[155] Plachta 'Aut Dedere Aut Judicare' (n 2) 332

complicit in a crime, efficiency may deteriorate if there is a general indifference of a state towards the crimes taking place abroad or if practical difficulties exist in their prosecution.[156] The former issue came to the fore in *Lockerbie* case where the US and UK refused to cooperate with Libya in sharing information regarding the investigation, on account of their reservations about fairness of a trial in Libya.[157]

To address this problem, some scholars recommend that the option not to extradite should be forfeited in situations where either of two factors—i.e. complicity or lack of interest—is established.[158] This recommendation is impracticable however because it is unlikely that states would accept a limit on their sovereign right to determine the fate of the fugitive found in their territory.[159] Notably, states have consistently shown their reluctance to accept an absolute obligation to extradite because of the traditional norms against extradition of nationals and that of offenders found involved in political crimes.[160] In the words of Bassiouni and Wise, 'the right or privilege to refuse extradition is so deeply rooted in international law that there is something fundamentally wrong about trying to compel a state that is unwilling to do so to relinquish the privilege.'[161] Furthermore, the removal of the option not to extradite defies the alternative nature of *aut dedere aut judicare*. If *judicare* option is taken away, the obligation comes down to mandatory extradition.[162]

4.1.3) Alternative options

I shall now make some suggestions with respect to measures that could be taken to minimise difficulties associated with trial in lieu of extradition. These will neither be so radical as to compromise the alternative nature of *aut dedere aut judicare* nor so demanding as to appear inconsistent with national laws and bilateral treaties.

---

[156] ibid

[157] *Lockerbie* case (n 111) at para 148; See also Plachta 'Lockerbie' (n 138) 127, 129; Bassiouni & Wise (n 1) 58

[158] Elegab (n 98) at 299

[159] Bassiouni & Wise (n 1) 64

[160] Ibid; See also ICAO Doc 8979-LC/165-2 at 81, SA Doc. No.33, Rev.1 (1972)

[161] Bassiouni & Wise (n 1) 66

[162] Bassiouni & Wise (n 1) 66

A-Conditional extradition

State parties might be encouraged to allow the surrender of a fugitive, subject to the condition that if convicted the offender will be returned to the requested state to serve his sentence. This option provides a way out of the situation where extradition could not be granted due to concerns such as harsh punishments in the requesting state and a trial could not be held because of the requested state lacked extraterritorial jurisdiction to punish crimes committed abroad by non-nationals. A modified version of this option appears in the Organised Crime Convention 2000 and the UN Convention against Corruption 2003.[163] Its scope is, however, limited to extradition of nationals only—and then only where domestic law allows it. Hence, it is recommended that the option should not only be disentangled from the limitation of national law permissibility but its ambit should also be enlarged to cover non-nationals as well.

Interestingly, some domestic laws have already incorporated such provisions. For example, New Zealand's extradition law empowers the government to grant conditional extradition: (1) when a mandatory restriction on the surrender of a person applies under the relevant bilateral treaty or national law, and (2) when it appears that the person, if surrendered, would be subjected to torture in the requesting state.[164] The law facilitates extradition by overcoming traditional hurdles such as the non-extradition of nationals and the fear of human rights violations in the requesting state.

B-Sending observers to custodial state

This option was presented by the Institute of International law in 1981.[165] According to it, a state in the territory of which the offence is committed should be entitled to send observers to the requested state to witness the trial in lieu of extradition, unless serious grounds such as preservation of national security justify their non-admittance.[166] A major difficulty in the implementation of this option relates to the cost involved in sending observers. Other challenges include inadequate security arrangements for

---

[163] See (n 137) above

[164] See Sc. 54 Extradition Act 1999 (1999 No. 55) [hereinafter New Zealand's Extradition Act 1999]; See also Sc. 26-a The Extradition For Criminal Offences Act (1957: 668) [hereinafter Swedish Extradition Law 1957]

[165] Resolution Adopted by the 121 Commission at its Session in Dijon,59 Institute of International Law Yearbook (1981) 176-177

[166] ibid

observers.[167] Arguably, if the option is included in the international conventions on terrorism and organised crime, at least the parties which can afford to meet these challenges will have an extra tool at their disposal to ensure the application of *aut dedere aut judicare*.

C-Surrender to third state

States can be encouraged to surrender the fugitive to a third state which does not have an interest in the prosecution that is adverse to that of the requested state.[168] The legal basis for including such an option already exists under the international conventions on terrorism and organised crime as they provide that the offence should not only be deemed to have occurred in the territory of the state in which it actually takes place but also in the territory of every state having jurisdiction under the conventions .[169]

Notably, the option was finally adopted by the parties to the *Lockerbie* case when all other measures had failed to end the standoff between Libya and the US and the UK.[170] Acting upon this formula, Libya agreed to surrender the suspects to Netherlands to be tried by a court comprised of Scottish Judges applying Scottish law.[171] In the same way, Afghanistan and Saudi Arabia had nearly struck a deal with respect to surrender of Bin Laden to Saudi Arabia when the incident of the bombings of the US embassies took place in 1998. This led to airstrikes against Afghanistan resulting in breakdown of talks.[172] In this case, the surrender was demanded by the US on the basis of an indictment issued by one of its courts, however, the host state Afghanistan refused to extradite him either to the US or the UK.[173] The frustrated negotiations between Saudi Arabia and Afghanistan proved that the Taliban, then the government of Afghanistan, was willing to consider the option of surrendering the fugitive to a third state, i.e. Saudi Arabia.

---

167 Plachta 'Aut Dedere Aut Judicare'(n 2) 337

168 Plachta 'Lockerbie' (n 138) 131

169 See text to (n 216-219) Chapter 2 above; See also article 8(4) Hague Convention 1970

170 Plachta 'Lockerbie' (n 138) 125

171 ibid

172 ibid at 137

173 Indictment, *US v. Usama Bin Laden* S(2) 98 Cr.1023 (LSB) (SDNY 4 Nov. 1998) <www.heroes.net/pub/heroes/indictment.html> [date accessed 21/03/13

4.1.4) The problem of competing jurisdictions and the absence of hierarchy in the alternative obligations

In cases involving ordinary crimes such as murder, the requested state should normally have no hesitation in granting extradition because it is unlikely to have a parallel interest in the prosecution of the offender.[174] However, in transnational crimes like hijacking, since the crime spreads across national frontiers, the requested state may have a jurisdictional nexus with the crime, making it punishable under its own law.[175] Such situations may, for example, arise when the accused is a national of the requested state, when the crime occurs in part in its territory or when the crime is committed on an aircraft or vessel owned by it.[176] Equally, the requesting state may have its own compelling reasons to request extradition, such as the occurrence of the main part of the crime on its territory, threats to its national security or injury to its citizens. Thus, the prosecution of transnational crimes may involve an inherent clash of jurisdictional interests.[177] Although, the international conventions regulating these crimes oblige the requested state to submit the case for prosecution if extradition is refused, this option may not necessarily satisfy the requesting state, particularly when it has suffered greater injury or distrusts the proceedings in the requested state.[178]

To illustrate the problem, a hypothetical example of two states interacting in two different situations is given below.

4.1.4.1) Hypothetical example

a)-Suppose the US and India are partners to a bilateral extradition treaty.[179] An Indian national after committing murder of a fellow citizen in New Delhi, escapes to the US. Subsequently, India makes a request for extradition. In this situation, the US is expected to have no difficulty in accepting the request because the offender and the victim as well as the place of the commission are all based in India and the US has no parallel interest in the prosecution of the offender. Most importantly, the US has an extradition treaty with India which obliges it to extradite, provided, extradition is not barred under the grounds of refusal as established by the

[174] Abelson (n 154) at 110
[175] ibid at 125
[176] ibid at 102
[177] ibid at 125
[178] Elegab (n 98) 296
[179] See for example, US-India Extradition Treaty 1997

treaty.[180] The grounds of refusal include double jeopardy, political offence exception, lapse of time and capital punishment.[181] Assuming none of these issues are at stake, the US will most probably extradite the offender.

b)-A second hypothetical situation involves the crime of hijacking. Suppose the offender again an Indian national hijacks an Indian aircraft from New Delhi, carrying several American nationals, amongst passengers of other nationalities and escapes to the US. India makes a request for extradition on the bases of territoriality, nationality and flag state principles. This time the process of arriving at a decision is not likely to be as simple as it was in the case of murder. Although, the US is bound by the same extradition treaty, it has its own jurisdictional nexus with the act of hijacking, hence its own parallel interest in the prosecution. The basis of jurisdiction is presumably provided by the US law on hostage taking which makes it a federal crime to take hostages whether inside or outside the US when the victims or offender is a US national.[182]

The conflicting interests of India and the US in the prosecution may lead to a stalemate because the applicable multilateral convention, i.e. the Hague Convention 1970,[183] does not require extradition in all circumstances; rather, it allows refusal of the extradition, where the requested state prefers prosecution over extradition.[184] Nonetheless, the Convention does not provide guidance as to which state prevails.

The international conventions on terrorism and organised crime lack a mechanism by which the requested state may choose between extradition and prosecution in cases involving competing jurisdictional interests. As Clarke has observed, the conflict of concurrent jurisdiction has been downplayed in the negotiations leading to some of these conventions.[185] However, such a conflict remains a genuine possibility owing to the nature of offences and the absence of priority in the alternative obligations of extradition and prosecution.

---

[180] See article 1 ibid

[181] articles 4-8 ibid

[182] 18 U.S.C. Sc. 1203 (making it a federal crime to take hostages "whether inside or outside the United States," so long as "the offender or the person seized or detained is a national of the United States").

[183] See current status of the Hague Convention 1970
<http://www.icao.int/secretariat/legal/List%20of%20Parties/Hague_EN.pdf>

[184] See article 7 the Hague Convention 1970

[185] See Roger Clarke 'The United Nations Convention against Transnational Organized Crime' 50 Wayne Law Review (2004) 161-184 at 181

The decision to extradite or prosecute solely comes down to the discretion of the requested state. Although modern international conventions on terrorism and organised crime encourage the parties to consult with each other, this remains a recommendation only. Accordingly, in the *Lockerbie* case, all interested parties admitted before the ICJ that the Montreal Convention 1971 is silent on the matter of priority or exclusivity of jurisdiction.[186] In this case, the US and UK asserted jurisdiction on the basis of flag state and territorial principles respectively, whereas Libya claimed it on the basis of offender's presence in state territory. While the Montreal Convention establishes mandatory obligations to assert jurisdiction under territoriality and flag state principles, it refers to the offender's presence only as a secondary basis.[187] However, the ICJ in its judgement did not make any distinction between the theories of jurisdiction relied upon.[188]

Since the parties in this case could not arrive at a negotiated settlement, the Security Council had to intervene. This was interpreted by one commentator as world community's substantial loss of faith in the authority of the Montreal Convention to settle disputes.[189] It can thus be argued that under the existing scheme of the international conventions on terrorism and organised crime, the state in the territory of which the offender is found assumes de facto priority regardless of the strength or weakness of its jurisdictional claim vis-a-vis the requesting state.[190] As noted by Elegab, in *Lockerbie* case, the UK and the US had superior jurisdictional claims as compared to Libya. However, since Libya had custody of the offenders, the US and the UK had no choice but to wait until Libya voluntarily forfeited its authority to prosecute.[191]

According to some commentators, the decision to extradite or prosecute could be regulated by establishing a system of hierarchy amongst the bases of jurisdiction.[192] A resolution to this effect was actually adopted at the 17th Commission of the Institute of International Law at its 2005 Session. Paragraph 3(c) of the resolution provides:

---

186 Elegab (n 98) 296
187 See article 5 the Montreal Convention 1971
188 *Lockerbie* Case (n 111) at para 9
189 Plachta 'Aut Dedere Aut Judicare' (n 2) 331
190 ibid
191 Elegab (n 98) 296
192 Abramovsky' Hague Part 1' (n 126) 396

> Any state having custody over an alleged offender should, before commencing a trial … ask the state where the crime was committed or the state of nationality of the person concerned, whether it is prepared to prosecute that person…[193]

The idea however has not made its way to the international conventions on terrorism and organised crime because of the lack of necessary consensus. For example, during the drafting of the Hague Convention 1970, it was proposed that state of registration should be given priority, by making it mandatory for the requested state to accept its extradition request. The proposal was rejected after having been put to a vote.[194] Similarly, the Chinese proposal to subordinate the permissive bases of jurisdiction to mandatory bases was also rejected during the drafting of the Terrorist Bombing Convention.[195]

4.1.4.2) The rule of 'Reasonableness' as an alternative

As an alternative, a rule of reasonableness could be included in the international counterterrorism and organised crime conventions on the pattern of some domestic laws. In the words of Clarke, 'since general international law has not established a priority system among various jurisdictional theories, the solution is negotiation especially on the basis where the strongest case may be mounted.'[196]

Rule of reasonableness provides an efficient mechanism to determine the proprietary of contradictory jurisdictional claims. According to it, states are to weigh their interest in prosecuting a crime, relative to the interest of other states having concurrent jurisdiction over the same crime.[197] When the interest of one state proves stronger, the state having the lesser interest would be required to voluntarily abstain from exercising jurisdiction, regardless of the strength of its claim under the traditional rules of jurisdiction.[198]

---

[193] See Paragraph 3(c) of Resolution adopted at the 17th Commission of the Institute of International Law at its 2005 Krakow Session <http://www.idi-iil.org/idiE/resolutionsE/2005_kra_03_en.pdf> [Date accessed 21/03/23]
[194] ICAO Doc 8979-LC/165-2 at 81, SA Doc. No.33, Rev.1 (1972)
[195] See UN Doc. A/C.6/52/L.3, Written proposals to Ad hoc Committee.
[196] Clarke (n 185) 181
[197] P.M. Roth, 'Reasonable Extraterritoriality- Correcting the Balance of Interest' 41 ICLQ (1992) 254 at 258
[198] Ibid

Such a rule would require the state in the territory of which the offender is found to weigh its interest in prosecuting him vis-a-vis the interest of the requesting state when making a decision to extradite or prosecute. The rule appears in the Restatement Third of the US Foreign Policy Law.[199] It was also applied by the Canadian Supreme Court in the case of *Swystun v. United States*.[200]

Section 403 of the Restatement 3rd provides that regardless of the fact that a state is competent to establish jurisdiction on any of the bases provided under international law the exercise of jurisdiction will be subject to the requirement that one state may not act in unreasonable manner towards another.[201] Section 403(2) contains a list of factors on the basis of which reasonableness can be determined.[202] These are:

i) The link of the activity to be regulated with the territory of the regulating state.
ii) The connections between the regulating state and the persons responsible for activity to be regulated or for whom regulation is designed.
iii) The character of the activity to be regulated and the importance of such regulation to regulating state and degree to which such regulation is generally accepted.
iv) Whether justified expectations would be hurt or protected by such regulation.
v) The extent to which such regulation is consistent with the international system and traditions.
vi) The extent to which another state may have an interest in such regulation and the likelihood it will conflict with regulations imposed by other states.

Based on this approach, the state which has maximum interest in the prosecution would get the custody of the offender.

---

199 See Restatement of the Law, Third, Foreign Relations Law of the United States 1987 <http://internationalcriminallaw.org/Restatement(Third)_of_Foreign_Relations_Law/RSecs334_401-04_411_432_442.PDF> [Date accessed 21/03/23]

200 *Swystun v. United States of America* (1988) 40 C.C.C (3d) 222, 227-228 (Man. Q.B)

201 See Sc.403 Restatement Third (n 199)

202 ibid

It has been argued that a majority of these factors are subjective and give enormous discretion to national authorities of the requested state to interpret them in line with its local interests.[203] Furthermore, the factors outlined by Restatement 3rd make no distinction between civil and criminal proceedings; hence, their utility in the specific context of criminal law is questionable. Accordingly, one scholar has proposed an amended list of factors which not only appears more precise but is also more relevant in the specific context of criminal law.[204] These are:

i) Which state which has suffered the greatest injury as a result of the crime?
ii) In which state were the effects of the crime most felt?
iii) Which state provides the stronger guarantees of procedural fairness?
iv) Which state is the place of offender's or victim's nationality?
v) In which state did the major part of the crime occur?

The above factors alone may not, however, prove sufficient to arrive at a fair decision in cases involving transnational crimes. This is so because transnational crimes differ from ordinary crimes in that their occurrence does not necessarily imply the greatest injury to the territorial state; they may have larger repercussions for the targeted state.[205] For example, the offence of terror financing may have lesser implications for the state in the territory of which the act of financing has been committed as compared to the state in the territory of which the actual terrorist attack was to be committed.[206] Similarly, in cases involving conspiracies to export narcotics, the state where the conspiracy was hatched may have a lesser interest in prosecution as compared to the state where the narcotics were planned to be received.[207] Likewise in hijacking and hostage taking, the state which is the object of coercion or whose nationals have been targeted may have a greater interest in the prosecution as compared to the state of registration of the aircraft or state of the offender's nationality.[208]

---

[203] Roth (n 197) 256
[204] Abelson (n 154) 129
[205] ibid
[206] See article 2 Terrorism Financing Convention 1999
[207] See article 3 the Drugs Convention 1988; See also Plachta 'Aut Dedere Aut Judicare' (n 2) 339
[208] See article 1 The Hostages Convention 1979; See also Joseph J. Lambert, *Terrorism and Hostages in international law- A Commentary on the Hostages Convention 1979* (Grotius publications 1990) 150

To counter these challenges, two additional factors can be added to the list of factors indicating reasonableness. Firstly, jurisdiction might be assessed on case by case basis by balancing the interest of the requesting and requested states.[209] Secondly, a new factor of *forum conveniens*, i.e., the place where it would be most convenient to hold the trial, should also be introduced.[210] Convenience may be determined with respect to the collection of evidence, the availability of witnesses or the ability to bring together all of the accused and witnesses in one place.[211]

Notably, the rule of reasonableness does not make it obligatory for the requested state to extradite the offender when the interest of the requesting state is clearly greater. The power to decide whether or not to extradite still remains with the requested state. What it does, however, is invite states to consider various factors when making their decision whether or not to extradite. It therefore brings harmony in national laws with respect to matters to be considered when making a decision to extradite or prosecute the offender in cases involving competing jurisdictions.

Considering the explanation above, it is clear that the application of trial in lieu of extradition cannot be facilitated simply by requiring the parties to implement *aut dedere aut judicare*. It requires further, international guidance with respect to resolution of the problems inherent in this option such as, lack of extraterritorial jurisdiction to prosecute non-nationals and the issue of competing and concurrent jurisdictions.

4.2) Facilitating the application of extradition option of *aut dedere aut judicare*

Since transnational criminality differs from ordinary crimes, the rules of extradition governing ordinary crimes may not be suitable for surrender of suspects involved in these crimes. To facilitate the extradition of transnational offenders, some bilateral and regional treaties include special rules. It is recommended that corresponding rules should be included in the international conventions on terrorism and organised crime to facilitate the application of extradition option of *aut dedere aut judicare* in the specific context of transnational criminality.

---

209 Abelson (154) 129
210 ibid at 134
211 ibid

4.2.1) Restricted application of the principle of speciality

As explained in chapter 3 above, speciality is a rule of extradition law which prohibits the requesting state from trying the offender for an offence other than that for which his extradition was granted.[212] The rule creates complications in the trial of transnational offenders whose crimes tend to aggregate and compound.[213] For instance, if an accused is extradited for the import of drugs, he may subsequently be found to have been involved in organised drug trafficking activities. In such cases, the strict application of speciality will prevent the requesting state from prosecuting the offender for subsequently disclosed offences.

To counter this difficulty, some bilateral treaties limit the application of speciality. For instance, article 18(3) of Canada-France Extradition Treaty 1988 provides:

> When the legal nature of an offence for which a person has been extradited is changed, the person shall not be prosecuted or tried unless the new description of the offence … (b) relates to the same conduct as the offence for which extradition was granted.[214]

Similarly, article 18 (1) of Australia-China Extradition Treaty 1993 provides that the rule of speciality shall not prevent the requesting state from trying the offender for:

> (b) any lesser offence however described, disclosed by the facts in respect of which return was ordered provided such an offence is an offence for which the person sought can be returned under this Agreement.[215]

Likewise article 18 (1) of the US-UK Extradition Treaty 2003 provides:

> A person extradited under this treaty may not be detained, tried or punished in the requesting state except for: a) any offense for which extradition was granted or a differently denominated offense based on the same facts as the offense on which extradition was granted provided such

---

[212] See text to (n 92-95) Chapter 3 above

[213] Bruce Zagaris, 'US International Cooperation against Transnational Organised Crime' 44 Wayne State Law Review (1998-1999) 1401 at 1425-1426

[214] See article 18 (3) Canada-France Extradition Treaty 1988; Also see article 13 of US-Israel Extradition Treaty 1962, article 17 UK-UAE Extradition Treaty 2008; article 13 Thailand-China Extradition Treaty 1993 and article 16 India-China Extradition Treaty 1997

[215] See article 18(1)(b) Australia-China Extradition Treaty 1997

> offense is extraditable or is a lesser included offense; (b) any offense committed after the extradition of the person…[216]

In the same way, article XVI (1) of the US-Italy Extradition Treaty 1983 provides:

> A person extradited under this Treaty may not be detained, tried or punished in the Requesting Party except for: (a) the offense for which extradition has been granted or when the same facts for which extradition was granted constitute a differently denominated offense which is extraditable…[217]

The above provisions make clear that the rule of speciality will not prevent the requesting state from prosecuting the offender for new charges arising out of the same conduct which led to his extradition. In this way, the provisions facilitate the trial of transnational offenders for a broader range of offences.

4.2.2) Surrender of property and mutual legal assistance in extradition

Some extradition treaties impose a mandatory obligation upon the requested state to surrender the proceeds and instrumentalities of crime to the requesting state along with the accused. For example, article 17 of Australia-China Extradition Treaty 1993 provides:

> (1) When a request for surrender is granted, the requested party shall as far as its law allows, hand over upon request, to the requesting party all articles including sums of money: (a) which may serve as a proof of offence (b) which may have been acquired by the person sought as a result of the offence and are in that person's possession or discovered subsequently.[218]

Similarly, article XVIII of the US-Italy Extradition Treaty 1983 provides:

> 1. All articles instruments, objects of value, documents or other evidence relating to the offence may be seized and surrendered to the Requesting party. Such property may be surrendered when extradition cannot be effected. The rights of 3rd parties in such property shall be respected.
>
> 2. The Requested party may condition the surrender of property upon satisfactory assurance from the Requesting party that the property will

---

216 See article 18(1) US-UK Extradition Treaty 2003
217 See article XVI US-Italy Extradition Treaty 1983
218 See article 17 Australia-China Extradition Treaty 1997

> be returned to the Requested party as soon as practicable, and may defer its surrender if it is needed as evidence in the Requested party.[219]

Apart from this, some bilateral treaties also enjoin the requested state to gather evidence in its territory for the requesting state relating to the offence for which extradition is sought. Thus, article XX of the Canada-Spain Extradition Treaty 1989 provides:

> the requested state agrees upon request, to the extent permitted by its law, to gather evidence within its own territory for the requesting state relating to the offence for which extradition is requested.[220]

Since many of the crimes proscribed by the international conventions on terrorism and organised crime lead to the generation of proceeds, the availability of such proceeds in trial proceedings is necessary to establish a link between the crime and the offender.[221] The above provisions oblige the requested state not only to provide assistance to the requesting state as regards the identification and tracing of proceeds, but also to deliver such proceeds to the requesting state along with the fugitive.

Although the two provisions are widely applied in extradition treaties, they do not find expression in the international conventions on terrorism and organised crime. One reason for this could be that the conventions establish separate provisions on mutual legal assistance and surrender of property is regarded a matter of legal assistance rather than extradition. However, since extradition treaties are much greater in number as compared to mutual assistance treaties,[222] such provisions should be included in international conventions, so that if the requesting and requested states do not have a mutual assistance treaty, the conduct of trial

---

[219] See article XVIII US-Italy Extradition Treaty 1988; Also see article 16 US-UK Extradition Treaty 2003; article 16 US-Israel Extradition Treaty 1962; article 14 UK-UAE Extradition Treaty 2008; article 20 the European Convention on Extradition 1957; article 13 the UN Model Treaty on Extradition 1990; article 14 Thailand-China Extradition Treaty 1993; article 15 India-China Extradition Treaty 1997 and article 18 Australia-Germany Extradition Treaty 1988

[220] See article XX of Canada-Spain Extradition Treaty 1989; See also article XVIII of the US-Italy Extradition Treaty 1983

[221] Jimmy Gurule, 'The 1988 UN Convention against Illicit Traffic in Narcotic Drugs and Psychotropic Substances-A Ten Years Perspective: Is International Cooperation Merely Illusory?' 22 Fordham International law Journal (1998-1999) 74 at 77; See also Technical Guide for implementing the UNCAC 2003 (n 151) at 92

[222] M. Cherif Bassiouni, Multilateral and Bilateral Enforcement (n 103) 14

will not suffer. Because extradition is to be granted subject to the procedural requirements of the requested state's law, if the law of the requested state includes no enabling provision, it will be in no position to offer such assistance.

In view of the above, it is clear that the imposition of a mandatory obligation to implement *aut dedere aut judicare* is not sufficient to facilitate the application of the mechanism. To achieve this objective, there must be regulation of trial in lieu of extradition with a view to make it a viable option and simplification of extradition in the specific context of transnational crimes. For this purpose, the above bilateral treaties, domestic laws and practices provide excellent examples. It is suggested that corresponding provisions should be imported in the international conventions on terrorism and organised crime to enable the parties to apply rather than to merely include the maxim in national laws.

Conclusions

The international conventions on terrorism and organised crime aim to facilitate state cooperation in bringing to justice the offenders involved in borderless crimes. For this purpose, they establish the mandatory obligation to implement the mechanism of *aut dedere aut judicare.* The obligation is designed to bring harmony to national laws with a view to facilitating the application of the mechanism.

Pursuant to this obligation, the parties are required to implement domestically the alternative enforcement measures of extradition or prosecution, so that the offenders involved in these crimes may not find refuge on the territory of any state party. However, the application of both enforcement measures depends upon the requesting state fulfilling the domestic law conditions of the requested state. For there to be an obligation, harmony is needed as regards the domestic law conditions governing extradition and trial. If the laws of the two states differ substantially in regard to these conditions, the realisation of the obligation becomes doubtful. This could result in the offender avoiding punishment for his crime altogether. Consequently, it can be argued that the obligation in its present form, while bringing harmony to the extent of requiring the inclusion of the maxim in national laws, is insufficient to facilitate its application. To do so, it is essential that the international conventions on terrorism and organised crime must regulate and simplify the domestic law conditions of extradition and trial.

The conditions of law enforcement cooperation, including those of extradition and of prosecution in lieu thereof, have been discussed in Chapters 1 2 and 3, this chapter has focused on procedure of applying these measures. Although the international conventions on terrorism and organised crime have made some inroads with respect to regulating the procedure of extradition, these inroads have been insufficient to facilitate the application of *aut dedere aut judicare* as whole, particularly, in the specific context of transnational crimes. Furthermore, the conventions include more than one versions of *aut dedere aut judicare*. Since the parties are allowed to implement any of these, the application of the mechanism might become problematic whenever it involves states following different formulas.

As opposed to the international conventions on terrorism and organised crime, some bilateral treaties and domestic laws on extradition focus on simplifying the procedure of extradition and trial in the specific context of transnational crimes. In the first place, they require the parties to make trial in lieu of extradition more credible by implementing options such as allowing observers to witness the trial and to consider holding trial in a third state. Secondly, they recommend that parties adopt the rule of reasonableness in order to deal with the problem of competing jurisdictions peculiar to transnational crimes. Thirdly, they enjoin the parties to create new powers to respond to the requests of extradition involving multi-jurisdictional and financial crimes.

This technique appears to be far more useful in facilitating the application of *aut dedere aut judicare,* than merely requiring the parties to include the maxim in their national law. It therefore merits being tested in the international conventions on terrorism and organised crime with a view to giving it a global effect.

In sum, it is suggested that the aim of bringing to justice transnational offenders cannot be realised effectively just by establishing the international obligation to implement *aut dedere aut judicare*. Doing so requires the regulation and simplification of the domestic law procedure relating to extradition and trial.

CHAPTER 6

FACILITATION OF LAW ENFORCEMENT COOPERATION BY IMPOSING DUTY TO CONFISCATE, IDENTIFY AND FREEZE THE PROCEEDS OR INSTRUMENTALITIES OF CRIME

Introduction

The UN-sponsored international conventions on terrorism and organised crime deal with a kind of criminality which spreads across national frontiers. Since it is not possible for any one state to single-handedly prevent and punish these crimes, their suppression demands state cooperation in law enforcement.

Confiscation of the proceeds and instrumentalities of crime represents an important tool of law enforcement to combat sophisticated transnational criminality. Accordingly, the international conventions proscribing these crimes establish mandatory obligation for the parties to implement the mechanism of confiscation upon foreign request. The obligation is designed to bring harmony to national legal systems in order to ensure that the domestic laws of states parties will accommodate foreign requests for confiscation. This chapter is concerned with analysing the nature of the obligation and the question of the extent to which it contributes to facilitation of state cooperation in confiscation.

It will be explained that the obligation besides having been left vague is required to be implemented to the extent permissible under national laws. Hence, its translation into national laws is likely to be inconsistent. The reason is that the international counterterrorism and organised crime conventions are universal in scope, and states parties to them represent diverse legal systems. When they implement these rules subject to national legal principles, the resultant domestic legislation inevitably reflects this diversity. The ensuing dissimilarity in national procedures leads to denial of a foreign request of confiscation. Thus, the obligation, in its present form, may only bring harmony to the extent of including confiscation in national laws as a law enforcement tool, which is insufficient to facilitate its application upon foreign request. To facilitate the application of confiscation, as a device of inter-state cooperation, it is important that the conventions bring harmony in national procedures of confiscation.

The dissimilar national procedures have time and again led to a foreign request not having been accepted or its acceptance having been declared unlawful by the courts of the requested state. For example, in *Noriega* case, when the US government, pursuant to a request made by the Columbian government, froze the assets of the General Noriega in spite of his difficulties in paying his attorney's fee, the Court regarded it a violation of the sixth amendment to the US constitution which protects the right to be defended by the attorney of one's own choice. Consequently, the assets had to be unfrozen.

The imprecise nature of the obligation and the allowance for implementing it subject to national legal principles leave enough gaps in the national procedures to make possible the refusal of state cooperation in confiscation, based upon the non-existence of enabling provisions in the laws of the requested state or the request being inconsistent with its national law. This calls into question the effectiveness of the reliance on mandatory obligations to facilitate the application of confiscation pursuant to foreign request.

As an alternative, the makers of the international conventions may wish to consider simplifying the procedure of confiscation upon foreign request, by including elaborate provisions, giving extra tools to states to offer inter-state assistance when their existing procedures prove insufficient. Although states have been reluctant to accept absolute and overriding international obligation, they are less likely to oppose detailed provisions on the procedure of confiscation which are only meant to serve as models for domestic legislation. Interestingly, this approach has already been adopted in some bilateral/ regional treaties and domestic laws on mutual legal assistance and merits being experimented with at international level.

The chapter has been divided into three sections. Section 1 gives an introduction to confiscation and its significance for bringing to justice transnational offenders. Section 2 analyses the provisions of the international counterterrorism terrorism and organised crime conventions concerning the empowerment of national law enforcement authorities and the execution of foreign requests of confiscation. Section 3 examines provisions of the conventions concerning mutual legal assistance.

Section 1: Introduction to confiscation and its significance for bringing to justice transnational offenders

1.1) Transnational criminality and the importance of confiscation for its suppression

The enforcement modality of confiscation targets the financial aspect of the crime.[1] Its evolution is based on the concept that offenders must be made to realise that 'crime never pays'.[2] Punishment in the form of imprisonment is ill-suited to discouraging sophisticated serious crimes because even if imprisoned, the offender will be in a position to benefit from his unlawful wealth.[3] Accordingly, confiscation aims at the permanent deprivation of the property to keep the offenders from enjoying the fruits of their crime.[4] Since the terms 'forfeiture' and 'confiscation' have been used interchangeably in multilateral and bilateral treaties, the same approach has been adopted in this chapter.[5]

As the crimes established by the international conventions on terrorism and organised crime essentially involve the element of border crossing, it frequently happens that the crime is committed in one state while its proceeds or instrumentalities are transferred to another to avoid their seizure by law enforcement authorities.[6] For example, when drugs are

---

[1] Bruce Zagaris and Elizabeth Kingma, 'Asset Forfeiture International and Foreign Law: An Emerging Regime' 5 Emory International Law Review (1990) 445 at 448

[2] UNODC'S Technical Guide for the implementation of the UN Convention against Corruption 2003 at 92 <www.unodc.org/documents/corruption/Technical_Guide_UNCAC.pdf > [Date accessed 21/03/23]

[3] Cherif Bassiouni, 'Effective National and International Action against Organised Crime and Terrorist Criminal Activities' 4 Emory International Law Review (1990) 9 at 21; See also UNODC'S Legislative Guide for implementing the Organized Crime Convention 2000 at 136 <http://www.unodc.org/pdf/crime/legislative_guides/Legislative%20guides_Full%20version.pdf> [Date accessed 21/03/23]

[4] See article 1(f) the Drugs Convention 1988; See also Technical Guide to the UN Convention against Corruption (n 2) at 92

[5] See article 2(1) (b) of 2004 Mutual Legal Assistance Treaty among eight far-eastern states. See also article 1(f) the Drugs Convention 1988

[6] Jimmy Gurule, 'The 1988 UN Convention against Illicit Traffic in Narcotic Drugs and Psychotropic Substances-A Ten Years Perspective: Is International

imported into a country, huge financial profits are made by their importers. If an investigation is launched into the offence, the offenders come to know of it because the due process laws of many states allow public access to information concerning the investigation of crimes.[7] To avoid the seizure of their illicit profits, the offenders might immediately transfer them abroad where they are inter-mingled with lawful wealth or converted into some other form of property.[8] Once introduced into banking system or converted into new property, it becomes extremely difficult to trace their illicit origin.[9]

To ensure the seizure of funds which are transferred abroad, it is essential that states must cooperate with each other in identification, tracing, freezing and forfeiture of the proceeds of crime regardless of the place of the commission of crime which led to their generation. Accordingly, the international conventions regulating the acts of transnational terrorism and organised crime establish mandatory obligation for the parties to implement the mechanism of confiscation pursuant to foreign request.

It is thus apparent that confiscation of the proceeds and instrumentalities of crime represents an important law enforcement measure to combat transnational crimes.[10] The cross-border nature of these crimes necessitates state cooperation in law enforcement. This in turn demands confiscation of the proceeds upon foreign request. Since the object of the international conventions regulating these crimes is to facilitate state cooperation in law enforcement, they establish mandatory obligation for the parties to implement the mechanism of confiscation upon foreign request.

The international community's seriousness in putting to use confiscation to root out transnational criminality can be gauged from the fact that state cooperation in confiscation is not only required by the international conventions on terrorism and organised crime, but has also been focused in the Security Council's binding resolutions on countering terrorism and in the Financial Action Task Force (FATF) recommendations on money laundering. For example, resolution 1373 (2001) of the Security Council

---

Cooperation Merely Illusory?' 22 Fordham International Law Journal (1998-1999) 74 at 77; See also M. Sornarajah, 'Extraterritorial Criminal Jurisdiction' 2 Singapore Journal of International and Comparative Law (1998) 1 at 1,4

[7] Gurule ibid

[8] Gurule ibid at 75

[9] Technical Guide to the UN Convention against Corruption (n 2) 92

[10] Zagaris 'Asset Forfeiture' (n 1) 446

requires states to freeze without delay funds and other financial assets belonging to persons involved in terrorist acts.[11] Similarly, Special recommendation III of FATF calls upon states to target financial wealth of the offenders by enabling their courts to exercise power of forfeiture.[12] FATF is an inter-governmental body whose purpose is the development and promotion of policies both at national and international level to combat money laundering and terror financing. FATF is in existence since 1989 and its 40 + 9 Recommendations provide the international standard for combating money laundering and terror financing.[13]

1.2) Introduction to the different steps in the process of state cooperation in confiscation

Elaborate provisions on the process of confiscation upon foreign request can be found in four international conventions on terrorism and organised crime. These include the UN Convention against Narcotics Drugs 1988,[14] the Terrorism Financing Convention 1999,[15] the Organised Crime Convention 2000 [16] and the UN Convention against Corruption 2003.[17] In the other conventions under consideration herein, the obligation is implicit in their mutual legal assistance provisions.[18]

According to the aforementioned four conventions, the obligation is comprised of five steps. Firstly, the parties are required to criminalise money laundering.[19] Secondly, they are required to control the movement

---

[11] See paragraph 1 (c) S/RES/1373 (2001); See also paragraph 4, S/RES/1267 (1999)

[12] See Special Recommendation III of FATF <www.fatf-gafi.org/document/44/0,3746,en_32250379_43751788_1_1_1_1,00.htm> [Date accessed 21/03/23]

[13] See FATF 40 + 9 Recommendations <www.fatf-gafi.org/document/44/0,3746,en_32250379_43751788_1_1_1_1,00.htm> [Date accessed 21/03/23]

[14] See article 5 the Drugs Convention 1988

[15] See article 8 the UN Convention against Financing of Terrorism 1999

[16] See article 12-13 Organised Crime Convention 2000

[17] See article 31 & 55 UN Convention against Corruption 2003

[18] See for instance article 11 the Montreal Convention 1971, article 11 the Hostages Convention 1979 and article 12 the Rome Convention 1988. For Corresponding provisions of other Conventions, see (n 10) Chapter 4 above

[19] See article 3 the Drugs Convention 1988, article 6 the Organised Crime Convention 2000 and article 23 the UN Convention against Corruption 2003

of money across national borders.[20] Thirdly, they are obliged to empower their law enforcement authorities to identify, seize, trace, freeze and forfeit the proceeds, property and instrumentalities of crimes.[21] Fourthly, the parties are required to carry out these measures upon the request of another state having jurisdiction over the crime.[22] Lastly, extensive provisions are laid down on mutual legal assistance requiring the parties to apply them as the legal basis for providing assistance to each other.[23]

The first step regarding criminalisation of money laundering has been discussed at length in chapter 3 above.[24] The second step relating to the control of money movement is outside the scope of this book because it relates to the financial and administrative aspects of money laundering, whereas, this book is concerned with its criminal aspects only. A number of scholars make a clear distinction between the two.[25] According to them, the incompatibility between the administrative and penal aspects of money laundering and the necessity of blending them together represents one of the greatest hurdles in the establishment of an effective control regime.[26]

I shall now consider the remaining three steps, the way they have been expressed in the international counterterrorism and organised crime conventions and how far the obligations imposed in relation to them advance the cause of facilitating state cooperation in law enforcement.

---

[20] See article 52 & 58 the UN Convention against Corruption 2003, article 7 the Organised Crime Convention 2000 and article 18(b) the Terrorism Financing Convention 1999

[21] See article 5 the Drugs Convention 1988, article 8 the Terrorism Financing Convention 1999, article 12 the Organised Crime Convention 2000 and article 31 the UN Convention against Corruption 2003

[22] See article 5 the Drugs Convention 1988, article 8 the Terrorism Financing Convention 1999, article 13 the Organised Crime Convention 2000 and article 55 the UN Convention against Corruption 2003

[23] See article 46 UN Convention against Corruption 2003, article 18 the Organised Crime Convention 2000, article 7 the Drugs Convention 1988 and article 12 the Terrorism Financing Convention 1999

[24] See text to (n 143-147 and 159-168) Chapter 3 above

[25] See for instance Zagaris 'Asset Forfeiture' (n 1); See also Cherif Bassiouni, *International Criminal Law Vol 2: Multilateral and Bilateral Enforcement Mechanisms* (3rdedn. Martnus Nijhoff-2008) 17

[26] ibid

Section 2: Analysis of provisions of the conventions concerning empowerment of national law enforcement authorities and execution of foreign requests of confiscation

2.1) Empowerment of national law enforcement authorities to identify, trace, freeze and confiscate the proceeds of crime

As a preliminary measure, the process of state cooperation in confiscation demands the empowerment of national law enforcement authorities to identify, trace, freeze and confiscate the proceeds and instrumentalities of crime. Giving these powers to national authorities is essential to responding to foreign requests of confiscation.[27] The UN Convention against Drugs 1988 represents the forerunner of the conventions establishing the provisions relating to confiscation.[28] Article 5(1) of the Convention requires the parties to enable their judicial and executive authorities to order the confiscation of the proceeds derived from drug trafficking, as well as the property and instrumentalities used or intended to be used in the commission of the crime.[29] Article 5(2) requires the parties to authorise their law enforcement authorities to identify, trace, freeze and seize the proceeds, property or instrumentalities of crime.[30]

The above provisions have been reproduced in the Terrorism Financing Convention 1999, the Organised Crime Convention 2000 and the UN Convention against Corruption 2003.[31]

2.1.1) Meanings of the terms used in the provisions

The term 'proceeds of crime' refers to the property derived by the commission of crime whereas 'instrumentalities' mean the property used in the commission of crime.[32] The expression 'identification and tracing' entails securing evidence as to the status, location or value of the forfeitable property.[33] 'Freezing and seizing' implies temporarily prohibiting the transfer of the property and temporarily assuming its custody or control under the

[27] See also Legislative Guide to the Organised Crime Convention (n 3) at 137
[28] Zagaris 'Asset Forfeiture' (n 1) 456
[29] See article 5(1) the Drugs Convention 1988
[30] See article 5(2) the Drugs Convention 1988
[31] See article 8 the Terrorism Financing Convention 1999, article 12 the Organised Crime Convention 2000 and article 31 UN Convention against Corruption 2003
[32] See article 1 the Drugs Convention 1988 and article 1 (a) & (c) Convention on Laundering, Search, Seizure and Confiscation of the Proceeds of Crime. Strasbourg, 8.XI.1990 [hereinafter the European Laundering Convention 1990]
[33] See article 8 the European Laundering Convention 1990

order of the competent authority. The word 'confiscation' denotes permanent deprivation of the property by the order of the court or competent authority.[34]

In view of this, it is clear that provisions require the creation of legal powers for national law enforcement authorities to secure evidence of forfeitable property, to immobilise it temporarily and to take it permanently from the offender.

2.1.2) Provisions to be implemented to the extent permissible under national law

The international conventions on terrorism and organised crime require the parties to create these powers to the extent permissible under national laws. For example, article 31 (1) of the UN Convention against Corruption 2003 provides:

> [e]ach party shall take, to the extent possible within its domestic legal systems, such measures as may be necessary to enable confiscation of: (a) Proceeds of crime derived from offences established in accordance with this Convention or property the value of which corresponds to that of such proceeds; (b) Property, equipment or other instrumentalities used in or destined for use in offences established in accordance with this Convention.[35]

Similar provisions can be found in the Organised Crime Convention 2000 and Terrorism Financing Convention 1999.[36] Although the Drugs Convention 1988 carries no such qualification, its unqualified wording is counter-balanced by a separate paragraph of the same article which provides:

> Nothing contained in this article shall affect the principle that the measures to which it refers shall be defined and implemented in accordance with and subject to the provisions of the domestic law of a party.[37]

In the light of above, it is evident that the obligation to empower national law enforcement authorities is required to be discharged in accordance with, and to the extent permissible, under national laws. Accordingly, its domestic implementation is likely to be inconsistent pursuant to the

---

[34] See article 1(f) the Drugs Convention 1988

[35] See article 31(1) the UN Convention against Corruption 2003

[36] See article 12 the Organised Crime Convention 2000 and article 8 Terrorism Financing Convention 1999

[37] See article 5(9) the Drugs Convention 1988

diverse national legal principles of states parties. In the words of Zagaris, '[b]ecause of the rapid rise of new asset forfeiture laws, approaches to the legislation differ and pose difficulties for cooperation in some cases. Much of the problem is caused by divergences among legal systems...'[38] This contradicts the common objective of the conventions to facilitate law enforcement cooperation through harmonisation of national legal systems. The allowance for implementing the obligation subject to national legal principles is likely to leave enough gaps in national laws as to allow refusal of cooperation based upon non-existence of enabling provisions under the law of the requested state.

2.1.3) Inconsistent domestic implementation and its implications

Some states subscribe to a civil forfeiture system according to which the conviction of an offender is not a pre-condition for confiscation of the property; it is sufficient if the property represents proceeds or instrumentalities of crime.[39] For example, Indian counterterrorism law, the Unlawful Activities (Prevention) Act 1967 provides:

> (2) Proceeds of terrorism, whether held by a terrorist or [terrorist organisation or terrorist gang or] by any other person and whether or not such terrorist or other person is prosecuted or convicted for any offence under Chapter IV or Chapter VI, shall be liable to be forfeited to the Central Government or the State Government, as the case may be, in the manner provided under this Chapter.[40]

Similarly, US law enforcement authorities are empowered under various national statutes to confiscate criminally tainted property whether or not an offender has been previously convicted in relation to its accumulation.[41] Conversely, the majority of states follow a criminal forfeiture system, according to which, forfeiture is applied as a punishment for the commission of crime. For instance, the laws of Pakistan apply forfeiture as a penalty and empower courts to impose it in addition to deprivation of liberty, upon conviction of the offender.[42] Hence, Pakistani law enforcement authorities lack statutory powers to confiscate property in the absence of a

---

[38] Zagaris 'Asset Forfeiture' (n 1) 447

[39] Ibid at 448

[40] See Sc. 24 (2) of The Unlawful Activities (Prevention) Act 1967 of India

[41] 28 U.S.C 1782; 21 USC 881(1991); 19 U.S.C 1602 est. seq (1991);31 U.S.C 5316,5317

[42] See Sc. 4 Anti-Money Laundering Act 2010 of Pakistan; Sc. 19 of the Control of Narcotics Substances Act 1997 of Pakistan and Sc. 12 National Accountability Bureau Ordinance1997 of Pakistan.

previous conviction. A number of states, such as India apply civil forfeiture to a restricted category of offences such as terrorism.[43]

In view of these discrepancies, if a state like the US makes a request of forfeiture without conviction to a state which does not have civil forfeiture laws, the request is likely to be denied because the acceptance of such a request will violate the domestic law of the requested state.[44] According to UNODC's legislative guide to the Organised Crime Convention 2000:

> [P]roblems may arise when a request from a country with one system is directed at a state using the other unless the domestic law of the requested state has been framed in sufficiently flexible manner.[45]

This possibility puts a question mark on the efficacy of the technique adopted by the international conventions on terrorism and organised crime to facilitate state cooperation, i.e. harmonisation of national laws by imposing mandatory obligations.[46] Since the obligations are required to be implemented in accordance with and to the extent permissible under national laws, state parties are entitled to adjust them to suit the needs of their domestic legal system. Consequently, discrepancies such as civil and criminal forfeiture systems are likely to remain intact despite the imposition of a mandatory obligation to give powers to national authorities to identify freeze and confiscate criminally- tainted property.

2.1.3.1) Alternative option

As an alternative, the international conventions on terrorism and organised crime may require a party to include provisions in its domestic law along the lines of those contained in the Criminal Code of Canada. This law

---

[43] For example, Indian Money Laundering Law applies criminal forfeiture. Hence, it empowers the court to forfeit criminally tainted property when the offender has been charged for having committed a scheduled offence. However, its Anti-Terrorism Law applies civil forfeiture. It therefore empowers the court to confiscate proceeds of crime whether or not an accused has been charged or convicted for an offence. See Sc.5 & 8(6) Prevention of Money Laundering Act 2002 of India and section 24 of The Unlawful Activities (Prevention) Act of India 1967

[44] According to Zagaris, a central difficulty in judicial assistance in asset forfeiture cases arises from civil /criminal dichotomy. See Zagaris 'Asset Forfeiture' (n 1) 448

[45] UNODC'S Legislative Guide to the Organised Crime Convention (n 3) 144

[46] The adoption of this technique has been confirmed by the UNODC's Legislative Guides for the implementation of transnational treaties. See ibid at 130

focuses on reducing procedural hurdles to state cooperation in confiscation while preserving the fundamental principles of the national justice system.

According to Canadian Criminal Code, forfeiture is applied as a penalty upon the conviction for an 'enterprise crime'.[47] However, if the court does not find that an 'enterprise crime' was committed in relation to the property but does find that the property was a yield of another crime, it 'may' forfeit the property.[48] An 'enterprise crime' is a crime where each member of an organised group could be held individually liable for crimes committed by group within the common plan or purpose.[49] For example, if three people commit a bank robbery and one kills a person in the process, the law considers all guilty of murder. This could be considered domestic law equivalent of the crime defined by article 5 of the Organised Crime Convention 2000.[50]

Clearly, the above law does not require the abandonment of the criminal forfeiture system; it rather applies civil forfeiture as an option only. In other words, it does away with the rule that forfeiture may only occur after conviction. Where a property used in or derived from any crime has been recovered but no individual is convicted for an 'enterprise crime' involving the use or accumulation of such property, the court 'may' order its forfeiture. The existence of such a mechanism would enable a state following criminal forfeiture system to act upon a civil forfeiture request, while maintaining the individuality of its national legal system. Evidently, the approach taken in the Criminal Code of Canada provides a better mechanism to facilitate state cooperation as compared to the one adopted by the international conventions on terrorism and organised crime.

Interestingly, the inclusion of such provisions in national laws has been advocated by the UNODC's legislative guide to the implementation of Organised Crime Convention 2000. According to it, the drafters need to constantly review national laws to ensure that any current procedures which are more expeditious or extensive than those required by the Convention are not adversely affected.[51]

---

[47] See Criminal Code of Canada R.S.C,1985,C.C-46 Sc. 426-37

[48] ibid

[49] See Gunel Guliyeva, 'The Concept of Joint Criminal Enterprise and the ICC Jurisdiction' <http://www.americanstudents.us/Pages%20from%20Guliyeva.pdf> [date accessed 21/03/23]

[50] See (n 141-142) Chapter 3 above

[51] Legislative Guide to the Organised Crime Convention (n 3) 145

2.2) Execution of foreign requests

The next step in the process of state cooperation in confiscation relates to the execution of foreign requests. It represents a multi-task procedure. According to it, the parties are first required to confiscate the criminally-tainted property upon the request of a foreign state. Secondly, they are obliged to assist foreign states in the identification, tracing, seizure and freezing of the proceeds or instrumentalities of crime. Thirdly, they are required to provide inter-state assistance in the confiscation of converted, transferred or inter-mingled proceeds and the income derived there from. Finally, they are called upon to protect the rights of *bona fide* third parties.[52] I shall now consider each of these requirements in detail, including their subordination to national law, complications arising as a result of their inconsistent implementation and suggestions to overcome difficulties.

2.2.1) Execution of a foreign confiscation order: either to execute or to submit for consideration

Article 5(4)(a) of the 1988 Drugs Convention stipulates that when a request is made by a state having jurisdiction over a crime, the state in the territory of which proceeds, property or instrumentalities of crime are located shall either (i) submit the request to its competent national authorities for the purpose of obtaining an order of confiscation and, if such order is granted, give effect to it; or (ii) submit to its competent authorities, with a view to giving effect to it to the extent requested, an order of confiscation issued by the requesting party.[53] Similar provisions can be seen in the Organised Crime Convention 2000 and the UN Convention against Corruption 2003.[54]

The provision requires that parties either execute a foreign request of confiscation or submit the same before competent authorities for consideration. The first option presupposes a judicial or administrative proceeding wherein the competent authorities of the requested state shall consider whether and to what extent the request shall be executed.[55] According to the second option, the competent authorities may straight

[52] See article 5 the Drugs Convention 1988, article 13 the Organised Crime Convention 2000 and article 55 the UN Convention against Corruption 2003

[53] See article 5(4)(1) of the Drugs Convention 1988

[54] See article 13(1) the Organised Crime Convention 2000 and article 55(1) UN Convention against Corruption 2003

[55] Legislative Guide to the Organised Crime Convention 2000 (n 3) 145

away execute the request without looking into the merits of the foreign confiscation order.

The provision indicates that states parties were not willing to accept an unconditional obligation to execute a foreign forfeiture request. Thus, on the pattern of *aut dedere aut judicare*, they are given a choice either to carry out the request or to submit the same for appropriate orders of their national authorities.[56] The wording '[i]f the order is granted, it shall be given effect to', makes evident the discretionary nature of the obligation.[57] Apart from this, the subsequent paragraphs make it plain that confiscation is required to be enforced in accordance with and to the extent permissible under the national laws of the requested state and bilateral treaties binding it.[58]

2.2.1.1) Non-recognition of foreign criminal judgements as a hurdle to the execution of a foreign confiscation order

States tend to follow contrasting approaches with respect to recognition of foreign criminal judgements. While a few countries are able to enforce them, most are not.[59] Since a majority of states view forfeiture as a criminal judgement,[60] its execution upon foreign request becomes problematic when the requested state gives no recognition to foreign criminal judgements. Thus, during the drafting of the Organised Crime Convention 2000, one delegate pointed out that the national law of his state did not allow the execution of foreign penal judgements.[61] The following provisions of bilateral treaties bring to the fore divergent national approaches with respect to recognition of foreign criminal judgements.

Article 1(5) (b) of the 1995 Mutual Assistance Treaty between Australia and Indonesia provides that the execution of foreign criminal judgements is prohibited except to the extent permitted by the law of the requested

---

[56] D.W Sproule and Paul ST-Denis, 'The UN Drug Trafficking Convention: An Ambitious Step' 27 Canadian Yearbook of International Law (1989) 263 at 283
[57] David P. Stewart, 'Internationalizing the War on Drugs' 18 Denv. J. Int'l L. & Pol'y (1989-1990) 387 at 395
[58] See article 5(4)(c) and 5(9) of the Drugs Convention 1988
[59] Stewart (n 57) 395
[60] Zagaris 'Asset Forfeiture' (n 1) 448
[61] See UN Doc. E / Conf.82 / C.1 / S.R at 5

state.[62] Similarly, article 2(1) (b) of 2004 Mutual Assistance Treaty among eight far-eastern states provides that the treaty does not apply to the enforcement in the requested state of criminal judgements imposed in the requesting state except to the extent permitted by the law of the requested state.[63] This may be compared with the 2009 UK-Philippines Mutual Assistance Treaty which imposes no such restriction on the execution of foreign criminal judgements.[64]

2.2.1.2) Solution of the problem under the counterterrorism and organised crime conventions

The international conventions on terrorism and organised crime attempt to resolve this problem by giving a choice to the requested state to either execute the foreign request or to submit it before competent national authorities in order to obtain an order of confiscation.[65] As per the latter option, the competent authorities are required to only consider the request in accordance with national law. The obligation thus leads to three consequences: execution of the request, simple refusal and refusal along with the undertaking that fresh proceedings will be held in the requested state. Assuming that the law of the requested state bars the enforcement of foreign criminal judgements, its competent authorities will have no choice but to refuse the execution. In case the authorities decide to hold fresh proceedings, they will be faced with multiple difficulties of procuring evidence from the requesting state and deciding afresh the ancillary issues such as rights of third parties and the application of value and substitute confiscation.[66] The settlement of all these issues is likely to be so time consuming as to make the requesting state lose its interest or to frustrate the purpose behind confiscation proceedings. So practically speaking, apart from the execution of foreign requests, no viable option exists and this option may only be exercised if the national law makes allowance for the same.

---

[62] See article 1(5)(b) of the Australia- Indonesia Legal Mutual Assistance Treaty 1995

[63] See article 2(1)(b) of 2004 Mutual Legal Assistance Treaty among eight far-eastern states

[64] See article 1, Treaty on Mutual Legal Assistance in Criminal Matters between the United Kingdom of Great Britain and Northern Ireland and the Republic of the Philippines. Signed at London 18 September 2009 [hereinafter UK-Philippines Mutual Legal Assistance Treaty 2009]

[65] See text to (n 53) above

[66] For definition of value and substitute confiscation see text to (n 82) below. See also Zagaris 'Asset Forfeiture' (n 1) 503

In light of the above, it is difficult to see how international conventions on terrorism and organised crime, by giving choice to states to either execute the request or submit it before competent national authorities, may be said to have overcome the traditional hurdle of states giving no recognition to foreign criminal judgements.

2.2.1.3) Solution under bilateral treaties on mutual legal assistance

As a substitute, states might be encouraged to exempt forfeiture from the operation of the rule against recognition of foreign penal judgements. As noted by Bassiouni, forfeiture not only represents a punishment but also embodies an investigative proceeding.[67] Hence, a sufficient legal basis exists to exempt it from the operation of the rule against enforcement of foreign penal judgements. Notably, the proposal has already been adopted in certain bilateral treaties on mutual legal assistance. For example, article 1(2) of the 1998 Mutual Assistance Treaty between the US and France provides 'this treaty does not apply to: (b) the enforcement of criminal judgements except for forfeiture.'[68] This arrangement has also been approved by the UN Model Treaty on Mutual Assistance in Criminal Matters 1990.[69] Hence, it merits consideration for inclusion in the international conventions on terrorism and organised crime.

2.2.2) Execution of a foreign freezing, tracing and seizure order

Article 5(4)(b) of the Drugs Convention requires the parties to identify, trace, seize and freeze the proceeds and instrumentalities of crime for the purposes of their eventual confiscation, following a request by another state having jurisdiction over the crime.[70] Corresponding provisions can be

---

[67] Bassiouni 'Multilateral and Bilateral Enforcement' (n 25) 13

[68] See article 1(2)(b) of Mutual Legal Assistance Treaty Between the United States of America and France, Signed at Paris December 10, 1998 [hereinafter US-France Mutual Legal Assistance Treaty 1998]

[69] See article 1(3) (b) of UN Model Treaty on Mutual Legal Assistance in Criminal Matters 1990 G.A. Res. 117, 45th Sess., Annex, at 215-19, U.N. Doc. A/Res/117 (1990) [hereinafter the UN Model Treaty on Mutual Legal Assistance 1990]. The article provides that the present treaty does not apply to the enforcement in the requested state of criminal judgements rendered in the requesting state except to the extent permitted by the law of the requested state and article 18 of the present treaty. Since article 18 relates to forfeiture, the treaty clearly exempts forfeiture from the rule against execution of foreign judgements in the requested state.

[70] See article 5(4)(b) the Drugs Convention 1988

seen in the Organised Crime Convention 2000 and the UN Convention against Corruption 2003.[71]

The provision requires a party in the territory of which proceeds, property or instrumentalities of a crime are located to provide assistance to another state having jurisdiction over that crime in securing evidence as to status, location or value of such property and to place it under temporary restraint, pending the judgement of forfeiture. The purpose of temporary restraint is to prevent the offenders from transferring or removing the forfeitable property from the territory of the requested state.[72]

Unlike the provision on confiscation, this provision does not give an option to the requested state to either carry out the request or to submit the same for appropriate orders of national authorities. It rather obliges the parties to take these measures upon foreign request. However, subsequent paragraphs indicate that the obligation is required to be performed in accordance with and to the extent permissible, under national laws and bilateral treaties.[73]

2.3) Confiscation of intermingled, converted proceeds and protection of third party rights

Article 5(6) of the Drugs Convention 1988 requires the parties to empower national law enforcement authorities to identify, freeze and confiscate the proceeds and instrumentalities which have been transformed or converted into other property, inter-mingled with lawful property and income or other benefits derived from such property.[74] It further obliges the parties to carry out these measures upon the request of a foreign state. Identical provisions can be found in the Organised Crime Convention 2000 and UN Convention against Corruption 2003.[75]

---

[71] See article 13(2) the Organised Crime Convention 2000 and article 55(1) the UN Convention against Corruption 2003

[72] Gurule (n 6) 77

[73] See article 5(4)(c) of the Drugs Convention 1988; For comparable provisions; see article 55(4) UN Convention against Corruption 2003 and article 13(4) Organised Crime Convention 2000; Also See article 5 (4)(d) the Drugs Convention 1988, article 7(6) and 7(12) of the Drugs Convention 1988; For corresponding provisions, see articles 46(6) and 46(12) of the UN Convention against Corruption 2003 and article 18(6) and 18(17) of the Organised Crime Convention 2000

[74] See article 5(6) of the Drugs Convention 1988

[75] See article 31 the UN Convention against Corruption 2003 and article 12 the Organised Crime Convention 2000

In the same way, article 5(8) provides that the provisions of this article shall not be construed as prejudicing the rights of *bona fide* third parties.[76] Corresponding provisions can be seen in the Organised Crime Convention 2000, the UN Convention against Corruption 2003 and the Terrorism Financing Convention 1999.[77]

Whereas the two provisions themselves leave little room for discretion, they are however subject to the general requirements of article 5(4) (c) of the Drugs Convention 1988 which provides that the decisions and actions concerning confiscation, identification and freezing of proceeds or instrumentalities of crime shall be made in accordance with the domestic law of the requested state and bilateral or multilateral treaties to which it may be bound.[78] Furthermore, article 5(4) (d) provides that a state, while taking these measures upon foreign request, shall be guided by the provisions of article 7 of the Drugs Convention 1988, which relates to mutual legal assistance. Article 7 suggests that the assistance is to be provided in accordance with, and subject to the provisions of, domestic law and bilateral treaties of the requested state.[79]

These paragraphs make it obvious that article 5 as a whole is subordinate to national law and each of its requirements, including confiscation of converted or intermingled proceeds and protection of third party rights, is governed by this principle.

2.3.1) Meanings of intermingled and converted proceeds

The international conventions on terrorism and organised crime oblige the parties to enable their law enforcement authorities to order the forfeiture of not only the proceeds of crime but also the property into which such proceeds have been transferred or converted as well as income derived from such property. Furthermore, the parties are required to carry out these measures upon the request of another state having jurisdiction over the

[76] See article 5(8) of the Drugs Convention 1988

[77] See article 8(5) the Terrorism Financing Convention 1999, article 31(9) the UN Convention against Corruption 2003 and article 12(8) the Organised Crime Convention 2000

[78] See article 5(4) (c) of the Drugs Convention 1988. See also article 55(4) UN Convention against Corruption 2003 and article 13(4) Organised Crime Convention 2000

[79] See article 7(6) and 7(12) of the Drugs Convention 1988; For corresponding provisions see articles 46(6) and 46(12) the UN Convention against Corruption 2003 and article 18(6) and 18(17) the Organised Crime Convention 2000

crime.[80] According to this requirement, when the property which is eligible for confiscation has been transformed, converted or inter-mingled with other property, governments can seize the new property.[81] The provision incorporates two modern theories of confiscation, namely value and substitute confiscation. Under the substitute confiscation theory, the property into which the proceeds have been transferred or converted can be confiscated. According to value confiscation, a sum of money equivalent to the value of proceeds can be confiscated.[82]

2.3.1.1) Impact on national laws and bilateral treaties

Since the obligation is required to be carried out in accordance with national law, its domestic implementation may vary. Whereas some states give power to their law enforcement authorities to confiscate the new property, others do not. For example, the UK's Drug Trafficking Offences Act 1986 allows the court to order a person convicted of drug trafficking to pay to the court the value of the benefit he or another person has derived in connection with drug trafficking.[83] Similarly, a Canadian Court may fine the convicted party for the value of the property subject to forfeiture if the property cannot be located or has been transferred outside Canada, has diminished in value or has irretrievably inter-mingled with other property.[84] Likewise, the Australian Proceeds of Crimes Act 1987 empowers the court to impose a penalty equivalent to the value of the benefit derived from the offence.[85] All these provisions reflect the implementation of value confiscation theory.

Conversely, the organised crime laws of both India and Pakistan make no allowance for either value or substitute confiscation.[86] As a result, a

---

[80] See article 5(6) of the Drugs Convention 1988, article 12(2)(3)(4)&(5) the Organised Crime Convention 2000 and article 31(4)(5)&(6) the UN Convention against Corruption 2003

[81] Zagaris 'Asset Forfeiture' (n 1) 499

[82] ibid

[83] See Part I, Sc. 1(4) the Drug Trafficking Offences Act 1986, 1986 Chapter 32, 12 Halsbury's Stats 933 (1989 re-issue) [hereinafter UK's Drug Trafficking Offences Act 1986]

[84] Criminal Code of Canada R.S.C Ch C-46 S 462.37 (1985)

[85] Australian Proceeds of Crime Act 1987 Vol.I S.26, 2 Austl. Acts p. 1764 (1987)

[86] For instance, under the law of Pakistan, the punishment for money laundering is 10 years imprisonment and forfeiture of the property involved. Similarly, according to Indian Anti-Terrorism law, the punishment for holding or possessing the proceeds of terrorism is forfeiture of such proceeds. Both these enactments are silent with respect to confiscation of the proceeds which have been transferred,

request made by Canada, Australia or the UK to Pakistan or India to confiscate the property equivalent to the value of forfeitable property, is unlikely to succeed because the laws of the latter states contain no enabling provisions to carry out the request.[87] However, the parties not implementing substitute or value confiscation may not be held responsible for breach of their convention obligation because the provisions are required to be implemented in accordance with, and to the extent permissible, under national laws. This calls into question the utility of the provisions in regard to harmonising national laws and thereby to facilitate state cooperation in confiscation.

2.3.1.2) Absence of any universal procedure of confiscating intermingled, substituted and converted proceeds

Another area of concern is that the international conventions on terrorism and organised crime provide no guidance with respect to the procedure for employing value and substitute confiscation. In other words, the conventions are silent with respect to procedure to be adopted by states in forfeiting inter-mingled, substituted and converted proceeds. If a procedure adopted by the requesting state when issuing the order of confiscation does not correspond to the law of requested state, the latter may be compelled to refuse execution of the order.[88] For example, it has been asserted that confiscation of attorney's fee violates the presumption of innocence as contained in the ECHR.[89] If the ECHR applies in the requested state and if the defendant were to raise it as a defence against a

converted into new property or inter-mingled with legitimate property. See Sc. 4 of Anti-Money Laundering Act 2010 of Pakistan; See also Sc. 24 of the Unlawful Activities (Prevention) Act of India 1967

[87] See section 5 and 8 of Prevention of Money Laundering Act 2002 of India; the two sections only relate to attachment and confiscation of the proceeds of crime not to their value or substitution.

[88] It can be so because Mutual Assistance Treaties (MLATs) generally require the provision of assistance on the basis of reciprocity which means the requesting state must be in a position to provide similar assistance if the circumstances are reversed. See article 3(1) (g) of 2004 Mutual Legal Assistance Treaty among eight far-eastern states. The article includes amongst the grounds of refusal of assistance the non-fulfilment of the principle of reciprocity 'the requested state shall refuse assistance if … the requesting party fails to undertake that it will be able to comply with a future request of a similar nature by the requested party for assistance in a criminal matters.'

[89] Zagaris 'Asset Forfeiture' (n 1) 511

foreign confiscation request, the execution of the request may have to be refused.[90]

The *Noriega* case of 1990 highlights the problem.[91] Here, the government of Panama filed a $6.5 billion law suit in the US against General Noriega, while simultaneously seeking in another case to restrain him from transferring his assets. The US government froze his assets, despite Noriega's difficulties in obtaining money for legal fee. The US District Court held that the act of freezing his assets amounted to a denial of the right to be defended by the counsel of one's choice. Since the right was protected under the Sixth Amendment to the US constitution, the Court had no choice but to order the unfreezing of the assets.[92]

2.3.1.3) Alternative option

In contrast to the international conventions on terrorism and organised crime, some domestic laws provide specific and detailed rules with respect to procedure of forfeiting intermingled, converted and substituted proceeds. For example, under Australian law, the Criminal Property Confiscation Act 2000, the property liable to confiscation has been classified into three distinct categories: 1) unexplained wealth 2) - criminal benefits and 3)-crime used property.[93] The Act defines unexplained wealth as any property that is constituent of a respondent's wealth.[94] The value of such property would be equal to difference between: (a) total value of respondent's wealth and (b) the value of respondent's lawfully acquired wealth.[95] Similarly, the Act defines criminal benefits as property derived as a result of respondent's involvement in the commission of confiscable offence.[96] If such property is given away or is no longer available, its

---

90 See article 6(2) ECHR 1950

91 See *U.S v. Noriega* 746 F. Supp. 1541 (1990) <http://www.leagle.com/decision/19902287746FSupp1541_12092> [date accessed 21/03/23]

92 ibid; See also David Johnston, 'With Millions Frozen in Banks, Noriega Might Be Tried as a Pauper' NY Times, Nov 14, 1990 at B6, C.13 <http://www.nytimes.com/1990/11/14/us/with-millions-frozen-in-banks-noriega-might-be-tried-as-pauper.html> [date accessed 21/03/23]

93 See Part 3, Divisions 1,2,3 of the Criminal Property Confiscation Act 2000, the Act as at 9 December 2005 [Australian Confiscation Act 2000] <http://www.austlii.edu.au/au/legis/wa/consol_act/cpca2000333/> [date accessed 21/03/23]

94 See Sc. 12 Australian Confiscation Act 2000

95 See Sc. 13 ibid

96 See Sc. 16 ibid

value would be the greater of: (a) its value at the time it was acquired and (b) its value at the time it was given away or used or consumed.[97] Likewise, the Act provides that the value of a property used in the commission of crime would be the amount equal to value of the property at the time the relevant confiscation offence was or is likely to have been committed.[98] The Act provides further that when making a freezing order the court may provide for meeting the reasonable living and business expenses of the owner of property.[99]

Clearly, the above enactment not only lays down a logical formula to confiscate intermingled, converted and substituted proceeds, but also empowers the court to make allowance for necessary expenses such as attorney's fee when making a freezing order. By following this approach, much needed clarity could be brought in the provisions of the international conventions relating to intermingled, converted and substituted proceeds. Furthermore, it provides better model for modernising national laws in line with the requirements of suppressing sophisticated financial crimes.

2.3.2) Meanings of third party protection

The international conventions on terrorism and organised crime, while requiring the parties to provide interstate assistance in the confiscation of proceeds or instrumentalities of crime, stipulate that nothing in these conventions shall be construed to prejudice the rights of *bona-fide* third parties.[100] The provision is meant to protect the rights of innocent third parties who have acquired property through legitimate purchase without notice of its illicit origin. However, it carries no guideline with respect to the extent or manner of protection to be afforded. As a result, the laws and treaties implementing the provision diverge.

2.3.2.1) Inconsistent implementation

For example, the UK's Criminal Justice (International Cooperation) Act 1990 requires the court to give notice to third parties when the property is seized and detained.[101] Likewise the Criminal Justice Act 1988 requires

---

[97] See Sc. 19 ibid

[98] See Sc. 23 ibid

[99] See Sc. 45 ibid

[100] See article 5(8) the Drugs Convention 1988, article 12(8) the Organised Crime Convention 2000, article 8 (5) Terrorism Financing Convention and article 31(9) the UN Convention against Corruption 2003

[101] Criminal Justice (International Cooperation) Act 1990 Part III S. 28

that, prior to releasing property that is under confiscation order, anyone holding any interest in the property should be given a 'reasonable opportunity' of being heard.[102] Canada has a very specific protection mechanism for the rights of third parties. It provides that before issuing a restraining order a judge may require notice and hearing for any person who appears to have a valid interest in the property. To dispense with the requirement to provide notice, the Attorney General must provide an undertaking with respect to payment of damages for disappearance or reduction of the value of property in question. Once property has been seized, any interested person may apply for revocation of the seizure order. If it is established that the applicant is lawfully entitled and is not complicit in the crime, the judge may return the property to him.[103] Similarly, the Anti-money Laundering Act 2010 of Pakistan provides not only the opportunity of being heard but also the right of appeal to third parties aggrieved by the order of attachment or forfeiture.[104] In the same way, section 30 of the Unlawful Activities (Prevention) Act of India 1967 requires, where a claim is preferred that a property is not liable to seizure or attachment, the designated authority will investigate it unless the authority considers that the claim is designed to cause delay. Where the objector establishes his claim, the notice of attachment shall be cancelled.[105]

Clearly, different levels of protection are afforded by states to third parties. At one extreme are states like the UK requiring that the objectors should merely be given notice or reasonable opportunity of being heard; at the other are states like Canada affording not only the right of hearing and appeal but also compensation in case notice of hearing is dispensed with.[106] Needless to say, if the requested state provides greater protection as compared to the requesting state, this disparity might result in the delay or refusal of a confiscation request.

---

[102] Criminal Justice Act 1988, Part II, S 80, 12 Halsbury Stat 1154 (1989 re-issue)

[103] Criminal Code of Canada R. S.C Ch. C-46, S 462.32(5), 462.33(3) 1985

[104] See section 10 and 23 of the Anti-Money Laundering Act 2010 of Pakistan

[105] See also Sc. 8 of the Prevention of Money Laundering Act 2002 of India

[106] Similar discrepancies can be seen with respect to the stages of affording protection to third parties. For example, article 18(2) of the UK-Philippines Mutual Assistance Treaty 2009 stipulates that the rights claimed by *bona fide* 3rd parties over the confiscated assets shall be respected at the stage of return of assets. On the other hand, article 17 of UN Model Treaty on Mutual legal Assistance 1990 obliges the requested state to protect the rights of *bona fide* third parties at every stage of confiscation process including search and seizure and delivery of any material for evidentiary purposes.

This brings into question the rationale of the obligation under the international counterterrorism and organised crime conventions to protect 3rd party rights. If the obligation is designed to harmonise national laws with a view to facilitating state cooperation in confiscation, it has clearly fallen short of the target by failing to prescribe minimum standards of protection. As per the existing arrangement, each party is supposed to have its own standards. A foreign court, when making the confiscation order is bound to apply its own law, which may substantially differ from that of the requested state. The resulting discrepancies may compel the requested state to refuse the execution of the order.

2.3.2.2) Expeditious determination of third party rights as an alternative to the existing provisions

As a substitute, the makers of the international conventions on terrorism and organised crime may wish to consider including provisions which encourage the parties to determine third party rights 'expeditiously'. This technique would not require the adoption of similar standards of protection. However, it would expedite the determination of third party rights and consequently facilitate the execution of foreign requests of confiscation. It would therefore present a more convincing technique of facilitating state cooperation in confiscation as compared to the existing open-ended obligation. The following proposals might be considered when framing such a provision:

(a)- Taking into account the urgency of attachment and confiscation proceedings, states might be advised to fix a certain time period within which their courts must hear and determine the claims of third parties. For example, section 13 of National Accountability Ordinance of Pakistan 1999 fixes a time limit of 14 days for filing claims or objections against orders of freezing property.[107] Similarly, the Unlawful Activities (Prevention) Act 1967 of India sets forth a time limit of one month for any aggrieved person to file an appeal against an order of confiscation.[108]

(b)- States might be asked to recognise the decision of the court of the requesting state concerning the rights of third parties, subject to its fairness. This proposal is likely to save time by relieving the requested state of the burden of acquiring overseas evidence and deciding afresh technical issues such as the application of value and substitute confiscation. Thus, article 22 of the European Laundering Convention

[107] See Section 13 (a) National Accountability Bureau Ordinance 1999 of Pakistan
[108] See Sc.28 the Unlawful Activities (Prevention) Act 1967 of India

1990 provides that a requested state is bound to give effect to the court order of the requesting state concerning the rights of third party unless the decision was taken without giving opportunity of being heard to third parties or it is contrary to the law of the requested state.[109]

In the light of above, it is clear that the allowance for implementing the rules established by the international counterterrorism and organised crime conventions subject to national legal principles leaves enough disharmonies in the national laws to make possible the refusal of state cooperation in confiscation based upon non-existence of enabling provisions under the law of the requested state or the request not being in conformity with its national law. These dissimilarities may for example relate to civil and criminal forfeiture systems, the non-recognition of foreign penal judgements, the protection of third party rights and the mechanism for and application of value or substitute confiscation. As noted by Shehu, one of the central criticisms against the international counterterrorism and organised crime conventions is that most of their critical provisions are left to the discretion of states.[110]

If it was not possible for the makers of the conventions to establish unqualified obligations, they could have resorted to simplifying the procedure of confiscation by including elaborate provisions, to serve as models for domestic legislation. This appears to be a more convincing strategy to facilitate state cooperation because it offers guidance to states to modernise their laws in line with the requirements of sophisticated transnational crimes.

---

[109] See article 2 of the European Laundering Convention 1990. Paragraph 1 of the article provides, when dealing with a request for cooperation concerning asset freezing or forfeiture, the requested party shall recognize any judicial decision taken in the requesting state regarding rights claimed by a 3rd party. Paragraph 2 sets forth an exception to this rule. It provides that the recognition of the foreign decisions concerning rights of third parties may be refused when: (a) a third party did not have adequate opportunity to assert their rights, (b) the decision is incompatible with decision already taken in the requested party on the same matter, (c) it is incompatible with order public of the requested state, (d) the decision is contrary to the provisions on exclusive jurisdiction provided for by the law of the requested party.

[110] See Abdullah Y. Shehu, 'International Initiatives against Corruption and Money Laundering: An Overview' 12 Journal of Financial crime (2005) 221 at 226

Section 3: Obligation to provide Mutual Legal Assistance under the international conventions on terrorism and organised crime

3.1) Explanation of mutual legal assistance

The final step in the process of state cooperation in confiscation involves mutual legal assistance. Mutual legal assistance denotes a practice among states whereby they assist each other in the investigation, prosecution and adjudication of crimes which spread across national frontiers. The practice has been explained by Bassiouni in these words:

> [T]he courts of one state address a request to those of another state for judicial assistance in the form of taking of the testimony of a witness or securing tangible evidence. The [requested] courts then transmit the oral or tangible evidence to the requesting court, certifying that the evidence has been secured in accordance with the legal requirements of the requested state.[111]

The importance of mutual legal assistance can hardly be exaggerated for the purposes of combating transnational crimes. As observed by Stewart,

> [the suppression of borderless criminality] … requires a means for the acquisition of evidence abroad in a form admissible in the court of the requesting state.[112]

The confiscation of proceeds upon foreign request embraces two modalities of state cooperation: enforcement of foreign criminal judgements and inter-state assistance in the collection of evidence.[113] The former refers to forfeiture or permanent deprivation of property and the latter to identification, tracing, seizure and freezing of the property.[114] Both measures are taken by utilising the legal device of mutual legal assistance.[115]

Mutual legal assistance is usually provided on the basis of mutual assistance treaties (MLATs) and unilateral legislation.[116] A typical mutual legal assistance treaty comprises a list of offences with respect to which the assistance might be provided, the respective rights and obligations of the requesting and requested states, the rights of the offender and the

---

[111] Bassiouni 'Multilateral and Bilateral Enforcement' (n 25) 8
[112] Stewart (n 57) 398
[113] Bassiouni 'Multilateral and Bilateral Enforcement'(n 25) 13
[114] ibid
[115] Sproule (n 56) 285
[116] Zagaris 'Asset Forfeiture' (n 1) 466, 478

procedure of making and reviewing a request of mutual legal assistance.[117] MLATs are generally divided into two parts, one dealing with the execution of foreign criminal judgements or forfeiture, and the other with the collection of evidence that is identification, tracing, freezing and seizure of criminally tainted property.

3.2) Mutual legal assistance provisions of the international conventions on terrorism and organised crime

The international conventions on terrorism and organised crime, in particular those concluded recently, lay down extensive provisions on mutual legal assistance.[118] These provisions are meant to supplement their provisions relating to the execution of foreign requests. Thus, article 13(3) of the Organised Crime Convention 2000 provides, '[t]he provisions of article 18 of this Convention are applicable, mutatis mutandis, to this article.'[119] Article 13 deals with the execution of foreign requests, while article 18 concerns mutual legal assistance.[120] This implies that a state, while executing a foreign request of confiscation, identification and freezing of the proceeds of crime under article 13, shall be guided by the provisions of article 18 concerning mutual legal assistance. Corresponding provisions can be seen in the UN Convention against Drugs 1988 as well as the UN Convention against Corruption 2003.[121]

By virtue of article 18 of the Organised Crime Convention 2000, state parties are obliged to provide each other with the widest measure of mutual legal assistance in matters concerning investigation, prosecution and judicial proceedings relating to the offences set forth by the Convention.[122] The assistance might be provided on the basis of bilateral

[117] Legislative Guide to the Organised Crime Convention 2000 (n 3) 200

[118] See article 7 the Drugs Convention 1988, article 18(21) the Organised Crime Convention 2000, article 46(21) the UN Convention against Corruption 2003 and article 12 of the Terrorism Financing Convention 1999

[119] See article 13(3) the Organised Crime Convention 2000

[120] See article 13(3) and 18 of the Organised Crime Convention 2000

[121] See article 55(3) the UN Convention against Corruption 2003 and article 5(4)(d) the Drugs Convention 1988

[122] 'States Parties shall afford one another the widest measure of Mutual Legal Assistance in investigations, prosecutions and judicial proceedings in relation to the offences covered by this Convention …' See article 18(1) of the Organised Crime Convention 2000. See also article 7(1) the Drugs Convention 1988 and article 46 (1) the UN Convention against Corruption 2003

and regional treaties or unilateral legislation.[123] In case the cooperating states do not have a bilateral treaty between them and the domestic law of the requested state makes the provision of assistance conditional upon the existence of such a treaty, parties are obliged to consider the Organised Crime Convention 2000 as a legal basis of assistance.[124]

Article 18 of the Organsied Crime Convention 2000 further points out the type of assistance which might be offered by one state to another. It inter alia includes the identification, seizure, freezing and tracing of the proceeds, property and instrumentalities of crime, pursuant to a foreign request.[125] Apart from this, the article requires the parties to enable their competent national authorities to call for and seize the records of financial institutions operating within their jurisdiction, following the request of another state.[126] The contracting parties are also obliged to make sure that their bank secrecy laws and laws relating to fiscal crimes are not used as an excuse to refuse the production of such records.[127] Additionally, the parties are called upon to consider concluding agreements concerning sharing and disposal of the proceeds of crime,[128] and providing voluntary information about money laundering activities.[129] Finally, article 18 of the Organised Crime Convention 2000 lays down the grounds on which the mutual legal assistance could be denied.[130]

---

[123] See article 7(7) the Drugs Convention 1988, article 18(7) the Organised Crime Convention 2000, article 46(6) the UN Convention against Corruption 2003 and article 12(5) the Terrorism Financing Convention 1999

[124] ibid

[125] See article 18 (3) the Organised Crime Convention 2000; For corresponding provisions see article 46(3) the UN Convention against Corruption 2003 and article 7(2) the Drugs Convention 1988

[126] See article 5(3) the Drugs Convention 1988, article 12(6) the Organised Crime Convention 2000 and article 31(7) the UN Convention against Corruption 2003

[127] See article 7(1) the Drugs Convention 1988, article 18(8) the Organised Crime Convention 2000 and article 46(8) the UN Convention against Corruption 2003

[128] See article 14 the Organised Crime Convention 2000, article 5(5) the Drugs Convention 1988 and article 57 the UN Convention against Corruption 2003

[129] See article 5(4)(g) the Drugs Convention 1988, article 46(4) the UN Convention against Corruption 2003 and article 18(4) the Organised Crime Convention 2000

[130] See article 7(15) the Drugs Convention 1988, article 18(21) the Organised Crime Convention 2000 and article 46 (21) the UN Convention against Corruption 2003

3.2.1) Subordination to national law and bilateral treaties

Provisions of the international counterterrorism and organised crime conventions concerning mutual legal assistance are as much subordinate to national law as their provisions on money laundering, confiscation and execution of foreign requests although, apparently, they have been expressed in mandatory language.

For example, while article 7(1) of the Drugs Convention 1988 provides that state parties 'shall' afford to one another the widest measures of mutual legal assistance,[131] later paragraphs indicate that the assistance is to be provided in accordance with national law and bilateral treaties. Thus, article 7(6) provides that the convention shall not affect any bilateral or multilateral treaty which governs mutual legal assistance between the requesting and requested state.[132] Similarly, article 7(12) provides that the request shall be executed in accordance with and to the extent permissible under the domestic law of the requested state.[133]

I shall now analyse the impact of mutual legal assistance provisions of the counterterrorism and organised conventions on national law and bilateral treaties. For this purpose, only those mutual legal assistance provisions which directly relate to state cooperation in the confiscation of the proceeds of crime will be discussed.

---

[131] See article 7(1) the Drugs Convention 1988.For corresponding provisions, see article 18(1) the Organised Crime Convention 2000, article 46(1) the UN Convention against Corruption 2003 and article 12(1) the Terrorism Financing Convention 1999

[132] See article 7(6) the Drugs Convention 1988. For corresponding provisions, see article 18(7) the Organised Crime Convention 2000, article 46(6) the UN Convention against Corruption 2003 and article 12(5) the Terrorism Financing Convention 1999. In addition, the grounds of refusal suggest that a request might be denied if its execution will be contrary to the legal system of the requested state concerning mutual legal assistance. See article 7(15) the Drugs Convention 1988, article 18(21) the Organised Crime Convention 2000 and article 46(21) the UN Convention against Corruption 2003

[133] See article 7(12) the Drugs Convention 1988. For corresponding provisions, see article 46(17) the UN Convention against Corruption 2003, article 18(17) the Organised Crime Convention 2000 and article 12(5) the Terrorism Financing Convention 1999

3.2.2) Mutual Legal assistance provisions concerning identification, tracing, seizure and freezing

3.2.2.1) Mandatory obligation to provide legal assistance in identification and freezing

The international organised crime conventions establish mandatory obligations for the parties to assist each other in the identification, tracing, search and seizure of the proceeds and instrumentalities of crime.[134] These measures are required to be taken in accordance with and to the extent permissible under the national law of the requested state and bilateral and regional treaties to which it is bound.[135] The language of the provisions is unclear with respect to meanings of the terms 'identification', 'tracing', 'search' and 'seizure'. Furthermore, the provisions leave it entirely up to states to determine the procedure of taking these measures.

3.2.2.2) Inconsistent implementations of the obligation

Due to discretionary and ambiguous nature of the obligation, multiple approaches are being followed by states to implement it in national laws and bilateral treaties. For example, the US-France Mutual Assistance Treaty 1998 sets forth the obligation in these words:

> [a]t the request of requesting state, the requested state based on facts that would constitute an offence under the laws of both states, and to the extent permitted by its law, may take protective measures to immobilize

[134] See article 18(3(c)& (g) the Organised Crime Convention 2000, article 46(3)(c) &(g) the UN Convention against Corruption 2003 and article 7(2)(g) the Drugs Convention 1988

[135] See article 18(17) the Organised Crime Convention 2000:

> A request shall be executed in accordance with the domestic law of the requested State Party and, to the extent not contrary to the domestic law of the requested State Party and where possible, in accordance with the procedures specified in the request.

For Corresponding provisions, see article 7(12) the Drugs Convention 1988, article 46(17) the UN Convention against Corruption 2003 and article 12(5) the Terrorism Financing Convention 1999

See also paragraph 18(6) the Organised Crime Convention 2000, 'The provisions of this article shall not affect the obligations under any other treaty, bilateral or multilateral, that governs or will govern, in whole or in part, mutual legal assistance.' For Corresponding provisions, see article 7(6) the Drugs Convention 1988 and article 46(6) the UN Convention against Corruption 2003

> temporarily such proceeds or instrumentalities to ensure their availability for forfeiture.[136]

As we can see, the obligation to seize or freeze property upon the request of a contracting party is subject to the double criminality condition.

By contrast, 2004 Mutual Assistance Treaty among eight far-eastern states does not require the fulfilment of double criminality. Instead, it demands that the requesting state must provide all the information which the requested party considers necessary for giving effect to a foreign request of forfeiture.[137]

These may be compared with the 2009 Mutual Assistance Treaty between the UK and Philippines which simply provides that the request shall be carried out in accordance with domestic law of the requested state. Article 17(1) reads:

> [t]he contracting states shall assist each other in proceedings involving identification, tracing, restraint, seizure and confiscation of the proceeds and instrumentalities of crime in accordance with domestic law of the Requested state.[138]

So, three different approaches have been adopted to implement the obligation concerning the execution of foreign requests of identification, tracing, search and seizure of the proceeds and instrumentalities of crime. The first approach requires fulfilment of double criminality condition, the second demands provision of information concerning the crime and the third only requires that the assistance be provided in accordance with domestic law of the requested state.

This variation in bilateral treaties casts doubt on the utility of mutual legal assistance provisions of the international organised crime conventions. If each bilateral or regional treaty has separate rules, it will reinforce bilateral rather than international approaches to state cooperation. However, the bilateral or regional treaties cannot be blamed for deviating from the international conventions because the latter leave it entirely up to states to determine the procedure of providing inter-state assistance.

---

[136] See article 11(3) US-France Mutual Assistance Treaty 1998

[137] See article 22 of 2004 Mutual Legal Assistance Treaty among eight far-eastern states

[138] See article 17(1) of UK- Philippines Mutual Legal Assistance Treaty 2009

3.2.2.3) Elaboration of procedure as an alternative

In contrast to the international conventions, some bilateral and regional treaties adopt the technique of laying down comprehensive procedure of providing legal assistance in identification, tracing and freezing of the proceeds of crime. For example, the European Laundering Convention 1990 divides the process of mutual legal assistance into two parts. The first part relates to investigation which embraces the measures of identification and tracing. It requires the parties to assist each other in securing evidence as to location, movement, nature, legal status or value of the property liable to confiscation.[139] The second part concerns provisional measures. It obliges the parties to assist each other in freezing and seizing of the property by imposing prohibition against dealing in, transfer or disposal of property which at a later stage may be the subject of a request for confiscation.[140] It further stipulates that the requested party shall, wherever possible, give the requesting party an opportunity to present its reasons in favour of continuing the measure, before lifting any provisional measures.[141]

The procedure of identification and tracing has been elaborated further by the UN Model Treaty on Mutual Legal Assistance 1990. According to it:

> The requested state shall upon request endeavour to ascertain whether any proceeds of crime are located within its jurisdiction and shall notify to the requesting state of the result of its inquiries. In making the request the requesting state shall notify to the requested state of the basis of its belief that such proceeds may be located within its jurisdiction.[142]

Clearly, the aforementioned bilateral and regional treaties not only define the terms 'identification', 'tracing', 'freezing' and 'seizure' but also lay down extensive rules for applying them in practice. Accordingly, it can be suggested that these treaties establish specific rules whereas the organised crime conventions lay down general obligations only.[143] Since mandatory obligations under the international conventions are as deferential to national laws as the above referred provisions of bilateral and regional

---

[139] See article 8 European Laundering Convention 1990

[140] See article 11 European Laundering Convention 1990

[141] See article 12(2) the European Laundering Convention 1990

[142] See article 18(2) UN Model Treaty on Mutual Legal Assistance 1990

[143] For instance, articles 9 & 12 of the European Laundering Convention 1990 provide that while executing the request relating to investigation or provisional measures, the requested state shall be governed by its own domestic law and the request shall be executed to the extent permissible under such law.

treaties, the latter at least provide better models for framing effective national laws, which amounts to creating enabling powers to offer more comprehensive assistance in suppression of transnational crimes.

3.2.3) Voluntary or spontaneous information

Mutual assistance provisions of the international counterterrorism and organised crime conventions stipulate that the contracting parties may, subject to their national law, provide information to each other, without prior request, if the information is likely to facilitate criminal proceedings or trigger a request for freezing or confiscation under these conventions.[144] This is an important provision because it enables one party voluntarily to bring to the notice of another the existence of property that is liable to confiscation under latter's domestic law.

The provision has been criticised for its discretionary nature. As noted by Gurule, the use of the discretionary 'may' instead of obligatory 'shall' has turned the provision into a recommendation or suggestion rather than a specific duty. Therefore, it is not likely to have the desired harmonising impact on national legal systems.[145]

3.2.3.1) Impact on bilateral and regional treaties

The 1995 Mutual Assistance Treaty between Australia and Indonesia contains no provision with respect to the transmission of voluntary or spontaneous information. Under this treaty, the information could only be provided pursuant to a request made by one of the contracting parties.[146] This may be compared with the European Laundering Convention 1990, which stipulates that a party may, without prior request, forward to another party the information on instrumentalities and proceeds when it considers that the disclosure of such information might assist the receiving party in the investigation or prosecution or lead to initiation of a request by the receiving party for provision of legal assistance.[147]

The inconsistent national approaches towards the inclusion of voluntary information clauses in bilateral and regional treaties runs counter to the

---

[144] See article 18(4) the Organised Crime Convention 2000; See also article 46 (4) the UN Convention against Corruption 2003 and article 18 (3) the Terrorism Financing Convention 1999

[145] Gurule (n 6) 92

[146] See article 18, Australia-Indonesia Mutual Assistance Treaty 1995; See also article 11 US-France Mutual Assistance Treaty 1998

[147] See Article 10 of the European Laundering Convention 1990

objective of facilitating state cooperation in law enforcement through harmonisation of national legal systems. Seemingly, states not having the enabling clauses are not in a position to transmit spontaneous information. However, such states cannot be held accountable for violating their convention obligation because the relevant clauses of the conventions are only recommendatory.

While the decision as to whether a provision is recommendatory or obligatory will depend upon states parties, it is nonetheless possible for the drafters of the conventions to make such a provision more precise, with a view to providing a better model for domestic legislation. In this regard, the 2009 UK- Philippines Mutual Assistance Treaty provides a useful example. This treaty makes it plain that the information may not only be provided with respect to proceeds found in the informing state, but also those found in the receiving state. Such information either results in the receiving state initiating proceedings within its own territory or forwarding a request for confiscation to the informing state under the provisions of this treaty. The treaty provides further that the informing state may impose conditions on the use of such information by the receiving state and the latter shall be bound by those conditions.[148] It is suggested that corresponding provisions be included in international counterterrorism and organised crime conventions to simplify the procedure of state cooperation in confiscation of the proceeds of crime. This strategy at least provides better guidelines to states to legislate effective mutual legal assistance laws to offer more comprehensive assistance in the suppression of transnational crimes.

3.2.4) Disposal and sharing of the proceeds

Article 5(5) of the Drugs Convention 1988 makes recommendations about the disposal of confiscated proceeds or property. Identical provisions can be found in the Organised Crime Convention 2000, UN Convention against Corruption 2003 and Terrorism Financing Convention 1999.[149] Article 5(5) (a) explains that proceeds or property confiscated by a state party shall be disposed of according to its domestic law and administrative procedure. Article 5(5)(b) encourages parties to consider concluding agreements: (i) to contribute the proceeds or property to inter-governmental bodies specialising in the fight against drug trafficking (ii)

---

[148] See also article 25 of the UK-Philippines Mutual Assistance Treaty 2009

[149] See article 14 the Organised Crime Convention 2000, article 57 the UN Convention against Corruption 2003 and article 8(3) the Terrorism Financing Convention 1999

to share with other parties on a regular or case-by-case basis property or proceeds derived from drug trafficking in accordance with their domestic law, administrative procedures and multilateral agreements.

3.2.4.1) Inconsistent implementation

The provisions of article 5(5) (b) are designed to enhance the efforts of law enforcement officials and concerned governments by offering them the financial incentive of sharing in the proceeds of crime.[150] Nonetheless, they have been expressed in a recommendatory fashion. Consequently, domestic laws reflect variation in their implementation. For example, Pakistan's money laundering law provides that the confiscated proceeds shall vest in the federal government exclusively unless it has a bilateral agreement with the requesting state for the return of such proceeds.[151] Similarly, the Indian law provides that the confiscated proceeds shall vest in the Indian government even if confiscation has taken place upon the request of a foreign state.[152] On the other hand, the Australian Proceeds of Crime Act stipulates that while the proceeds of crime shall vest in the Commonwealth, the Attorney General is authorised to order the disposal of proceeds under a foreign confiscation order.[153] This may be compared with the Canadian law which provides that the items seized pursuant to a foreign request 'will be' transferred to the requesting state, if, upon a hearing subsequent to the seizure, the judge finds that the warrant was properly executed and issued.[154]

Thus, at one extreme are domestic enactments such as Indian money laundering law which leave no room for sharing of proceeds, at the other are the Canadian Proceeds of Crime Act which make it obligatory to return the confiscated proceeds to the requesting state or the victims of crime.

Similar discrepancies exist in bilateral treaties. For example, the 1995 Mutual Assistance Treaty between Australia and Indonesia makes it obligatory for the requested party to return the confiscated property or its value to the requesting state.[155] Likewise, 2004 Mutual Assistance Treaty

---

[150] Zagaris 'Asset Forfeiture' (n 1) 506

[151] See sections 10 & 30 Anti-Money Laundering Act 2010 of Pakistan

[152] Sc. 60 of the Indian Prevention of Money Laundering Act 2002

[153] Sc. 70(1) & Sc.23(2) Australian Proceeds of Crime Act 1987 Vol 1, 2 Austl. Acts p.1800 (1987)

[154] Sc. 15(a)(i) & (ii) Mutual Assistance in Criminal Matters Act 1998, 36-37 Eliz II, Vol II [hereinafter Canadian Mutual Assistance in Criminal Matters Act 1988]

[155] See Article 18(5) of the Australia-Indonesia Mutual Assistance Treaty 1995

among eight far- eastern states provides that the requested party 'shall', subject to its national law and pursuant to any agreement with the requesting party, transfer to the latter the agreed share of the confiscated property subject to payment of the cost incurred by the requested state in the enforcement of the forfeiture order.[156] These may be compared with the US-France Mutual Assistance Treaty 1998 which only recommends the requested state to return or share the proceeds. Article 11 of the treaty provides that the requested state shall dispose of the proceeds in accordance with its domestic law. 'As it determines appropriate', the requested state may also transfer the confiscated property, or the proceeds of its sale, to the requesting state.[157]

Diverse national approaches towards disposal and sharing of proceeds repudiate the convention objective of facilitating state cooperation in confiscation of crime proceeds. Obviously, states not having enabling laws or treaties are not in a position to offer inter-state assistance in the disposal or sharing of proceeds. However, they cannot be held liable for violating their convention obligation because the obligation is not mandatory.

3.2.4.2) Elaboration of procedure as an alternative

The 2009 UK-Philippines Mutual Assistance Treaty presents a substitute arrangement. The treaty divides the obligation to share proceeds into two parts. The first part relates to the return of assets to the state where the crime was committed or the conviction was obtained. The second part deals with the sharing of the confiscated property with a state whose cooperation has led to final confiscation. Thus, article 18(1) of the treaty explains that confiscated assets may be returned to the requesting state if the offence is committed and a conviction has been obtained in the requesting state. Moreover, it stipulates that the return of the confiscated property shall take place in accordance with the law of the requested state.[158] Articles 20-21 enumerate the circumstances under which the

---

[156] See article 22 (5) of 2004 Mutual Legal Assistance Treaty among eight far-eastern

[157] See article 11(5) US-France Mutual Assistance Treaty 1998. The article provides further:

> … [i]nsofar as cooperation between two states contributed to a final forfeiture decision, the forfeiting state to the extent permitted by its national law and upon such terms and conditions as it deems to be appropriate, may transfer all or part of such assets or proceeds of their sale to other state.

[158] See article 18(1) UK Philippines Mutual Assistance Treaty 2009

confiscated property may be shared with states other than the one where the offence was committed or the conviction was obtained. According to them, where it appears to the confiscating/holding state that cooperation has been extended by another contracting state which has led to confiscation of the assets, the confiscating/holding state may upon the request of such cooperating state consider whether to share assets. The outcome of the deliberation shall be conveyed to the cooperating state.

The above provisions bring much needed procedural clarity and serve as better models for domestic legislations as compared to the vague provisions of international counterterrorism and organised crime conventions. They are expected to facilitate state cooperation in confiscation by assisting states in framing enabling laws. Accordingly, their inclusion in the conventions in place of the existing provisions would be an improvement.

3.2.5) Grounds for refusal of mutual legal assistance

The mutual assistance provisions of the international counterterrorism and organised crime conventions establish grounds on the basis of which assistance may be refused. Article 18(21) of the Organised Crime Convention 2000 provides that mutual legal assistance may be refused: (a) if the request is not made in conformity with the provisions of the article (b) if the requested state considers that the execution of the request is likely to prejudice its sovereignty, security, public order or other essential interests (c) if the authorities of the requested State Party would be prohibited by its domestic law from carrying out the action requested with regard to any similar offence, had it been subject to investigation, prosecution or judicial proceedings under their own jurisdiction (d) if it would be contrary to the legal system of the requested state party relating to mutual legal assistance for the request to be granted.[159] Corresponding provisions can be seen in the Drugs Convention 1988 and the UN Convention against Corruption 2003.[160]

3.2.5.1) Non-exhaustive list of grounds

Whereas some of these grounds are specific, others are fairly general. The latter include grounds such as *essential national interests* and the request being *incompatible with the national legal system*. It can be argued that broad terms such as these give open authorisation to states to incorporate

---

[159] See article 18(21) the Organised Crime Convention 2000

[160] See article 7(15) the Drugs Convention 1988 and article 46(21) the UN Convention against Corruption 2003

any ground of refusal in their national laws.[161] An interpretive note attached to the Organised Crime Convention 2000 supports this argument. According to this note, the term 'essential interests', includes the political offence exception and non-discrimination.[162]

This implies that the grounds for refusal set forth by the international conventions are not exhaustive and can be tailored to suit the needs of domestic legal systems.[163] The assumption is reinforced by two common provisions of the conventions. One stipulates that a request for mutual legal assistance shall be executed in accordance with the domestic law of the requested party and to the extent it is not contrary to such law.[164] The other provides, '[t]he provisions of this article shall not affect the obligations under any other treaty, bilateral or multilateral, that governs or will govern, in whole or in part, mutual legal assistance.'[165] Both these provisions make it evident that the manner and procedure of executing a foreign request of mutual legal assistance is to be determined by the national law of the requested state and the bilateral treaty to which it is bound. In view of this, the harmonising impact of the grounds for refusal listed by the international counterterrorism and organised crime convention is expected to be minimal.

3.2.5.2) Additional grounds for refusal under bilateral and multilateral treaties

The European Laundering Convention 1990, in addition to the grounds for refusal enumerated by the international counterterrorism and organised crime conventions, authorises the parties to refuse assistance where: (a) in the opinion of the requested party the importance of the case to which the request relates does not justify the action sought, (b) the offence to which the request relates is a political or fiscal offence, (c) the compliance with the action requested would be contrary to the principle of *ne bis in idem,* (d) confiscation may no longer be enforced under the law of the requested state due to lapse of time, (e) the request for confiscation does not relate to

---

161 See Legislative Guide to the Organised Crime Convention (n 3) 211

162 See A/55/383/Add.1, para.42

163 See Zagaris 'Asset Forfeiture' (n 1) 487

164 See article 18(17) the Organised Crime Convention 2000, article 7(12) the Drugs Convention 1988, article 46(17) the UN Convention against Corruption 2003 and article 12(5) the Terrorism Financing Convention 1999

165 See article 18(6) the Organised Crime Convention 2000. See also article 7(6) the Drugs Convention 1988 and article 46(6) the UN Convention against Corruption 2003

a previous conviction, (f) confiscation is not enforceable in the requesting state or is still subject to ordinary means of appeal, and (g) the request relates to a confiscation order passed in absence of defendant.[166]

Similarly, 2004 Mutual Assistance Treaty among eight far-eastern states lays down some new grounds, including non-discrimination, political and military crime exception, and double jeopardy.[167] The above grounds are also found in the 1998 US-France Mutual Assistance treaty,[168] the 2009 Mutual Assistance Treaty between the UK and the Philippines[169] and the UN Model Treaty on Mutual Legal Assistance 1990.[170] Thus, it is clear that bilateral and multilateral treaties do not confine themselves to the grounds for refusal set forth by the international conventions; they rather establish new and additional grounds.

3.2.5.3) Implications of additional grounds for refusal

The varying grounds for refusal of mutual legal assistance under bilateral and regional treaties raise a question about the utility of the grounds listed by the international counterterrorism and organised crime conventions. Since these grounds are non-exhaustive, they are unlikely to bring harmony in national laws and thereby to facilitate mutual legal assistance. Consequently, even if the requesting state satisfies each ground for refusal identified by the international counterterrorism and organised crime conventions, the request may still be denied for not having satisfied the additional grounds expressed under the law of the requested state or the bilateral treaty to which the parties are bound.

As an alternative, the makers of the international counterterrorism and organised crime conventions may wish to shift their focus towards factors on the basis of which mutual legal assistance may not be refused. This approach also aims at facilitating state cooperation; nonetheless, it takes the route of minimising procedural constraints.

---

166 See article 18(1) the European Laundering Convention 1990

167 See article 3 of 2004 Mutual Legal Assistance Treaty among eight far-eastern states

168 See article 6, US-France Mutual Legal Assistance Treaty 1998

169 See article 2, UK- Philippines Mutual Legal Assistance Treaty 2009

170 See article 4 UN Model Treaty on Mutual Legal Assistance 1990

3.2.6) Factors on the basis of which mutual legal assistance may not be refused

Besides establishing grounds on the basis of which mutual legal assistance could be denied, the international counterterrorism and organised crime conventions also lay down factors which cannot be used as reasons to refuse assistance. Thus, article 18(22) of the Organised Crime Convention 2000 provides that states parties 'shall' not decline to render mutual legal assistance on the grounds of bank secrecy[171] and fiscal offence exception.[172] The object of this provision is to simplify the procedure of mutual legal assistance rather than to restrict the freedom of states in refusing assistance. Bank secrecy laws and fiscal offence exception provide legal basis to refuse the production of the records of banks and financial institutions before the courts and competent authorities. Accordingly, these factors make it difficult for the requested state to seize, identify, trace, freeze and confiscate the proceeds of crime pursuant to a foreign request.[173]

States appear to be more willing to embrace factors on the basis of which mutual legal assistance may not be refused instead of common grounds for refusal of assistance. For example, prohibition against the use of bank secrecy laws finds expression in a majority of bilateral and regional treaties including the European Laundering Convention 1990, 2004 Mutual Legal Assistance Treaty among eight far-eastern states and the UN Model Treaty on Mutual Legal Assistance 1990.[174] Similarly, the prohibition against fiscal offence exception is widely applied in national laws and bilateral treaties.[175]

---

[171] See article 18(8) the Organised Crime Convention 2000; See also article 46(8) the UN Convention against Corruption 2003 and 7(5) the Drugs Convention 1988

[172] See article 18(22) the Organised Crime Convention 2000; See also article 46(22) the UN Convention against Corruption 2003

[173] See text to (n 125-126) above

[174] See article 18(7) the European Laundering Convention 1990; article 3(5) of 2004 Treaty on Mutual Legal Assistance Treaty among eight far-eastern states and article 4(2) UN Model Treaty on Mutual Legal Assistance 1990

[175] See for instance article 2(2) UK-Philippines Mutual Assistance Treaty 2009. Noticeably, the impact of this provision has been inconsistent. For example, refusal of assistance on this ground is allowed under article 18 of the European Laundering Convention 1990 and section 41 the Anti-Money Laundering Act 2010 of Pakistan.

So far, the international counterterrorism and organised crime conventions have identified only two factors on the basis of which mutual legal assistance cannot be refused: a fiscal offence exception and bank secrecy laws. To make this provision more effective, the list of these factors could be expanded on the pattern of the European Laundering Convention 1990. The 1990 Convention provides that the assistance may not be refused on the ground that the request for confiscation is directed against a legal entity.[176] Furthermore, it stipulates that death of a natural person and insolvency of a legal entity shall not be used as reasons to refuse mutual legal assistance.[177] The two factors have been implemented in the money laundering laws of India and Pakistan which constitute unilateral legislations for providing mutual legal assistance upon foreign request.[178]

The benefit of including these factors can be gauged from the *Rodriquez Gachsa* case. In this case, Gachsa, a notorious drug trafficker was indicted on heroin trafficking charges in the Southern District of New York. However, subsequently, he was killed by the Colombian law enforcement authorities.[179] As a result, it became difficult to forfeit his assets worth $ 60 million because the governments could not try him in death. Nevertheless, since the US law applied civil forfeiture systems, his estate was finally forfeited.[180] This led to sharing of substantial proceeds of crime between the US and Colombia. [181] Had Gachsa been prosecuted by a state applying criminal forfeiture, it would not have been possible to confiscate his assets unless the law of the prosecuting state included a provision to the effect that forfeiture shall not be precluded on account of a defendant's death.

---

[176] See article 18(8)(a) the European Laundering Convention 1990

[177] See article 18(8)(b) the European Laundering Convention 1990

[178] See Section 26 & 38 Anti Money Laundering Act 2010 Pakistan; See also Sc.70 & 72 The Prevention of Money Laundering Act 2002 of India

[179] Douglas Jehl, 'Colombian Police Kill Drug Lord: War on Narcotics: Rodriguez Gacha was a leader of the Medellin cartel. U.S. hails the 'first big break we've had.'Los Angeles Times Nov 8, 1989<http://articles.latimes.com/1989-12-16/news/mn-228_1_medellin-cartel>[date accessed 21/03/23]

[180] Douglas Jehl and Ronald J. Ostrow, '5 Countries Freeze Drug Kingpin's $60 Million : Cocaine: Secret funds of Gonzalo Rodriguez Gacha are uncovered--the biggest strike yet in the war against traffickers' Los Angeles Times Nov 8, 1989 <http://articles.latimes.com/1989-11-08/news/mn-929_1_gonzalo-rodriguez-gacha> [date accessed 21/03/23]

[181] Sharing of Proceeds by the US in *Gachsa* case <http://www.justice.gov/opa/pr/2004/March/04_crm_180.htm> [Date accessed 21/03/23]; See also Zagaris 'Asset Forfeiture' (n 1) 510

Grounds on the basis of which mutual legal assistance may not be denied would be as much subject to national law as grounds for refusal of assistance. Hence they might not lead to synchronisation of national laws immediately. However, once they would appear in a significant numbers of multilateral treaties and model legislations, states might consider it expedient to implement them in view of their usefulness in modernising national laws in keeping with demands of state cooperation in suppressing sophisticated serious crime. According to Zagaris, this represents the process of turning soft law obligations into hard law ones.[182]

It is pertinent to note that state cooperation in extradition and mutual legal assistance has always been a voluntary proceeding and states have jealously guarded their right not to cooperate. However, in the wake of borderless crimes, they have shown their willingness to collectively lower the barriers to state cooperation. For example, states have agreed not to apply political and fiscal offence exception to extradition and mutual legal assistance proceedings involving these crimes. Listing of the grounds on the basis of which the assistance may not be denied represents a step in that direction.

Conclusion

Transnational crimes represent a criminal phenomenon which spreads across national frontiers. Its suppression is only possible through state cooperation in law enforcement. To facilitate state cooperation, the international conventions proscribing these crimes establish certain mandatory obligations. These include the obligation to implement the mechanism of identification, freezing and confiscation of the proceeds and instrumentalities of crime upon foreign request.

The purpose of the obligation is to bring harmony in national justice systems, which is needed because the absence of compatible rules of procedure under the laws of the requesting and requested states leads to refusal of a foreign confiscation. However, since the obligation is imprecise and is required to be implemented to the extent permissible under national laws, its domestic implementation varies in line with diverse national legal principles of state parties. As a result, enough discrepancies arise in the laws of states parties to allow refusal of confiscation based upon the non-existence of the enabling rules under the law of the requested state or the request not being consistent with its

[182] Zagaris 'Asset Forfeiture' (n 1) 452

confiscation procedure. These discrepancies may, for example, relate to civil and criminal forfeiture systems, sharing and disposal of proceeds, provision of voluntary information and the non-existence of a mechanism to undertake value and substitute confiscation.

Clearly, the makers of the international conventions are not in a position to impose overriding and unconditional obligations unless the necessary consensus builds amongst state parties. As an alternative, they might wish to consider shifting their focus towards simplifying the procedure of confiscation upon foreign request by including elaborate provisions, to serve as models for domestic legislation. Although the implementation of proposed elaborate provisions would be as much subject to national law, as that of the existing general provisions, states might consider it expedient to implement the former on account of their usefulness in modernising national laws in keeping with demands of suppressing sophisticated serious crimes. Notably, states have, in the context of transnational criminality, shown their willingness to collectively lower the barriers to law enforcement cooperation. The inclusion of elaborate provisions on confiscation in the international conventions regulating transnational crimes represents a step in that direction.

CHAPTER 7

CONCLUDING APPRAISAL

It has been argued that the UN sponsored international conventions regulating the acts of transnational terrorism and organised crime evidence the emergence of a new regime of state cooperation, the object of which is to subject sovereign discretion to collective law enforcement.[1] The argument implies that conventions supersede national laws and bilateral treaties on extradition and mutual legal assistance. The formulation of the conventions, however, disproves this theory, according to which the conditions and procedure of extradition and mutual legal assistance are to be determined in accordance with national law of the requested state and bilateral treaties to which it is bound. It is thus clear that the international conventions are meant to complement rather than supersede these laws and treaties.

The laws and treaties on extradition and mutual legal assistance lay down certain requirements which necessitate harmony in the justice systems of the requesting and requested states. These are: 'double conditions' associated with principle of reciprocity and similarity in the procedures of applying *aut dedere aut judicarè* and confiscation. Since the object of the international counterterrorism and organised crime conventions is to facilitate state cooperation in law enforcement and since they do not override national laws and bilateral treaties on extradition and mutual legal assistance, it can be argued that their mandatory obligations are directed towards facilitating the fulfilment of these requirements through establishing

---

[1] See Kofi A Annan, Foreword to the UNTOC 2000 at p.iii; Neil Boister, 'Transnational Criminal Law' 14 EJIL (2003) 953 at 953; Carrie Lyn Donigan Guymon, 'International Legal Mechanisms for Combating Transnational Organised Crime: The Need for a Multilateral Convention' 18 Berkeley J. Int'l L (2000) 53 at 86-87; D.W. Sproule and Paul St-Denis, 'The UN Drug Trafficking Convention: An Ambitious Step' 27 Canadian Yearbook of International Law (1989) 263 at 266; UNODC's Technical Assistance Guide 2009 to the UN Convention against Corruption 2003 at 133 <http://www.unodc.org/documents/corruption/Technical_Guide_UNCAC.pdf> [Date accessed 21/03/23]

harmony. However, as we have seen, the obligations set forth by the conventions may not produce a level of harmony needed to achieve this goal.

1.1 Suggestions for improvement

Recognising that the mandatory obligations set forth by the counterterrorism and organised crime conventions are subject to various limitations, the book recommends that alternative techniques of facilitating law enforcement cooperation should be looked for. One such technique could be to regulate the requirements of law enforcement cooperation, i.e. 'double conditions' and procedure of applying *aut dedere aut judicare* and confiscation.

This technique does not require the abolishment or replacement of the requirements necessitating harmony. Instead, it aims at simplifying the procedure of enforcing *aut dedere aut judicare* and confiscation and defining with precision and clarity 'double conditions', with a view to bringing about consistency in their application.

It is hoped that by adopting this approach, the international counterterrorism and organised crime conventions will achieve their objective of facilitating law enforcement cooperation more effectively than the existing technique of imposing mandatory obligations. As noted by Bassiouni:

> These values and interests must be defined with sufficient specificity, applied with high level of consistency that would provide needed predictability in order to contribute to the preservation of world public order. The consistent application of uniform standards of practice between states and the relator is self-evidently a sound policy...[2]

The suggestions made here are not required to be expressed in the form of mandatory obligations; their purpose is to serve as models for national legislation. If states are unwilling to accept unqualified mandatory obligations, the international conventions could at least provide comprehensive guidelines to modernise national laws in keeping with the demands of bringing to justice transnational offenders.

Although states have traditionally been reluctant to part with their discretion not to cooperate, they have nonetheless indicated their

---

[2] Cherif Bassiouni, 'The "Political Offence Exception" Revisited: Extradition between the US and the UK- A Choice between Friendly Cooperation among Allies and Sound Law and Policy' 15 Denv. J. Int'l L. Pol'y (1986-1987) 255 at 260

willingness to collectively lower the barriers to law enforcement cooperation in the specific context of transnational crimes. The consensus of states not to apply political and fiscal offence exception to extradition and mutual legal assistance proceedings involving these crimes provides but one example of their willingness. The proposed relaxation of 'double conditions' and simplification of procedure of applying *aut dedere aut judicare* and confiscation signifies a step in that direction.

One criticism against the suggestions made here could be that the proposed technique suffers from same weaknesses which are found in the existing technique. If harmony could not be established with respect to making national justice systems conducive to the requirements of law enforcement cooperation, how could it be established in regard to relaxing 'double conditions' and simplifying procedure of applying *aut dedere aut judicare* and confiscation? The argument overlooks the fact that the existing technique is focused on harmonising the entire 'justice systems' of states parties which involves amendments to their laws on terrorism and organised crime as well as constitutions and criminal codes. Since it purports to supersede local norms of prosecution, trial, punishment, forfeiture, criminalisation, jurisdiction and treatment of offenders, states consider it an interference with their sovereignty. On the other hand, the proposed regulation of 'double conditions' and procedure of applying *aut derere aut judicare* and confiscation impacts only one aspect of national justice systems i.e. state cooperation in law enforcement. This amounts to collectively lowering the barriers to law enforcement cooperation which cannot be equated to harmonisation of the entire 'justice systems'. According to the existing technique, states are in a way required to surrender their sovereign right to conduct criminal proceedings in accordance with their local norms, whereas the proposed technique requires them to surrender a portion of their sovereignty, to the extent of state cooperation in law enforcement. Summary of the measures for improvement suggested in the book are set out immediately below.

1.1.1) Relaxing the application of special use of double criminality

The book recommends that the principle of special use of double criminality might be relaxed in view of the specific nature of transnational criminality. According to this principle, when assistance is sought in relation to a crime taking place outside state territory, the theory of jurisdiction applied by the requesting state must correspond to the theory applied by the requested state in respect of the crime in question. Simply put, the principle requires that the theory of jurisdiction applied by the state seeking assistance in respect of an extraterritorial crime must be accepted under the legal system of the requested state. To facilitate the satisfaction of this condition, the international counterterrorism and organised crime conventions impose mandatory obligations upon states to implement the bases of jurisdiction outlined by them. The obligation is, however, inconclusive because there is no rule of international law which restricts the right of states to apply their laws extraterritorially under any theory of jurisdiction recognised by their national law. Accordingly, it is unlikely to produce the level of harmony needed to satisfy the special use of double criminality.

As an alternative, the makers of the conventions may recommend that states consider the non-fulfilment of special use condition a mandatory ground of refusal only, where it has been expressed in obligatory language in the relevant law or bilateral treaty. Likewise, they can encourage states to reserve powers for their competent authorities to grant extradition, notwithstanding, the non-fulfilment of special use condition by the requesting state. A more radical approach could be to make it altogether irrelevant for the purposes of surrender, which theory is applied by the requesting state to assert jurisdiction over crime. Extradition should be granted if the offence is extraditable as per the terms of the relevant bilateral treaty or under the law of the requested state.

1.1.2) Relaxing the application of double criminality

A major complication arises in the surrender or interrogation of suspects on account of the requesting state not being able to fulfil the double criminality condition of extradition and mutual legal assistance laws. According to this condition, the act in respect of which the assistance is sought must constitute a criminal offence under the laws of both the requesting and requested state, not only at the date of making of the request but also at the date of alleged commission of crime. Since crimes set forth by the modern counterterrorism and organised crime conventions are complex aggregate crimes, it is possible that the definition of a crime or its constituent elements may differ under the laws of the requesting and requested states. This allows the offender to raise an objection of double criminality in extradition and mutual assistance proceedings. To address this problem, the recent conventions adopt the technique of imposing mandatory obligation upon states to legislate against universal definitions of crimes set forth by them. However, the obligation is riddled with exceptions and safeguards; hence, it is unlikely to produce the level of harmony needed to satisfy the demands of double criminality, which has more than one interpretation at the national level.

As an alternative arrangement, the conventions may require states to apply double criminality only in those proceedings which represent steps towards punishment, such as extradition and confiscation. In other forms of law enforcement cooperation, which are investigative in nature, like asset freezing, identification and seizure, states may be encouraged not to insist upon the fulfilment of the double criminality rule. Another technique could be to encourage states not to insist that the act in respect of which surrender or interrogation is sought must have constituted a crime under the laws of both, the requesting and requested states, at the date of commission, it should be sufficient if the act was a crime at the date of making extradition request. Yet another strategy would be to require states not to insist upon exact similarity in the definitions of crimes under the laws of the requesting and requested states. It should be sufficient if the act in respect of which cooperation is sought constitutes a crime under the law of the requested state regardless of its denomination.

1.1.3) Regulating the double punishability requirement

Extradition and interrogation may be refused when the act in respect of which the inter-state assistance is sought is deemed non-punishable under the laws of the requested state due to actual or anticipated violation of human rights of the offender in the requesting state. Thus, a requesting state while seeking inter-state assistance is required to provide such evidence of criminality as would justify the trial of the offender in both the requesting and requested states. To facilitate the fulfilment of this requirement, the international counterterrorism and organised crime conventions impose mandatory obligation upon states to provide fair treatment to the relators in accordance with national and international law, including human rights law. However, since the obligation does not define the rights to be guaranteed, it is unlikely to produce a level of harmony sufficient to satisfy multiple applications of these rights under extradition and mutual assistance laws, as grounds for refusal of assistance.

The book recommends that instead of focusing on bringing harmony as regards provision of human rights to the offender, the conventions should emphasise on the consistent application of these rights, under extradition and mutual assistance laws, as grounds for refusal of assistance. The application of human rights as grounds for refusal of assistance varies in extradition and mutual assistance laws, with respect to matters such as:

what constitutes political persecution, under what circumstances the possibility of torture represents a ground for refusal of assistance, which state's limitation law is relevant for blocking assistance under the rule of time- barred prosecutions and when double jeopardy can be raised as a ground for denying assistance.

To reconcile the use of torture as a ground of refusal with severe punishment requirement of transnational criminality, the book suggests that states should be encouraged to surrender the fugitive subject to obtaining diplomatic assurances from the requesting state. To bring consistency in the application of time-barred prosecutions as a ground for refusal, the book recommends that only the requesting state's limitation law should be deemed relevant for the purposes of refusing cooperation on this ground. Since it is the interests of that state which are at stake, it should not be forced to comply with the limitation law of its treaty partner. Likewise, the conventions may encourage states to follow uniform rules with respect to the forum whose previous judgement may lead to denial of surrender or interrogation on the ground of double jeopardy. Additionally, the conventions may recommend that previous conviction or acquittal should block surrender or interrogation in relation to specific offences rather than to an entire criminal transaction. Since the crimes set forth by the conventions tend to aggregate, if a previous conviction or acquittal for one offence is considered a ground for refusing assistance for the whole transaction, the offender may escape punishment for more serious offences.

1.1.4) Simplifying the procedure of *aut dedere aut Judicare*

To ensure the denial of safe heavens, the counterterrorism and organised crime conventions oblige states to implement the mechanism of *aut dedere aut judicare*. The obligation is designed to make sure that states have in place the alternative enforcement measures of extradition or prosecution, so that if one fails the other can be applied to offer inter-state assistance. Nonetheless, both alternative measures are to be applied in accordance with the national law of the requested state. Since these laws differ, the obligation is unlikely to bring about a level of harmony sufficient to ensure that one of the measures would be applied in every situation. As a result, the offender may avoid punishment altogether for his crime, under certain circumstances. Furthermore, the conventions contain more than one formula of *aut dedere aut judicare* and states are entitled to implement any one of these. Hence, the obligation may only establish harmony to the extent of including the maxim in national laws, which is insufficient to facilitate its application.

To facilitate the application of *aut dedere aut judicare*, the book recommends that states should be encouraged to take measures such as sending observers to witness the trial and holding trial in a third state. These measures are designed to make the option of trial in lieu of extradition—which currently suffers from weaknesses such as the inability of the requested state to prosecute foreign nationals for crimes committed abroad and the complicity of the requested state in the commission of crime—more effective. Additional difficulties in the application of *aut dedere aut judicare* include the problem of competing jurisdictions and absence of hierarchy in the alternatives of extradition or prosecution. To address these, the book recommends that states be encouraged to adopt a rule of reasonableness with a consensual list of factors to be considered when making a decision about surrender or trial in a given situation. Likewise, to facilitate the extradition option of *aut dedere aut judicare,* the book recommends that states be encouraged to adopt innovative rules such as the provision of mutual legal assistance in extradition.

1.1.5) Simplifying the procedure of confiscation upon foreign request

To deprive the offenders of their illicit wealth, the international counterterrorism and organised crime conventions oblige the parties to implement the mechanism of confiscation and asset freezing. The obligation leaves it up to states to determine the procedure of confiscation, in accordance with their national laws. Moreover, it stipulates that measures prescribed therein should be implemented to the extent permissible under national laws. In view of this, it is unlikely to produce the level of harmony sufficient to facilitate the enforcement of confiscation upon foreign request. At most, it may lead to the inclusion of confiscation as a law enforcement measure in national laws. Thus, despite the establishment of a mandatory obligation, a request for confiscation remains under the threat of being refused on account of national law disparities in areas such as civil and criminal forfeiture systems, application of value and substitute confiscation and the determination of third party rights.

To facilitate the enforcement of confiscation upon foreign request, the book recommends that following provisions might be considered for inclusion in the international counterterrorism and organised crime conventions:

1. States might be encouraged to include civil forfeiture as an option in their national laws. Additionally, it might be suggested that they exempt forfeiture from domestic law rule against enforcement of foreign criminal judgements.
2. To determine the value of proceeds which are lost or are no longer available, the book recommends that a consensual formula be provided on the pattern of some domestic laws to apply value and substitute confiscation. It further recommends that states be encouraged to empower their courts to provide reasonable allowance to offenders with a view to avoid human rights complications such the offender having been deprived of the right to choose attorney of his own choice.
3. To minimise the likelihood of a foreign request being delayed on account of disparity in national procedures as regards protection of third party rights, the book recommends that states parties be encouraged to determine these rights expeditiously.
4. As regards mutual legal assistance, the book recommends that the conventions should elaborate a procedure concerning the sharing and disposal of proceeds and the provision of voluntary information. The existing provisions of the conventions are silent with respect to sharing of proceeds with third parties whose cooperation has led to confiscation. Similarly, no guideline exists concerning the scope of voluntary information. These deficiencies could be removed by borrowing suitable provisions from bilateral treaties and domestic laws on mutual legal assistance.
5. To bring consistency in national approaches towards the refusal of mutual legal assistance, the book recommends that the conventions should focus on the grounds on which the assistance *may not* be refused. The grounds on the basis of which the assistance *may* be denied are non-exhaustive and are unlikely to produce the desired harmony. Conversely, the national implementing laws indicate that states are more willing to implement factors on the basis of which the assistance *may not* be denied. So far the conventions have indicated only two such factors, i.e. bank secrecy laws and the fiscal offence exception. The list might be expanded to include additional factors such as involvement of legal entities and the death or insolvency of the offender.

1.2) Compatibility of the proposed technique with aims and purposes of the counterterrorism and organised crime conventions and its utility in regard to modernisation of extradition and mutual assistance laws

It might be argued that the proposed technique of facilitating state cooperation, i.e. relaxing 'double conditions' and simplifying procedure of *aut dedere aut judicare* and confiscation is not in consonance with the nature of the international counterterrorism and organised crime conventions. Since the conventions are multilateral instruments of universal scope, their role is to provide broad guidelines only. Thus, the proposed regulation must be carried out by other instruments such as the UN Model Treaties on extradition and mutual legal assistance. The argument can be refuted on two grounds. Firstly, the aim of the counterterrorism and organised crime conventions is to facilitate state cooperation in law enforcement; thus the regulation of the conditions of extradition/mutual legal assistance and procedure of applying *aut dedere aut judicare* and confiscation is very much in line with this objective. Secondly, model treaties provide guidelines for states having regional and bilateral arrangements. Since the counterterrorism and organised crime conventions are universal in scope, not all states parties to them can be expected to have bilateral and regional treaties. For states not having such arrangements, guidelines have to come from the international conventions.

The proposed technique offers a further advantage of bringing laws and treaties on extradition and mutual legal assistance in consonance with the requirements of sophisticated serious crimes. It has been argued that extradition laws belong to the age of the horse and buggy and steamship, not to the age of jet airliners and high speed communications.[3] Hence, they are ill-suited for bringing to justice the offenders involved in sophisticated multi-jurisdictional crimes. Under these laws several difficulties arise in the surrender of offenders involved in borderless crimes. For example, the lack of extraterritoriality, dissimilar crime definitions and incompatible human rights safeguards, can all lead to the refusal of surrender. Thus, the technique of relaxing 'double conditions' and simplifying procedures of

---

[3] The present extradition laws belong to "the world of the horse and buggy and the steamship, not in the world of commercial jet air transportation and high speed telecommunications." From a letter to Senator Edward Kennedy from US Attorney General Benjamin R. Civiletti. See 126 CONG.RECORD Sc.13233 at S.13235 Col.2. See also Geoff Gilbert, *Transnational Fugitive Offenders in International law: Extradition and other mechanics* (Netherlands Martinus Nijhoff Publishers 1998) 1

aut dedere aut judicare and confiscation offers the added incentive of modernising extradition and mutual assistance laws in line with the peculiar requirements of transnational criminality. Finally, it is reiterated that states have, by agreeing not to apply political and fiscal offence exception to extradition and mutual legal assistance proceedings involving the crimes set forth by the counterterrorism and organised crime conventions, clearly shown their willingness to depart from traditional rules of surrender and interrogation in the specific context of transnational crimes.

BIBLIOGRAPHY

Books

Ballentine, J.A. A Law Dictionary of words, terms, abbreviations and phrases (New Jersey: The Law book exchange Ltd 2005)

Bassiouni, M.C. and Wise, E.M. Aut dedere Aut Judicare: The Duty to Extradite or Prosecute in International Law (Netherlands: Matinus Nijhoff Publishers 1995)

Bassiouni, M.C. International Criminal Law Vol 1: Sources, Subjects and Contents (3rd edn, Martnus Nijhoff-Netherlands 2008)

Bassiouni, M.C. International Criminal Law, Volume II: Multilateral and Bilateral Enforcement Mechanisms (3rd edn, Martinus Nijhoff, Netherlands, 2008)

Bedi, S.D. Extradition: A Treatise on the Laws Relevant to the Fugitive Offenders (2002-USA)

Evans, M.D. International law (2nd edn Oxford University Press 2006)

Gilbert, G. Transnational Fugitive Offenders in International law: Extradition and other mechanics (Netherlands Martinus Nijhoff Publishers 1998)

Gobert J. and Punch, M. 'Rethinking Corporate Crimes' (UK Butterworth's 2003)

ILC's Commentary on 1973 Convention on Protection of Diplomats, 1972 Yearbook of the International Law Commission (YBILC) Vol. II, Documents of twenty fourth session including the report of the Commission to General Assembly (United Nations Publications-New York 1974)

Lambert, J.J. Terrorism and Hostages in International Law, A Commentary on Hostages Convention 1979 (Cambridge: Grotius Publications Limited 1990)

Lowe, V. International Law (New York: Oxford University Press 2007)

Plachta, M. The Role of Double Criminality in International Cooperation in Penal Matters in N. Jareborg, ed., Double Criminality. Studies in International Criminal Law (Uppsala, 1989)

Stessens, G. Money Laundering a New International Law Enforcement Model (UK Cambridge University Press 2004)

Walter, C. Voneky, S., et al, Terrorism as a Challenge for national and international law: Security versus liberty (Max-Planck Germany-2004)

Zagaris, B. International White Collar Crime: Cases and materials (New York: Cambridge University Press 2010)

Implementation kits of transnational treaties

Commonwealth Implementation kits for the International Counter Terrorism Conventions <http://www.thecommonwealth.org/internal/38061/documents/>

UNODC's Legislative Guide 2004 for implementation of the Organized Crime Convention 2000 <http://www.unodc.org/pdf/crime/legislative_guides/Legislative%20guides_Full%20version.pdf>

UNODC's Legislative Guide For Implementation of the Human Trafficking Protocol to the UN Convention against Transnational Organized Crime 2000 <http://www.unodc.org/pdf/crime/legislative_guides/Legislative%20guides_Full%20version.pdf>

UNODC's Legislative Guide for implementing the UN Convention against Corruption 2003 <www.unodc.org/.../LegislativeGuide/UNCAC_Legislative_Guide_A.pdf >

UNODC's Legislative Guide to the Universal Anti-terrorism Conventions & Protocols (2003) <http://www.unodc.org/pdf/crime/terrorism/explanatory_english2.pdf>

UNODC's Legislative Guide to the Universal Legal Regime against Terrorism 2008 <www.unodc.org/unodc/en/treaties/CAC/legislative-guide.html>

UNODC's Technical Assistance Guide 2009 for implementing UN Convention against Corruption 2003 <http://www.unodc.org/documents/corruption/Technical_Guide_UNCAC.pdf>

Official Reports

A) - Reports presented to international bodies

Amnesty International's Report on the Obligation to Extradite or Prosecute 2009 <http://www.amnesty.org/ar/library/asset/IOR40/001/2009/en/a4761626-f20a-11dd-855f-392123cb5f06/ior400012009en.pdf>

Fourth Annual Report of the International Tribunal for the Prosecution of Persons Responsible for Serious Violations of International Humanitarian Law Committed in the Territory of Former Yugoslavia Since 1991, 150 U.N. Doc A/52/375-S/ 1997/729 (Sept. 18 1997)

Report of the ILC on the work of its 24th session, UN Doc.A/8710/Rev.1 <www.un.org/law/ilc/index/htm>

S/2001/1232.Letter dated 19 December 2001 from the Permanent Representative of the United Kingdom of Great Britain and Northern Ireland to the United Nations addressed to the Chairman of the Committee established pursuant to resolution 1373 (2001) concerning Counterterrorism. <http://www.refworld.org/pdfid/46d571150.pdf> .

S/2002/689.Supplementary Report of the Republic of Cyprus to the Counterterrorism Committee (CTC) established pursuant to the Security Council Resolution 1373 (2001) concerning Counterterrorism, in reply to the letter dated 1 April 2002 from the Chairman of the CTC. See S/2002/689 <http://www.mfa.gov.cy/mfa/mfa2006.nsf/All/F91E0D83B87C299CC22571D3002497CB/$file/Terrorism%20Report%202.pdf>

Galicki, Z. '4th Report on the Obligation to Extradite or Prosecute submitted in the 63rd session of the ILC' A/CN.4/648

Galicki, Z. 'Preliminary Report on the Obligation to Extradite or Prosecute presented in the 58th Session of the International Law Commission (ILC) held in Geneva,1 May-9 June and 3 July-11 August 2006'. A/CN.4/571

b) - Reports Presented to Domestic Legislative bodies

A Review of the United Kingdom's Extradition Arrangements (following Written Ministerial Statement by the Secretary of State for the Home Department of 8 September 2010). Presented to the Home Secretary on 30 September 2011 <http://www.homeoffice.gov.uk/publications/police/operational-policing/extradition-review?view=Binary>

Doyle, C. 'Extraterritorial Application of American Criminal Law' CRS Report to Congress 2010 <http://www.fas.org/sgp/crs/misc/94-166.pdf>

Doyle,C. 'Statutes of Limitation in Federal Criminal Cases: An Overview' CRS Report for Congress (April 9, 2007) <http://www.fas.org/sgp/crs/misc/RL31253.pdf>

Letter to Senator Edward Kennedy from US Attorney General Benjamin R. Civiletti. See 126 CONG.RECORD Sc.13233 at S.13235 Col.2.

Money Laundering and the Financing of Terrorism, 19th Report of the House of Lords on its 2008-09 Session, published 22 July 2009 <http://www.coe.int/t/dghl/monitoring/moneyval/activities/UK_Parlrep.pdf>

Rollins, J. and Wyley, L.S. 'International Terrorism and Transnational Crime, Security threats, US Policy & Considerations for Congress' <www.fas.org/sgp/crs/terror/R41004.pdf>

International Documents

A/55/383/Add.1, para.42; an interpretive note attached to the Organised Crime Convention 2000

Financial Action Task Force (FATF) 40 + 9 Recommendations. <www.fatf- gafi.org/document/44/0,3746,en_32250379_43751788_1_1_1_1,00.htm>

ICAO Doc 8979-LC/165-2 at 81, SA Doc. No.33, Rev.1(1972); the Hague Convention 1970

Kofi A Annan, Foreword to the Organised Crime Convention 2000 at iii <www. unodc.org>

Problematic Reservations and Declarations to Counterterrorism Conventions, Government of Pakistan's Declaration dated 13 August 2002 to the Terrorist Bombings Convention 1997; Egypt's Declaration to the Terrorist Financing Convention 1999 dated 1 March 2005; Syria's Declaration to the Terrorist Financing Convention 1999 dated 24th April 2005 <www.unodc.org>

Resolution adopted at the 17th Commission of the Institute of International Law at its 2005 Krakow Session <http://www.idi-iil.org/idiE/resolutionsE/2005_kra_03_en.pdf>

Resolution Adopted by the 121 Commission at its Session in Dijon,59 Institute of International Law Yearbook (1981) 176-177

UN Doc. E/Conf.82/C.1/S.R at 5; Document of the United Nations Economic and Social Council E/CONF.82/15

UN GAOR, 34th Sess. (13th mtg.) A/C.6/SR.13(1979)

UN Doc. A/C.6/52/L.3; Written proposals to Ad hoc Committee; Terrorist Bombing Convention 1997

Introductory Comment, 'Jurisdiction With Respect to Crime-Research in International Law' 29 AJIL (1935) Supp.443-445

Articles

Abelson, A. 'The Prosecute / Extradite Dilemma: Concurrent Criminal Jurisdiction and Global Governance' 16 University of California, Davis (2010) pp.102-138

Abeyratne, R. 'The Beijing Convention of 2010 on the Suppression of Unlawful Acts relating to International Civil Aviation—an Interpretative Study' 4 Journal of Transport Security (2011) pp.131-143

Abeyratne, R.I.R, 'Attempts at Ensuring Peace and Security in International Aviation' 24 Transp. L.J. (1996-1997) pp. 27-71

Abramovsky, A. 'Extraterritorial Jurisdiction: The United States Unwarranted Attempt to Alter International Law' 15 Yale J. Int'l L. (1990) pp.121-161

Abramovsky, A. 'Multilateral Conventions for Suppression of Unlawful Seizure and Interference with Aircraft Part 1: Hague Convention' 13 Colum. J. Transnat'l L. (1974) pp. 381-405

Abramovsky, A. 'Multilateral Conventions for the Suppression of Unlawful Seizure and Interference with the Aircraft Part II- The Montreal Convention' 14 Colum. J. Transnat'l L. (1975) pp. 268-300

Akehurst, M., 'Jurisdiction in International law' 46 British Yearbook of International Law (1972-73) pp.145-259

Bassiouni, M P. 'The Political Offence Exception Revisited: Extradition between the US and UK- A Choice between Friendly Cooperation among Allies' 15 Denv. J. Int'l L. & Pol'y (1986-1987) pp. 255-282

Bassiouni, M P. 'Ideologically Motivated Offenses and the Political Offenses Exception in Extradition - A Proposed Juridical Standard for an Unruly Problem' 19 DePaul L. Rev. (1969-1970) pp. 217-265

Bassiouni, M P. 'Effective National and International Action against Organised Crime and Terrorist Criminal Activities' 4 Emory Intl L. Review (1990) pp. 9-42

Bassiouni, M.C., 'Policy Considerations on Interstate Cooperation in Criminal Matters' 4 Pace Y.B.Int'l L. (1992) pp.123-145

Basso, K.A., 'The 1985 US-UK Supplementary Extradition Treaty: A Superfluous Effort' 12 Boston College International and Comparative Law Review (1989) pp. 301-333

Beku, O. 'A case for the Review of Article 88 of the ICC Statute: Strengthening a Forgotten Provision' 12 New Criminal Law Review (2009) pp.468-483

Bewley-Taylor, D.R. 'Challenging the UN Drug Control Conventions: Problems and Possibilities' 14 International Journal of Drug Policy (2003) pp.171-179

Bibes, P., 'Transnational Organised Crime and Terrorism - Columbia a Case Study' 17 Journal of Contemporary Criminal Justice (2001) pp. 243-258

Bissouni, M.C., 'Theories of Jurisdiction and their Application in Extradition Law and Practice' 5 Cal W. Int'l L.J 1 (1974-75) pp.1-61

Blakesley, C. L., 'A Conceptual Framework For Extradition and Jurisdiction over Extraterritorial Crime' 1984 Utah Law Review (1984) pp. 685-762

Blakesley, C. L., 'The Autumn of the Patriarch: The Pinochet Extradition Debacle and Beyond - Human Rights Clauses Compared to Traditional Derivative Protections Such as Double Criminality' 91 Journal of Criminal Law and Criminology (200-2001) pp. 1-98

Blakesley, C. L., 'The Law of International Extradition: A Comparative Study' 62 Revue Internationale De Droit Penal (1991) pp. 381-389

Blakesley, C. L., 'United States Jurisdiction over Extraterritorial Crime' 73 J. Crim. L. & Criminology (1982) pp.1109-1163

Blakesley, C. L., 'Wings For Talon: The Case for Extraterritorial Jurisdiction Over Sexual Exploitation of Children Through Cyberspace' 50 Wayne State L. Rev (2004) pp.109-159

Boister, N., 'Transnational Criminal Law' 14 EJIL (2003) pp. 953-976

Boister, N., 'Treaty Crimes, International Criminal Court?' 12 New Criminal Law Review (2009) pp. 341-365

Cantrell, C.L 'The Political Offense Exemption in International Extradition' 60 Marquette Law Review (1977) pp. 777-824

Christopher C. Joiner, 'Countering Nuclear Terrorism: A Conventional Response' 18 EJIL (2007) pp. 225-251

Clarke, R. S. 'The United Nations Convention against Transnational Organised Crime' 50 Wayne State Law Review (2004) pp. 161-184

Colangelo, A.J. 'Constitutional Limits on Extraterritorial Jurisdiction' 48 Harv.Int'l. L. J. (2007) pp.121-201

Corbonneau, T.E., 'Terrorist Acts - Crimes or Political infractions? An appraisal of recent French Extradition Cases' 3 Hastings International and Comparative Law Review (1980) pp. 265-298

Davies, G. 'Extradition post the NatWest Three' 156 New Law Journal (2006) 1542

Duffy, A. 'Expulsion to face Torture? Non-Refoulment in International Law' 20 Int'l. J. of Refugee law (2008) pp. 373-390

Dugard, J. and Wyngaert, C., 'Reconciling Extradition with Human Rights' 92 AJIL (1998) pp. 187-212

Elegab, O.Y., 'The Hague as the Seat of Lockerbie Trial: Some Constraints' 34 The International Lawyer (2000) pp.289-306

Feller, S.Z. 'Reflections on the nature of the Specialty Principle in Extradition Relations' 12 Isr .L. Rev (1977) pp. 466-524
Feller, S.Z., 'The Significance of the Requirement of Double Criminality in the Law of Extradition' 10 IsrL.Rev (1975) pp. 51-80
Finkelman, P., 'International Extradition and Fugitive Slaves: The John Anderson Case' 18 Brook. J. Int'l L. (1992) pp. 765-810
Gardocki, L. 'Double Criminality in Extradition Law' 27 Isr. L. Rev (1993) pp.288-296
Gaynes, J. 'Bringing the terrorist to Justice: A Domestic Law Approach' 11 Cornell Int'l L.J (1978) pp. 71-84
Gilbert, G, 'Terrorism and Political Offence Exemption Reappraised' 34 ICLQ (1985) pp. 695-723
Gilbert, G. 'Crimes Sans Frontiers: Jurisdictional Problems in English Law' 63 BYBIL (1992) pp. 415-442
Green, A.B. 'Convention on the Prevention and Punishment of Crimes against Internationally Protected Persons, including Diplomatic Agents: An analysis' 14 Virginia Journal of International Law (1973-74) pp. 703-728
Gunel, G., 'The Concept of Joint Criminal Enterprise and the ICC Jurisdiction' 2008 CASIN pp.49-51 <http://www.americanstudents.us/Pages%20from%20Guliyeva.pdf>
Gurule, J., 'The 1988 UN Convention against Illicit Traffic in Narcotic Drugs and Psychotropic Substances-A Ten Years Perspective: Is International Cooperation Merely Illusory?' 22 Fordham International law Journal (1998-1999) pp.74-121
Guymon, C.L.D. 'International Legal Mechanisms for Combating Transnational Organised Crime: The Need for a Multilateral Convention' 18 Berkeley J. Int'l L (2000) pp. 53-101
Hamid, A.G. 'Jurisdiction Over Person Abducted From a Foreign Country: Alvarez Machain Case Revisited' 4 Journal of Malaysian and Comparative Law (2004) <http://www.commonlii.org/my/journals/JMCL/2004/4.html>
Horlick, G.N. 'The Developing Law of Air Hijacking' 12 Harv.Int'l. L. J. (1971) pp. 33-70
Iraola, R. 'The Doctrine of Speciality and Federal Criminal Prosecutions' 83 Valparaiso University Law Review (2008) pp. 89-112
Izumo, A. 'Diplomatic Assurances Against Torture & Ill treatment European Court of Human Rights Jurisprudence' 42 Columbia Human Rights Law Review (2010) pp. 233- 277
Jennings, R. 'Extraterritorial Jurisdiction and the United States Antitrust Laws' 33 BYBIL (1957) pp. 146-175

Kirk W. Munroe, 'Canadian Appeals Court refuses to Extradite for US Money Laundering Sting' 12 Int'l Enforcement L.Rep (1996) 138

Lavelle, R. 'The International Convention for the Suppression of Financing of Terrorism' 60 Heidelberg Journal of International law (2000) pp.492-510

Mann, F.A. 'The Doctrine of Jurisdiction in International law' 111 Recuil Des Cours (1964) pp.1-162

Mendelson, A.I. 'The International and Domestic Picture under the Tokyo Convention' 53 Virginia Law Review (1967) pp. 509-563

Nathan Rasiah, 'To Prosecute or to Extradite? A Duty to Consider the Appropriate Venue in Cases of Concurrent Criminal Jurisdiction' Law Reform Essay Competition (2008) pp. 1-11 <www.barcouncil.org.uk/media/61922/nathan_rasiah__32_.pdf>

O.Hafen, J., 'International Extradition: Issues arising under Dual Criminality Requirement' Brigham Young University Law Review (1992) pp.191-230

O'Keefe, R. 'Universal Jurisdiction - Clarifying the Basic Concept' 2 Journal of International Criminal Justice (2004) pp. 735-760

Onyeneke, O.H.C, 'Extradition: International Law and Domestic Law: Gary McKinnon v.Natwest Three' SSRN (December 4, 2009) <http://ssrn.com/abstract=1589502 or <http://dx.doi.org/10.2139/ssrn.1589502>

Orlova, A.V. and James W. Moore, 'Umbrellas or Building Blocks? Defining International Terrorism and Transnational Organised Crime in International Law' 27 Houston Journal of International Law (2004-2005) pp.268-310

Pieth, M., 'Criminalizing the Financing of Terrorism' 4 Journal of International Criminal Justice (2006) pp. 1074-1086

Piragoff, D.K., and Marcia V.J Kran, 'The Impact of Human Rights Principles on Extradition from Canada and the US: Role of National Court' 3 Crim Law Forum (1992) pp. 225-270

Plachta, M., 'Aut Dedere Aut Judicare: An Overview of Modes of Implementation and Approaches' 6 Maastricht J. Eur. & Comp. L. (1991) pp. 331-365

Plachta, M., 'Contemporary Problems of Extradition: Human Rights, Grounds for Refusal and Principle of Aut dedere' 114th International Training Course Visiting Experts Papers pp. 64-86 <www.or.jp/english/pdf/PDF_rms/no57/57-16pdf>

Plachta, M., 'The Lockerbie Case: The Role of Security Council in Enforcing the Principle of Aut Dedere aut Judicare' 12 EJIL (2001) pp.125-140

Roth, P.M., 'Reasonable Extraterritoriality: Correcting the Balance of Interest' 41 ICLQ (1992) pp.245-286

Rozaqis, C. L., 'Terrorism and the Internationally Protected Persons in the Light of ILC's Draft Articles' 23 ICLQ (1974) pp. 32-72

Rychlak, R. J. '*Humberto Alvarez-Machain v. United States*: The Ninth Circuit Panel Decision of September 11' <http://www.fed-soc.org/publications/detail/humberto-alvarez-machain-v-united-states-the-ninth-circuit-panel-decision-of-september-11

SBetti, S. 'Duty to Bring Terrorists to Justice and Discretionary Prosecution' 4 Journal of International Criminal Justice (2006) pp. 1104-1116

Scharf, M P. 'Application of Treaty Based Universal Jurisdiction to Nationals of Non-Party States' 35 New Eng. L. Rev. (2000-2001) pp.363-382

Shehu, A.Y. 'International Initiatives against Corruption and Money Laundering: An Overview' 12 Journal of Financial crime (2005) pp. 221-245

Shelley, L., 'The Unholy Trinity: Transnational Crime, Corruption and Terrorism' 11 Brown J. World Aff. (2004-2005) pp. 101-112

Shelly, L., 'The Nexus of Organised Crime and Terrorism: Two Case Studies in Cigarette Smuggling' 32 International Journal of Comparative and Applied Criminal Justice (2008) pp.43-63

Shubber, S. 'Aircraft Hijacking under the Hague Convention 1970 - A New Regime?' 22 ICLQ (1973) pp. 687-726

Sornarajah, M., 'Extraterritorial Criminal Jurisdiction: British, American and Commonwealth Perspectives' 2 Singapore Journal of International and Comparative Law (1998) pp. 1-36

Sproule D.Q., and Paul St-Denis, 'The UN Drug Trafficking Convention: An Ambitious Step' 27 Canadian Yearbook of International Law (1989) pp. 263-294

Stewart, D.P. 'Internationalizing the War on Drugs' 18 Denv. J. Int'l L. & Pol'y (1989-1990) pp. 387-404

The Abu Doud Affair, 'The Note' 11 J.Int'l L.& Econ (1977) pp.539-582

Webb, P., 'The UN Convention against Corruption: Global achievement or missed opportunity' 8 Journal of International Economic Law (2005) pp. 191-229

Williams, S. 'Human Rights Safeguards and International Cooperation in Extradition: Striking in Balance' 3 Criminal Law Forum (1992) pp.191-224

Williams, S. 'The Double Criminality Rule and Extradition: A Comparative Analysis' 15 Nova Law Review (1991) pp. 581-623

Wise, E.W. 'Rico and its Analogues: Some Comparative Considerations' 27 Syracuse J. Int'l L. & com (2000) pp. 303-324

Wise, E.W. 'Some Problems of Extradition' 15 Wayne Law Review (1968-69) pp.709-231

Witten, S.M. 'International Convention for the Suppression of Terrorist Bombings' 92 AJIL (1998) pp. 774-781

Wyngaert C. and Guy Steesens, 'The International Non Bis in Idem Principle: Resolving Some of the Unanswered Questions' 48 ICLQ (1999) pp. 779-804

Zagaris, B. 'US Cooperation against Transnational Organised Crime' 44 Wayne State Law Review (1998-1999) pp.1401-1464

Zagaris, B. 'Asset Forfeiture International and Foreign Law-An Emerging Regime' 5 Emory International Law Review (1991) pp. 445-514

Zagaris, B. and Jay Rosenthal, 'United States Jurisdictional Consideration in International Criminal Law' 15 California Western International Law Journal (1985) pp.303-338

Newspaper Articles & Blogs

Christopher Tappin: A History of Extradition Cases' *The Telegraph* (24/02/12) <http://www.telegraph.co.uk/news/uknews/law-and-order/9102825/Christopher-Tappin-a-history-of-extradition-cases.html>

Newsmax.com, 'Marcos Juror Among Stewart Jury Finalists' (25 January 2004) <http://archive.newsmax.com/archives/articles/2004/1/25/74621.shtm>

BBC News 'Call for Over-haul of UK Extradition Rules' *BBC News UK* (June 22, 2011) <http://www.bbc.co.uk/news/uk-politics-13867921>

Mohammed Rizwan 'Switzerland Ready to Cooperate in Zardari Graft Cases'. *The Express Tribune* (*January 18th, 2012*) <http://tribune.com.pk/story/323226/switzerland-ready-to-cooperate-in-zardari-graft-cases/>

Umar Cheema 'Experts Confused at Swiss Time Bar' *The News Pakistan* (January 20, 2012) <http://www.thenews.com.pk/Todays-News-2-88577-Experts-confused-at-Swiss-time-bar>

Terence J Sigamony 'Will Swiss Cases Follow Zardari When He Leaves Office?' *The Nation Pakistan* (June 27 2012) <http://www.nation.com.pk/pakistan-news-newspaper-daily-english-online/national/27-Jun-2012/will-swiss-cases-follow-zardari-when-he-leaves-office>

Vikram Dodd 'Abu Hamza Can Be Extradited to US, Human Rights Court Rules' *The Guardian UK (*10/04/2012) <http://www.guardian.co.uk/uk/2012/apr/10/abu-hamza-extradited-us-court>

PA/Huffington Post UK 'Abu Hamza Extradition: Human Rights Judges Set To Rule Over Terrorist Charges' *The Huffington Post UK* (10/04/2012) <http://www.huffingtonpost.co.uk/2012/04/10/abu-hamza-extradition-america-terrorist-human-rights_n_1413907.html>

PTI New Delhi 'Abu Salem's Extradition: Portugal's SC rejects CBI plea' *Daily News and Analysis India* (17/01/2012) <http://www.dnaindia.com/india/report_abu-salem-s-extradition-portugal-s-sc-rejects-cbi-plea_1638666 >

The Indian Express 'India Has No Locus Standi in Abu Salem Matter: Portugal Court' *The Indian Express* (10/07/12) <http://www.indianexpress.com/news/india-has-no-locus-standi-in-abu-salem-matter-portugal-court/972654/2>

David Johnston, 'With Millions Frozen in Banks, Noriega Might Be Tried as a Pauper' *NY Times*, Nov 14, 1990 at B6, C.13 <http://www.nytimes.com/1990/11/14/us/with-millions-frozen-in-banks-noriega-might-be-tried-as-pauper.html>

Douglas Jehl, 'Colombian Police Kill Drug Lord: War on Narcotics: Rodriguez Gacha was a leader of the Medellin cartel. U.S. hails the 'first big break we've had.' *Los Angeles Times* Nov 8, 1989 <http://articles.latimes.com/1989-12-16/news/mn-228_1_medellin-cartel>

Douglas Jehl and Ronald J. Ostrow, '5 Countries Freeze Drug Kingpin's $60 Million : Cocaine: Secret funds of Gonzalo Rodriguez Gacha are uncovered—the biggest strike yet in the war against traffickers' *Los Angeles Times* Nov 8, 1989 <http://articles.latimes.com/1989-11-08/news/mn-929_1_gonzalo-rodriguez-gacha>

Sharing of Proceeds by the US in *Gachsa* case <http://www.justice.gov/opa/pr/2004/March/04_crm_180.htm>

The NatWest Three/ Norris <http://www.simmonsandsimmons.com/docs/feb_06_the_natwest_three_norris.pdf>

James Barron, 'Swiss Extradite Khashoggi to US' (July 20, 1989) *The New York Times* <http://www.nytimes.com/1989/07/20/world/swiss-extradite-khashoggi-to-us.html>

ANI (23rd January, 2012) David Cameron to Confront Court over Extraditing Suspected Osman; Europe News.net <http://www.europenews.net/story/202878694>

Foreman (2012, February 13) 'US Cites United Nations Treaty in Mega upload case' *International Extradition Lawyers*. <http://internationalextraditionblog.com/2012/02/13/us-cites-united-nations-treaty-in-megaupload-case/>

The Guardian UK (February 22, 2012) 'Kim Dotcom Granted Bail in Mega upload case' <http://www.guardian.co.uk/technology/2012/feb/22/kim-dotcom-granted-bail-megaupload>

The News Pakistan (June 19, 2012) Graft Cases against President Zardari cannot be reopened : Swiss authorities <http://www.pakistantoday.com.pk/2013/06/18/news/national/graft-cases-against-president-zardari-cannot-be-reopened-swiss-authorities>

Hasnaat Malik, *Daily Times Pakistan* (Wednesday, June 19, 2013) Swiss money laundering case buried once and for all <http://www.dailytimes.com.pk/default.asp?page=2013%5C06%5C19%5Cstory_19-6-2013_pg1_2.>

Web Resources

The United Nations office at Vienna (UNOV) Library <http://www.unvienna.org/unov/en/faq.html>

International Civil Aviation Organization (ICAO) Secretariat <http://www.icao.int/secretariat/legal/List%20of%20Parties/Hague_EN.pdf>

Centre for International Law (CIL) National University of Singapore <http://cil.nus.edu.sg/1971/1971-convention-for-the-suppression-of-unlawful-acts-against-the-safety-of-civil-aviation/>

United Nations Treaty Collection <http://treaties.un.org/Pages/ViewDetails.aspx?src=IND&mtdsg_no=XVIII-7&chapter=18&lang=en>

The Free Dictionary by Farlex <http://legal dictionary.thefreedictionary.com/Period+of+prescription>

Council of Europe <http://www.coe.int/t/dghl/monitoring/moneyval/activities/UK_Parlrep.pdf>

Security Council, Counter Terrorism Committee <http://www.un.org/en/sc/ctc/>

United Nations Office on Drugs and Crime < http://www.unodc.org/ >
United Nations High Commission for Refugees (UNCHR) <http://www.refworld.org/ >